## Get the eBooks FREE!

(PDF, ePub, Kindle, and liveBook all included)

We believe that once you buy a book from us, you should be able to read it in any format we have available. To get electronic versions of this book at no additional cost to you, purchase and then register this book at the Manning website.

Go to https://www.manning.com/freebook and follow the instructions to complete your pBook registration.

## That's it!
## Thanks from Manning!

D0731572

# *Testing Microservices with Mountebank*

BRANDON BYARS

MANNING
SHELTER ISLAND

Manning Publications Co.
20 Baldwin Road
PO Box 761
Shelter Island, NY 11964

| | |
|---|---|
| Development editor: | Elesha Hyde |
| Technical development editor: | John Guthrie |
| Review editor: | Ivan Martinović |
| Project manager: | Vincent Nordhaus |
| Copy editor: | Carl Quesnel |
| Proofreader: | Keri Hales |
| Technical proofreader: | Alessandro Campeis |
| Typesetter and cover designer: | Marija Tudor |

ISBN 9781617294778
Printed in the United States of America
1 2 3 4 5 6 7 8 9 10 – SP – 23 22 21 20 19 18

# brief contents

PART 1 FIRST STEPS ........................................................ 1

    1 ▪ Testing microservices   3

    2 ▪ Taking mountebank for a test drive   22

PART 2 USING MOUNTEBANK ........................................ 41

    3 ▪ Testing using canned responses   43

    4 ▪ Using predicates to send different responses   65

    5 ▪ Adding record/replay behavior   87

    6 ▪ Programming mountebank   108

    7 ▪ Adding behaviors   130

    8 ▪ Protocols   153

PART 3 CLOSING THE LOOP ........................................ 177

    9 ▪ Mountebank and continuous delivery   179

    10 ▪ Performance testing with mountebank   201

# contents

*preface   ix*
*acknowledgments   x*
*about this book   xii*
*about the author   xv*
*about the cover illustration   xvi*

**PART 1   FIRST STEPS** ..................................................... **1**

## 1   *Testing microservices   3*

1.1   A microservices refresher   4

*The path toward microservices   5 ▪ Microservices and organizational structure   7*

1.2   The problem with end-to-end testing   9

1.3   Understanding service virtualization   11

*Test-by-test setup using an API   13 ▪ Using a persistent data store   14 ▪ Record and replay   14*

1.4   Introducing mountebank   16

1.5   The service virtualization tool ecosystem   20

## 2   *Taking mountebank for a test drive   22*

2.1   Setting up the example   23

2.2   HTTP and mountebank: a primer   24

v

2.3    Virtualizing the product catalog service   27

2.4    Your first test   33

PART 2    USING MOUNTEBANK ....................................... 41

3    *Testing using canned responses   43*

3.1    The basics of canned responses   44

*The default response   46 ▪ Understanding how the default
response works   49 ▪ Changing the default response   49
Cycling through responses   50*

3.2    HTTPS imposters   52

*Setting up a trusted HTTPS imposter   56 ▪ Using mutual
authentication   58*

3.3    Saving the responses in a configuration file   59

*Saving multiple imposters in the config file   61*

4    *Using predicates to send different responses   65*

4.1    The basics of predicates   66

*Types of predicates   68 ▪ Matching object request fields   74
The deepequals predicate   75 ▪ Matching multivalued
fields   76 ▪ The exists predicate   77 ▪ Conjunction
junction   78 ▪ A complete list of predicate types   80*

4.2    Parameterizing predicates   80

*Making case-sensitive predicates   80*

4.3    Using predicates on JSON values   81

*Using direct JSON predicates   81 ▪ Selecting a JSON value
with JSONPath   82*

4.4    Selecting XML values   83

5    *Adding record/replay behavior   87*

5.1    Setting up a proxy   88

5.2    Generating the correct predicates   91

*Creating predicates with predicateGenerators   91 ▪ Adding
predicate parameters   93*

5.3    Capturing multiple responses for the same request   96

5.4    Ways to replay a proxy   100

5.5 Configuring the proxy 102

*Using mutual authentication 102 ▪ Adding custom headers 103*

5.6 Proxy use cases 105

*Using a proxy as a fallback 105 ▪ Converting HTTPS to HTTP 106*

## 6 Programming mountebank 108

6.1 Creating your own predicate 109

6.2 Creating your own dynamic response 114

*Adding state 116 ▪ Adding async 117 ▪ Deciding between response vs. predicate injection 126*

6.3 A word of caution: security matters 127

6.4 Debugging tips 128

## 7 Adding behaviors 130

7.1 Understanding behaviors 131

7.2 Decorating a response 132

*Using the decorate function 132 ▪ Adding decoration to saved proxy responses 134 ▪ Adding middleware through shellTransform 137*

7.3 Adding latency to a response 139

7.4 Repeating a response multiple times 140

7.5 Replacing content in the response 141

*Copying request data to the response 141 ▪ Looking up data from an external data source 148*

7.6 A complete list of behaviors 152

## 8 Protocols 153

8.1 How protocols work in mountebank 154

8.2 A TCP primer 155

8.3 Stubbing text-based TCP-based RPC 157

*Creating a basic TCP imposter 158 ▪ Creating a TCP proxy 159 ▪ Matching and manipulating an XML payload 161*

8.4 Binary support 162

*Using binary mode with Base64 encoding 162 ▪ Using predicates in binary mode 163*

8.5 Virtualizing a .NET Remoting service   164

    *Creating a simple .NET Remoting client   165* • *Virtualizing the .NET Remoting server   167* • *How to tell mountebank where the message ends   171*

PART 3   CLOSING THE LOOP ...................................... 177

9   *Mountebank and continuous delivery   179*

9.1   A continuous delivery refresher   180

    *Testing strategy for CD with microservices   182* • *Mapping your testing strategy to a deployment pipeline   185*

9.2   Creating a test pipeline   186

    *Creating unit tests   187* • *Creating service tests   191 Balancing service virtualization with contract tests   194 Exploratory testing   198*

10   *Performance testing with mountebank   201*

10.1   Why service virtualization enables performance testing   202

10.2   Defining your scenarios   204

10.3   Capturing the test data   206

    *Capturing the responses   207* • *Capturing the actual latencies   208* • *Simulating wild latency swings   209*

10.4   Running the performance tests   210

10.5   Scaling mountebank   212

    *index   217*

# *preface*

Pete Hodgson used to joke that building your own mocking framework was a rite of passage for ThoughtWorks developers. Those days are past, not because ThoughtWorks doesn't care about testing anymore (we do, very much), but because the tooling around testing is a lot better, and because we have more interesting problems to focus on nowadays. In the winter of 2014, I had a testing problem, and it turns out that not being able to test prevents you from focusing on those more interesting problems.

We had adopted a microservices architecture but were limited by some of the legacy service code we were strangling out. The idea of service virtualization—using tests to mock up downstream network dependencies—was not new to us, even if the term wasn't common in the open source world. It seemed like every time a new developer joined the team, they recommended using VCR (a Ruby tool) or WireMock (a Java tool) to solve the problem. Those are great tools, and they are in great company. By that time, ThoughtWorkers had contributed a couple more quality tools to the mix (stubby4j and Moco), and tools like Hoverfly would be coming soon. You wouldn't have been wrong to pick any of them if you needed to virtualize HTTP services.

Unfortunately, our downstream service was not HTTP. The way new team members kept suggesting the same type of tooling provided good evidence that the approach worked. The fact that without such tooling, we were unable to gain the confidence we needed in our tests which provided the need for mountebank. Over that winter break, buoyed by red wine and Jon Stewart jokes, I wrote mountebank.

This book is about mountebank, but it is also about testing and about continuous delivery and about microservices and architecture. You may be able to do your job without mountebank, but if you run into trouble, service virtualization may just be able to help you focus on the more interesting problems.

# *acknowledgments*

The advantage of working for a company like ThoughtWorks is that a lot of people I know have written technical books. The disadvantage is that every single one of them told me that writing a book is, like, really hard. (Thanks Martin Fowler, Neal Ford, and Mike Mason.)

Fortunately, Pete Hodgson wasn't one of them. He has, however, written several articles, including one on testing JavaScript on Martin Fowler's bliki. I didn't really understand it the first 10 times I read it, and, not being a JavaScript developer myself, tried to implement a synchronous promise library based on a naive interpretation of promises. A few weeks later, when I untangled my frontal cortex from my corpus callosum before realizing what a Bad Idea trying to write my own promise library was, I asked Pete for help. He provided the first contribution to mountebank, showing me how to *actually* test JavaScript. I felt that was a good thing to know because I was writing a testing tool. Thanks, Pete.

Paul Hammant was another one who never told me how hard writing a book is. Unfortunately, he also never bothered to tell me how hard managing a popular open source project is. A long-time open sourcer himself (he kicked off Selenium, one of the early inversions of control frameworks, and a host of other initiatives), he likely assumed everyone suffered from the same desire to leave work every night to code and blog and manage a community like he does. Nonetheless, Paul has been both an incredibly helpful promoter of mountebank and an incredibly helpful mentor, even if I don't always do a good job of listening to him.

Of course, none of this would have been possible without the support of that first team, named SilverHawks after some cartoon that, despite being age-appropriate for me, I never watched. I owe my thanks to Shyam Chary, Bear Claw, Gonzo, Andrew

Hadley, Sarah Hutchins, Nagesh Kumar, Stan Guillory, and many others. The mounte-bank community has grown from those humble beginnings, and I owe a debt of grati-tude to all the many folks who have dedicated their free time to improving the product.

I was in Oklahoma City when Manning called to suggest writing a book. It was, like, really hard. Elesha Hyde, my developmental editor, was amazing, even when I'd go silent for weeks at a time because work and life and kids didn't wait. I wrote this book in Oklahoma, Dallas, Toronto, Vancouver, San Francisco, San Antonio, Houston, Aus-tin, São Paulo, and Playa del Carmen. That's right—I wrote parts of this book while drinking mojitos on the beach (and chapter 4 is better off for it).

Which brings me to Mona. You let me write on weekends and on vacations. You let me write at family events and when your damn Patriots were playing in another damn Super Bowl (or whatever they call that last game, I don't follow baseball that much anymore). You let me write at the spa and at the pool while you kept our kids from drowning. Thank you.

# *about this book*

I wrote *Testing Microservices with Mountebank* to show how service virtualization helps you test microservices, and how mountebank is a powerful service virtualization tool. That necessarily requires building a deep familiarity with mountebank—the middle section of this book is dedicated to the subject—but many of the lessons apply with any service virtualization tool.

## Who should read this book

Mountebank is a developer-friendly tool, which makes developers a primary audience of *Testing Microservices with Mountebank*. Some familiarity with test automation is expected, but I avoid using any advanced language features throughout this book to keep the focus on the tool and the approach. Automation-friendly QA testers also will find value in this book, as will those who specialize in performance testing. Finally, service virtualization is increasingly an architectural concern, and within these pages I hope to arm solution architects with the arguments they need to make the right decisions.

## How this book is organized

You'll find three parts and 10 chapters in this book.

- Part 1 introduces the overall testing philosophy of distributed systems.
  - Chapter 1 provides a brief refresher of microservices, as well as a critique of traditional end-to-end testing. It helps explain how service virtualization fits in a microservices world and provides a mental model for mountebank.
  - Chapter 2 sets up an example architecture that we will revisit a few times throughout the book and shows how you can use mountebank to automate deterministic tests despite a distributed architecture.

- Part 2 deep dives into mountebank, giving you a comprehensive overview of its capabilities.
  - Chapter 3 provides foundational material for understanding basic mountebank responses in the context of HTTP and HTTPS. It also describes basic ways of managing test data through configuration files.
  - Chapter 4 explores predicates—mountebank's way of responding differently to different types of requests. It also introduces mountebank's capability around matching XML and JSON.
  - Chapter 5 looks at mountebank's record and replay capability. Mountebank uses proxies to real systems to let you capture realistic test data.
  - Chapter 6 shows you how to program mountebank itself, by using a feature called injection to write your own predicates and responses in JavaScript. We look at how injection helps solve some thorny problems around CORS and OAuth handshakes, including virtualizing GitHub's public API.
  - Chapter 7 rounds out the core capabilities of the mountebank engine by looking at behaviors—postprocessing steps applied to responses. Behaviors let you add latency, look up data from external sources, and perform a host of other transformation steps.
  - Chapter 8 shows how all of the concepts in chapters 3–7 extend beyond HTTPS. The engine of mountebank is protocol-agnostic, and we show TCP-based examples, including an extended .NET Remoting test scenario.
- Part 3 takes a step back to put service virtualization in a broader context.
  - Chapter 9 explores an example test pipeline for microservices, from unit tests to manual exploratory tests, and shows where service virtualization does and doesn't fit.
  - Chapter 10 shows how service virtualization helps with performance testing. It includes a fully worked out example virtualizing a publicly available API.

### About the code

This book uses a number of code examples to help illustrate the concepts. Some of them are whimsical (see chapter 4), some are based on virtualizing real public APIs (see chapters 6 and 10), and some are just downright gnarly (see chapter 8). I tried my best to keep the examples interesting across the wide range of problems that service virtualization can help with. This was no easy task. Some problems are easily understood. Some, like virtualizing a .NET Remoting service returning binary data, are not. My hope is that I've maintained enough of a sense of humor to keep you interested with the easy problems, and with the complex behavior, I've given you enough of a sense of what's possible that you'll be capable of innovating on your own.

Source code for the book is publicly available at https://github.com/bbyars /mountebank-in-action.

## Book Forum

Purchase of *Testing Microservices with Mountebank* includes free access to a private web forum run by Manning Publications where you can make comments about the book, ask technical questions, and receive help from the author and other users. To access the forum go to www.manning.com/books/testing-microservices-with-mountebank. You can also learn more about Manning's forums and the rules of conduct at https:// forums.manning.com/forums/about.

Manning's commitment to its readers is to provide a venue where a meaningful dialog between individual readers and between readers and the author can take place. It is not a commitment to any specific amount of participation on the part of the author, whose contributions to the forum remain voluntary (and unpaid). We suggest you ask the author challenging questions, lest his interest stray.

## Online resources

Need additional help?

The mountebank website at https://www.mbtest.org provides the most up-to-date documentation for the tool.

The Google group site is https://groups.google.com/forum/#!forum/mounte bank-discuss. Feel free to ask any questions about the tool there.

# *about the author*

BRANDON BYARS is a principal consultant at ThoughtWorks and the creator and maintainer of mountebank. He has 20 years of experience in IT, with roles ranging from developer to DBA to architect to account manager. When he is not geeking out over test automation, he has an interest in applying systems thinking to large-scale development and in finding ways to rediscover what it means to be human in a world where we have opened Pandora's technobox.

# about the cover illustration

The figure on the cover of *Testing Microservices with Mountebank* is captioned "A Man from Slovenia." This illustration is taken from a recent reprint of Balthasar Hacquet's *Images and Descriptions of Southwestern and Eastern Wends, Illyrians, and Slavs*, published by the Ethnographic Museum in Split, Croatia, in 2008. Hacquet (1739–1815) was an Austrian physician and scientist who spent many years studying the botany, geology, and ethnography of many parts of the Austrian Empire, as well as the Veneto, the Julian Alps, and the western Balkans, inhabited in the past by peoples of the Illyrian tribes. Hand-drawn illustrations accompany the many scientific papers and books that Hacquet published.

The rich diversity of the drawings in Hacquet's publications speaks vividly of the uniqueness and individuality of the eastern Alpine and northwestern Balkan regions just 200 years ago. This was a time when the dress codes of two villages separated by a few miles identified people uniquely as belonging to one or the other, and when members of a social class or trade could be easily distinguished by what they were wearing. Dress codes have changed since then and the diversity by region, so rich at the time, has faded away. It is now often hard to tell the inhabitant of one continent from another, and today the inhabitants of the picturesque towns and villages in the Slovenian Alps or Balkan coastal towns are not readily distinguishable from the residents of other parts of Europe.

We at Manning celebrate the inventiveness, the initiative, and the fun of the computer business with book covers based on costumes from two centuries ago, brought back to life by illustrations such as this one.

# Part 1

# First Steps

Welcome, friend.

Those words adorn the welcome mat near my front door, and they are the first words you will see when you visit the mountebank website (https://www.mbtest.org). I'd very much like them to be the first words you read in this book, as I welcome you to the wonderful world of service virtualization in general and mountebank in particular.

This first part aims to provide context behind that introduction, setting the stage for introducing mountebank as part of your testing and continuous delivery stack. Because one of the main drivers behind service virtualization is the increasingly distributed nature of computing, chapter 1 starts with a brief review of microservices, with a focus on how they change the way we test software. It puts service virtualization in context and provides a gentle introduction to the main components of mountebank.

Chapter 2 demonstrates mountebank in action. You'll get some dirt under your nails as you write your first test using service virtualization, providing a simple launching point to explore the full capabilities of mountebank in part 2.

# Testing microservices

**This chapter covers**

- A brief background on microservices
- The challenges of testing microservices
- How service virtualization makes testing easier
- An introduction to mountebank

Sometimes, it pays to be fake.

I started developing software in the days when the web was starting to compete with desktop applications in corporate organizations. Browser-based applications brought tremendous deployment advantages, but we tested them in almost the same way. We wrote a monolithic application, connected it to a database, and tested exactly like our users would: by using the application. We tested a *real* application.

Test-driven development taught us that good object-oriented design would allow us to test at much more granular levels. We could test classes and methods in isolation and get feedback in rapid iterations. Dependency injection—passing in the dependencies of a class rather than instantiating them on demand—made our code both more flexible and more testable. As long as we passed in test dependencies that had the same interface as the real ones, we could completely isolate the bits of code we wanted to test. We gained more confidence in the code we wrote by being able to inject fake dependencies into it.

Before long, clever developers produced open-source libraries that made creating these fake dependencies easier, freeing us to argue about more important things, like what to call them. We formed cliques based on our testing styles: the mockists reveled in the purity of using mocks; the classicists proudly stood by their stubborn reliance on stubs.[1] But neither side argued about the fundamental value of testing against fake dependencies.

It turns out when it comes to design, what's true in the small is also true in the large. After we made a few halting attempts at distributed programming, the ever-versatile web gave us a convenient application protocol—HTTP—for clients and servers to talk to each other. From proprietary RPC to SOAP to REST and back again to proprietary RPC, our architectures outgrew the single codebase, and we once again needed to find ways to test entire services without getting tangled in their web of run-time dependencies. The fact that most applications were built to retrieve the URLs for dependent services from some sort of configuration that varied per environment meant dependency injection was built in. All we needed to do was configure our application with URLs of *fake* services and find easier ways to create those fake services.

Mountebank creates fake services, and it's tailor-made for testing microservices.

## 1.1 A microservices refresher

Most applications are written as *monoliths*, a coarse-grained chunk of code that you release together with a shared database. Think of an e-commerce site like Amazon.com. A common use case is to allow a customer to see a history of their orders, including the products they have purchased. This is conceptually easy to do as long as you keep everything in the same database.

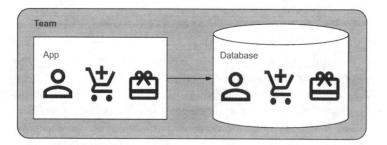

**Figure 1.1  A monolithic application handles view, business, and persistence logic for multiple domains.**

---

[1]  You probably have better things to spend your time on than reading about the differences between classicists and mockists, but if you can't help yourself, you can read more at http://martinfowler.com/articles/mocks ArentStubs.html.

In fact, Amazon did this in their early years, and for good reason. The company had a monolithic codebase they called "Obidos" that looked quite similar to figure 1.1. Configuring the database that way makes it easy to join different domain entities, such as customers and orders to show a customer's order history or orders and products to show product details on an order. Having everything in one database also means you can rely on transactions to maintain consistency, which makes it easy to update a product's inventory when you ship an order, for example.

This setup also makes testing—the focus of this book—easier. Most of the tests can be in process, and, assuming you are using dependency injection, you can test pieces in isolation using mocking libraries. Black-box testing the application only requires you to coordinate the application deployment with the database schema version. Test data management comes down to loading the database with a set of sample test data. You can easily solve all of these problems.

### 1.1.1 The path toward microservices

It's useful to follow the history of Amazon.com to understand what compels organizations to move away from monolithic applications. As the site became more popular, it also became bigger, and Amazon had to hire more engineers to develop it. The problems started when the development organization was large enough that multiple teams had to develop different parts of Obidos (figure 1.2).

The breaking point came in 2001, as the company struggled to evolve pieces of the application because of the coupling between teams. By CEO mandate, the engineering organization split Obidos into a series of services and organized its teams around

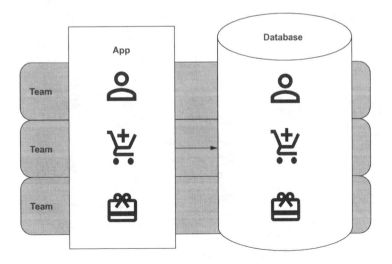

**Figure 1.2  Scaling a monolith means multiple teams have to work in the same codebase.**

them.[2] After the transformation, each team was able to change the code relevant to the domain of their service with much higher confidence that they weren't breaking other teams' code—no other team shared their codebase. Amazon now has tremendous ability to develop different parts of the website experience independently, but the transformation has required a change of paradigm. Whereas Obidos used to be solely responsible for rendering the site, nowadays a single web page at Amazon.com can generate over a hundred service calls (figure 1.3).

The upshot is that each service can focus on doing one thing well and is much easier to understand in isolation. The downside is that such an architecture pushes the complexity that used to exist inside the application into the operational and runtime environment. Showing both customer details and order details on a single screen changes from being a simple database join to orchestrating multiple service calls and combining the data in the application code. Although each service is simple in isolation, the system as a whole is harder to understand.

Netflix was one of the first companies of its size to migrate its core business to Amazon's cloud services, which significantly influenced the way the company thought

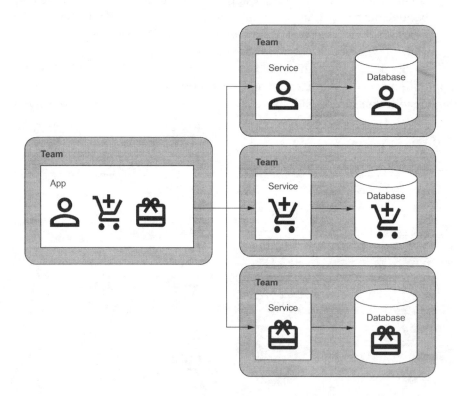

**Figure 1.3   Services use different databases for different domains.**

---

[2]   See https://queue.acm.org/detail.cfm?id=1142065 for details.

about services. Once again, the need to scale its development efforts is what drove this change. Adrian Cockcroft, formerly the Netflix lead cloud architect, noted two opposing tensions.[3] First, demands on IT had increased by a factor of 1,000 in recent years as technology moved from managing payroll and a few enterprise services to becoming the core differentiator for digitally native companies. Second, as the number of engineers increased, the communication and coordination overhead of activities like troubleshooting a broken build became a significant slowdown to delivering software.

Netflix experienced this slowdown once the organization grew to about 100 engineers, with multiple teams competing in the same codebase. Like Amazon, the company solved the problem by breaking the monolithic application into services, and it made a conscious effort to make each service do only one thing. This architectural approach—what we now call microservices—supported development teams working independently of each other, allowing the company to scale its development organization.

Although scaling development efforts is the primary force leading us toward microservices, it has a welcome side effect: it's much easier to release a small service than it is to release a large application. If you can release services independently, you can release features to the market much more quickly. By removing the need for release coordination between teams, microservices provide an architectural solution for what would normally have to be solved manually. Customers are the beneficiaries. Both Amazon and Netflix are known for the ability to rapidly innovate in the marketplace but to do so required rethinking how they organized to deliver software and how they tested software.

### 1.1.2 *Microservices and organizational structure*

Before we get into how mountebank makes testing microservices easier, you need to understand how microservices require a different testing mentality. It all starts with team organization and ends with a full-frontal assault on traditional QA approaches that gate releases through coordinated end-to-end testing.

Microservices require you to rethink traditional organizational structures. Silos exist in any large organization, but some silos are anathema to the goal of microservices, which is to allow independent releases of small services with minimal coordination. Traditional organizations use certain silos as "gates" that validate a deployment before it's released. Each gate acts as a point of coordination. Coordination is one way to gain confidence in a release, but it's slow and couples teams together. Microservices work best when you silo the organization by business capability and allow the development team to own the release of its code autonomously.

A useful metaphor to explain the concept is to imagine your IT organization as a highway. When you need to increase throughput—the number of features released over a given timeframe—you do so by adding lanes to the highway. Having more

---

[3] See https://www.infoq.com/presentations/migration-cloud-native.

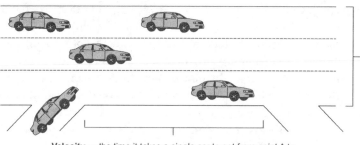

Throughput —
the number of cars that
get from point A
to point B in a given
timeframe — is defined
by the number of lanes.

Velocity — the time it takes a single car to get from point A to
point B — is defined by the speed limit.

**Figure 1.4   During normal traffic, the number of lanes and speed limit define throughput and velocity.**

lanes means you can support more cars at the same time (figure 1.4). This is analogous to hiring more developers to do more work in parallel. You also may want to be able to release a single feature more quickly. This is equivalent to raising the speed limit on the highway, enabling a single car to get from point A to point B in less time. So far, so good.

One thing will kill both throughput *and* velocity, no matter how many lanes you have or what the speed limit is: congestion. Congestion also has an indirect cost that you have almost certainly experienced if you live in a big city. Navigating through stop-and-go traffic is a soul-crushing experience. It's demotivating. It's hard to get excited to get in your car and drive. Many large IT organizations that, with the best of intentions, create unintended congestion, suffer from a real motivational cost.

They create congestion in two ways. First, they overuse the highway, having too many cars given the space available. Second, they add coordination that creates congestion. This second way is harder to eradicate.

One way to require coordination on the highway is to add a toll gate (especially those old-timey ones, before an automated camera replaced the need to pay physical money to a real person). Another way is to have fewer upstream lanes than you have downstream, where "upstream" refers to the section of the highway closer to the exit in highways, and closer to a production release in IT. Reducing the number of upstream lanes throttles traffic by requiring merging multiple lanes into one (figure 1.5). Sometimes this reduction happens by design or because of road construction. Other times it happens because of an accident, which results from an unfortunate degree of coupling between two cars.

Like all models, the highway metaphor is imperfect, but it highlights some useful points. As you saw earlier in the Amazon and Netflix examples, microservices often originate from an organization's desire to increase feature throughput. A helpful side effect is that a smaller codebase has a higher speed limit, increasing velocity. But both of these advantages are negated if you don't change the organization to remove congestion.

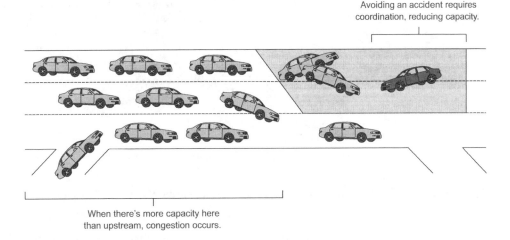

Figure 1.5  **Having fewer upstream lanes increases congestion.**

In organizational terms, fixing overutilization is easy in principle, though it's often politically challenging. You can either hire more people (add more lanes to the highway) or reduce the amount of work in progress (throttle entry to the highway).

The other reasons for congestion are harder to fix. It's common to see organizations with less upstream capacity than downstream capacity. One toll gate example would be increasing coordination by requiring releases to go through a central release management team that throttles development throughput. Accidents are even more common. Every time someone discovers a bug or the build breaks in a codebase that multiple teams share, you have an accident requiring coordination, and both throughput and velocity suffer. Adrian Cockcroft cited this exact reason for driving Netflix toward microservices.

Microservices provide a technical solution for reducing congestion caused by accidents. By not sharing the same codebase, broken builds don't affect multiple teams, effectively creating different lanes for different services. But toll gates are still a problem, and to fully unlock the throughput and velocity advantages we hope to gain through microservices, we have to address organizational complexity. That comes in many forms (for example, from operations to database schema management), but there's one form of upstream congestion that's particularly relevant to this book: our QA organization. Microservices fundamentally challenge the way you test.

## 1.2  *The problem with end-to-end testing*

Traditionally, a central QA team could partner with a central release management team to coordinate a schedule of changes that needed to be deployed into production. They could arrange it such that only one change went through at a time, and that change could be tested against the production versions of its runtime dependencies before being released. Such an approach is perfectly reasonable up to

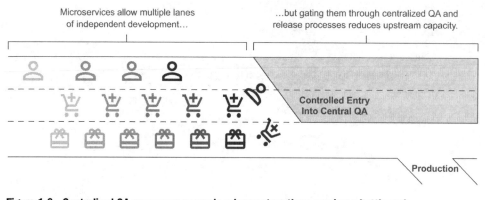

**Figure 1.6  Centralized QA processes recouple releases together, causing a bottleneck.**

a point. Beyond that—and this is often where organizations turn to microservices—it's inappropriate.

You still need confidence that the entire system will work when you release part of it. Gaining that confidence through traditional end-to-end testing and coordinated releases couples all of the services together, moving the coupling bottleneck from the development organization to the QA organization (figure 1.6).

Coordinated integration testing between services recouples codebases that have been decoupled through service decomposition, destroying the scaling and rapid delivery advantages of microservices. As soon as you couple the releases of services together, you have reintroduced the communication and coordination overhead you were trying to avoid. It doesn't matter how many services you have; when you have to release them at the same time, you have a monolith.

The only way to truly scale the technology organization is to decouple releases, so that it can deploy a service independently of the service's dependencies (figure 1.7).

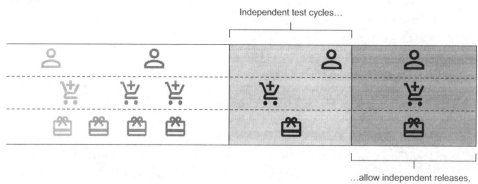

**Figure 1.7  Independent testing works to avoid release congestion.**

This requires a fundamental rethinking of the test strategy for microservices. End-to-end testing doesn't completely disappear, but relying on it as a gate to releasing software becomes another sacrifice on the path toward microservices. The question remains: how do you gain the confidence you need in your changes before releasing them?

## 1.3 Understanding service virtualization

*The problem with dependencies is that you can't depend on them.*

— Michael Nygard, "Architecture Without an End State"

Additional problems exist besides coordination, as shown in figure 1.8. Running in a shared environment means tests may pass or fail for reasons that have nothing to do with either the service you are testing or the tests themselves. They could fail because of resource contention with other teams who are touching the same data, overwhelming the server resources of a shared service, or environmental instability. They could

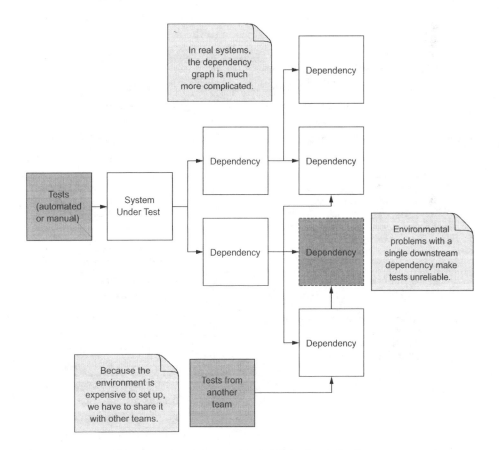

**Figure 1.8   End-to-end testing introduces several problems of coordination.**

fail, or be nearly impossible to write to begin with, because of an inability to get consistent test data set up in all of the services.

It turns out that other industries have already solved this problem. A car, for example, is made up of a multitude of components, each of which can be released to the market independently of the car as a whole. By and large, nobody buys an alternator or a flywheel for anything other than to fix a car. All the same, it's common for companies to manufacture and sell those parts separately *even though they have never tested them in your specific car.*

A car battery comes standard with negative and positive terminals. You can test the battery—outside the car—by using a voltmeter attached to those two terminals and verifying that the voltage is between 12.4 and 12.7 volts. When you start the car, the alternator is responsible for charging the battery, but you can verify the behavior of the battery independently of the alternator by providing a current as input to the battery and measuring the voltage. Such a test tells you that, *if* the alternator is behaving correctly, *then* the battery also behaves correctly. You can gain most of the confidence you need to verify the battery is working by using a *fake* alternator.

*Service virtualization* involves nothing more than using test doubles that operate over the wire and is analogous to how you test car batteries without a real alternator. You silo the runtime environment into the bits relevant to test a single service or application and fake the rest, assuming standard interfaces. In traditional mocking and stubbing libraries, you would stub out a dependency and inject that into your object's constructor, allowing your tests to probe the object under test in isolation. With service virtualization, you virtualize a service and configure the service under test to use the virtualized service's URL as a runtime dependency (figure 1.9). You can set up the virtual service with a specific set of canned responses, allowing you to probe the service under test in isolation.

Service virtualization lets you do black box testing of the service while tightly controlling the runtime environment in which it operates. Although it falls short of the end-to-end confidence that integration tests give you, it does make testing much easier. If you need to test what your shopping cart will do if you try to submit the order when you are out of inventory, you don't have to figure out how to change the inventory system to run your test. You can virtualize the inventory service and configure it to respond with an out-of-inventory message. You can take full advantage of the reduced coupling that the narrow service interface provides to dramatically reduce the amount of test setup required.

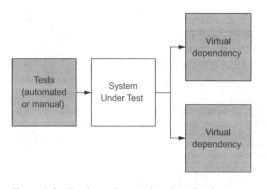

**Figure 1.9  Testing using service virtualization**

*Deterministic* tests are tests that always pass or fail when given the same code to test. Nondeterminism is a tester's worst enemy. Every time you try to "fix" a broken test by re-running it because it worked last time, the devil on your shoulder does a little dance while the angel on your other shoulder lets out a big sigh. Automated tests create a social contract for a team: when a test breaks, you fix the code. When you allow flaky tests, you chip away at that social contract. All kinds of bad behavior might occur when teams lose confidence that their tests are giving them meaningful feedback, including completely ignoring the output of a build.

For your tests to run deterministically, you need to control what the virtual service returns. You can seed the response in several ways, depending on the type and complexity of the tests. What works for writing automated behavioral tests against your service and for testing edge cases likely won't work when running performance tests where you need to execute thousands of requests against the virtual service.

### 1.3.1 Test-by-test setup using an API

The simplest approach is to mirror what mocking libraries do: directly collude with the mocked objects. The unit testing community often speaks about the *3A pattern*, which is to say that each test has three components: arrange, act, and assert. First you set up the data needed for the test to run (arrange), then you execute the system under test (act), and finally you assert that you got the expected response (figure 1.10). Service virtualization can support this approach through an API that lets you configure the virtual service dynamically.

This approach supports creating a laboratory environment for each test, in order to strictly control the inputs and dependencies of the service under test. However, it does make a couple of fundamental assumptions. First, it expects each test to start with a clean slate, which means that each test must remove the test data it added to prevent that data from interfering with subsequent tests. Second, the approach doesn't work if multiple tests are run in parallel. Both of these assumptions fit nicely into automated behavioral tests, as test runners typically ensure tests are run serially.

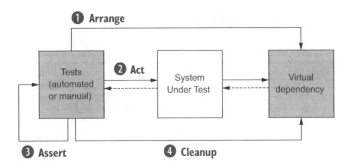

**Figure 1.10   Service virtualization supports a standard unit testing pattern.**

As long as each developer runs their own virtual service, you can avoid the resource contention that comes with concurrent test runs.

### 1.3.2    Using a persistent data store

Creating test data test-by-test doesn't work well for manual testers, it doesn't work if multiple testers are hitting the same virtual service, and it doesn't work in situations (like performance testing) where you need a large batch of data. To address these concerns, you can configure the virtual service to read the test data from a persistent store. With the test-by-test approach to test data creation, all you have to do is tell the virtual service what the next response should look like. With a data store, you will need some way of deciding which response to send based on something from the request. For example, you might send back different responses based on identifiers in the request URL (figure 1.11).

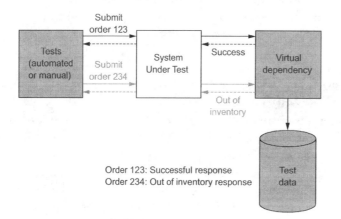

**Figure 1.11   Using persistent test data from a data store**

The downside of this approach is that the arrange step is removed from the test, meaning that to understand what each test is trying to do, you need some information that it doesn't directly specify. If you are testing what happens when you submit orders under various scenarios, for example, you'd have to know that order 123 should have appropriate inventory, whereas order 234 should experience an out-of-inventory situation. The configuration that sets that up is in a data store instead of in the arrange section of your test.

### 1.3.3    Record and replay

Once you have determined where to store the test data, the next question is how to create it. This is rarely an issue for automated behavioral tests because you would

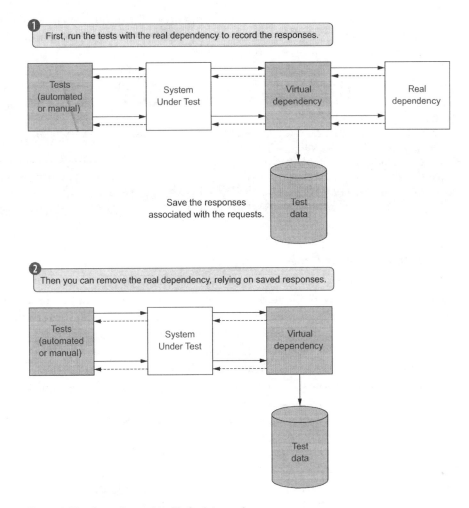

**Figure 1.12  Capturing real traffic for later replay**

create the data specific to the testing scenario. But if you are using a persistent data store, creating the test data is often a significant challenge, especially when you want large quantities of realistic data. The solution is often to record interactions with the real dependency in a way that allows you to play them back through a virtual service (figure 1.12).

The trick with recording responses is that you still have to specify some condition on the request that has to match before playing back the recorded response. You need to know that the order identifier in the URL is what's used to separate the successful order submit response from the out-of-inventory response.

Service virtualization isn't a silver bullet, and by itself it's not enough to cover the confidence gap created by giving up end-to-end testing. But it's a critical component of a modern test strategy in a distributed world, and we'll explore ways of closing that confidence gap in chapters 9 and 10, when we combine service virtualization with other techniques to create a continuous delivery pipeline.

---

**Service virtualization isn't just for microservices!**

Although the focus here is on microservices and the changes in test strategy they require, service virtualization is a useful tool in many other contexts. A common use case is mobile development, where the mobile team needs to be able to develop independently of the team building the API. The need to compete in the mobile ecosystem has driven many organizations to change their integration approach to one based on HTTP-based APIs, and mobile developers can take advantage of that fact to virtualize the APIs as they develop the front-end code.

---

## 1.4    *Introducing mountebank*

*Mountebank* means a charlatan. It comes from Italian words meaning, literally, to mount a bench, which captures the behavior of snake oil salesmen who duped uninformed consumers into forking over money for quack medicine. It's a useful word for describing what mountebank[4] the tool does, which is to conspire with your tests to dupe the system under test into believing that mountebank is a real runtime dependency.

Mountebank is a service virtualization tool. It supports all of the service virtualization scenarios we have looked at: behavioral testing using the API test-by-test, using a persistent data store, and acting as a proxy for record and replay situations. Mountebank also supports the ability to pick a response based on certain criteria of the request and to select which request fields you want to differentiate the responses during the playback stage of record-playback. Most of the remainder of this book explores those scenarios and more to help you build a robust test strategy for microservices, because a robust test strategy is the key to unlocking release independence.

Mountebank is a standalone application that provides a REST API to create and configure virtual services, which are called *imposters* in the API (figure 1.13). Rather than configuring the service that you are testing to point to URLs of real services, you configure it to point to the imposters you create through mountebank.

Each imposter represents a socket that acts as the virtual service and accepts connections from the real service you are testing. Spinning up and shutting down imposters is a lightweight operation, so it's common to use the arrange step of automated tests to create the imposter, then shut it down in the cleanup stage of each

---

[4]   Since its initial release, I have always preferred to lowercase the "m" in "mountebank" when writing about the tool. Largely this has to do with the way the documentation is written—in a personified voice from a snake oil salesman who claims false humility by, among other things, not capitalizing his name. Whatever the historical origins, it's now a mildly unexpected stylistic twist. Sorry about that.

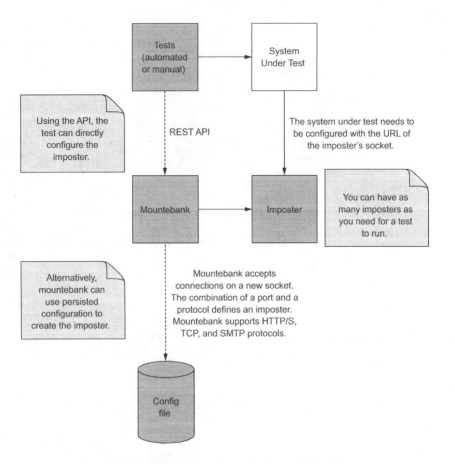

**Figure 1.13   Configuring virtual services with a simple mountebank imposter**

test. Although we will use HTTP/S for most examples in this book, mountebank supports other protocols, including binary messages over TCP, and more protocols are expected soon.

As Larry Wall, the creator of the Perl scripting language, once said, the goal of a good tool is to make the easy things easy and the hard things possible.[5] Mountebank tries to accomplish this with a rich set of request-matching and response-generation capabilities, balanced by as many defaults as reasonably possible. Figure 1.14 shows how mountebank matches a request to a response.

---

[5]  Most developers who have had the misfortune of using many "enterprise" tools will realize that this statement is far from the truism it may sound like.

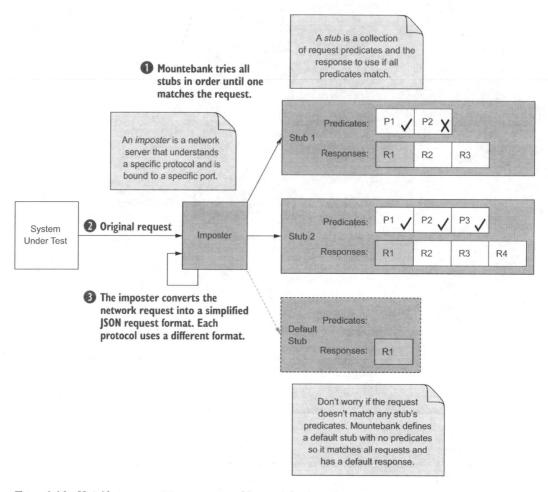

**Figure 1.14   Matching a request to a response with mountebank**

Network protocols are complicated beasts. The first job of the imposter is to simplify a protocol-specific request into a JSON structure so that you can match the request against a set of predicates. Each protocol gets its own request JSON structure; we will look at HTTP's structure in the next chapter.

You configure each imposter with a list of stubs. A *stub* is nothing more than a collection of one or more responses and, optionally, a list of predicates. *Predicates* are defined in terms of request fields, and each one says something like "Request field X must equal 123." No self-respecting mocking tool would leave users with a simple *equals* as the only comparison operator, and mountebank ups the game with special predicate extensions to make working with XML and JSON easier. Chapter 4 explores predicates in detail.

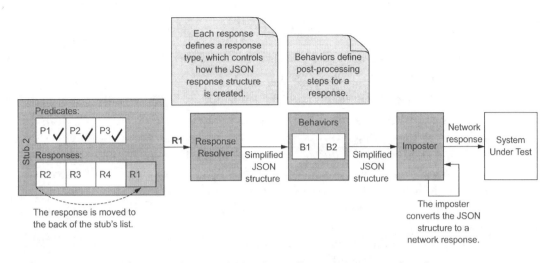

**Figure 1.15   Response generation in mountebank using predicates and responses in stubs**

Mountebank passes the request to each stub in list order and picks the first one that matches all the predicates. If the request doesn't match any of the stubs defined, mountebank returns a default response. Otherwise, it returns the first response for the stub, which brings us to how responses are generated (figure 1.15).

The first thing that happens is that the selected response shifts to the back of the list. This allows you to cycle through the responses in order each time a request matches the stub's predicates. Because mountebank moves the request to the back instead of removing it, you never run out of responses—you can start reusing them. This data structure is what the academics call a *circular buffer*, because a circle prefers to start over rather than end.

The response resolver box in figure 1.15 is a bit of a simplification. Each response is responsible for generating a JSON structure representing the protocol-specific response fields (like the HTTP status code), and you can generate those fields in different ways. Mountebank has three different response types that take entirely different approaches to generating the JSON:

- An *is* response type returns the provided JSON as-is, creating a canned response. We explore canned responses in chapter 3.
- A *proxy* response type forwards the request on to a real dependency and converts its response into a JSON response structure. You use proxies for record-playback functionality, and we describe them in chapter 5.
- An *inject* response type allows you to programmatically define the response JSON using JavaScript. Injection is how you can extend mountebank when its built-in capabilities don't quite do what you need, and we cover that in chapter 6.

Once the response is resolved, mountebank passes the JSON structure to behaviors for post-processing. *Behaviors*, which we discuss in chapter 7, include, among others:

- Copying values from the request into the response
- Adding latency to the response
- Repeating a response, rather than moving it to the back of the list

Up to this point, mountebank has dealt only with JSON, and every operation (with the exception of forwarding a proxy request) has been protocol-agnostic. Once the response JSON is finalized, the imposter converts the JSON to a protocol-aware network response and sends it over the wire. Although we will spend much of our time in this book looking at HTTP requests and responses, all of the core capabilities of mountebank work with any supported network protocol (even binary ones), and in chapter 8, we will show some non-HTTP examples.

To keep simple things simple, nearly everything in mountebank is optional. That allows you to get started gently, which we will do in the next chapter.

## 1.5   *The service virtualization tool ecosystem*

This book is about two things: mountebank and how service virtualization fits into your microservices test strategy. Although both topics are valuable, the second one is much broader than mountebank.

The service virtualization ecosystem offers several quality tools, both open source and commercial. Commercial tooling is still quite popular in large enterprises. HP, CA, and Parasoft all offer commercial service virtualization tools, and SmartBear took the (originally noncommercial) SoapUI and converted it into part of their commercial service virtualization toolkit. Many of the commercial tools are high quality and offer a richer set of capabilities than the open source tooling, such as broader protocol support, but in my experience, they both devalue the developer experience and hinder true continuous delivery. (Chapter 9 offers a fuller critique.) Of the open source tools, I believe that mountebank comes the closest to the full feature set of commercial tools.

The open source tooling offers a rich set of options primarily aimed at virtualizing HTTP. WireMock is probably the most popular alternative to mountebank. Whereas mountebank aims to be cross-platform by having its public API be REST over HTTP, WireMock (and many others) optimizes for a specific platform. Although this involves tradeoffs, WireMock is easier to get started with in a purely Java-based project, as you don't have to worry about calling an HTTP API or any complicated wiring into the build process.

Mountebank has an ecosystem of language bindings and build plugins, but you will have to search for them, and they may not expose the full capabilities of the tool. (In the next chapter, you will see an example using JavaScript to wrap the REST API, and chapter 8 has an example using a pre-built C# language binding.) That said, mountebank has broader portability than WireMock.

Another popular example is Hoverfly, a newer Go-based service virtualization tool that baked in middleware as part of the toolchain, allowing a high degree of customization. Mountebank offers middleware in the form of the `shellTransform` behavior, which we look at in chapter 7. Moco and stubby4j are other popular options that are Java-based, although stubby4j has been ported to multiple languages.

As you will see in part 3 of this book, service virtualization helps in a number of scenarios, and one tool isn't always right for every scenario. Many of the commercial tools aim for centralized testing, including performance tests. Many of the open source tools aim for a friendly developer experience when doing functional service tests as part of the development process. I believe mountebank is unique in the open source world in that it aspires to support the full spectrum of service virtualization use cases, including performance testing (which we look at in chapter 10). That said, you won't hurt my feelings if you use another tool for certain types of testing, and I hope that this book helps you identify what you need in the different types of tests to thrive in a microservices world.

## Summary

- Microservices represent an architectural approach that can increase both delivery throughput and velocity.
- To realize the full potential of microservices, you must release them independently.
- To gain release independence, you must also test independently.
- Service virtualization allows independent black-box testing of services.
- Mountebank is an open source service virtualization tool for testing microservices.

# Taking mountebank
# for a test drive

**This chapter covers**

- Understanding how mountebank virtualizes HTTP
- Installing and running mountebank
- Exploring mountebank on the command line
- Using mountebank in an automated test

In trying to do for pet supplies what Amazon did for books, Pets.com became one of the most spectacular failures of the dot-com bust that occurred around the turn of the millennium. On the surface, the company had everything it needed to be successful, including a brilliant marketing campaign that featured a famous sock puppet. Yet it flamed out from IPO to liquidation in under a year, becoming synonymous with the bursting of the dot-com bubble in the process.

Business-minded folk claim that Pets.com failed because no market existed for ordering pet supplies over the internet. Or it failed because of the lack of a viable business plan...or maybe because the company sold products for less than it cost to buy and distribute them. But as technologists, we know better.

Pets.com made only two mistakes that mattered. They didn't use microservices, and, more importantly, they didn't use mountebank.[1] In an era in which social media and meme generators have conspired to bring cat picture innovation to new heights, it's clear that we need internet-provided pet supplies now more than ever. The time to correct the technical mistakes of Pets.com is long overdue. In this chapter, we will get started on a microservices architecture for a modern pet supply company and show how you can use mountebank to maintain release independence between services.

## 2.1 Setting up the example

Though building an online pet supply site is a bit tongue-in-cheek, it will serve as a useful reference to get comfortable with mountebank. As an e-commerce platform, it looks similar to the Amazon.com example you saw in chapter 1.

The architecture shown in figure 2.1 is simplified, but it's complex enough to work with. Each of the services on the right have its own set of runtime dependencies, but

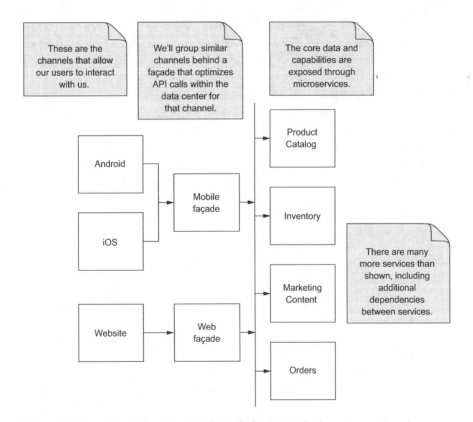

**Figure 2.1   Your reference architecture for exploring mountebank**

---

[1]   I am, of course, joking. Neither microservices nor mountebank existed back then.

we will look at the architecture from the perspective of the website team. One of the hallmarks of a good architecture is that, although you will need to understand something about your dependencies, you shouldn't need to know anything about the other teams' dependencies. I have also introduced a *façade* layer that represents presentational APIs relevant to a specific channel. This is a common pattern to aggregate and transform downstream service calls into a format optimized for the channels (mobile, web, and so on).

An advantage of using HTTP for integration is that, unlike libraries and frameworks, you can use an API without knowing what language the API was written in.[2] It would be perfectly acceptable, for example, for you to write the product catalog service in Java and the inventory service in Scala. Indeed, having the ability to make new technology adoption easier is another side benefit of microservices.

## 2.2    HTTP and mountebank: a primer

HTTP is a text-based request-response network protocol. An HTTP server knows how to parse that text into its constituent parts, but it's simple enough that you can parse it without a computer. Mountebank assumes that you are comfortable with those constituent parts. After all, you can't expect to provide a convincing fake of an HTTP service if you don't first understand what a real one looks like.

Let's deep-dive into HTTP using one of the first features you need to support: listing the available products. Fortunately, the product catalog service has an endpoint for retrieving the products in JSON format. All you have to do is make the right API call, which looks like figure 2.2 in HTTP-speak.

The first line of any HTTP request contains three components: the method, the path, and the protocol version. In this case, the method is GET, which denotes that you are retrieving information rather than trying to change state on some server resource.

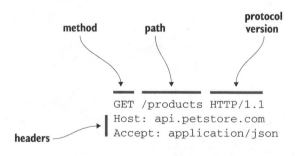

**Figure 2.2   Breaking down the HTTP request for products**

---

[2]    It's this fact that makes mountebank usable in any language.

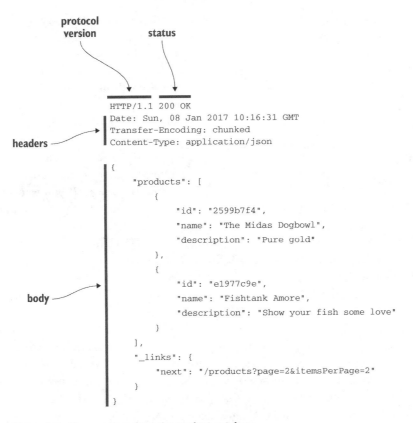

protocol
version        status

```
HTTP/1.1 200 OK
Date: Sun, 08 Jan 2017 10:16:31 GMT
Transfer-Encoding: chunked
Content-Type: application/json
```

headers

body

```
{
    "products": [
        {
            "id": "2599b7f4",
            "name": "The Midas Dogbowl",
            "description": "Pure gold"
        },
        {
            "id": "e1977c9e",
            "name": "Fishtank Amore",
            "description": "Show your fish some love"
        }
    ],
    "_links": {
        "next": "/products?page=2&itemsPerPage=2"
    }
}
```

**Figure 2.3   The response from the product catalog**

Your path is /products, and you are using version 1.1 of the HTTP protocol. The second line starts the headers, a set of newline-separated key-value pairs. In this example, the Host header combines with the path and protocol to give the full URL like you would see in a browser: http://api.petstore.com/products. The Accept header tells the server that you are expecting JSON back.

When the product catalog service receives that request, it returns a response that looks like figure 2.3. A real service presumably would have many more data fields and many more items per page, but I have simplified the response to keep it digestible.

A high degree of symmetry exists between HTTP requests and responses. As with the first line of the request, the first line of the response contains metadata, although for responses the most important metadata field is the status code. A 200 status is HTTP-speak for success, but in case you forgot, it tells you with the word OK following the code. Other codes have other words that go with them, like BAD REQUEST for a 400, but the text doesn't serve any purpose other than a helpful hint. The libraries that you use for integrating with HTTP services only care about the code, not the text.

```
GET /products?page=2&itemsPerPage=2 HTTP/1.1
Host: api.petstore.com
Accept: application/json
```

**Figure 2.4    Adding a query parameter to an HTTP request**

The headers once again follow the metadata, but here you see the HTTP body. The body is always separated from the headers by an empty line, and even though your HTTP request did not have a body, you will see plenty of examples in this book that do.

This particular body includes a link to the next page of results, which is a common pattern for implementing paging in services. If you were to craft the HTTP request that follows the link, it would look similar to the first request, as shown in figure 2.4.

The difference appears to be in the path, but every HTTP library that I'm aware of would give you the same path for both the first and second request. Everything after the question mark denotes what is called the *querystring*. (Mountebank calls it the *query*.) Like the headers, the query is a set of key-value pairs, but they are separated by the & character and included in the URL, separated from the path with a ? character.

HTTP can attribute much of its success to its simplicity. The textual format makes it almost as easy for pizza-fueled computer programmers to read as it is for electricity-fueled computers to parse. That's good for you because writing virtual services requires you to understand the protocol-specific request and response formats, which are treated as simple JSON objects that mimic closely the standard data structures used by HTTP libraries in any language. To generalize, figure 2.5 shows how mountebank translates an HTTP request.

```
POST /products?page=2&itemsPerPage=2 HTTP/1.1
Host: api.petstore.com
Content-Type: application/json

{
    "key": "abc123"
}
```

```
{
    "method": "POST",
    "path": "/products",
    "query": {
        "page": "2,
        "itemsPerPage": "2"
    },
    "headers": {
        "Host": "api.petstore.com",
        "Content-Type": "application/json"
    },
    "body": "{\n    \"key\": \"abc123\"\n}"
}
```

**Figure 2.5    How mountebank views an HTTP request**

Notice in figure 2.5 that even though the body is represented in JSON, HTTP itself doesn't understand JSON, which is why the JSON is represented as a simple string value. In later chapters, we will look at how mountebank makes working with JSON easier.

Figure 2.6 shows how mountebank represents an HTTP response.

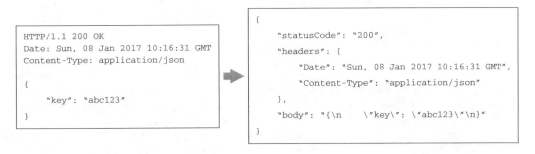

```
HTTP/1.1 200 OK
Date: Sun, 08 Jan 2017 10:16:31 GMT
Content-Type: application/json

{
    "key": "abc123"
}
```

```
{
    "statusCode": "200",
    "headers": {
        "Date": "Sun, 08 Jan 2017 10:16:31 GMT",
        "Content-Type": "application/json"
    },
    "body": "{\n    \"key\": \"abc123\"\n}"
}
```

**Figure 2.6   How mountebank represents an HTTP response**

This type of translation happens for all the protocols mountebank supports—simplifying the application protocol details into a JSON representation. Each protocol gets its own JSON representation for both requests and responses. The core functionality of mountebank performs operations on those JSON objects, blissfully unaware of the semantics of the protocol. Aside from the servers and proxies to listen to and forward network requests, the core functionality in mountebank is protocol-agnostic.

Now that you've seen how to translate HTTP semantics to mountebank, it's time to create your first virtual service.

## 2.3   *Virtualizing the product catalog service*

Once you understand how to integrate your codebase with a service, the next step is to figure out how to virtualize it for testing purposes. Continuing with our example, let's virtualize the product catalog service so you can test the web façade in isolation (figure 2.7).

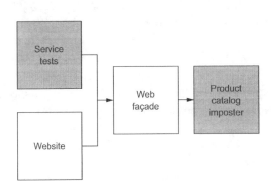

**Figure 2.7   Virtualizing the product catalog service to test the web facade**

Remember, an *imposter* is the mountebank term for a virtual service. Mountebank ships with a REST API that lets you create imposters and write tests against them in any language.

---

### Mountebanks, imposters, and funny sounding docs

Much of the mountebank documentation is written in the voice of a true mountebank, prone to hyperbole and false modesty, where even the word "mountebank" shifts from describing the tool itself to the author of the documentation (yours truly). When I originally wrote the tool, I made *imposters* the core domain concept, in part because it fit the theme of using synonyms for charlatans to describe fake services, and in part because it self-deprecatingly made fun of my own Impostor Syndrome, a chronic ailment of consultants like myself. And yes, as Paul Hammant (one of the original creators of the popular Selenium testing tool and one of the first users of mountebank) pointed out to me, impostor (with an "or" instead of "er" at the end) is the "proper" spelling. Now that mountebank is a popular tool used all over the world, complete with a best-selling book (the one you are holding), Paul also helpfully suggested that I change the docs to remove the hipster humor. Unfortunately, he has yet to indicate where I'm supposed to find the time for such pursuits.

---

Before you start, you will need to install mountebank. The website, http://www.mbtest .org/docs/install, lists several installation options, but you'll use npm, a package manager that ships with node.js, by typing the following in a terminal window:

```
npm install -g mountebank
```

The -g flag tells npm to install mountebank globally, so you can run it from any directory. Let's start it up:

```
mb
```

You should see the mountebank log on the terminal:

```
info: [mb:2525] mountebank v1.13.0 now taking orders -
➥ point your browser to http://localhost:2525 for help
```

The log will prove invaluable in working with mountebank in the future, so it's a good idea to familiarize yourself with it. The first word (info, in this case) tells you the log level, which will be either debug, info, warn, or error. The part in brackets (mb:2525) tells you the protocol and port and is followed by the log message. The administrative port logs as the mb protocol and starts on port 2525 by default. (The mb protocol is HTTP, but mountebank logs it differently to make it easy to spot.) The imposters you create will use different ports but log to the same output stream in the terminal. The startup log message directs you to open http://localhost:2525 in your web browser, which will provide you the complete set of documentation for the version of mountebank you are running.

To demonstrate creating imposters, you will use a utility called `curl`, which lets you make HTTP calls on the command line. `curl` comes by default on most Unix-like shells, including Linux and macOS. You can install it on Windows using Cygwin, or use PowerShell, which ships with modern versions of Windows. (We will show a PowerShell example next.) Open another terminal window and run the code shown in the following listing.[3]

---

**Listing 2.1 Creating an imposter on the command line**

```
curl -X POST http://localhost:2525/imposters --data '{        ◁──── Creates new
    "port": 3000,                                                     imposters
    "protocol": "http",              Minimally defines
    "stubs": [{                      each imposter by a
      "responses": [{                port and a protocol
        "is": {
          "statusCode": 200,
          "headers": {"Content-Type": "application/json"},
          "body": {
            "products": [
              {
                "id": "2599b7f4",
                "name": "The Midas Dogbowl",
                "description": "Pure gold"
              },
              {
                "id": "e1977c9e",
                "name": "Fishtank Amore",
                "description": "Show your fish some love"      Defines a canned
              }                                                HTTP response
            ],
            "_links": {
              "next": "/products?page=2&itemsPerPage=2"
            }
          }
        }
      }]
    }]
}'
```

---

An important point to note is that you are passing a JSON object as the body field. As far as HTTP is concerned, a response body is a stream of bytes. Usually HTTP interprets that stream as a string, which is why mountebank typically expects a string as well.[4] That said, most services these days use JSON as their *lingua franca*. Mountebank, being itself a modern JSON-speaking service, can properly accept a JSON body.

---

[3] To avoid carpal tunnel syndrome, you can download the source at https://github.com/bbyars/mountebank-in-action.

[4] Mountebank supports binary response bodies, encoding them with Base64. We look at binary support in chapter 8.

The equivalent command on PowerShell in Windows expects you to save the request body in a file and pass it in to the `Invoke-RestMethod` command. Save the JSON after the `--data` parameter from the `curl` command code above into a file called imposter.json, then run the following command from the same directory:

```
Invoke-RestMethod -Method POST -Uri http://localhost:2525/imposters
➥ -InFile imposter.json
```

Notice what happens in the logs:

```
info: [http:3000] Open for business...
```

The part in brackets now shows the new imposter. As you add more imposters, this will become increasingly important. You can disambiguate all log entries by looking at the imposter information that prefixes the log message.

You can test your imposter on the command line as well, using the `curl` command we looked at previously, as shown in figure 2.8.

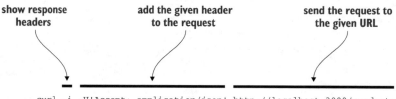

**Figure 2.8   Using `curl` to send a request to your virtual product catalog service**

The `curl` command prints out the HTTP response as shown in the following listing.

**Listing 2.2   The HTTP response from the `curl` command**

```
HTTP/1.1 200 OK
Content-Type: application/json
Connection: close
Date: Thu, 19 Jan 2017 14:51:23 GMT
Transfer-Encoding: chunked

{
  "products": [
    {
      "id": "2599b7f4",
      "name": "The Midas Dogbowl",
      "description": "Pure gold"
    },
    {
      "id": "e1977c9e",
      "name": "Fishtank Amore",
```

```
          "description": "Show your fish some love"
        }
    ],
    "_links": {
      "next": "/products?page=2&itemsPerPage=2"
    }
}
```

That HTTP response includes a couple of extra headers, and the date has changed, but other than that, it's exactly the same as the real one returned by the service shown in figure 2.3. You aren't accounting for all situations though. The imposter will return exactly the same response no matter what the HTTP request looks like. You could fix that by adding predicates to your imposter configuration.

As a reminder, a *predicate* is a set of criteria that the incoming request must match before mountebank will send the associated response. Let's create an imposter that only has two products to serve up. We will use a predicate on the query parameter to show an empty result set on the request to the second page. For now, restart mb to free up port 3000 by pressing Ctrl-C and typing mb again. (You will see more elegant ways of cleaning up after yourself shortly.) Then use the command shown in the following listing in a separate terminal.

> **Listing 2.3  An imposter with predicates**

```
curl -X POST http://localhost:2525/imposters --data '{
  "port": 3000,
  "protocol": "http",
  "stubs": [                           ◁──┐ Using two stubs allows different
    {                                       │ responses for different requests.
      "predicates": [{
        "equals": {                          Requires that the request
          "query": { "page": "2" }           querystring include page=2
        }
      }],
      "responses": [{
        "is": {
          "statusCode": 200,                             Sends this response if
          "headers": {"Content-Type": "application/json"},  the request matches
          "body": { "products": [] }                     the predicate
        }
      }]
    },
    {
      "responses": [{
        "is": {
          "statusCode": 200,
          "headers": { "Content-Type": "application/json" },
          "body": {                                      Otherwise, sends
            "products": [                                 this response
              {
                "id": "2599b7f4",
                "name": "The Midas Dogbowl",
```

```
          "description": "Pure gold"
        },
        {
          "id": "e1977c9e",
          "name": "Fishtank Amore",
          "description": "Show your fish some love"
        }
      ],
      "_links": {
        "next": "/products?page=2&itemsPerPage=2"
      }
    }
  }
}]
}
]
}'
```

Otherwise, sends this response

Now, if you send a request to the imposter without a querystring, you'll get the same response as before. But adding page=2 to the querystring gives you an empty product list:

```
curl -i http://localhost:3000/products?page=2

HTTP/1.1 200 OK
Content-Type: application/json
Connection: close
Date: Sun, 21 May 2017 17:19:17 GMT
Transfer-Encoding: chunked

{
    "products": []
}
```

Exploring the mountebank API on the command line is a great way to get familiar with it and to try sample imposter configurations. If you change the configuration of your web façade to point to http://localhost:3000 instead of https://api.petstore.com, you will get the products we have defined and can manually test the website. You have already taken a huge step toward decoupling yourself from the real services.

### Postman as an alternative to the command line

Although using command-line tools like curl is great for lightweight experimentation and perfect for the book format, it's often useful to have a more graphical approach to organize different HTTP requests. Postman (https://www.getpostman.com/) has proven to be an extremely useful tool for playing with HTTP APIs. It started out as a Chrome plugin but now has downloads for Mac, Windows, and Linux. It lets you fill in the various HTTP request fields and save requests for future use.

That said, the real benefit of service virtualization is in enabling automated testing. Let's see how you can wire up mountebank to your test suite.

## 2.4 Your first test

To properly display the products on the website, the web façade needs to combine the data that comes from the product catalog service with marketing copy that comes from a marketing content service (figure 2.9). You will add tests that verify that the data that gets to the website is valid.

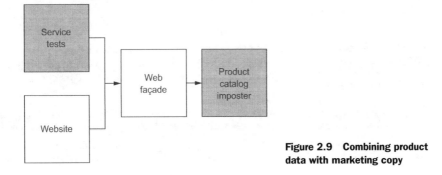

Figure 2.9 Combining product data with marketing copy

The data that the web façade provides to the website should show both the product catalog data and the marketing content. The response from the web façade should look like the following listing.

### Listing 2.4 Combining product data with marketing content

```
HTTP/1.1 200 OK
Content-Type: application/json
Date: Thu, 19 Jan 2017 15:43:21 GMT
Transfer-Encoding: chunked
{
  "products": [
    {
      "id": "2599b7f4",          ◄─┐
      "name": "The Midas Dogbowl",
      "description": "Pure gold",
      "copy": "Treat your dog like the king he is",
      "image": "/content/c5b221e2"
    },
    {
      "id": "e1977c9e",
      "name": "Fishtank Amore",
      "description": "Show your fish some love",
      "copy": "Love your fish; they'll love you back",
      "image": "/content/a0fad9fb"
    }
  ],
  "_links": {
    "next": "/products?page=2&itemsPerPage=2"
  }
}
```

**Comes from the product catalog service, but also will be used to look up content**

**Comes from the product catalog service**

**Comes from the marketing content service**

Let's write a service test that validates that *if* the product catalog and content services return the given data, *then* the web façade will combine the data as shown above. Although mountebank's HTTP API allows you to use it in any language, you will use JavaScript for the example. The first thing you will need to do is make it easy to create imposters from your tests. A common approach to make building a complex configuration easier is to use what is known as a fluent interface, which allows you to chain function calls together to build a complex configuration incrementally.

The code in listing 2.5 uses a fluent interface to build up the imposter configuration in code. Each `withStub` call creates a new stub on the imposter, and each `matchingRequest` and `respondingWith` call adds a predicate and response, respectively, to the stub. When you are done, you call `create` to use mountebank's REST API to create the imposter.

> **Listing 2.5    Using a fluent interface to build imposters in code**

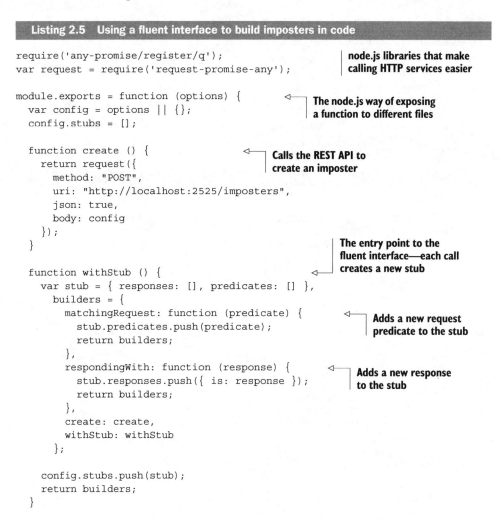

```
require('any-promise/register/q');                      node.js libraries that make
var request = require('request-promise-any');           calling HTTP services easier

module.exports = function (options) {                   The node.js way of exposing
  var config = options || {};                           a function to different files
  config.stubs = [];

  function create () {                                  Calls the REST API to
    return request({                                    create an imposter
      method: "POST",
      uri: "http://localhost:2525/imposters",
      json: true,
      body: config
    });
  }
                                                        The entry point to the
                                                        fluent interface—each call
  function withStub () {                                creates a new stub
    var stub = { responses: [], predicates: [] },
      builders = {
        matchingRequest: function (predicate) {         Adds a new request
          stub.predicates.push(predicate);              predicate to the stub
          return builders;
        },
        respondingWith: function (response) {           Adds a new response
          stub.responses.push({ is: response });        to the stub
          return builders;
        },
        create: create,
        withStub: withStub
      };

    config.stubs.push(stub);
    return builders;
  }
```

```
    return {
        withStub: withStub,
        create: create
    };
};
```

**JavaScript: ES5 vs. ES2015**

Modern JavaScript syntax is defined in the version of the EcmaScript (ES) specification. At the time of this writing, ES2015, which adds a bunch of syntactic bells and whistles, is seeing wide adoption, but ES5 still has the broadest support. Although those syntactic bells and whistles are nice once you get used to them, they make the code a little more opaque for non-JavaScript developers. Because this isn't a book on JavaScript, I use ES5 here to keep the focus on mountebank.

You will see how the fluent interface makes the consuming code more elegant shortly. The key to making it work is exposing the `create` and `withStub` functions in the builder, which allows you to chain functions together to build the entire configuration and send it to mountebank.

Assuming you saved the code above in a file called imposter.js, you can use it to create the product catalog service response on port 3000. The code in listing 2.6 replicates what you did earlier on the command line and shows how the function chaining that the fluent interface gives you makes the code easier to follow. Save the following code in test.js.[5]

**Listing 2.6   Creating the product imposter in code**

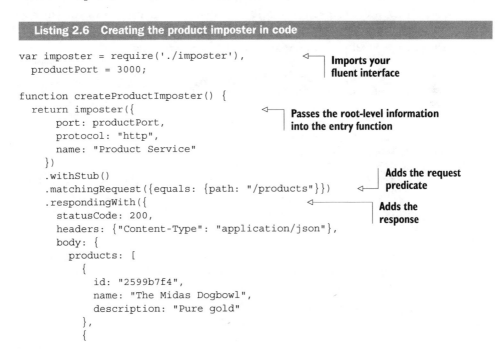

```
var imposter = require('./imposter'),          ◄─┐  Imports your
    productPort = 3000;                            │  fluent interface

function createProductImposter() {
    return imposter({                          ◄─┐  Passes the root-level information
        port: productPort,                         │  into the entry function
        protocol: "http",
        name: "Product Service"
    })
    .withStub()
    .matchingRequest({equals: {path: "/products"}})   ◄─┐  Adds the request
    .respondingWith({                              ◄─┐      predicate
        statusCode: 200,                               │  Adds the
        headers: {"Content-Type": "application/json"}, │  response
        body: {
            products: [
                {
                    id: "2599b7f4",
                    name: "The Midas Dogbowl",
                    description: "Pure gold"
                },
                {
```

```
            id: "e1977c9e",
            name: "Fishtank Amore",
            description: "Show your fish some love"
        }
      ]
    }
  })
  .create();                          Sends a POST to the mountebank
}                                     endpoint to create the imposter
```

It's worth noting a couple of points about the way you are creating the product catalog imposter. First, you have added a name to the imposter. The name field doesn't change any behavior in mountebank other than the way the logs format messages. The name will be included in the text in brackets to make it easier to understand log messages by imposter. If you look at the mountebank logs after you create this imposter, you will see the name echoed:

```
info: [http:3000 Product Service] Open for business...
```

That's a lot easier than having to remember the port each imposter is running on.

The second thing to note is that you are adding a predicate to match the path. This isn't strictly necessary, as your test will correctly pass without it if the web façade code is doing its job. However, adding the predicate makes the test better. It not only verifies the behavior of the façade given the response, it also verifies that the façade makes the right request to the product service.

We haven't looked at the marketing content service yet. It accepts a list of IDs on a querystring and returns a set of content entries for each ID provided. The code in the following listing creates an imposter using the same IDs that the product catalog service provides. (Add this to the test.js file you created previously.)

---

**Listing 2.7   Creating the content imposter**

```
var contentPort = 4000;

function createContentImposter() {
  return imposter({
      port: contentPort,
      protocol: "http",
      name: "Content Service"
    })
    .withStub()
    .matchingRequest({
      equals: {
        path: "/content",              Only respond if the path
        query: { ids: "2599b7f4,e1977c9e" }    and query match as shown.
      }
    })
    .respondingWith({
      statusCode: 200,
      headers: {"Content-Type": "application/json"},
```

```
      body: {
        content: [
          {
            id: "2599b7f4",
            copy: "Treat your dog like the king he is",
            image: "/content/c5b221e2"
          },
          {
            id: "e1977c9e",
            copy: "Love your fish; they'll love you back",
            image: "/content/a0fad9fb"
          }
        ]
      }
    })
    .create();
}
```

The entries that the content service would return

Armed with the `createProductImposter` and `createContentImposter` functions, you now can write a service test that calls the web façade over the wire and verifies that it aggregates the data from the product catalog and marketing content services appropriately (figure 2.10).

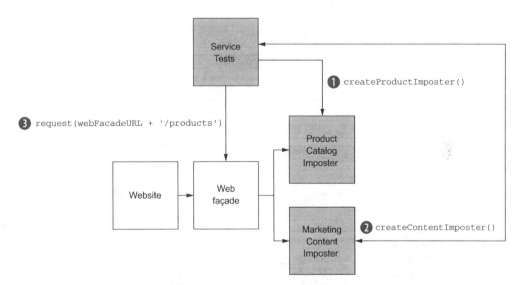

**Figure 2.10  The steps of the service test to verify web façade's data aggregating**

For this step, you will use a JavaScript test runner called Mocha, which wraps each test in an `it` function and collections of tests in a `describe` function (similar to a test class in other languages). Finish off the test.js file you have been creating by adding the code in the following listing.

**Listing 2.8   Verifying the web façade**

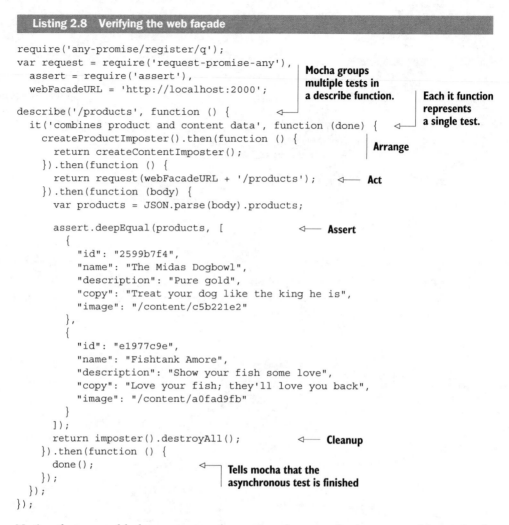

```
require('any-promise/register/q');
var request = require('request-promise-any'),
    assert = require('assert'),
    webFacadeURL = 'http://localhost:2000';

describe('/products', function () {
  it('combines product and content data', function (done) {
    createProductImposter().then(function () {
      return createContentImposter();
    }).then(function () {
      return request(webFacadeURL + '/products');
    }).then(function (body) {
      var products = JSON.parse(body).products;

      assert.deepEqual(products, [
        {
          "id": "2599b7f4",
          "name": "The Midas Dogbowl",
          "description": "Pure gold",
          "copy": "Treat your dog like the king he is",
          "image": "/content/c5b221e2"
        },
        {
          "id": "e1977c9e",
          "name": "Fishtank Amore",
          "description": "Show your fish some love",
          "copy": "Love your fish; they'll love you back",
          "image": "/content/a0fad9fb"
        }
      ]);
      return imposter().destroyAll();
    }).then(function () {
      done();
    });
  });
});
```

Mocha groups multiple tests in a describe function.

Each it function represents a single test.

Arrange

Act

Assert

Cleanup

Tells mocha that the asynchronous test is finished

Notice that you added one step to the test to clean up the imposters. Mountebank supports a couple ways of removing imposters. You can remove a single imposter by sending a DELETE HTTP request to the /imposters/:port URL (where :port represents the port of the imposter), or remove all imposters in a single call by issuing a DELETE request to /imposters. Add them to your imposter fluent interface in imposter.js, as shown in the following listing.

**Listing 2.9   Adding the ability to remove imposters**

```
function destroy () {
  return request({
    method: "DELETE",
    uri: "http://localhost:2525/imposters/" + config.port
  });
}
```

Passes in the config object, as in listing 2.5

```
function destroyAll () {
  return request({
    method: "DELETE",
    uri: "http://localhost:2525/imposters"
  });
}
```

Whew! You now have a complete service test that verifies some fairly complex aggregation logic of a service in a black-box fashion by virtualizing its runtime dependencies. (You had to create some scaffolding, but you will be able to reuse the imposters.js module in all of your tests moving forward.) The prerequisites for running this test are that both the web façade and mountebank are running, and you have configured the web façade to use the appropriate URLs for the imposters (http://localhost:3000 for the product catalog service, and http://localhost:4000 for the marketing content service).[6]

---

### JavaScript promises

Your test code relies on a concept called *promises* to make it easier to follow. JavaScript hasn't traditionally had any I/O, and when node.js added I/O capability, it did so in what is known as a nonblocking manner. This means that system calls that need to read or write data to something other than memory are done asynchronously. The application requests the operating system to read from disk, or from the network, and then moves on to other activities while waiting for the operating system to return. For a web service like the kind you are building, "other activities" would include processing new HTTP requests.

The traditional way of telling node.js what to do when the operating system has finished the operation is to register a callback function. In fact, the `request` library that you are using to make HTTP calls works this way by default, as shown in this callback-based HTTP request:

```
var request = require('request');
request('http://localhost:4000/products', function (error, response, body) {
  // Process the response here
})
```

The problem with this approach is that it gets unwieldy to nest multiple callbacks, and downright tricky to figure out how to loop over a sequence of multiple asynchronous calls. With promises, asynchronous operations return an object that has a `then` function, which serves the same purpose as the callback. But promises add all kinds of simplifications to make combining complex asynchronous operations easier. You will use them in your tests to make the code easier to read.

---

Part 3 of this book will show more fully worked-out automated tests and how to include them in a continuous delivery pipeline. First, though, you need to get familiar with the capabilities of mountebank. Part 2 breaks down the core mountebank capabilities step by step, starting in the next chapter by exploring canned responses in depth and adding HTTPS to the mix.

## *Summary*

- Mountebank translates the fields of the HTTP application protocol into JSON for requests and responses.
- Mountebank virtualizes services by creating *imposters*, which bind a protocol to a socket. You can create imposters using mountebank's RESTful API.
- You can use mountebank's API in automated tests to create imposters returning a specific set of canned data to allow you to test your application in isolation.

# Part 2

# Using mountebank

The test in chapter 2 was a behavioral test, but service virtualization can satisfy a wide spectrum of testing needs. Understanding how mountebank fits into that spectrum requires exploring the full capabilities of the tool.

The test we just looked at used basic building blocks of service virtualization—and indeed of any stubbing tool—the ability to evaluate the request to determine how to respond. We'll look at these capabilities over the course of the next two chapters, including additional context around HTTPS, managing configuration files, and taking advantage of mountebank's built-in XML and JSON parsing.

Chapters 5 and 6 demonstrate more advanced response generation, allowing a more interesting set of test scenarios. By adding record and replay capability, you can generate test data dynamically to perform large-scale tests and to build the foundation for performance testing (which we'll examine in part 3). The ability to programmatically change responses gives you key flexibility to support hard-to-test scenarios like OAuth.

Behaviors, or postprocessing steps, provide advanced functionality. From managing test data in a CSV file to adding latency to your responses, behaviors give you a robust set of tools both to simplify testing and to support a wider range of testing scenarios. We explore behaviors in chapter 7.

We round out this section by looking at mountebank's support for protocols, which is the glue that makes everything else possible. Although we spend much of the book exploring HTTP use cases, mountebank supports multiple protocols, and in chapter 8 we explore how it works with additional TCP-based protocols.

# Testing using
# canned responses

**This chapter covers**

- The `is` response type, which is the fundamental building block for a stub
- Using `is` responses in secure scenarios, with HTTPS servers and mutual authentication
- Persisting your imposter configuration using file templates

During a famous U.S. White House scandal of the 1990s, then-president Bill Clinton defended his prior statements by saying "It depends on what the meaning of *is* is." The grand jury and politicians ultimately failed to come to an agreement on the question, but, fortunately, mountebank has no uncertainty on the matter.

It turns out that *is* is quite possibly the most important, and the most foundational, concept in all of mountebank. Although an imposter, capturing the core idea of binding a protocol to a port, might beg to differ, by itself it adds little to a testing strategy. A response that looks like the real response—a response that, as far as the system under test is concerned, *is* the real response—changes everything.

*Is* is the key to being fake. Without *is*, a service binding a protocol to a port is a lame beast at best. Adding the ability to respond, and to respond as if the service *is* the real service, turns that service into a genuinely useful imposter.

In mountebank, the is response type is how you create *canned responses*, or responses that simulate a real response in some static way that you configure. Although it is one of three response types (proxy and inject being the other two), it's the most important one. In this chapter, we will explore is responses both by using the REST API and by persisting them in configuration files.

We will also start to layer in key security concerns. Although all of our examples so far have assumed HTTP, the reality is that any serious web-based service built today will use HTTPS, layering transport layer security (TLS) onto the HTTP protocol. Because security—especially authentication—is generally one of the first aspects of any microservice implementation you run into when writing tests, we will look at using an HTTPS server that uses certificates to validate the client.

Finally, we will explore how to persist imposter configurations. As you have no doubt realized by now, stubbing out services over the wire can be significantly more verbose than stubbing out objects in-process. Figuring out how to lay out that configuration in a maintainable way is essential to using service virtualization to shift tests earlier in the development life cycle.

## 3.1    *The basics of canned responses*

It's a bit rude for any book on software development to skip out on the customary "Hello, world!" example.[1] A "Hello, world!" response looks like the following listing in HTTP.

> **Listing 3.1    Hello world! in an HTTP response**

```
HTTP/1.1 200 OK
Content-Type: text/plain

Hello, world!
```

As you saw in the last chapter, returning this response in mountebank is as simple as translating the response you want into the appropriate JSON structure, as follows.

> **Listing 3.2    The HTTP response structure in JSON**

```
{
  "statusCode": 200,
  "headers": { "Content-Type": "text/plain" },
  "body": "Hello, world!"
}
```

---

[1]   Brian Kernighan and Dennis Ritchie showed how to print "Hello, world!" to the terminal in their venerable book *The C Programming Language*. It has become a common introductory example.

To create an HTTP imposter, listening on port 3000, that will return this response, save the following code in a helloWorld.json file.

**Listing 3.3 The imposter configuration to respond with Hello, world!**

```
{
  "protocol": "http",          ◁──┐  Protocol defines
  "port": 3000,                   │  response structure
  "stubs": [{
    "responses": [{                         ┐  Tells mountebank to
      "is": {               ◁────────────────┘  use an is response
        "statusCode": 200,
        "headers": { "Content-Type": "text/plain" },  ┐ Defines the canned response
        "body": "Hello, world!"                       │ to be translated into HTTP
      }
    }]
  }]
}
```

You represent the JSON response you want from listing 3.2 inside the is response and expect mountebank to translate that to the HTTP shown in listing 3.1 because you've set the protocol to http. With mb running, you can send an HTTP POST to http://localhost:2525/imposters to create this imposter. You will use the curl command, introduced in chapter 2, to send the HTTP request:[2]

```
curl -d@helloWorld.json http://localhost:2525/imposters
```

The -d@ command-line switch reads the file that follows and sends the contents of that file as an HTTP POST body. You can verify that mountebank has created the imposter correctly by sending any HTTP request you want to port 3000:[3]

```
curl -i http://localhost:3000/any/path?query=does-not-matter
```

The response is almost, *but not quite*, the same as the "Hello, world!" response shown in listing 3.1:

```
HTTP/1.1 200 OK
Content-Type: text/plain
Connection: close
Date: Wed, 08 Feb 2017 01:42:38 GMT
Transfer-Encoding: chunked

Hello, world!
```

Three additional HTTP headers somehow crept in. Understanding where these headers came from requires us to revisit a concept described in chapter 1 as the *default response.*

---

[2] Feel free to follow along using Postman or some graphical REST client. The examples are also available at https://github.com/bbyars/mountebank-in-action.

[3] In the examples that follow, I will continue to use the -i command-line parameter for curl. This tells curl to print the response headers to the terminal.

### *3.1.1   The default response*

You may recall the diagram shown in figure 3.1, which describes how mountebank selects which response to return based on the response.

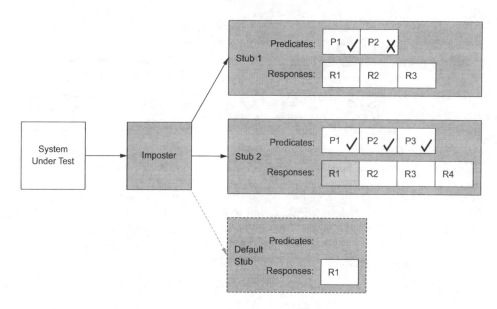

**Figure 3.1   How mountebank selects a response**

This diagram implies that if the request doesn't match any predicate, a hidden *default stub* will be used. That default stub contains no predicates, so it always matches the request, and it contains exactly one response—the default response. You can see this default response if you create an imposter without any stubs:

```
curl http://localhost:2525/imposters --data '
{
  "protocol": "http",
  "port": 3000
}'
```

> **NOTE**  Because you're using port 3000 across multiple examples, you may find that you have to shut down and restart mountebank between examples to avoid a port conflict. Alternatively, you can use the API to clean up the previous imposter(s) by sending an HTTP DELETE command to http://local host:2525/imposters (to remove all existing imposters) or to http://localhost:2525/imposters/3000 (to remove only the imposter on port 3000). If you're using curl, the command would be curl -X DELETE http://local host:2525/imposters.

You have not defined *any* responses with that lame beast of an imposter; you have only said you want an HTTP server listening on port 3000. If you send any HTTP request to that port, you get the default response shown in the following listing.

```
HTTP/1.1 200 OK
Connection: close
Date: Wed, 08 Feb 2017 02:04:17 GMT
Transfer-Encoding: chunked
```

We looked at the first line of the response in chapter 2, and the 200 status code indicates that mountebank processed the request successfully. The Date header is a standard response header that any responsible HTTP server sends, providing the server's understanding of the current date and time. The other two headers require a bit more explanation.

#### HTTP CONNECTIONS: TO REUSE OR NOT TO REUSE?

HTTP is an application protocol built on top of the hard work of a few lower level network protocols, the most important of which (for our purposes) is TCP. TCP is responsible for establishing the connection between the client and the server through a series of messages often referred to as the TCP handshake (figure 3.2).

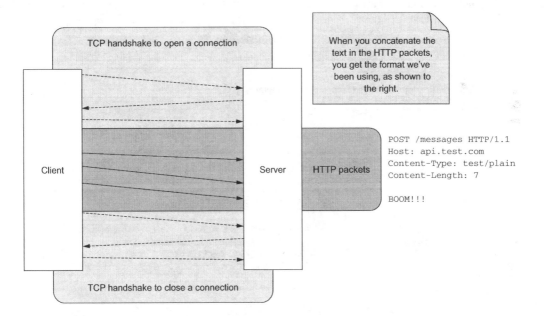

**Figure 3.2  TCP making the connection for HTTP messages**

Although the TCP messages to establish the connection (represented by the dashed lines) are necessary, they aren't necessary for *every* request. Once the connection is established, the client and server can reuse it for multiple HTTP messages. That ability is important, particularly for websites that need to serve HTML, JavaScript, CSS, and a set of images, each of which requires a round trip between the client and the server.

HTTP supports *keep-alive connections* as a performance optimization. A server tells the client to keep the connection open by setting the `Connection` header to `Keep-Alive`. Mountebank defaults it to `close`, which tells the client to negotiate the TCP handshake for every request. If you are writing service tests, performance likely doesn't matter, and you may prefer the determinism that comes with a fresh connection for each request. If you are writing performance tests, where the services you are virtualizing should be tuned with keep-alive connections, or if your purpose is to ensure your application behaves well with keep-alive connections, you should change the default.

### KNOWING WHERE AN HTTP BODY ENDS

Notice in figure 3.2 that a single HTTP request may consist of multiple packets. (The operating system breaks up data into a series of packets to optimize sending them over the network.) The same is true of a server response: what looks to be a single response may get transmitted in multiple packets. A consequence of this is that clients and servers need some way of knowing when an HTTP message is complete. With headers, it's easy: the headers end when you get a blank header line. But there's no way to predict where blank lines will occur in HTTP bodies, so you need a different strategy. HTTP provides two strategies, as shown in figure 3.3.

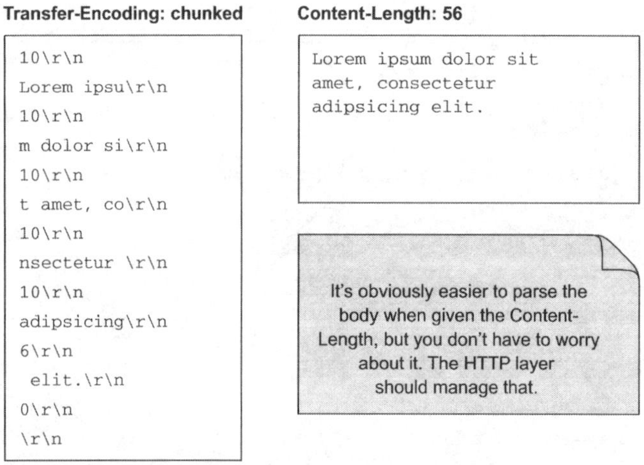

**Transfer-Encoding: chunked**

```
10\r\n
Lorem ipsu\r\n
10\r\n
m dolor si\r\n
10\r\n
t amet, co\r\n
10\r\n
nsectetur \r\n
10\r\n
adipsicing\r\n
6\r\n
 elit.\r\n
0\r\n
\r\n
```

**Content-Length: 56**

```
Lorem ipsum dolor sit
amet, consectetur
adipsicing elit.
```

It's obviously easier to parse the body when given the Content-Length, but you don't have to worry about it. The HTTP layer should manage that.

**Figure 3.3   Using chunked encodings or content length to calculate where the body ends**

The default imposter behavior sets the `Transfer-Encoding: chunked` header, which breaks the body into a series of chunks and prefixes each one with the number of bytes it contains. Special formatting delineates each chunk, making parsing relatively easy. The advantage of sending the body a chunk at a time is that the server can start streaming data to the client before the server has all of the data. The alternative strategy is to calculate the length of the entire HTTP body before sending it and provide that information in the header. To select that strategy, the server sets a `Content-Length` header to the number of bytes in the body.

When I created mountebank, I had to choose one default strategy. In truth, the web framework mountebank is written in chose it for me, which is the only reason mountebank imposters default to chunked encoding. The two strategies are mutually exclusive, so if you need to set the `Content-Length` header, the `Transfer-Encoding` header won't be set.

### 3.1.2 Understanding how the default response works

Now that you have seen what the default response looks like, it is probably a good time to admit that there is no such thing as a default stub in mountebank. That's a bald-faced lie. I'm sorry—I *did* feel a little guilty writing it—but it's a useful simplification for situations where no stub matches the request. And in case you haven't noticed yet, lying is exactly what mountebank does.

The reality is that mountebank merges the default response into *any* response you provide. Not providing a response is the same as providing an empty response, which is why you see the purest form of the default response in listing 3.4. But you also could provide a partial response; for example, the following response structure doesn't provide all of the response fields:

```
{
  "is": {
    "body": "Hello, world!"
  }
}
```

Not to worry. Mountebank will still return a full response, helpfully filling in the blanks for you:

```
HTTP/1.1 200 OK
Connection: close
Date: Sun, 12 Feb 2017 17:38:39 GMT
Transfer-Encoding: chunked

Hello, world!
```

### 3.1.3 Changing the default response

Mountebank's ability to merge in defaults for the response is a pleasant convenience. As I suggested, it means you only need to specify the fields that are different from the defaults, which simplifies the response configuration. But that's only useful if the defaults represent what you typically want. Fortunately, mountebank allows you to change the default response to better suit your needs.

Imagine a test suite that only wants to test error paths. You can default the statusCode to a 400 Bad Request to avoid having to specify it in each response. Although you can't get rid of the Date header (it's required for valid responses), you'll go ahead and change the other default headers to use keep-alive connections and set the Content-Length header, as in the following listing.

**Listing 3.5   Changing the default response**

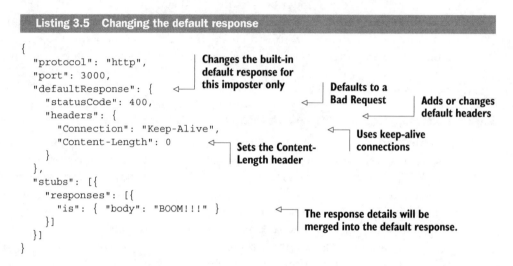

```
{
  "protocol": "http",                ⎫ Changes the built-in
  "port": 3000,                      ⎬ default response for
  "defaultResponse": {   ◁────────── ⎭ this imposter only
    "statusCode": 400,     ◁───────────── Defaults to a
    "headers": {                          Bad Request    ⎤ Adds or changes
      "Connection": "Keep-Alive",      ◁──────────────── ⎦ default headers
      "Content-Length": 0   ◁───┐                ⎤ Uses keep-alive
    }                           │ Sets the Content- ⎦ connections
  },                           Length header
  "stubs": [{
    "responses": [{
      "is": { "body": "BOOM!!!" }    ◁───┐ The response details will be
    }]                                   ┘ merged into the default response.
  }]
}
```

If you now send a test request to the imposter, it merges the new default fields into the response, as follows.

**Listing 3.6   A response using the new defaults**

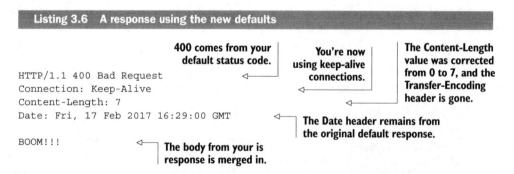

```
                              ⎤ 400 comes from your   ⎤ You're now  ⎤ The Content-Length
                              ⎦ default status code.  ⎦ using keep-alive ⎦ value was corrected
HTTP/1.1 400 Bad Request   ◁───────────────────────── using keep-alive  from 0 to 7, and the
Connection: Keep-Alive   ◁─────────────────────── connections.          Transfer-Encoding
Content-Length: 7   ◁───────────────────────────────────────            header is gone.
Date: Fri, 17 Feb 2017 16:29:00 GMT   ◁───┐ The Date header remains from
                                          ┘ the original default response.
BOOM!!!     ◁───┐ The body from your is
                ┘ response is merged in.
```

Notice in particular that mountebank set the Content-Length header to the correct value. Mountebank imposters won't send out invalid HTTP responses.

### 3.1.4   Cycling through responses

Let's imagine one more test scenario: this time, you will test what happens when you submit an order through an HTTP POST to an order service. Part of the order submission process involves checking to make sure inventory is sufficient. The tricky part, from a testing perspective, is that inventory is sold and restocked—it doesn't stay static for the same product. This means that the exact same request to the inventory service can respond with a different result each time (figure 3.4).

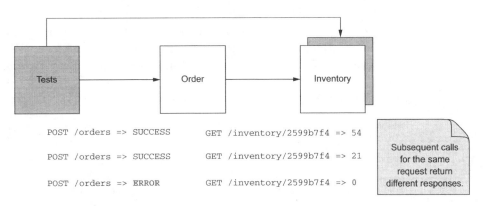

**Figure 3.4**  **Inventory checks return volatile results for the same request.**

In chapter 2, you saw a similar example with requests to the product catalog service, which returned different responses for the same path. In that example, you were able to use different predicates to determine which response to send based on the page query parameter, but in the inventory example, nothing about the request allows you to select one response over the other.

What you need is a way to cycle through a set of responses to simulate the volatility of the on-hand inventory for a fast-selling product. The solution is to use the fact that each stub contains a *list* of responses, as shown in the following listing. Mountebank returns those responses in the order provided.[4]

**Listing 3.7  Returning a list of responses for the same stub**

```
{
  "port": 3000,
  "protocol": "http",
  "stubs": [
    {
      "responses": [
        { "is": { "body": "54" } },          Responses that are
        { "is": { "body": "21" } },          returned in order
        { "is": { "body": "0" } }
```

---

[4]  Note that in the following example and several others throughout the book, I will use an overly simplified response to save space and remove some of the noise. No self-respecting inventory service would ever return only a single number, but it makes the intent of the example stand out more clearly, allowing you to focus on the fact that *some* data is different for each response.

```
          ]
        }
      ]
}
```

The first call returns 54, the second call returns 21, and the third call returns 0. If your tests need to trigger a fourth call, it will once again return 54, then 21, and 0. Mountebank treats the list of responses as an infinite list, with the first and last entries connected like a circle, the *circular buffer* data structure discussed in chapter 1.

As shown in figure 3.5, the illusion of an infinite list is maintained by shifting each response to the end of the list when it is returned. You can cycle through them as many times as you need to.

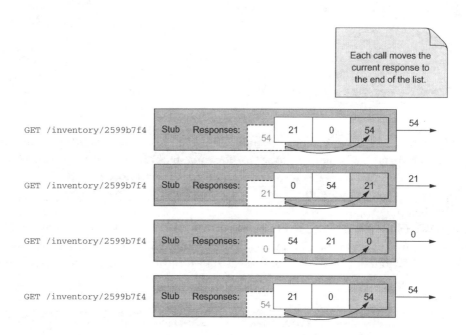

**Figure 3.5   Each stub cycles through the responses forever.**

In chapter 7, we'll look at all kinds of interesting post-processing actions you can take on a response, but for now, you don't need to know anything more about canned responses. Let's switch gears and see how to layer in security.

## 3.2   *HTTPS imposters*

To keep things simple, we've focused on HTTP services so far. The reality is that real services require security, and that means using HTTPS. The S stands for SSL/TLS,

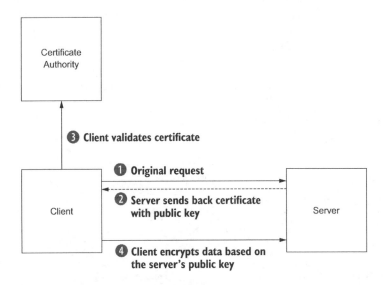

**Figure 3.6  The basic structure of SSL/TLS**

which adds encryption, and, optionally, identity verification to each request. Figure 3.6 shows the basic structure for SSL.

The infrastructure handles the SSL layer of HTTPS so that, as far as the application is concerned, each request and response is standard HTTP. The details of how the SSL layer works are a bit complex, but the key concepts that make it work are the server's *certificate* and the server's *keys*. The HTTPS server presents the client an SSL certificate during the handshake process, which describes the server's identity, including information such as the owner, the domain it's attached to, and the validity dates.

It's entirely possible that a malicious server may try to pass itself off as, say, Google, in the hopes of you passing it confidential information that you would only intend to pass to Google. That's why Certificate Authorities (CAs) exist. Trust has to start somewhere, and CAs are the foundation of trust in the SSL world. By sending a certificate, which contains a digital signature, to a CA that your organization trusts, you can confirm that the certificate is in fact from Google.

The certificate also includes the server's *public key*. The easiest approach to encryption is to use a single key for both encryption and decryption. Because of its efficiency, most of the communication relies on single-key encryption, but first the client and server have to agree on the key used without anyone else knowing it. The type of encryption SSL relies on during this handshake uses a neat trick that requires different keys for those two operations: the public key is used for encryption, and a separate *private key* is used for decryption (figure 3.7). This allows the server to share its public

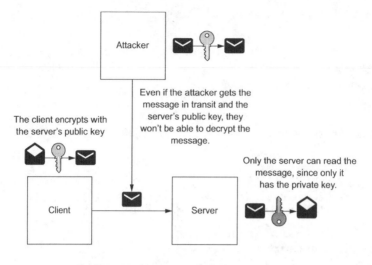

**Figure 3.7    Using two keys prevents attackers from reading messages in transit even when the encryption key is shared.**

key and the client to use that key for encryption, knowing that only the server will be able to decrypt the resulting payload because only it has the private key.

The good news is that creating an HTTPS imposter can look exactly like creating an HTTP imposter. The only required difference is that you set the protocol to `https`:

```
{
  "protocol": "https",
  "port": 3000
}
```

This is great for quickly setting up an HTTPS server, but it uses a default certificate (and key pair) that ships with mountebank. That certificate is both insecure and untrusted. Although that may be OK for some types of testing, any respectable service call should validate that the certificate is trusted, which, as shown in figure 3.6, involves a call to a trusted CA. By default, the HTTPS library that your system under test is using should reject mountebank's built-in certificate, meaning that it won't be able to connect to your virtual HTTPS service.

That leaves three options. The first is that you could configure the service you're testing not to validate that the certificate is trusted. Don't do this. You don't want to risk leaving code like that in during production, and you don't want to test one behavior for your service (that doesn't do a certificate validation) and deploy a completely different behavior to production (that does validation). The whole point of testing, after all, is to gain confidence in what you're sending to production, which requires that you actually *test* what's going to production.

The second option is to avoid testing with HTTPS. Instead, create an HTTP imposter and configure your system under test to point to it. The networking libraries that your system under test uses should support that change without any code changes, and you usually can trust them to work with HTTPS. This is a reasonable option to use when you are testing on your local machine.

The third option, shown in figure 3.8, is to use a certificate that is trusted, at least in the test environment. Organizations can run their own CA, making trust part of the environment rather than part of the application. That allows you to set up the test instances of your virtual services with appropriately trusted certificates.

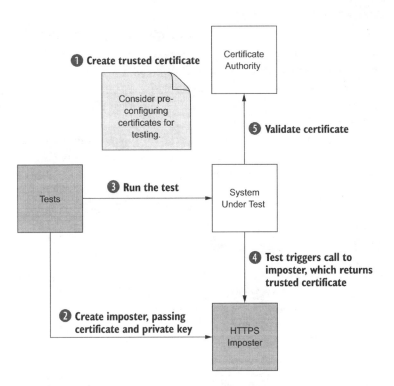

**Figure 3.8 Setting up a test environment with HTTPS**

With this approach, the test creates the imposter with both the certificate and the private key, as shown in the following listing. You can pass them in what is known as PEM format; we will look at how to create them shortly.

**Listing 3.8 Creating an HTTPS imposter**

```
{
  "protocol": "https",
  "port": 3000,
```

```
    "key": "-----BEGIN RSA PRIVATE KEY-----\n...",
    "cert": "-----BEGIN CERTIFICATE-----\n..."
}
```

**Much abbreviated from the actual text**

This setup is still insecure. The test needs to know the private key to create the imposter, so the imposter will know how to decrypt communication from the system under test. The certificate is tied to the domain name in the URL, so as long as you segment that domain name to your test environment, you aren't risking leaking any production secrets. With appropriate environment separation, this approach allows you to test the system under test without changing its behavior to allow untrusted certificates.

### 3.2.1 Setting up a trusted HTTPS imposter

Historically, getting certificates trusted by a public CA has been a painful and confusing process, and it cost enough money to discourage their use in exactly the kind of lightweight testing scenarios that mountebank supports. Using SSL is such a cornerstone of internet security that major players are pushing to change that process to the point where it's easy for even hobbyists without a corporate purse to create genuine certificates for the domains they register.

Let's Encrypt (https://letsencrypt.org/) is a free option that supports creating certificates for domains with minimal fuss, backed by a public CA. Every CA will require validation from the domain owner to ensure that no one is able to grab a certificate for a domain they don't own. Let's Encrypt allows you to completely automate the process by round-tripping a request based on a DNS lookup of the domain listed in the certificate (figure 3.9).

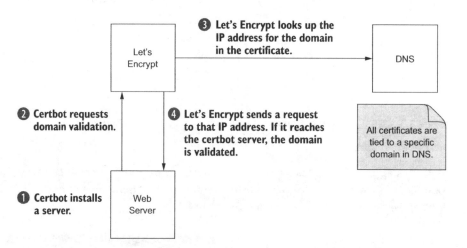

Figure 3.9  How Let's Encrypt validates the domain

Let's Encrypt uses a command-line tool called Certbot (https://certbot.eff.org) to automate the creation of certificates. Certbot expects you to install a client on the machine receiving the SSL request. The client stands up a web server and sends a request to a Let's Encrypt server. Let's Encrypt in turn looks up the domain for which you are requesting a certificate in DNS and sends a request to that IP address. If that request reaches the certbot server that created the first request, Let's Encrypt has validated that you own the domain.

The `certbot` command depends on the web server you are using, and because it is constantly evolving, you should check the documentation for details. In the general case, you might run:

```
certbot certonly --webroot -w /var/test/petstore -d test.petstore.com
```

That would create a certificate for the test.petstore.com domain that is served out of a web server running in /var/test/petstore. Simplifications are available if you're using a common web server like Apache or Nginx. See https://certbot.eff.org/docs/using .html#getting-certificates-and-choosing-plugins for details.

By default, the directory that certbot stores the SSL information in is /etc/lets encrypt/live/$domain, where $domain is the domain name of your service. If you look in that directory, you will find a few files, but two are relevant for our purposes: privkey.pem contains the private key, and cert.pem contains the certificate. The contents of those two files are what you would put in the `key` and `cert` fields when creating the HTTPS imposter.

A PEM file has newlines. An example certificate might look like the following:

```
-----BEGIN CERTIFICATE-----
MIIDejCCAmICCQDlIe97PDjXJDANBgkqhkiG9w0BAQUFADB/MQswCQYDVQQGEwJV
UzEOMAwGA1UECBMFVGV4YXMxFTATBgNVBAoTDFRob3VnaHRXb3JrczEMMAoGA1UE
CxMDT1NTMRMwEQYDVQQDEwptYnRlc3Qub3JnMSYwJAYJKoZIhvcNAQkBFhdicmFu
ZG9uLmJ5YXJjzQGdtYWlsLmNvbTAeFw0xNTA1MDMyMDE3NTRaFw0xNTA2MDIyMDE3
NTRaMH8xCzAJBgNVBAYTAlVTMQ4wDAYDVQQIEwVUZXhhczEVMBMGA1UEChMMVGhv
dWdodFdvcmtzMQwwCgYDVQQLEwNPU1MxEzARBgNVBAMTCm1idGVzdC5vcmcxJjAk
BgkqhkiG9w0BCQEWF2JyYW5kb24uYnlhcnNAZ21haWwuY29tMIIBIjANBgkqhkiG
9w0BAQEFAAOCAQ8AMIIBCgKCAQEA5V88ZyZ5hkPF7MzaDMvhGtGSBKIhQia2a0vW
6VfEtf/Dk80qKaalrwiBZlXheT/zwCoO7WBeqh5agOs0CSwzzEEie5/J6yVfgEJb
VROpnMbrLSgnUJXRfGNf0LCnTymGMhufz2utzcHRtgLm3nf5zQbBJ8XkOaPXokuE
UWwmTHrqeTN6munoxtt99olzusraxpgiGCil2ppFctsQHle49Vjs88KuyVjC5AOb
+P7Gqwru+R/1vBLyD8NVNl1WhLqaaeaopb9CcPgFZClchuMaAD4cecndrt5w4iuL
q91g71AjdXSG6V3R0DC2Yp/ud0Z8wXsMMC6X6VUxFrbeajo8CQIDAQABMA0GCSqG
SIb3DQEBBQUAA4IBAQCobQRpj0LjEcIViG8sXauwhRhgmmEyCDh57psWaZ2vdLmM
ED3D6y3HUzz08yZkRRr32VEtYhLldc7CHItscD+pZGJWlpgGKXEHdz/EqwR8yVhi
akBMhHxSX9s8N8ejLyIOJ9ToJQOPgelI019pvU4cmiDLihK5tezCrZfWNHXKw1hw
Sh/nGJ1UddEHCtC78dz6uIVIJQCOPkrLeGLKyAFrFJp4Bim8W8fbYSAffsWNATC+
dVKUlunVLd4RX/73nY5EM3ErcDDOCdUEQ2fUT59FhQF89DihFG4xW4OLq42/pgmW
KQBvwwfJxIFqg4fdnJUkHoLX3+glQWWrz80cauVH
-----END CERTIFICATE-----
```

You'll want to keep the newlines, escaped in typical JSON fashion with `'\n'`, in the strings you send mountebank. In this example, shortening the field for clarity, the resulting imposter configuration might look like this:

```
{
  "protocol": "https",
  "port": 3000,
  "key": "-----BEGIN RSA PRIVATE KEY-----\nMIIEpAIBAAKC...",
  "cert": "-----BEGIN CERTIFICATE-----\nMIIDejCCAmICCQD..."
}
```

Note that, although it's awkward to show in book format, the string would include all the way up to the end of the file (from the example, "…\nWWrz80cauVH\n—END CERTIFICATE—") for the certificate.

And…that's it. Everything else about your imposter remains the same. Once you have set the certificate and private key, the SSL layer is able to convert encrypted messages into HTTP requests and responses, which means the `is` responses you have already created continue to work. It may seem like a lot of work to set up the certificates, but that's the nature of SSL. Fortunately, tools like Let's Encrypt and shortcuts like using wildcard certificates simplify the process considerably.

> **Using wildcard certificates to simplify testing**
>
> A typical certificate is associated with a single domain name, such as `mypet store.com`. By adding a wildcard in front of the domain, the certificate becomes valid for all subdomains. You could, for example, create a `*.test.mypetstore .com` certificate, and that certificate would be valid for `products.test.mypet store.com` as well as `inventory.test.mypetstore.com`. It wouldn't be valid for production domains that don't include `test` as part of their domain name.
>
> A wildcard certificate is ideal for testing scenarios. You may find it easy to manually add a wildcard certificate to the CA, tied exclusively to a testing subdomain, and reuse the certificate and private key for all imposters.

### 3.2.2   *Using mutual authentication*

It turns out that certificates aren't only valid for HTTPS servers; they're also a common way to validate the identity of clients (figure 3.10). You don't see this when browsing the internet, because public websites have to assume the validity of the browsers that access them, but in a microservices architecture, it's important to validate that only authenticated clients can make a request to a server.

If the service you are testing expects to validate its identity with your imposter using a client certificate, you need to be able to configure your imposter in a way that expects that certificate. This is as simple as adding a `mutualAuth` field to the configuration set to `true`, as shown in the following listing.

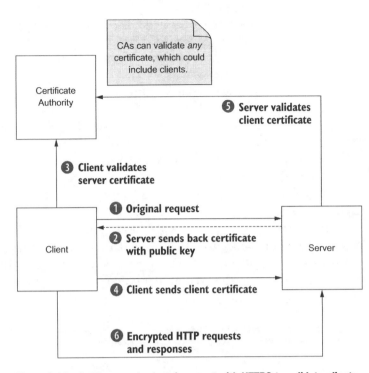

**Figure 3.10 Setting up a test environment with HTTPS to validate clients as well as servers**

---

**Listing 3.9 Adding mutual authentication to an imposter**

```
{
  "protocol": "https",
  "port": 3000,
  "key": "-----BEGIN RSA PRIVATE KEY-----\nMIIEpAIBAAKC...",
  "cert": "-----BEGIN CERTIFICATE-----\nMIIDejCCAmICCQD...",
  "mutualAuth": true
}
```

The server will expect a client certificate.

Now the server will challenge the client with a certificate request. Using certificates, both for HTTPS and for mutual authentication, allows you to virtualize servers in secure environments. But the fact that you have to escape the PEM files in JSON gets quite clunky. Let's look at how to make maintaining that data a bit easier using configuration files.

## 3.3 Saving the responses in a configuration file

By now, you're probably realizing that, as the complexity of the responses and security configuration increases, the JSON that you send mountebank can be quite complex.

```
├── inventory.ejs
└── ssl
    ├── cert.pem
    └── key.pem

1 directory, 3 files
```

**Figure 3.11  The tree structure for the secure inventory imposter configuration**

This is true even for a single field, like the multiline PEM files that need to be encoded as a JSON string. Fortunately, mountebank has robust support for persisting the configuration in a friendly format.

Now that you've added an inventory service and seen how to convert it to HTTPS, let's see how you would format the imposter configuration in files to make it easier to manage. The first bit of ugliness you'll want to solve is storing the certificate and private key in separate PEM files so you can avoid a long JSON string. If you store those as `cert.pem` and `key.pem` in the `ssl` directory, then you can create a file for the inventory imposter as `inventory.ejs` (figure 3.11).

Mountebank uses a templating language called EJS (http://www.embeddedjs .com/) to interpret the config file, which uses a fairly standard set of templating primitives. The content between `<%-` and `%>`, as shown in the following listing, is dynamically evaluated and interpolated into the surrounding quotes. Save the following in `inventory.ejs`.

**Listing 3.10  Storing the inventory service in a configuration file**

```
{
  "port": 3000,
  "protocol": "https",
  "cert": "<%- stringify(filename, 'ssl/cert.pem') %>",     Converts the multiline file
  "key": "<%- stringify(filename, 'ssl/key.pem') %>",       content into a JSON string
  "stubs": [
    {
      "responses": [
        { "is": { "body": "54" } },
        { "is": { "body": "21" } },
        { "is": { "body": "0" } }
      ]
    }
  ]
}
```

The inventory service will be available at startup, if you start mountebank with the appropriate command-line flag:

```
mb --configfile inventory.ejs
```

Mountebank adds the `stringify` function to the templating language, which does the equivalent of a JavaScript `JSON.stringify` call on the contents of the given file. In this case, the `stringify` call escapes the newlines. The benefit to you is that the configuration is much easier to read. (The `filename` variable is passed in by mountebank. It's a bit of a hack needed to make relative paths work.)

With those two templating primitives—the angle brackets that will be replaced by dynamic data and the `stringify` function to turn that data into presentable JSON—

you can build robust templates. Storing the SSL information separately is useful, but I intentionally oversimplified the inventory imposter to focus on the behavior of the responses array. Let's add in the product catalog and marketing content services you saw in chapter 2.

### 3.3.1 Saving multiple imposters in the config file

As you saw, templating allows you to break up your configuration into multiple files. You'll take advantage of that to revisit the product catalog and marketing content imposter configurations you saw in chapter 2, putting each imposter in one or more files. The first thing you need to do is define the root configuration, which now needs to take a list of imposters. The tree structure will look like figure 3.12.

```
├── content.ejs
├── imposters.ejs
├── inventory.ejs
├── product.ejs
└── ssl
    ├── cert.pem
    └── key.pem

1 directory, 6 files
```

**Figure 3.12   The tree structure for multiple services**

Save the following listing as `imposters.ejs`.

**Listing 3.11   The root configuration file, referencing other imposters**

```
{
  "imposters": [
    <% include inventory.ejs %>,          Interpolates content
    <% include product.ejs %>,            from other files as is
    <% include content.ejs %>
  ]
}
```

The `include` function comes from EJS. Like the `stringify` function, it loads in content from another file. Unlike `stringify`, the `include` function doesn't change the data; it brings the data as is from the referenced file. You can use the `include` EJS function and the `stringify` mountebank function to lay out your content any way you like. For complex configurations, you can store the response bodies—JSON, XML, or any other complex representation—in different files with newlines and load them in as needed. To keep it simple, you'll save each imposter in its own file, loading in the same wildcard certificate and private key. Save the product catalog imposter configuration that you saw in listing 2.1 in `product.ejs`, with some modifications as shown in the following listing.

**Listing 3.12   The updated version of the product catalog imposter configuration**

```
{
  "protocol": "https",          ◁── Converts to HTTPS
  "port": 3001,                                          Uses a different
  "cert": "<%- stringify(filename, 'ssl/cert.pem'); %>",  port to avoid a
  "key": "<%- stringify(filename, 'ssl/key.pem'); %>",    port conflict
  "stubs": [{
    "responses": [{
      "is": {                    Same stub configuration
        "statusCode": 200,       as in chapter 2
```

```
            "headers": { "Content-Type": "application/json" },
            "body": {
              "products": [
                {
                  "id": "2599b7f4",
                  "name": "The Midas Dogbowl",
                  "description": "Pure gold"
                },
                {
                  "id": "e1977c9e",
                  "name": "Fishtank Amore",
                  "description": "Show your fish some love"
                }
              ]
            }
          }
        }],
        "predicates": [{
          "equals": { "path": "/products" }
        }]
      }]
}
```

Finally, save the marketing content imposter configuration you saw in listing 2.7 in a
file called content.ejs, with the modifications shown in the following listing.

**Listing 3.13   The updated version of the marketing content imposter configuration**

```
{
  "protocol": "https",
  "port": 3002,                                                    ◁────  Uses a
  "cert": "<%- stringify(filename, 'ssl/cert.pem'); %>",                 different
  "key": "<%- stringify(filename, 'ssl/key.pem'); %>",                   port
  "stubs": [{
    "responses": [{
      "is": {
        "statusCode": 200,
        "headers": { "Content-Type": "application/json" },
        "body": {
          "content": [
            {
              "id": "2599b7f4",
              "copy": "Treat your dog like the king he is",
              "image": "/content/c5b221e2"
            },
            {
              "id": "e1977c9e",
              "copy": "Love your fish; they'll love you back",
              "image": "/content/a0fad9fb"
            }
          ]
        }
      }
    }
```

```
    }],
    "predicates": [{
      "equals": {
        "path": "/content",
        "query": { "ids": "2599b7f4,e1977c9e" }
      }
    }]
  }]
}
```

Now you can start mountebank by pointing to the root configuration file:

```
mb --configfile imposters.ejs
```

Notice what happens in the logs:

```
info: [mb:2525] mountebank v1.13.0 now taking orders -
➡ point your browser to http://localhost:2525 for help
info: [mb:2525] PUT /imposters
info: [https:3000] Open for business...
info: [https:3001] Open for business...
info: [https:3002] Open for business...
```

All three imposters are up and running. Of interest is the log entry pointing out that an HTTP PUT command was sent the mountebank URL of http://localhost:2525/ imposters. After running the contents of the configuration file through EJS, the mb command sends the results as the request body of the PUT command, which creates (or replaces) all the imposters in one shot. Nearly every feature in mountebank is exposed via an API first, so anything you can do on the command line, you can implement using the API. If you had more advanced persistence requirements, you could construct the JSON and send it to mountebank using curl, as in the following listing.

> **Listing 3.14  Using curl to send the JSON to mountebank**

```
curl -X PUT http://localhost:2525/imposters --data '{
  "imposters": [
    {
      "protocol": "https",
      "port": 3000
    },
    {
      "protocol": "https",
      "port": 3001
    }
  ]
}'
```

For clarity, I've left out all the important bits of the imposter configuration. You may find the PUT command a convenience in automated test suites where a setup step overwrites the entire set of imposters with one API call, rather than relying on all of the individual tests to send the DELETE calls to clean up their imposters.

If you do load the imposters through a configuration file, the imposter setup is part of starting mountebank, which you're expected to do before running your tests. That arrangement allows you to remove some of the setup steps from the test itself—specifically, those related to configuring and deleting the imposters.

## *Summary*

- The `is` response type allows you to create a canned response. The fields you specify in the response object merge in with the default response. You can change the default response if you need to.
- One stub can return multiple responses. The list of responses acts like a circular buffer, so once the last response is returned, mountebank cycles back to the first response.
- HTTPS imposters are possible, but you have to create the key pair and certificate. Let's Encrypt is a free service that lets you automate the process.
- Setting the `mutualAuth` flag on an imposter means that it will accept client certificates used for authentication.
- Mountebank uses EJS templating for persisting the configuration of your imposters. You load them at startup by passing the root template as the parameter to the `--configfile` command-line option.

# Using predicates to send different responses

## This chapter covers

- Using predicates to send different responses for different requests
- Simplifying predicates on JSON request bodies
- Using XPath to simplify predicates on XML request bodies

During his younger years, Frank William Abagnale Jr. forged a pilot's license and traveled the world by deadheading.[1] Despite not being able to fly, his successful impersonation of a pilot meant that his food and lodging were fully paid for by the airline. When that well dried up, he impersonated a physician in New Orleans for nearly a year without any medical background, supervising resident interns. When he didn't know how to respond after a nurse said a baby had "gone blue," he realized the life and death implications of that false identity and decided to make yet another

---

[1] The term refers to a pilot riding as a passenger on a flight to get to work. For example, a pilot who took up an assignment to fly from New York to London would need to first ride as a passenger to New York if he lived in Denver.

change. After forging a law transcript from Harvard University, he kept taking the Louisiana bar exam until he passed it, then he posed as an attorney with the attorney general's office. His story was memorialized in the 2002 movie, *Catch Me If You Can.*

Frank Abagnale was one of the most successful imposters of all time.

Although mountebank cannot guarantee you Abagnale's indefatigable confidence, it does give you the ability to mimic one of the other key factors of his success: tailoring your response to your audience. Had Abagnale acted like a pilot when facing a room full of medical interns, he would have had a much shorter medical career. Mountebank uses *predicates* to determine which response to use based on the incoming request, giving your imposter the ability pretend to be a virtual pilot for one request and a virtual doctor for the next one.

## 4.1　The basics of predicates

Testing a service that depends on a fictional Abagnale service (figure 4.1) is hard work. It involves doing something that has almost certainly never been done before in the history of mocking frameworks: you have to create a *virtual* imposter that pretends to be a *real* imposter.

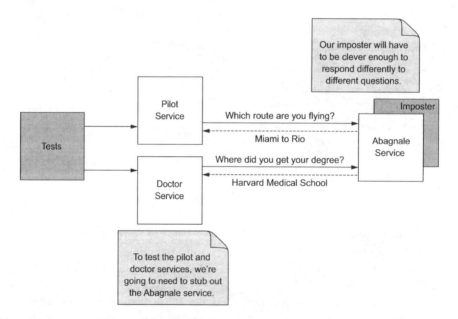

Figure 4.1　The Abagnale service adapts its response to the questions you ask it.

Fortunately, mountebank makes this easy. If you assume your system under test embeds the question it asks the Abagnale service inside the HTTP body, then your imposter configuration can look something like the following listing.[2]

---

[2]　To keep the examples as simple as possible, we'll use HTTP.

**Listing 4.1 Creating an Abagnale imposter**

```
{
  "protocol": "http",
  "port": 3000,
  "stubs": [
    {
      "predicates": [{
        "contains": { "body":
          ➡ "Which route are you flying?" }          ⟵  When asked a
      }],                                                 pilot question...
      "responses": [{
        "is": { "body": "Miami to Rio" }             ⟵  ...respond
      }]                                                 like a pilot.
    },
    {
      "predicates": [{
        "startsWith": { "body":
          ➡ "Where did you get your degree?" }       ⟵  When asked a
      }],                                                 doctor question...
      "responses": [{
        "is": { "body": "Harvard Medical School" }   ⟵  ...respond
      }]                                                 like a doctor.
    },
    {
      "responses": [{
        "is": { "body":
          ➡ "I'll have to get back to you" }         ⟵  If you don't know what type
      }]                                                 of question it is, stall!
    }
  ]
}
```

Each predicate matches on a request field. The examples in listing 4.1 all match the body, but any of the other HTTP request fields you saw in the previous chapter are fair game: method, path, query, and headers.

In chapter 2, we showed an example using equals predicates. Our simple Abagnale imposter shows off a couple more possibilities, using contains and startsWith. We'll look at the range of predicates shortly, but most of them are pretty self-explanatory. If the body contains the text "Which route are you flying?" then the imposter responds with "Miami to Rio," and if the body starts with the text "Where did you get your degree?" the imposter responds with "Harvard Medical School." This allows you to test the doctor and pilot services without depending on the full talents of Mr. Abagnale.

Note in particular the last stub, containing the "I'll have to get back to you" bit of misdirection. It contains no predicates, which means that all requests will match it, including those that match the predicates in other stubs. Because a request can match multiple stubs, mountebank always picks the first match, based on array order. This allows you to represent a fallback default response by putting it at the end of the stubs array without any predicates.

We haven't paid too much attention to stubs as a standalone concept because they only make sense in the presence of predicates. As you saw in the last chapter, it's possible to send different responses to the exact same request, which is why the responses field is a JSON array. This simple fact, combined with the need to tailor the response to the request, is the *raison d'etre* of stubs. Each imposter contains a list of stubs. Each stub contains a circular buffer for the responses. Mountebank selects which stub to use based on the stub's predicates (figure 4.2).

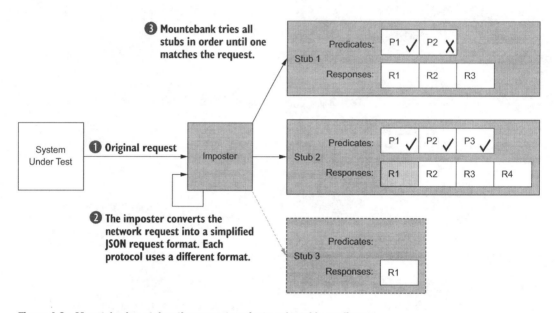

**Figure 4.2   Mountebank matches the request against each stub's predicates.**

Because mountebank uses a "first-match" policy on the stubs, having multiple stubs that could respond to the same request isn't a problem.

### 4.1.1   Types of predicates

Let's take a closer look at the simplest predicate operators (figure 4.3). These all behave much as you would expect. But a few more interesting types of predicates are available, starting with the incredibly useful matches predicate.

#### THE MATCHES PREDICATE

Your Abagnale service needs to respond intelligently to questions in both the present tense and the past tense. "Which route are you flying?" and "Which route did you fly?" should both trigger a response of "Miami to Rio." You could write multiple predicates, but the matches predicate lets you simplify your configuration with the use of a *regular expression* (or *regex*, as used in figure 4.4).

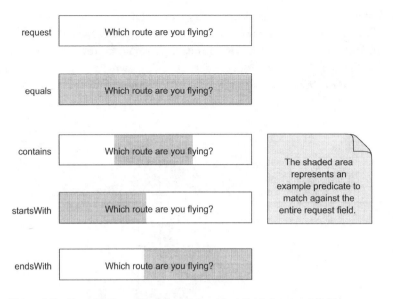

**Figure 4.3   How simple predicates match against the full request field**

Regular expressions include a wonderfully rich set of metacharacters to simplify pattern matching. This example uses three:

- . —matches any character except a newline
- * —matches the previous character zero or more times
- \ —escapes the following character, matching it literally

It may look like we had to double-escape the question mark, but that's only because \ is a JSON string escape character as well as a regular expression escape character. The first \ JSON-escapes the second \, which regex escapes the question mark, because it

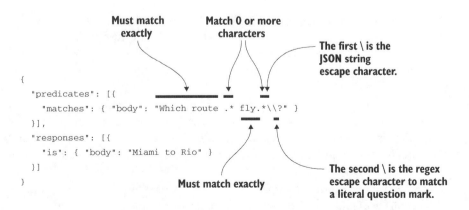

**Figure 4.4   Mountebank matches the request against each stub's predicates.**

turns out that a question mark is also a special metacharacter. Like the asterisk, it sets an expectation of the previous character or expression, but unlike the * metacharacter, ? matches it only zero times or one time. If you have never seen regular expressions before, that's a bit confusing, so let's break down your pattern against the request field value of "Which route did you fly?" (See figure 4.5.)

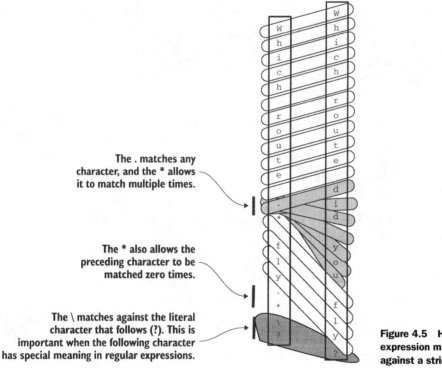

**The . matches any character, and the * allows it to match multiple times.**

**The * also allows the preceding character to be matched zero times.**

**The \ matches against the literal character that follows (?). This is important when the following character has special meaning in regular expressions.**

Figure 4.5   How a regular expression matches against a string value

Most characters match one-for-one against the request field. As soon as you reach the first metacharacters (.*), the pattern matches *as much as it can* until the next literal character (a blank space). The wildcard pattern .* is a simple way of saying "I don't care what they entered." As long as the rest of the pattern matches, then the entire regular expression matches.

The second .* matches because the * allows a zero-character match, which is another way of saying it can be satisfied even if it doesn't match anything. Conveniently, it also would have matched the "ing" if you had entered "flying" instead of "fly," which is why regular expressions are so flexible. Finally, the pattern \? matches the ending question mark.

The matches predicate is one of the most versatile predicates in mountebank. With a couple of additional metacharacters, it can completely replace the other predicates we've looked at so far. We will demonstrate that with another example.

### REPLACING OTHER PREDICATES WITH REGULAR EXPRESSIONS

A key to Abagnale's success is that he knew when it was time to run. After narrowly escaping arrest in New Orleans, he switched from being a pilot to a doctor with a new identity. When he realized the gravity of his medical ignorance, he switched again to being a lawyer. Recognizing when the jig is up requires seeing suspicious questions for what they are.

The Abagnale service responds with desperation when asked to see his driver's license, saying "Catch me if you can!" It gives the same response if the questioner asks for his "state's driver's license," or his "current driver's license," so you'll have to be a little loose with your matching.

You will need to match if the question *contains* the phrase "driver's license." You want to confirm that those characters represent a question by ensuring not only that they contain a question mark, but that they *end with* a question mark, and, to make absolutely sure that you are catching the right question, you will also ensure that the phrase *starts with* "Can I see your." Note that you can achieve all of this without regular expressions, but it would require combining multiple predicates, as follows:

```
{
  "predicates": [
    { "startsWith": { "body": "Can I see your" } },
    { "contains": { "body": "driver's license" } },
    { "endsWith": { "body": "?" } }
  ]
}
```

You can match exactly the same bodies with one `matches` predicate, as shown in the following listing.

> **Listing 4.2  Using the `matches` predicate to do the job of a set of `startsWith`, `contains`, and `endsWith` predicates**

```
{
  "predicates": [{
    "matches": { "body": "^Can I see your.*driver's license.*\\?" }
  }],
  "responses": [{
    "is": { "body": "Catch me if you can!" }
  }]
}
```

You've already seen how the `.*` metacharacters match any characters, or no characters at all. Wrapping text with those metacharacters on either side is equivalent to using a `contains` predicate (figure 4.6).

```
{
  "matches": { "body": ".*text to match.*" }
}
```
⟹
```
{
  "contains": { "body": "text to match" }
}
```

**Figure 4.6  Emulating the `contains` predicate with a regular expression**

The ^ metacharacter matches only if the following character occurs at the beginning of the string, which allows you to recreate the `startsWith` predicate (figure 4.7).

```
{                                              {
  "matches": { "body": "^text to match" }        "startsWith": { "body": "text to match" }
}                                              }
```

**Figure 4.7    Emulating the `startsWith` predicate with a regular expression**

Finally, the $ metacharacter matches only if the preceding character occurs at the end of the string, which mimics the `endsWith` predicate (figure 4.8).

```
{                                              {
  "matches": { "body": "text to match$" }        "endsWith": { "body": "text to match" }
}                                              }
```

**Figure 4.8    Emulating the `endsWith` predicate with a regular expression**

The beauty of regular expressions is that you can combine all of those criteria into a single pattern (figure 4.9).

```
                                               [
{                                                { "startsWith": { "body": "text" } },
  "matches": { "body": "^text.*to.*match$" }      { "contains": { "body": "to" } },
}                                                { "endsWith": { "body": "match" } }
                                               ]
```

**Figure 4.9    Emulating the `startsWith`, `contains`, and `endsWith` predicates with one regular expression**

If you remove the `.*` metacharacter but leave in the ^ and $ metacharacters that anchor a match at the beginning and end of a string of text, you create what equates to the `equals` predicate, although in this case the `equals` predicate is more readable (figure 4.10).

```
{                                              {
  "matches": { "body": "^text to match$" }        "equals": { "body": "text to match" }
}                                              }
```

**Figure 4.10    Emulating the `equals` predicate with a regular expression**

Regular expression patterns can greatly simplify your use of predicates. Let's look at a more common use case of the `matches` predicate next.

#### MATCHING ANY IDENTIFIER ON THE PATH

Although our predicates so far have focused on the http body field, predicates can work on any request field. A common pattern is to match the path field. Frank Abagnale took on a number of names, and in typical RESTful fashion, your Abagnale service allows you to query them by sending a GET request to /identities, or see the details about a single persona by looking at /identities/{id}, where {id} is the identifier for that particular identity. Let's start by matching the /identities/{id} path.

If you had a test scenario that involved hitting this endpoint, you could use the matches predicate to match any numeric identifier passed in, as shown in the following listing.

**Listing 4.3   Using the matches predicate to match any identity resource**

```
{
  "predicates": [{
    "matches": { "path": "/identities/\\d+" }
  }],
  "responses": [{
    "is": {
      "body": {
        "name": "Frank Williams",
        "career": "Doctor",
        "location": "Georgia"
      }
    }
  }]
}
```

The metacharacters used here, \d+, represent one or more digits, so the pattern will match /identities/123 and /identities/2 but not identities/frank-williams. Several other useful metacharacters are available, including (but not limited to!) the ones listed in table 4.1.

**Table 4.1   Regular expression metacharacters**

| Meta-character | Description | Example |
|---|---|---|
| \ | Unless it's part of a metacharacter like those described below, it escapes the next character, forcing a literal match. | 4 \* 2\? matches "What is 4 * 2?" |
| ^ | Matches the beginning of the string | ^Hello matches "Hello, World!" but not "Goodbye. Hello." |
| $ | Matches the end of the string | World!$ matches "Hello, World!" but not "World! Hello." |
| . | Matches any non-newline character | ..... matches "Hello" but not "Hi" |

**Table 4.1    Regular expression metacharacters** *(continued)*

| Meta-character | Description | Example |
|---|---|---|
| * | Matches the previous character 0 or more times | a*b matches "b" and "ab" and "aaaaaab" |
| ? | Matches the previous character 0 or 1 times | a?b matches "b" and "ab" but not "aab" |
| + | Matches the previous character 1 or more times | a+b matches "ab" and "aaaab" but not "b" |
| \d | Matches a digit | \d\d\d matches "123" but not "12a" |
| \D | Inverts \d, matching nondigit characters | \D\D\D matches "ab!" but not "123" |
| \w | Matches an alphanumeric "word" character | \w\w\w matches "123" and "abc" but not "ab!" |
| \W | Inverts \w, matching nonalphanumeric symbols | \W\W\W matches "!?." but not "ab." |
| \s | Matches a whitespace character (mainly spaces, tabs, and newlines) | Hello\sworld matches "Hello world" and "Hello  world" |
| \S | Inverts \s, matching any non-space character | Hello\Sworld matches "Hello-world" and "Hello—world" |

Regular expressions allow you to define robust patterns to match characters and are a rich subject in their own right. Several excellent books are available on the subject, and a number of internet sites provide tutorials. If you are looking for a quick start, I recommend the tutorials on http://www.regular-expressions.info/. We look at more examples in chapter 7.

### 4.1.2    *Matching object request fields*

Google supports full-text searching using the q querystring parameter, so, for example, https://www.google.com/?q=mountebank will show web pages that are somehow relevant to the search text "mountebank." Other web services, like the Twitter API, have adopted the q parameter as a search option even when searching more JSON-structured data like your Abagnale service. Having a single search parameter allows a Google-like user experience with a single text box, where the user doesn't have to specify the fields they are matching. They don't even have to match a field completely. Implementing a full-text search can be a little tricky, but you don't need to worry about that; you need to pretend to be a service that implements full-text searching.

The /identities path for your Abagnale service supports searching using the q querystring parameter. For example, /identities?q=Frank will search for all of Abagnale's identities that are somehow relevant to "Frank," which you can use as a shortcut to find those identities where he used his real first name. The predicate for querystring parameters looks a little different, but only because the querystring is an object field instead of a string field, as shown in the following listing.

**Listing 4.4 Adding a predicate for a query parameter**

```
{
  "predicates": [{
    "equals": {
      "query": { "q": "Frank" }          ◁──┐ Because query is an object field, the
    }                                         │ predicate value is also an object.
  }],
  "responses": [{
    "is": {
      "body": {
        "identities": [                   ◁──┐ Returns
          {                                   │ an array
            "name": "Frank Williams",
            "career": "Doctor",
            "location": "Georgia"
          },
          {
            "name": "Frank Adams",
            "career": "Brigham Young Teacher",
            "location": "Utah"
          }
        ]
      }
    }
  }]
}
```

For HTTP requests, both `query` and `headers` are object fields. To get to the right query parameter (or header), you have to add an extra level to your predicate.

### 4.1.3 *The deepequals predicate*

In some situations, you want to match only if *no* query parameters were passed; for example, sending a GET to /identities without any searching or paging parameters should return all identities. None of the predicates shown so far supports this scenario, as they all work on a single request field. For more complex key-value pair structures, like HTTP queries and headers, the other predicates expect you to navigate down to the primitive field inside, like the q parameter within the querystring we just looked at.

The deepEquals predicate matches an entire object structure, allowing you to specify an empty querystring:

```
{
  "deepEquals": { "query": {} }
}
```

Shortly you will see how it's possible to combine multiple predicates, which allows you to require two query parameters. But the deepEquals predicate is the only way to guarantee that those two query parameters *and nothing else* are passed:

```
{
  "deepEquals": {
```

```
      "query": {
        "q": "Frank",
        "page": 1
      }
    }
  }
```

With this predicate, a querystring of ?q=Frank&page=1 would match, but a query-string of ?q=Frank&page=1&sort=desc wouldn't.

### 4.1.4   *Matching multivalued fields*

Another interesting characteristic of HTTP query parameters and headers is that you can pass the same key multiple times. Your Abagnale service supports multiple q parameters and returns only those matches that satisfy all of the provided queries. For example, GET /identities?q=Frank&q=Georgia would return only Frank Williams, because Frank Adams worked in Utah.

```
{
  "identities": [{
    "name": "Frank Williams",
    "career": "Doctor",
    "location": "Georgia"
  }]
}
```

All of the predicates we looked at so far support multivalued fields, but, once again, deepEquals is significantly different from the others. If you use an equals predicate, the predicate will pass if *any* of the values equals the predicate value:

```
{
  "equals": {
    "query": {
      "q": "Frank"
    }
  }
}
```

The deepEquals predicate requires *all* of the values to match. Mountebank represents such multivalue fields as arrays in the request.[3] This particular request would look something like this in mountebank:

```
{
  "method": "GET",
  "path": "/identities",
  "query": {
    "q": ["Frank", "Georgia"]
  }
}
```

---

[3]  You also can use this trick when creating responses with multivalue fields. This is most commonly seen with the Set-Cookie response header.

The trick is to pass the array as the predicate value:

```
{
  "deepEquals": {
    "query": {
      "q": ["Georgia", "Frank"]
    }
  }
}
```

Note that the order of the values doesn't matter. You can use the array syntax for any predicate, not just `deepEquals`, but `deepEquals` is the only one that requires an exact match. The example in the following listing demonstrates the difference.

### Listing 4.5 Using predicate arrays

```
{
  "stubs": [
    {
      "predicates": [{
        "deepEquals": {
          "query": { "q": ["Frank", "Georgia"] }     Requires exact match
        }
      }],
      "responses": [{
        "is": { "body": "deepEquals matched" }
      }]
    },
    {
      "predicates": [{
        "equals": {
          "query": { "q": ["Frank", "Georgia"] }     Requires these elements
        }                                             to be present
      }],
      "responses": [{
        "is": { "body": "equals matched" }
      }]
    }
  ]
}
```

If you send a request to /identities?q=Georgia&q=Frank, the response body will show that the `deepEquals` predicate matched because all of the array elements matched *and* no additional array elements were present in the request. But if you send a request to /identities?q=Georgia&q=Frank&q=Doctor, the `deepEquals` predicate will no longer match because the predicate definition isn't expecting "Doctor" as an array element. The `equals` predicate *will* match, because it allows additional elements in the request array that aren't specified in the predicate definition.

### 4.1.5 The exists predicate

There's one more primitive predicate to look at. The `exists` predicate tests for either the existence or nonexistence of a request field. If you have a test that depends on the q parameter to be passed and the page parameter *not* being passed, then exists is what you want:

```
{
  "exists": {
    "query": {
      "q": true,
      "page": false
    }
  }
}
```

The exists predicate also comes in quite handy when you want to check for the presence of a header. For example, you may decide that for testing purposes, you want to verify that the service handles an HTTP challenge correctly (represented by a 401 status code) when the Authorization request header is missing, without worrying about whether the credentials stored in the Authorization header are correct, as shown here:

```
{
  "predicates": [{
    "exists": {
      "headers": { "Authorization": false }
    }
  }],
  "responses": [{
    "is": { "statusCode": 401 }
  }]
}
```

The headers field in this snippet specifies the condition that there's no Authorization header, and the is response returns a 401 status code.

The exists predicate works on string fields like the body, which is considered not to exist if it's an empty string. It's usually more useful in conjunction with the JSON or XML support described later in this chapter.

### 4.1.6   *Conjunction junction*

The predicates field is an array. Every predicate in the array must match for mountebank to use that stub. You can reduce the array to a single element by using the and predicate, so the following two sets of predicates will match the exact same requests (for example, one with a body of "Frank Abagnale"):

```
{
  "predicates": [
    { "startsWith": { "body": "Frank" } },
    { "endsWith": { "body": "Abagnale" } }
  ]
}
```

and

```
{
  "predicates": [{
    "and": [
      { "startsWith": { "body": "Frank" } },
      { "endsWith": { "body": "Abagnale" } }
    ]
  }]
}
```

By itself, the and predicate isn't very useful. But combined with its conjunction cousin, the or predicate, and its distant disjunction relative, the not predicate, you can create predicates of dizzying complexity in a festival of Booleanism. For example, the predicate in listing 4.6 matches requests that return Frank Williams, regardless of whether the system under test directly calls that persona URL (assumed to be /identities /123) or they search for him at /identities?q=Frank+Williams, but only if no page query parameter is added.

> **Listing 4.6  Combining multiple predicates using and, or, and not**

```
{
  "or": [
    { "equals": { "path": "/identities/123" } },          ◁── Matches if the request
                                                               goes directly to the URL...
    {
      "and": [
        { "equals": { "path": "/identities" } },          ◁── ...or if it
                                                               searches
        {
          "and": [
            {
              "contains": { "query": { "q": "Frank" } }   ◁── ...with a query
            },                                                containing Frank
            {
              "contains": { "query": { "q": "Williams" } } } ◁── ...and a query
            },                                                   containing Williams
            {
              "not": {
                "exists": { "query": { "page": true } }   } │ ...with no paging (you can
              }                                             │ get rid of the not predicate by
            }                                               │ changing the page value to false).
          ]
        }
      ]
    }
  ]
}
```

Sometimes it's necessary to create complex conditions, and the rich set of predicates mountebank supports enables you to specify such conditions. But to make your configuration readable and maintainable, it's good practice to make the predicates as simple as possible for your use case. The conjunctions are there when you need them, but you'll probably be happier if you can avoid using them too much.

### 4.1.7   A complete list of predicate types

There's one other predicate you haven't seen yet—the `inject` predicate—but you'll have to wait until chapter 6 to take a look at it. Before we proceed, let's review the predicates you have at your disposal. For your reference, table 4.2 provides the complete list of predicate operators that mountebank supports.

Table 4.2   All predicates that mountebank supports

| Operator | Description |
| --- | --- |
| equals | Requires the request field to equal the predicate value |
| deepEquals | Performs nested set equality on object request fields |
| contains | Requires the request field to contain the predicate value |
| startsWith | Requires the request field to start with the predicate value |
| endsWith | Requires the request field to end with the predicate value |
| Matches | Requires the request field to match the regular expression provided as the predicate value |
| exists | Requires the request field to exist as a nonempty value (if `true`) or not (if `false`) |
| not | Inverts the subpredicate |
| or | Requires any of the subpredicates to be satisfied |
| and | Requires all of the subpredicates to be satisfied |
| inject | Requires a user-provided function to return `true` (see chapter 6) |

## 4.2   Parameterizing predicates

Each predicate consists of an operator and zero or more parameters that alter the behavior of the predicate in certain ways. Two parameters, `xpath` and `jsonpath`, change the scope of the predicate to a value embedded in the HTTP body; we look at those shortly. The other parameter affects the way the predicate evaluates the request field.

### 4.2.1   Making case-sensitive predicates

All predicates are case-insensitive by default. The following predicate, for example, will be satisfied regardless of whether the q parameter is "Frank" or "frank" or "FRANK":

```
{
  "equals": {
    "query": { "q": "frank" }
  }
}
```

This is even true for the `matches` predicate. Regular expressions are case-sensitive by default, but mountebank changes their default to match the behavior of the other predicates. If you need case sensitivity, you can set the `caseSensitive` parameter to `true`, as follows.

**Listing 4.7  Using a case-sensitive predicate**

```
{
  "equals": {
    "query": { "q": "Frank" }
  },
  "caseSensitive": true
}
```

"FRANK" and "frank" will no longer satisfy the predicate.

Mountebank's default behavior also treats the keys in a case-insensitive manner, so that without the `caseSensitive` parameter, the predicate above also would match a querystring of ?Q=FRANK. This is often appropriate, especially for HTTP headers where the case of the headers shouldn't matter. Adding the `caseSensitive` parameter forces case sensitivity on both the keys and the values.

## 4.3   Using predicates on JSON values

JSON is the *lingua franca* of most RESTful APIs these days. As you have seen previously, it's possible to create mountebank responses that use JSON objects instead of strings for the body field. Mountebank also provides ample support for creating predicates against JSON bodies.

### 4.3.1   Using direct JSON predicates

Despite Frank Abagnale's cleverness, there's nothing magical about what he does. When he needs to add a new identity, for example, he POSTs the JSON representation of the identity to the /identities URL, like the rest of us.

Because the HTTP body is a string as far as mountebank is concerned, you can use a `contains` predicate to capture a particular JSON field. But doing so is inconvenient, as the white space has to match between the key and the value. The `matches` predicate gives you a lot more flexibility at the cost of readability. Fortunately for you, mountebank's willingness to treat HTTP bodies as JSON as well as strings allows you to navigate the JSON object structure like you have navigated the `query` object structure previously, as shown in the following listing.

**Listing 4.8  Using a direct JSON predicate on an HTTP body**

```
{
  "predicates": [{
    "equals": {
      "body": {
        "career": "Doctor"          The "career" field at the
      }                             root of the JSON body
    }                               has to equal "Doctor."
  }],
```

```
    "responses": [{
      "is": {
        "statusCode": 201,
        "headers": { "Location": "/identities/123" },
        "body": "Welcome, Frank Williams"
      }
    }]
}
```

You can navigate as many levels deep in the JSON object as you need to. Mountebank treats arrays no differently from how it treats the multivalued fields described in section 4.1.4, which used the example of a repeating key on the querystring. For complex queries, you are probably better off using JSONPath.

### 4.3.2  Selecting a JSON value with JSONPath

You can initialize the set of identities that the Abagnale service provides by sending a PUT command to the /identities path, passing in an array of identities, as shown here:

```
{
  "identities": [
    {
      "name": "Frank Williams",
      "career": "Doctor",
      "location": "Georgia"
    },
    {
      "name": "Frank Adams",
      "career": "Teacher",
      "location": "Utah"
    }
  ]
}
```

This test scenario requires you to send a 400 if the PUT command includes a career of "Teacher" as the last member of the array and a 200 otherwise. That is obviously a bit of a stretch, but it enables you to show off the power of JSONPath. JSONPath is a query language that simplifies the task of selecting values from a JSON document and excels with large and complex documents. Stefan Goessner came up with the idea and documented its syntax at http://goessner.net/articles/JsonPath/.

Let's look at the entire imposter configuration in the following listing.

Listing 4.9   Using JSONPath to match only the last element of an array

```
{
  "protocol": "http",
  "port": 3000,
  "stubs": [{
    "predicates": [
      { "equals": { "method": "PUT" } },          Only matches a PUT
      { "equals": { "path": "/identities" } },     request to /identities
      {
```

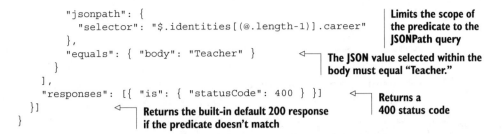

```
      "jsonpath": {
        "selector": "$.identities[(@.length-1)].career"
      },
      "equals": { "body": "Teacher" }
    }
  ],
  "responses": [{ "is": { "statusCode": 400 } }]
}]
}
```

**Limits the scope of the predicate to the JSONPath query**

**The JSON value selected within the body must equal "Teacher."**

**Returns a 400 status code**

**Returns the built-in default 200 response if the predicate doesn't match**

You set the predicate operator to have the `body` equal `Teacher`, even though the body contains an entire JSON document. The `jsonpath` parameter modifies its attached predicate and limits its scope to the result of the query. Let's take a look at the query as annotated in figure 4.11.

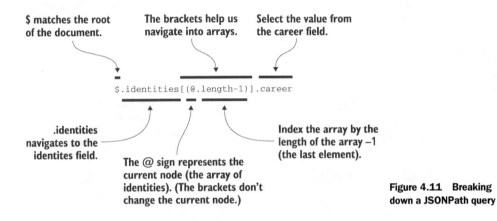

**$ matches the root of the document.**

**The brackets help us navigate into arrays.**

**Select the value from the career field.**

`$.identities[(@.length-1)].career`

**.identities navigates to the identites field.**

**The @ sign represents the current node (the array of identities). (The brackets don't change the current node.)**

**Index the array by the length of the array −1 (the last element).**

Figure 4.11 Breaking down a JSONPath query

JSONPath provides tremendous flexibility for selecting the value you need in a large JSON document. Its older cousin, XPath, does the same thing for XML documents.

## 4.4 Selecting XML values

Although XML isn't as common in services created in recent years, it's still a prevalent service format and is universally used for SOAP services. If you allowed sending XML as well as JSON with the PUT call to /identities that we just looked at—perhaps because Abagnale needs to impersonate an enterprise architect—you could expect a body that looks like this:

```xml
<identities>
  <identity career="Doctor">
    <name>Frank Williams</name>
    <location>Georgia</location>
  </identity>
  <identity career="Teacher">
    <name>Frank Adams</name>
```

```
        <location>Utah</location>
    </identity>
</identities>
```

Brigham Young University disputes Abagnale's account of teaching there. Our test scenario could detect Abagnale trying to claim he was a teacher in Utah and send a 400 status code. This is a complex enough query that the existing predicate operators are not up to the task.[4] It also involves using XML attributes in the query.

In the simple case shown in the following listing, the `xpath` parameter mirrors the `jsonpath` parameter, limiting the scope of what the predicate operator examines.

**Listing 4.10   Using XPath to prevent Abagnale from claiming he taught in Utah**

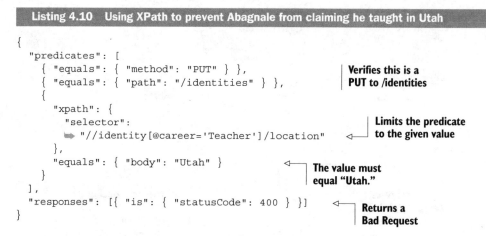

```
{
  "predicates": [
    { "equals": { "method": "PUT" } },          Verifies this is a
    { "equals": { "path": "/identities" } },     PUT to /identities
    {
      "xpath": {
        "selector":
    ➥ "//identity[@career='Teacher']/location"   Limits the predicate
      },                                          to the given value
      "equals": { "body": "Utah" }                The value must
    }                                             equal "Utah."
  ],
  "responses": [{ "is": { "statusCode": 400 } }]  Returns a
}                                                 Bad Request
```

XPath predates JSONPath, and unsurprisingly, their syntax is similar. Figure 4.12 breaks down the XPath expression.

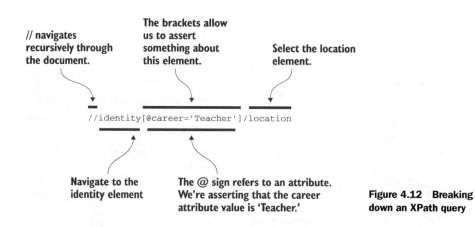

// navigates recursively through the document.

The brackets allow us to assert something about this element.

Select the location element.

```
//identity[@career='Teacher']/location
```

Navigate to the identity element

The @ sign refers to an attribute. We're asserting that the career attribute value is 'Teacher.'

**Figure 4.12   Breaking down an XPath query**

---

[4]  Not even the `matches` predicate, because you cannot parse XML (or HTML) with regular expressions. Trying to parse XML with regular expressions causes the unholy child to weep the blood of virgins: http://stackoverflow.com/questions/1732348/regex-match-open-tags-except-xhtml-self-contained-tags/1732454#1732454.

One of the most unfortunate design decisions in XML is the support for *namespaces*, which has caused needless harm to walls the world over as programmers everywhere banged their heads on them when confronted with namespaced documents. The idea is sensible enough: as you combine multiple XML documents, you need a way of resolving naming conflicts.[5]

Let's future-proof your XML document by adding namespaces:

```
<identities xmlns:id="https://www.abagnale-spec.com/identity"
            xmlns:n="https://www.abagnale-spec.com/name">
  <id:identity career="Doctor">
    <n:name>Frank Williams</n:name>
    <location>Georgia</location>
  </id:identity>
  <id:identity career="Teacher">
    <n:name>Frank Adams</n:name>
    <location>Utah</location>
  </id:identity>
</identities>
```

Despite your best attempts at future-proofing, you still require a breaking change in version 2 of the Abagnale service that moves the name value to an attribute instead of an XML tag:

```
<identities xmlns:id="https://www.abagnale-spec.com/identity"
            xmlns:n="https://www.abagnale-spec.com/name">
  <id:identity career="Doctor" n:name="Frank Williams">
    <location>Georgia</location>
  </id:identity>
  <id:identity career="Teacher" n:name="Frank Adams">
    <location>Utah</location>
  </id:identity>
</identities>
```

You need to write a test scenario that verifies that the Abagnale service responds with a 400 if you pass the name field in the wrong spot, as in the following listing. This is a great opportunity to use the `exists` predicate operator. You also have to add namespaces to your query, as name isn't the same as n:name in XML.

**Listing 4.11  Using XPath to assert that the name attribute exists and the name tag doesn't**

```
{
  "predicates": [
    { "equals": { "method": "PUT" } },          Verifies this is a
    { "equals": { "path": "/identities" } },    PUT to /identities
    {
      "or": [                          ←──┐ There are two
        {                                 │ possible scenarios.
```

---

[5]  At least we thought we did. Oddly, the same problem should exist with JSON documents, which lack namespaces, but...

```
        "xpath": {
          "ns": {
            "i":
              ➥ "https://www.abagnale-spec.com/identity",    Adds the namespace map
            "n": "https://www.abagnale-spec.com/name"
          },
          "selector": "//i:identity/n:name"              Matches if the
        },                                                n:name tag exists...
        "exists": { "body": true }
      },
      {
        "xpath": {
          "selector": "//i:identity[@n:name]",
          "ns": {                                         ...or if the
            "i": "https://www.abagnale-spec.com/identity",  n:name attribute
            "n": "https://www.abagnale-spec.com/name"     doesn't exist
          }
        },
        "exists": { "body": false }
      }
    ]
  }
],                                                        Sends a Bad Request
"responses": [{ "is": { "statusCode": 400 } }]            if the predicates match.
}
```

The `xpath` parameter allows you to pass in a namespace map in the `ns` field, which takes a prefix and a URL. The URL has to match the one defined in the XML document, but the prefix can be whatever you want. XPath namespace queries use the prefix in front of each element.

And with that beast of a stub, it's time to take a step back and review what you learned.

## Summary

- Predicates allow mountebank to respond differently to different requests. Mountebank ships with a full range of predicate operators, including the versatile `matches` operator, which matches request fields based on a regular expression.
- The `deepEquals` predicate operator is used to match an entire object structure, such as the query object. You also can match a single field within the object (for example, a single query parameter) with one of the standard predicate operators by navigating into the object structure.
- Predicates are case-insensitive by default. You can change that by setting the `caseSensitive` predicate parameter to `true`.
- `jsonpath` and `xpath` predicate parameters limit the scope on the request field to the part that matches the JSONPath or XPath selector.

# Adding record/replay behavior

The best imposters don't simply pretend to be someone else; they actively copy the person they impersonate. This mimicry requires both observation and memory: observation to study the behaviors of the person being impersonated and memory to be able to replay those behaviors at a later time. Satirists on comedy shows like *Saturday Night Live*, where actors and actresses often pretend to be famous U.S. political figures, base their performances on those skills.

Mountebank lacks the comedic flair of *Saturday Night Live* impersonators, but it does support a high-fidelity form of mimicry. Rather than creating a canned response for each request, an imposter can go directly to the source. It's as if the imposter is wearing an earpiece, and every time your system under test asks it a question, the real service whispers the answer in your imposter's ear. Better yet, mountebank imposters have a great memory, so once the imposter has heard a response, it can replay the response in the future even without the earpiece. Thanks to the magic of proxy responses, a mountebank imposter can be almost indistinguishable from the real thing.

## 5.1    Setting up a proxy

The proxy response type lets you put a mountebank imposter between the system under test and a real service that it depends on, saving a real response in the process (figure 5.1).

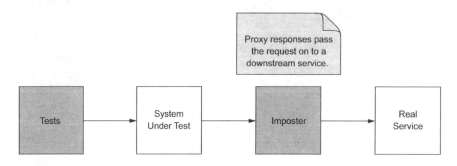

**Figure 5.1    An imposter acting as a proxy**

This arrangement allows capturing real data that you can replay in tests, rather than hand-creating it using canned responses. To illustrate, let's revisit the imaginary pet store architecture you first saw in chapter 3. The pet store, like all modern e-commerce shops, needs a service to keep track of inventory, and, to keep it simple, ours takes a product ID on the URL and sends back the on-hand stock for that product. In chapter 3, you virtualized it with hand-created is response types. Let's reimagine it using a proxy, which requires the real service to be available to capture the responses, as shown in figure 5.2.

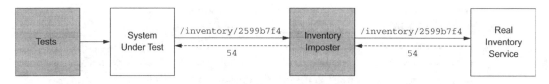

**Figure 5.2    Using a proxy to query the downstream inventory**

The simplest imposter configuration looks like the following listing.[1]

---

[1]  You can follow the examples from the GitHub repository at https://github.com/bbyars/mountebank-in-action.

**Listing 5.1  Imposter configuration for a basic proxy**

```
{
  "port": 3000,
  "protocol": "http",
  "stubs": [{
    "responses": [{
      "proxy": { "to": "http://api.petstore.com" }      ◁─┐  New response
    }]                                                        type
  }]
}
```

The difference is in the new response type. Whereas an `is` response tells the imposter to return the given response, a `proxy` response tells the imposter to fetch the response from the downstream service. The basic form of the `proxy` response shown in the listing passes the request unchanged to the downstream service and sends the response unchanged back to the system under test. By itself, that isn't a very useful thing, but the proxy remembers the response and will replay it the next time it sees the same request, rather than fetching a new response (figure 5.3).

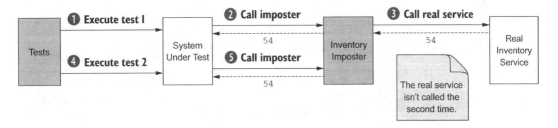

**Figure 5.3  By default, the proxy returns the first result as the response to all subsequent calls.**

Mountebank exposes the current state of each imposter through the API. If you send a GET request to http://localhost:2525/imposters/3000, you will see the saved response.[2] It's worth looking at the changed imposter configuration in some detail after the first call to the proxy, as shown in the following listing.

**Listing 5.2  Saved proxy responses change imposter state**

```
{
  "protocol": "http",
  "port": 3000,
  "numberOfRequests": 1,
  "requests": [],
  "stubs": [{                          No predicates? We'll
    "predicates": [],      ◁─┘         come back to that....?
```

---

[2]  The 3000 at the end of the URL is the imposter's port.

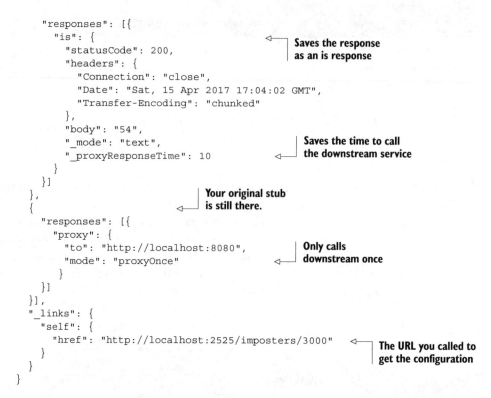

```
      "responses": [{
        "is": {
          "statusCode": 200,                          Saves the response
          "headers": {                                as an is response
            "Connection": "close",
            "Date": "Sat, 15 Apr 2017 17:04:02 GMT",
            "Transfer-Encoding": "chunked"
          },
          "body": "54",
          "_mode": "text",                            Saves the time to call
          "_proxyResponseTime": 10                    the downstream service
        }
      }]
    },                                          Your original stub
    {                                           is still there.
      "responses": [{
        "proxy": {
          "to": "http://localhost:8080",        Only calls
          "mode": "proxyOnce"                    downstream once
        }
      }]
    }],
    "_links": {
      "self": {
        "href": "http://localhost:2525/imposters/3000"     The URL you called to
      }                                                     get the configuration
    }
  }
}
```

There's a lot in there, and we aren't quite ready to get to all of it yet. Mountebank recorded the time it took to call the downstream service in the _proxyResponse-Time field; you can use this to add simulated latency during performance testing. We explore how to do that in chapters 7 and 10. The most important observations for now are:

- Mountebank proxies the first call to the base URL given in the to field of the proxy configuration. It appends the request path and query parameters and passes through the request headers and body unchanged.
- Mountebank captures the response as a new stub with an is response. It saves it *in front of* the stub with the proxy response. (This is what the proxyOnce mode means; we will look at the alternative shortly.)
- The newly created stub has no predicates. Because mountebank always uses the first match when iterating over stubs, it will never again call the proxy response, because a stub with no predicates always matches.

Proxies change the state of the imposter. By default, they create a new stub (figure 5.4).

The default behavior of a proxy (defined by the proxyOnce mode) is to call the downstream service the first time it sees a request it doesn't recognize, and from that point forward to send the saved response back for future requests that look similar. Unfortunately, the example we've been considering isn't discriminatory in how it recognizes requests; *all* requests match the generated stub. Let's fix that.

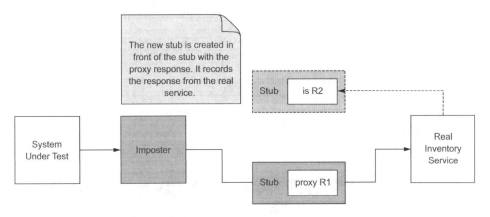

Figure 5.4  The proxy saves the downstream response in a new stub.

## 5.2 Generating the correct predicates

Proxies will create new responses formed from the downstream service response, but you need to give them hints on how to create the request predicates that determine when mountebank will replay those responses. We will start by looking at how you can replay different responses for different request paths.

### 5.2.1 Creating predicates with predicateGenerators

Your inventory service includes the product id on the path, so sending a GET to /inventory/2599b7f4 returns the inventory for product 2599b7f4, and a GET to /inventory/e1977c9e returns inventory for product e1977c9e. Let's augment the proxy definition you set up in listing 5.1 to save the response for each product separately. Because it's the path that varies between those requests, you need to tell mountebank to create a new is response with a path predicate. You do so using a proxy parameter called predicateGenerators. As the name indicates, the predicate-Generators are responsible for creating the predicates on the saved responses. You add an object for each predicate you want to generate underneath a matches key, as in the following listing.

---

**Listing 5.3  Imposter response that saves a different response for each path**

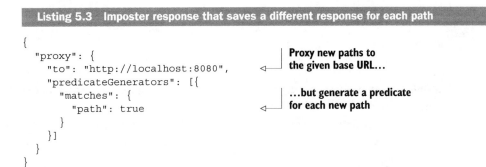

```
{
  "proxy": {
    "to": "http://localhost:8080",          Proxy new paths to
    "predicateGenerators": [{                the given base URL...
      "matches": {
        "path": true                         ...but generate a predicate
      }                                       for each new path
    }]
  }
}
```

You can test it out with a couple calls using different paths:

```
curl http://localhost:3000/inventory/2599b7f4
curl http://localhost:3000/inventory/e1977c9e
```

Let's look at the state of the imposter again after the change:

```
curl http://localhost:2525/imposters/3000
```

The stubs field contains the newly created responses with their predicates, as in the following listing.

**Listing 5.4   Saved proxy responses with predicates**

```
{
  "stubs": [
    {
      "predicates": [{
        "deepEquals": { "path": "/inventory/2599b7f4" }        ◁──┐ Saves the first call
      }],                                                           as the first stub
      "responses": [{
        "is": { "body": "54" }        ◁──┐ To save space, most of
      }]                                    the response isn't shown.
    },
    {
      "predicates": [{
        "deepEquals": { "path": "/inventory/e1977c9e" }        ◁──┐ Creates a new stub with
      }],                                                           a different predicate
      "responses": [{
        "is": { "body": "100" }        ◁──┐ The response
      }]                                    will be different.
    },
    {
      "responses": [{
        "proxy": {
          "to": "http://localhost:8080",
          "predicateGenerators": [{
            "matches": {
              "path": true
            }
          }],
          "mode": "proxyOnce"
        }
      }]
    }
  ]
}
```

The generated predicates use deepEquals for most cases. Recall that the deep-Equals predicate requires that all fields be present for object fields like query and headers, so if you include either of those using the simple syntax shown in listing 5.4, the complete set of querystring parameters or request headers would have to be present in a subsequent request for mountebank to serve the saved response:

```
{
  "predicateGenerators": [{
    "matches": {
      "path": true,
      "query": true          ⊲──┐  All query parameters
    }                            │  will need to match.
  }]
}
```

As you saw in the last chapter, when defining predicates for object fields, you can be more specific if you need to be. If, for example, you want to save a different response for each different `path` and `page` query parameter, regardless of what else is on the querystring, you navigate into the `query` object:

```
{
  "predicateGenerators": [{
    "matches": {
      "path": true,
      "query": {
        "page": true          ⊲──┐  Only the page parameter
      }                           │  needs to match
    }
  }]
}
```

## 5.2.2   Adding predicate parameters

The `predicateGenerators` field closely mirrors the standard `predicates` field and accepts all the same parameters. Each object in the `predicateGenerators` array generates a corresponding object in the newly created stub's `predicates` array. If, for example, you wanted to generate a case-sensitive match of the `path` and a case-*insensitive* match of the body, you could add two `predicateGenerators`, as shown in the following listing.

---

**Listing 5.5   Generating case-sensitive predicates**

```
{
  "responses": [{
    "proxy": {
      "to": "http://localhost:8080",
      "predicateGenerators": [
        {
          "matches": { "path": true },    Generates a case-
          "caseSensitive": true           sensitive predicate
        },
        {
                                          Generates a default case-
          "matches": { "body": true }     insensitive predicate
        }
      ]
    }
  }]
}
```

The newly created stub has both predicates:

```
{
  "predicates": [
    {
      "caseSensitive": true,
      "deepEquals": { "path": "..." }
    },
    {
      "deepEquals": { "body": "..." }
    }
  ],
  "responses": [{
    "is": { ... }
  }]
}
```

As you saw in the last chapter, more parameters are available beyond `case-Sensitive`. The `jsonpath` and `xpath` predicate parameters allow you to limit the scope of the predicate, and you can generate those too.

### GENERATING JSONPATH PREDICATES

In chapter 4, we demonstrated JSONPath predicates in the context of virtualizing the inimitable Frank Abagnale service, which showed a list of fake identities the famous (real) imposter had assumed. A partial list of identities might look like this:

```
{
  "identities": [
    {
      "name": "Frank Williams",
      "career": "Doctor",
      "location": "Georgia"
    },
    {
      "name": "Frank Adams",
      "career": "Teacher",
      "location": "Utah"
    }
  ]
}
```

If you needed a predicate that matched the `career` field of the last element of the `identities` array, then you could use the same JSONPath selector you saw in the previous chapter. Because you now want mountebank to *generate* the predicate, you specify the selector in the `predicateGenerators` object and rely on the proxy to fill in the value, as in the following listing.

> **Listing 5.6    Specifying a `jsonpath` `predicateGenerators`**

```
{
  "proxy": {
    "to": "http://localhost:8080",
    "predicateGenerators": [{
```

```
        "jsonpath": {
          "selector": "$.identities[(@.length-1)].career"    Saves the value defined
        },                                                     by the selector...
        "matches": { "body": true }    ◁──┐ ...from the
    }]                                      │ body field.
  }
}
```

Remember, `predicateGenerators` work on the incoming *request*, so the JSONPath selector saves off the value in the request body. If you sent the Abagnale JSON in listing 5.6 to your proxy, the generated stub would look something like this:

```
{
  "predicates": [{
    "jsonpath": {
      "selector": "$.identities[(@.length-1)].career"
    },
    "deepEquals": { "body": "Teacher" }    ◁── The value captured from the selector
  }],                                          in the incoming request body
  "responses": [{
    "is": { ... }
  }]
}
```

Future requests that match the given selector will use the saved response.

### GENERATING XPATH PREDICATES

The same technique works for XPath. If you translate Abagnale's list of identities to XML, it might look like:

```
<identities>
  <identity career="Doctor">
    <name>Frank Williams</name>
    <location>Georgia</location>
  </identity>
  <identity career="Teacher">
    <name>Frank Adams</name>
    <location>Utah</location>
  </identity>
</identities>
```

The `predicateGenerators` mirrors the xpath predicate you saw in chapter 4, so if you had a need for a predicate to match on the location where Abagnale pretended to be a teacher, the following listing would do the trick.

**Listing 5.7  Specifying an xpath predicateGenerators**

```
{
  "proxy": {
    "to": "http://localhost:8080",
    "predicateGenerators": [{
      "xpath": {
        "selector": "//identity[@career='Teacher']/location"    Saves the value defined
      },                                                          by the selector...
```

```
        "matches": { "body": true }
    }]
  }
}
```

⟵  …from the
    body field.

The predicates that the proxy creates show the correct location:

```
{
  "predicates": [{
    "xpath": {
      "selector": "//identity[@career='Teacher']/location"
    },
    "deepEquals": { "body": "Utah" }
  }],
  "responses": [{
    "is": { ... }
  }]
}
```

⟵  **The value captured from the selector
    in the incoming request body**

### CAPTURING MULTIPLE JSONPATH OR XPATH VALUES

JSONPath and XPath selectors both can capture multiple values. To take a simple example, look at the following XML:

```
<doc>
  <number>1</number>
  <number>2</number>
  <number>3</number>
</doc>
```

If you use the XPath selector of `//number` on this XML document, you get three values: 1, 2, and 3. The `predicateGenerators` field is smart enough to capture multiple values and save them using a standard predicate array, which requires all results to be present in subsequent requests to match but allows them to be present in any order.

## 5.3   *Capturing multiple responses for the same request*

The examples we looked at so far have been great for minimizing traffic to a downstream service while still collecting real responses. For each type of request, defined by the `predicateGenerators`, you only pass the request to the real service once. This is the promise of the default mode, appropriately called `proxyOnce`. The guarantee is satisfied by ensuring that mountebank creates new stubs before the stub with the proxy response (figure 5.5). Mountebank's first match policy will ensure that subsequent requests matching the generated predicates don't reach the proxy response.

A significant downside to `proxyOnce` is that each generated stub can have only one response. This is a problem for your inventory service, which returns different responses over time for the same request, reflecting volatility in stock for an item (figure 5.6).

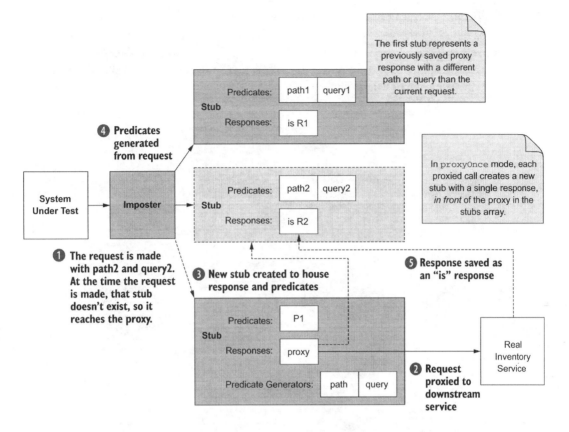

Figure 5.5  In `proxyOnce` mode, mountebank creates new stubs before the stub with the proxy.

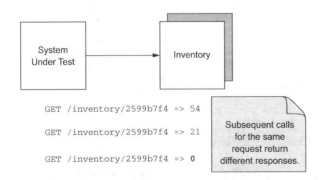

Figure 5.6  Volatile responses for the same request

In `proxyOnce` mode, mountebank captures only the first response (54). If your test cases relied on the volatility of inventory over time, you'd need a proxy that would let you capture a richer data set to replay. The `proxyAlways` mode ensures that *all* requests reach the downstream service, allowing you to capture multiple responses for a single request type (figure 5.7).

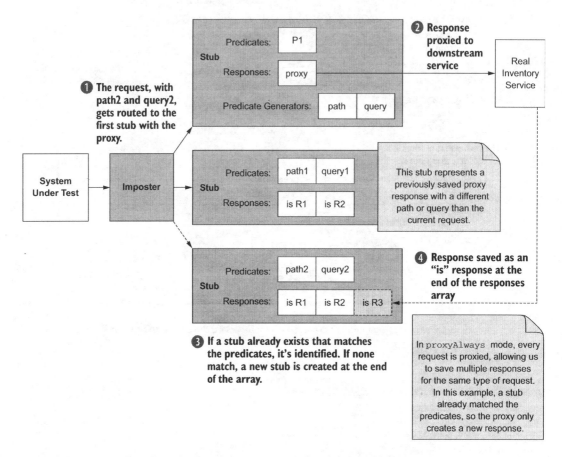

**Figure 5.7**   In `proxyAlways` mode, new stubs are created after the stub with the proxy

Creating this type of proxy is as simple as passing in the mode, as in the following listing.

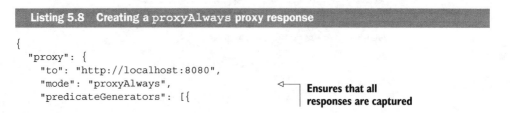

**Listing 5.8**   Creating a `proxyAlways` proxy response

```
{
  "proxy": {
    "to": "http://localhost:8080",
    "mode": "proxyAlways",                 ⟵  Ensures that all
    "predicateGenerators": [{                  responses are captured
```

```
      "matches": { "path": true }
    }]
  }
}
```

The key difference in the mechanics between `proxyOnce` and `proxyAlways`, as shown in figures 5.5 and 5.7, is that `proxyOnce` generates new stubs *before* the stub containing the proxy response, whereas `proxyAlways` generates stubs *after* the proxy stub. Both approaches rely on mountebank's first-match policy when matching a request to a stub. In the `proxyOnce` case, a subsequent request matching the generated predicates is guaranteed to match before the proxy stub, and in the `proxyAlways` case, the proxy stub is guaranteed to match before the generated stubs.

But `proxyAlways` does more than create new stubs. It first looks to see if a stub whose predicates already exists match the generated predicates, and, if so, it *appends* the saved response to that stub. This behavior allows multiple responses to be saved for the same request. You can see this by calling the imposter in listing 5.8 a few times and querying its state (by sending a GET request to http://localhost:2525/imposters/ 3000, assuming it was started on port 3000). To save space and make the salient bits stand out, I've omitted the full response inside each generated `is` response in the following listing.

---

**Listing 5.9 The imposter state after a few calls to a `proxyAlways` response**

```
{
  "stubs": [
    {
      "responses": [{
        "proxy": {
          "to": "http://localhost:8080",
          "mode": "proxyAlways",          ◁──┐ Ensures that all
          "predicateGenerators": [{          └ requests are proxied
            "matches": { "path": true }
          }]
        }
      }]
    },
    {
      "predicates": [{                       ┐ First request
        "deepEquals": { "path": "/inventory/2599b7f4" }  ◁─┘ type
      }],
      "responses": [
        { "is": { "body": "54" } },
        { "is": { "body": "21" } },      All responses saved
        { "is": { "body": "0" } }
      ]
    },
    {
      "predicates": [{                       ┐ Second request
        "deepEquals": { "path": "/inventory/e1977c9e" }  ◁─┘ type
      }],
```

```
      "responses": [{
        "is": { "body": "100" }
      }]
    }
  ]
}
```
<──┐ **Only one**
   │ **response**

A `proxyAlways` proxy allows you to capture a full set of test data that is as rich as your downstream service (at least for the requests sent to it). Although this is great for supporting complex test cases, it comes with a significant problem. As you can see in listing 5.9, none of the saved responses will ever get called. With `proxyOnce`, you don't need to worry about switching from recording to replaying; it happens automatically. Not so with `proxyAlways`, so it's time to look at how you can tell mountebank to replay all the data it has captured.

## 5.4    Ways to replay a proxy

Conceptually, the switch from recording to replaying is as simple as removing the proxy response (figure 5.8).

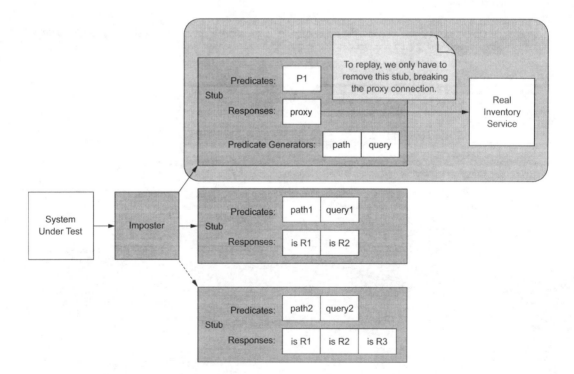

**Figure 5.8   Replaying involves removing the proxy**

All it takes to switch into replay mode is a single command, as follows:

```
mb replay
```

If you watch the logs after that command, you'll see something like the following:

```
info: [mb:2525] GET /imposters?replayable=true&removeProxies=true
info: [mb:2525] PUT /imposters
info: [http:3000] Ciao for now
info: [http:3000] Open for business...
```

The switch involves resetting all imposters, removing their proxies. You can see in the third line that you're shutting down the existing imposter (`Ciao for now`) and restarting it on the fourth line (`Open for business...`). The line before shows the API call to send the altered configuration; this is the same line you'd see if you started mountebank with the `--configfile` command-line option.

The first line shows a different part of the mountebank REST API. Just as you can query the state of a single imposter by sending a `GET` request to http://localhost:2525/imposters/3000 (assuming the imposter is on port 3000), you can query *all* imposters at http://localhost:2525/imposters. The `replay` command adds two query parameters to that call:

- Because the configuration for all imposters is quite possibly a considerable amount of data, it's trimmed by default. The `replayable` query parameter ensures that all data essential (and no more) for replay is returned.
- The `removeProxies` parameter removes the proxy responses, leaving only the captured `is` responses.

The `mb replay` command replays the responses as is. If you need to tweak the captured responses for any reason, you can always use the API call to get the data yourself and process it as appropriate. Even better, you can let mountebank's command line do the job for you. The following command saves the current state of all imposters, with proxies removed:

```
mb save --savefile imposters.json --removeProxies
```

The `mb save` command saves all imposter configuration to the given file. The `–savefile` argument specifies where to save the configuration, and the `--removeProxies` flag strips the proxy responses from the configuration. Functionally, the `mb replay` command is nothing but an `mb save` followed by a restart. The following command reimplements the replay command:

```
mb save --savefile imposters.json --removeProxies
mb restart --configfile imposters.json
```

The ability to save all responses to a downstream service in `proxyAlways` mode and replay them with a single command dramatically simplifies capturing data for rich test suites.

## 5.5    Configuring the proxy

Proxies are configurable, both on the request they send to the downstream service and the generated responses they send back to the system under test (figure 5.9).

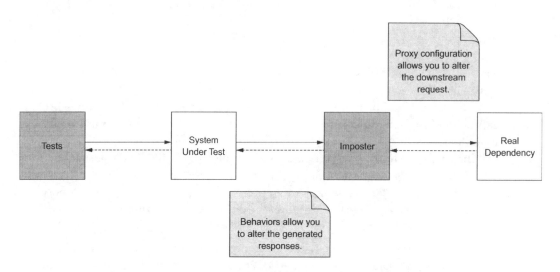

Figure 5.9   **You can configure both the proxy request and the generated response.**

We look at how to alter the responses in chapter 7 when we examine behaviors. You can apply two basic types of configuration to the proxied request: using certificate-based mutual authentication and adding custom headers.

### 5.5.1    Using mutual authentication

Recall from chapter 3 that you can configure imposters to expect a client certificate by setting the `mutualAuth` field to true. In that case, configuring the certificate and private key is the responsibility of the system under test. If the downstream service you are proxying to requires mutual authentication, then you have to configure the certificate on the proxy itself (figure 5.10).

In this case, setting up the proxy is similar to how you set HTTPS imposters. You set the certificate and private key in PEM format directly on the proxy, as shown in the following listing.

Listing 5.10   **A proxy configured to pass a client certificate**

```
{
  "proxy": {
    "to": "https://localhost:8080",
    "mode": "proxyAlways",
```

```
    "predicateGenerators": [{
      "matches": { "path": true }
    }],
    "key": "-----BEGIN RSA PRIVATE KEY-----\n...",
    "cert": "-----BEGIN CERTIFICATE-----\n..."
  }
}
```

| The actual text is
| much longer.

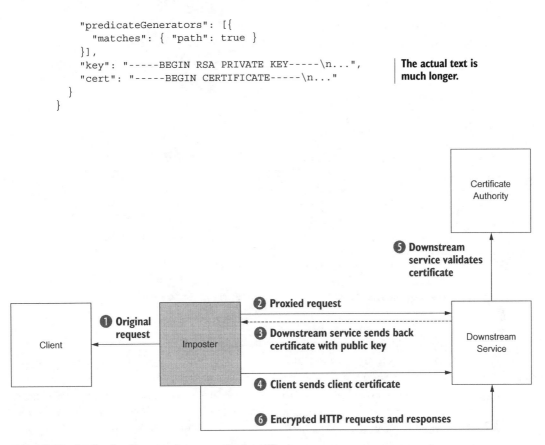

**Figure 5.10  Configuring the proxy to pass a client certificate**

Refer to chapter 3 for the full PEM format and how to create certificates.

### 5.5.2  *Adding custom headers*

Occasionally, it's useful to add another header that gets passed to the downstream service. For example, many services return compressed responses for efficiency. Although the original data may be human-readable JSON, after compression it turns into unreadable binary. By default, any proxies you set up will respond with the compressed data unchanged. Because negotiating gzipped compression through headers is a standard operation in HTTP, the HTTP libraries that the system under test uses would decompress the data, allowing the code that you're testing to see the plain text response (figure 5.11).

The standard proxy configurations that you've seen so far have no issues returning the compressed data to the system under test. The problem occurs when you want to actually *look* at the data, such as after saving it in a configuration file using the mb save command. You may want to examine the JSON bodies of the generated is responses

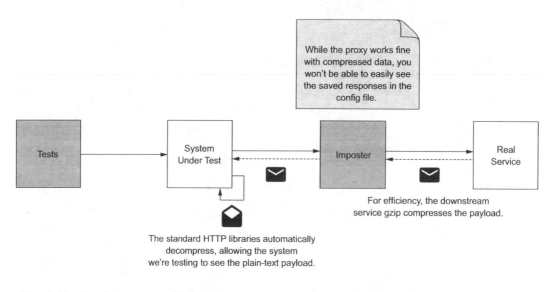

While the proxy works fine with compressed data, you won't be able to easily see the saved responses in the config file.

For efficiency, the downstream service gzip compresses the payload.

The standard HTTP libraries automatically decompress, allowing the system we're testing to see the plain-text payload.

**Figure 5.11   Proxying compressed responses**

and perhaps tweak them to better fit your test cases, but you won't be able to. All you will be able to see are encoded binary strings.[3]

HTTP provides a way for clients to tell servers not to send back compressed data by setting the `Accept-Encoding` header to `"identity"`. The original request from the system under test likely doesn't include this header, because it can handle the compressed data just fine (and using compressed data in production is a good idea anyway for efficiency reasons). Fortunately, you can inject headers into the proxied request, as shown in the following listing.

**Listing 5.11   Injecting a header into the request to prevent response compression**

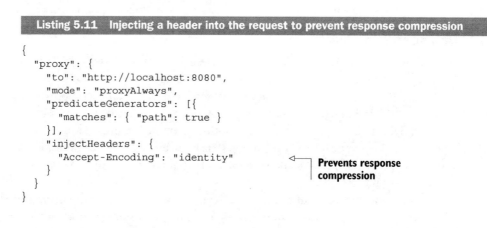

```
{
  "proxy": {
    "to": "http://localhost:8080",
    "mode": "proxyAlways",
    "predicateGenerators": [{
      "matches": { "path": true }
    }],
    "injectHeaders": {
      "Accept-Encoding": "identity"          ◁───┐ Prevents response
    }                                             │ compression
  }
}
```

---

[3]   We'll look at how mountebank handles binary data in chapter 8.

If you need to inject multiple headers, add multiple key/value pairs to the `inject-Headers` object. Each header will be added to the original request headers.

## 5.6 *Proxy use cases*

The examples so far in this chapter have focused on using proxies to record and replay. That is the most common use case for proxies, as it allows you to capture a rich set of test data for your test suite by recording real traffic. In addition, proxies have at least two other use cases: as a fallback response and as a way of presenting an HTTP face to an HTTPS service.

### 5.6.1 *Using a proxy as a fallback*

Though it isn't a common scenario, sometimes it's convenient to test against a real dependency when that dependency is stable, reliable, and highly available. One project I was on involved testing against a software-as-a-service (SaaS) credit card processor, and the SaaS provider supported a reliable preproduction environment for testing. In fact, it was perhaps *too* reliable. "Happy path" testing (testing the expected flow through the service) was easy, but the service was so reliable that testing error conditions was difficult.

You can get the best of both worlds by using a partial proxy. Most calls flow through to the credit card processing service, but a few special requests trigger canned error responses. Mountebank supports this scenario by relying on its first-match policy, putting the error conditions first and the proxy last (figure 5.12).

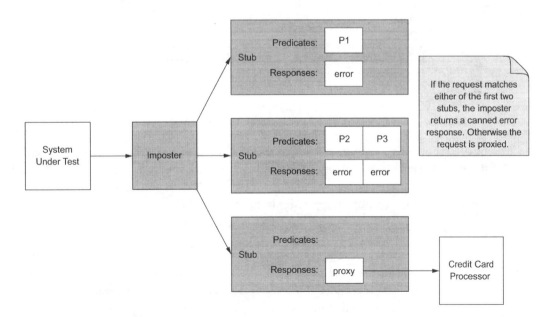

**Figure 5.12   Mixing canned responses with a fallback proxy**

Notice that proxy has no predicates, which means all requests that don't match the predicates on the previous stubs will flow through to the proxy. Ensuring that all requests flow through to the credit card processor involves putting the proxy in `proxyAlways` mode. In the following listing, the code to do this relies on putting the proxy stub last.

**Listing 5.12  Using a partial proxy**

```
{
  "port": 3000,
  "protocol": "http",
  "stubs": [
    {
      "predicates": [{
        "contains": { "body": "5555555555555555" }     If the body contains
      }],                                                this credit card #...
      "responses": [{
        "is": { "body": "FRAUD ALERT... " }           ...send a fraud-alert
      }]                                                response.
    },
    {
      "predicates": [{
        "contains": { "body": "4444444444444444" }     If it contains this
      }],                                                credit card #...
      "responses": [{
        "is": { "body": "INSUFFICIENT FUNDS..." }      ...send an over-
      }]                                                balance response.
    },
    {
      "responses": [{
        "proxy": {
          "to": "http://localhost:8080",        All other calls go
          "mode": "proxyAlways"                  to the real service.
        }
      }]
    }
  ]
}
```

In this scenario, you would not use `mb replay`, because you aren't trying to virtualize the downstream service. Mountebank still creates new stubs and responses, so for any long-lived partial proxy, you'll run into memory leaks. A future version of mountebank will support configuring proxies not to remember each response.

### 5.6.2  Converting HTTPS to HTTP

Another less common scenario is to make an HTTPS service easier to test against. When I've seen this done, it has been as a workaround in an enterprise test environment that hasn't configured SSL correctly, leading to certificates that don't validate against the Certificate Authority. As I mentioned in chapter 3, I strongly advise against changing the system under test to accept invalid certificates, because you risk releasing that configuration into production. Although the best solution is to fix the test environment certificates, the division of labor in some enterprises makes that difficult to do. Assuming that you're confident in the ability of the system under test to negotiate HTTPS with valid certificates (behavior that's nearly always provided by the core language libraries), you can rely on mountebank to bridge the misconfigured HTTPS to HTTP, as shown in the following listing.

**Listing 5.13 Using a proxy to bridge HTTPS to HTTP**

```
{
  "port": 3000,
  "protocol": "http",              ⟵┐ The imposter itself
  "stubs": [{                        │ is an HTTP server...
    "responses": [{
      "proxy": {
        "to": "https://localhost:8080",   ⟵┐ ...but forwards requests
        "mode": "proxyAlways"               │ to an HTTPS server.
      }
    }]
  }]
}
```

Because mountebank is designed to help test in environments that have yet to be fully configured, the imposter itself doesn't validate the certificate during the proxy call. This doesn't require any similar change in configuration in the system under test.

## Summary

- Proxy responses capture real downstream responses and save them for future replay. The default `proxyOnce` mode saves the response in front of the `proxy` stub, meaning you don't need to do anything to replay the response.
- The `proxyAlways` mode allows you to capture a full set of test data by capturing multiple responses for the same logical request. You have to explicitly switch from record mode to replay mode by using `mb replay`.
- The `predicateGenerators` field tells mountebank how to create the predicates based on the incoming request. All fields used to discriminate requests are listed under the `matches` object. You configure parameters no differently than you would for normal predicates.
- Proxies support mutual authentication. You are responsible for setting the `key` and `cert` fields.
- You can alter the request headers that your proxied request sends to the downstream service with the `injectHeaders` field. This is useful, for example, to disable compression so you can save a text response.

# *Programming mountebank*

**This chapter covers**

- Matching requests even when none of the standard predicates do the trick
- Adding dynamic data to mountebank responses
- Making network calls to create a stub response
- Securing mountebank against unwanted remote execution
- Debugging your scripts within mountebank

Most developers have the experience of a tool or framework that makes solving a problem harder than it should be or outright impossible. A primary goal in mountebank is to keep things that should be easy actually easy, and to make hard things possible. Comprehensive default settings, predicates, and simple is responses enable you to solve easy problems with simple solutions. Support for certificates, JSON, XML, and proxies help you to create solutions for a harder set of problems. But sometimes, that's not enough.

At times, the built-in features of mountebank may not directly support your use case. Matching predicates based on JSON and XML is nice, but what if your requests use CSV format? Or say you have a service that needs to replay information from an earlier request in a subsequent response, requiring stateful memory. Maybe your use case extends beyond what a proxy is capable of doing. Or perhaps you need to grab some data from outside mountebank itself and insert it into the stub response.

You need `inject`.

Mountebank ships with several scriptable interfaces, which we'll examine in chapters 7 and 8. The main scriptable interface comes in the form of a new predicate type and a new response type, both called `inject`, that allows you to match requests and create responses in ways mountebank wasn't designed to support.

## 6.1 Creating your own predicate

Like most technologists, I like to while away the idle hours pretending to be a rock star. Scaling that desire into a set of microservices requires both a manager service (to manage my itinerary) and a roadie service (to manage my instruments). The two services collaborate to protect my guitars against excess humidity (figure 6.1).

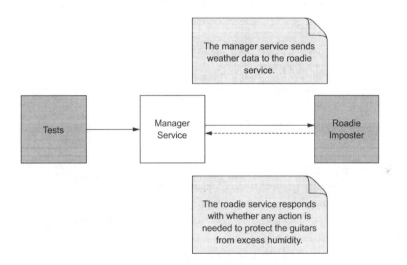

**Figure 6.1   Service collaboration used to protect my guitars**

Let's assume that the manager service (the system under test) is responsible for sending updated weather reports in CSV format to the roadie service, which uses that information to protect my guitars against dangerous humidity levels. Nice acoustic guitars are made of wood that generally wants to stay in the 40–60% humidity range, and the roadie service is responsible for alerting the manager service when a plan is needed to protect the guitars against excessive humidity.

Although virtualizing a roadie service is a bit fantastical, you'll run into services that use something other than JSON or XML as their *lingua franca* from time to time. CSV is still a relatively popular format in certain types of service integrations, particularly those that involve passing some bulk-style information between teams or organizations, such as:

- Retrieving an augmented set of customer information from a marketing research partner who has added (for example) demographic information to your customer information
- Retrieving an updated list of tax rates by ZIP code in the United States from an outside partner
- Retrieving bulk reporting information from an internal team

For this example, you'll expect the manager service to pass weather data showing the next 10 days of weather information in a format similar to what you might get on a site like weather.com, as shown in the following listing.

**Listing 6.1   A weather CSV service payload**

```
Day,Description,High,Low,Precip,Wind,Humidity
4-Jun,PM Thunderstorms,83,71,50%,E 5 mph,65%
5-Jun,PM Thunderstorms,82,69,60%,NNE 8mph,73%
6-Jun,Sunny,90,67,10%,NNE 11mph,55%
7-Jun,Mostly Sunny,86,65,10%,NE 7 mph,53%
8-Jun,Partly Cloudy,84,68,10%,ESE 4 mph,53%
9-Jun,Partly Cloudy,88,68,0%,SSE 11mph,56%
10-Jun,Partly Cloudy,89,70,10%,S 15 mph,57%
11-Jun,Sunny,90,73,10%,S 16 mph,61%
12-Jun,Partly Cloudy,91,74,10%,S 13 mph,63%
13-Jun,Partly Cloudy,90,74,10%,S 17 mph,64%
```

Mountebank doesn't natively support CSV, and it doesn't have a `greaterThan` predicate to look for humidity levels greater than 60%, so you are already outside of its built-in capabilities, but let's raise the stakes even higher. Your expectations of the roadie service are that it only presses the panic button if you are out of range for at least three consecutive days, *or* if you are more than 10% out of range for a single day (figure 6.2).

That makes for a complex predicate, but no one said becoming a rock star would be easy. You can create your own predicate using JavaScript and the `inject` predicate, but first you have to start mountebank with the `--allowInjection` command line flag:

```
mb --allowInjection
```

The logs show a warning at startup that hints at why injection is disabled by default:

```
info: [mb:2525] mountebank v1.13.0 now taking orders -
➥ point your browser to http://localhost:2525 for help
warn: [mb:2525] Running with --allowInjection set.
➥ See http://localhost:2525/docs/security for security info
```

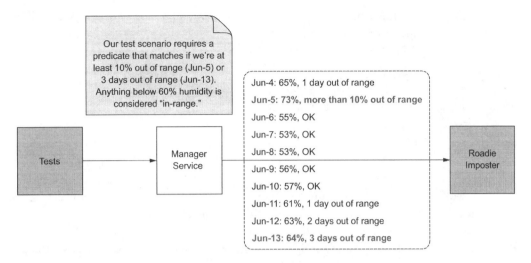

**Figure 6.2 A test scenario requiring advanced predicate logic**

You can go ahead and view the docs provided at the given URL now, or wait until you get to the topic of security later in this chapter. One thing you should *not* do is ignore the warning. It's great that you can do wonderfully complex feats of logic with Java-Script injection and mountebank. Unfortunately, so can malicious attackers on your network who can access your machine. They now have a remote execution engine listening on a socket. You can protect yourself, and we look at ways to do that at the end of this chapter. For now, the safest option is to add the `--localOnly` flag, which disallows remote connections:

```
mb restart --allowInjection --localOnly
```

All of the predicates we looked at in chapter 4 operate on a single request field. Not so with `inject`, which gives you complete control by passing the entire request object into a JavaScript function you write. That JavaScript function returns `true` if the predicate matches the request and `false` otherwise, as shown in the following listing.[1]

**Listing 6.2 The structure of an `inject` predicate**

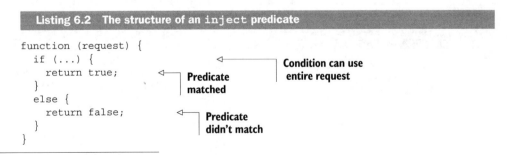

---

[1] JavaScript as a language has a lot of warts, and experts will tell you that you can return `truthy` or `falsy`. I never cared to learn what that meant, so I stick with `true` or `false` and recommend you do too.

Plugging the function into the `predicates` array of a stub involves JSON-escaping the function, which replaces newlines with `'\n'`, and escaping double quotes:

```
{
  "predicates": [{
    "inject": "function (request) {\n  if (...) {\n
    return true;\n  }\n  else {\n    return false;\n  }\n}"
  }],
  "responses: [{
    "is": { ... }
  }]
}
```

I wouldn't recommend doing the JSON-escaping by hand. In the examples that follow, you will use EJS templating and the `stringify` function mountebank adds to EJS. (Refer to chapter 3 for details on how to lay out configuration files.)[2] If you're building up the imposter configuration in code, your JSON libraries should manage the escaping for you.

All you have to do now is write the JavaScript function. I have intentionally created a complex example to show that injection is up to nearly any task. Let's look at the JavaScript bit by bit, starting with a function to parse CSV. You need a function that will take raw text, like that shown in listing 6.1, and convert it into an array of Java-Script objects:

```
[
  {
    "Day": "4-Jun",
    "Description": "PM Thunderstorms",
    "High": 83,
    "Low": 71,
    "Precip": "50%",
    "Wind": "E 5 mph",
    "Humidity": "65%"
  },
  ...
]
```

You will call the function shown in the following listing `csvToObjects`.

**Listing 6.3   A JavaScript function to parse CSV data—`csvToObjects`**

```
function csvToObjects (csvData) {
  var lines = csvData.split('\n'),                    csvData is the
      headers = lines[0].split(','),      Splits input by    raw text.
      result = [];                        line endings
```

---

[2] Browse the GitHub repo at https://github.com/bbyars/mountebank-in-action to see fully worked-out examples.

```
// Remove the headers
lines.shift();                          Removes first
                                        line (headers)
lines.forEach(function (line) {
  var fields = line.split(','),          Splits line
      row = {};                          by commas

  for (var i = 0; i < headers.length; i++) {
    var header = headers[i],
        data = fields[i];
    row[header] = data;                  Adds data
  }                                      keyed by header

  result.push(row);          Adds to
});                          array

  return result;
}
```

As far as CSV parsing functions go, this is as simple as it gets. It works for your data, but not for more complex data involving escaped commas inside quotes and other edge scenarios.

The next function you will need is one to look for three consecutive days of humidity over 60%, as shown in the following listing.

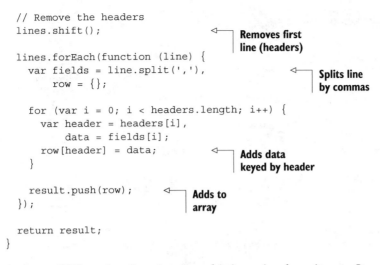

```
function hasThreeDaysOutOfRange (humidities) {       Accepts an array of integers
  var daysOutOfRange = 0,                            representing humidity level
      result = false;

  humidities.forEach(function (humidity) {
    if (humidity < 60) {
      daysOutOfRange = 0;          Resets counter if
      return;                      humidity is in range
    }

    daysOutOfRange += 1;
    if (daysOutOfRange >= 3) {          Sets result if humidity is
      result = true;                    out of range for three days
    }
  });

  return result;
}
```

Detecting three consecutive days of out-of-range humidity is complicated enough to extract into a separate function, but it isn't too difficult to code. The last check—looking for a single day more than 10% out of range—is simple enough that you can do it inline using the JavaScript some function of arrays, which returns true if the supplied function is true for any element of the array. The predicate function looks like the following listing.

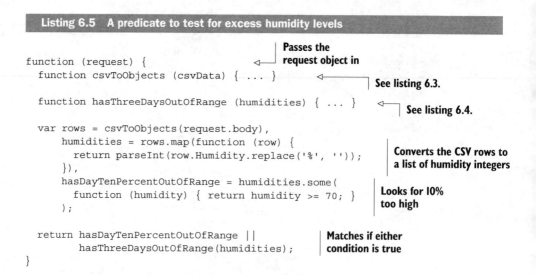

Listing 6.5   A predicate to test for excess humidity levels

```
function (request) {                          Passes the
  function csvToObjects (csvData) { ... }      request object in

  function hasThreeDaysOutOfRange (humidities) { ... }   See listing 6.3.

  var rows = csvToObjects(request.body),              See listing 6.4.
      humidities = rows.map(function (row) {
        return parseInt(row.Humidity.replace('%', ''));     Converts the CSV rows to
      }),                                                    a list of humidity integers
      hasDayTenPercentOutOfRange = humidities.some(
        function (humidity) { return humidity >= 70; }       Looks for 10%
      );                                                     too high

  return hasDayTenPercentOutOfRange ||            Matches if either
         hasThreeDaysOutOfRange(humidities);      condition is true
}
```

When you include an `inject` predicate in a stub, mountebank passes the entire request object to the provided function. You have included your `csvToObjects` and `hasThreeDaysOutOfRange` functions as subfunctions inside the parent predicate function. You can use this approach to include code of considerable complexity.

Adding this predicate allows you to mimic the roadie service effectively, virtualizing its behavior with high fidelity. Although that highlights the power of JavaScript injection, it also raises an important concern about service virtualization.

Virtualizing the roadie service has been a wonderful example to demonstrate the power of `inject`. However, it does come with two pretty serious drawbacks: it hasn't helped one bit in terms of making me an actual rock star, and it's likely the kind of thing you'd want to avoid virtualizing in a real application stack. Remember, service virtualization is a testing strategy that gives you determinism when testing a service that has runtime dependencies. It's not a way of reimplementing runtime dependencies in a different platform. Although mountebank provides advanced functionality to make your stubs smarter when you need them to be, your best bet is to not need them to be so smart. The dumber your virtual services can be, the more maintainable your test architecture will be.

## 6.2   *Creating your own dynamic response*

You also can create your own response in mountebank. The `inject` response joins `is` and `proxy` to round out the core response types, and it represents a dynamic response that JavaScript generates. In its simplest form, the response injection function mirrors that for predicates, accepting the entire request as a parameter. It's responsible for returning a response object that mountebank will merge with the default response. Think of it as creating an `is` response using a JavaScript function, as follows.

**Listing 6.6   The basic structure of response injection**

```
{
  "responses": [{
    "inject": "function (request) { return { statusCode: 400 }; }"
  }]
}
```

In this basic form, it's quite easy to replace your predicate injection you used to virtualize the roadie service with response injection. Because you're giving the response injection function the same request as the predicate injection function, you could remove the predicate injection and move the conditions to the function that generates the response, as shown in the following listing.

**Listing 6.7   A response injection function to virtualize the roadie service humidity checks**

```
function (request) {                                    ← Mountebank passes request in
  function csvToObjects (csvData) { ... }               ← See listing 6.3.

  function hasThreeDaysOutOfRange (humidities) { ... }  ← See listing 6.4.

  var rows = csvToObjects(request.body),
    humidities = rows.map(function (row) {
      return parseInt(row.Humidity.replace('%', ''));
    }),
    hasDayTenPercentOutOfRange = humidities.some(
      function (humidity) { return humidity >= 70; }
    ),
    isTooHumid = hasDayTenPercentOutOfRange ||          ← Capture condition
                 hasThreeDaysOutOfRange(humidities);

  if (isTooHumid) {
    return {
      statusCode: 400,                                  ⎫ Return failure
      body: 'Humidity levels dangerous, action required' ⎬ response
    };                                                   ⎭
  }
  else {
    return {
      body: 'Humidity levels OK for the next 10 days'   ⎫ Return happy
    };                                                   ⎬ path response
  }                                                      ⎭
}
```

Instead of returning `true` or `false` to determine whether a predicate matches, a response injection returns the response object, or at least the portion of it that isn't the default response. In this case, it returns a 400 status code and a body indicating action is required if the humidity check requires you to take action, or a default 200 code with a body letting you know that the humidity levels are OK.

### 6.2.1   *Adding state*

At first glance, there isn't much difference between using a predicate injection and using a response injection in this example. But for complex workflows, response injections have a key advantage: they can keep state. To see how that can be useful, imagine having to virtualize a scenario where your manager service sends *multiple* weather reports, and the roadie service needs to detect three consecutive days out of range even if they span two reports that the manager sent (figure 6.3).

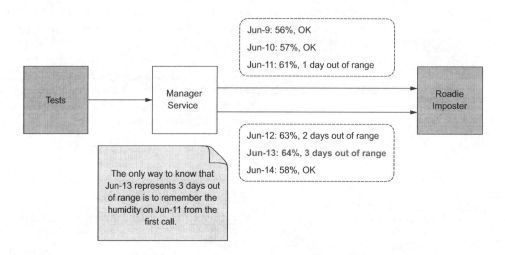

**Figure 6.3   Two reports need to be spanned to detect dangerous humidity.**

Mountebank passes a `state` parameter into your response injection functions that you can use to remember information across multiple requests. It's initially an empty object, but you can add whatever information you want to it each time the injection function executes. In this example, you will have to save the humidity results by day so you can detect dangerous humidity levels even if three consecutive days over 60% humidity span two requests from the manager service.

You start by adding the parameter to your function and initializing it with the variables you want to remember. In this case, `state` will remember the days, and if the roadie service sees the weather report for a day it hasn't seen yet, your function will add the humidity to a list:

```
function (request, state) {
  if (!state.humidities) {
    state.days = [];
    state.humidities = [];
  }

  ...
}
```

Now the rest of the function is nearly identical to listing 6.7. You only have to add to the `state.humidities` array at the appropriate time and do your checks on that array instead of a local variable, as in the following listing.

**Listing 6.8  Remembering state between responses**

```
function (request, state) {
  function csvToObjects (csvData) {...}

  function hasThreeDaysOutOfRange (humidities) {...}

  // Initialize state arrays
  if (!state.humidities) {
    state.days = [];
    state.humidities = [];
  }

  var rows = csvToObjects(request.body);

  rows.forEach(function (row) {                              Only adds to the list if it
    if (state.days.indexOf(row.Day) < 0) {          ◁──      hasn't seen this day before
      state.days.push(row.Day);
      state.humidities.push(row.Humidity.replace('%', ''));  ◁──  Adds new
    }                                                              humidity
  });

  var hasDayTenPercentOutOfRange =
    state.humidities.some(function (humidity) {    ◁──   Switches these functions
      return humidity >= 70;                              to use state variable
  });

  if (hasDayTenPercentOutOfRange ||
    hasThreeDaysOutOfRange(state.humidities)) {
    return {
      statusCode: 400,
      body: 'Humidity levels dangerous, action required'
    };
  }
  else {
    return {
      body: 'Humidity levels OK'
    };
  }
}
```

Voilà! Now the virtual roadie service can keep track of humidity levels across multiple requests. There is only one feature of injection left to look at, but it is a big topic: asynchronous operations.

### 6.2.2  Adding async

Asynchronicity is baked into JavaScript, to the extent that it is generally required to access any file or network resource used to craft a dynamic response. Understanding why requires a quick tour of how programming languages manage I/O, as JavaScript is fairly unusual in this regard. Until Microsoft introduced the `XMLHttpRequest` object that powers AJAX requests, JavaScript lacked any form of I/O found in the base class libraries of other languages. It took Node.js to add a full complement of I/O functions to JavaScript, but it did so following the AJAX pattern familiar to a generation of web developers: using callbacks.

Take a look at the following code to sort the lines in a file. This is in Ruby, but the code would be similar in Python, Java, C#, and most traditional languages.

> **Listing 6.9  Using traditional I/O to sort lines in a file**

```
lines = File.readlines('input.txt')
puts lines.sort
puts "The end..."
```

First you read all the lines in the input.txt file into an array, then you sort the array, printing the output to the console. Finally, you print "The end…" to the console. At first blush, nothing could be simpler, but the `File.readlines` function is hiding considerable complexity.

As shown in figure 6.4, under the hood, Ruby has to make a system call into the operating system (OS), because only the OS has the appropriate privileges to interact with the hardware, including the disk storing input.txt. To buy time while it waits on the results, the OS scheduler switches to another process to execute for a period of time. When the data from the disk is available, the OS feeds it back into the original process. Computers move fast enough that this is largely transparent to the user; for most I/O operations, the application will still feel quite responsive. It's also transparent to the developer, as the linear nature of the code matches a mental model, which

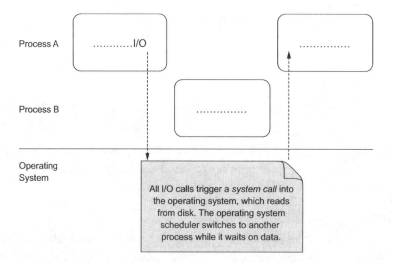

**Figure 6.4  What happens with traditional blocking I/O**

is why *blocking I/O*—having the process block until the operation completes—is the most common form of I/O.

JavaScript was born of the web, a programming environment rich with events, such as responding when a user presses a button or types in a text field. AJAX, which made web pages more responsive by allowing the user to fetch data from the server without refreshing the entire page (a form of I/O involving the network), maintained that event model, treating getting a response from the server as an event. When Ryan Dahl wrote Node.js to add more I/O capability to JavaScript, he intentionally maintained that event model because he wanted to explore *nonblocking I/O* in a mainstream language. The fact that developers were already used to AJAX events made JavaScript a natural fit (figure 6.5).

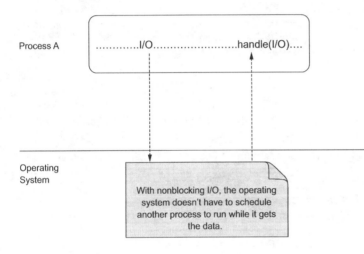

**Figure 6.5   Nonblocking I/O doesn't block the process.**

Each I/O operation registers a callback function that executes when the OS has data, and program execution continues immediately to the next line of code. Let's rewrite the Ruby file sort operation in JavaScript, using nonblocking I/O, as in the following listing.

**Listing 6.10   File sort using nonblocking I/O**

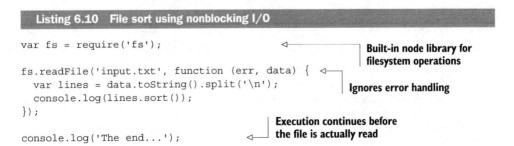

```
var fs = require('fs');                              ◁————————  Built-in node library for
                                                                filesystem operations
fs.readFile('input.txt', function (err, data) {  ◁——┐
  var lines = data.toString().split('\n');           │        Ignores error handling
  console.log(lines.sort());
});
                                                         ┌  Execution continues before
console.log('The end...');                         ◁——————┘  the file is actually read
```

The callback function is passed as a parameter to `fs.readFile`, and execution immediately continues to the next line of code. At some later point, when the OS has the contents of input.txt, the callback function will execute, providing the sorted lines. That flow means that, in this example, you will print "The end…" to the console *before* you print the sorted lines of input.txt.

As of this writing, predicate injection doesn't support asynchronous operations. But async support *is* important when it comes to response injection, as I/O operations are often valuable in scripting dynamic responses. Let's show an example by virtualizing a simple OAuth flow in mountebank.

### OAuth

OAuth is a delegated authorization framework. It allows one party (the resource owner) to allow another party (the client) to act on a resource held by a third party (the resource server), where the identity of the resource owner is guaranteed by a fourth party (the authorization server). You can often collapse these four roles in various ways, creating a number of alternative flows.

A standard use case is where a person (the resource owner) allows a web app (the client) to act on a resource held by a third party like GitHub (resource server) after presenting credentials to that third party (authorization server). This flow allows the web app to perform secure operations in GitHub on behalf of the user, even though the user never provided their GitHub credentials to that website.

This OAuth flow is common, and its mechanics are difficult to stub out. In the section "Virtualizing an OAuth-backed GitHub client," I use that as an opportunity to show how to manage async in an `inject` response by building a small GitHub web app and virtualizing the GitHub API for testing purposes.

### VIRTUALIZING AN OAUTH-BACKED GITHUB CLIENT

GitHub has a robust marketplace of client applications available at https://github .com/marketplace. Unfortunately, none of them solve an immediate problem of the readers of this book: adding a star to the mountebank repo.[3] But GitHub has a public RESTful API that allows you to build an app. You will treat that app as your system under test, requiring you to virtualize the GitHub API itself.

GitHub uses OAuth, which requires a complex set of interactions before GitHub will accept an API call to star a repo.[4] The first thing you need to do is to register your new application, which you can do at https://github.com/settings/applications/new (figure 6.6).

The OAuth flow expects to call back to complete the authentication and uses the URL you provided during registration to call back into. The general flow is shown in figure 6.7.

---

[3] For readers willing to star the old-fashioned way, you can do so by visiting the repo directly at https:// github.com/bbyars/mountebank.

[4] We will use a basic OAuth web flow described at https://developer.github.com/v3/guides/basics-of-authentication/.

**Application name**

mountebankTest

Something users will recognize and trust

**Homepage URL**

https://github.com/bbyars/mountebank-in-action/tree/master/ch

The full URL to your application homepage

**Application description**

A test app showing testing OAuth
using mountebank injection

This is displayed to all potential users of your application

The OAuth flow expects to
call back into the website to
complete authentication.

**Authorization callback URL**

http://localhost:3000/callback

Your application's callback URL. Read our OAuth documentation for more information.

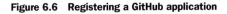

**Update application**    **Delete application**

**Figure 6.6    Registering a GitHub application**

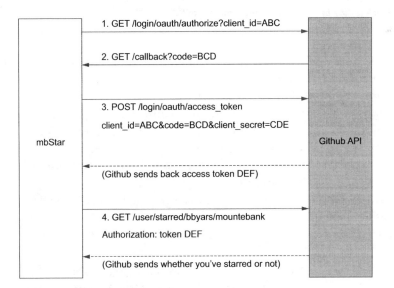

**Figure 6.7    Understanding the GitHub OAuth flow**

The application calls the /login/oauth/authorize endpoint, passing a `client_id`. GitHub calls the callback URL you provided during registration, passing a random code. The application is then expected to call a /login/oauth/access_token URL, sending the `client_id`, the `code` and a `client_secret`. If all of that is done correctly, GitHub sends back a token that the application can use to authorize subsequent calls. Although the fictional app is designed to star the mountebank repo if you haven't already done so, I will only show how to test whether you have already starred or not. (On the advice of my legal staff, I have decided to leave starring mountebank as an exercise for the reader.)

The `client_id` and `client_secret` are provided during registration on GitHub (figure 6.8). Like a private key, you should keep the `client_secret` super secret. You shouldn't store it in source control, and you most certainly shouldn't publish it in a book for millions to read.[5]

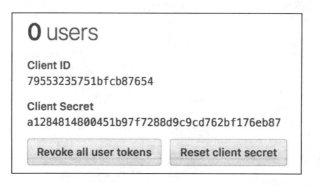

**Figure 6.8    Viewing the client secret to communicate to GitHub**

Your test case should validate this entire flow, requiring you to virtualize three GitHub endpoints. Structurally, the GitHub imposter needs to have three stubs representing those endpoints (figure 6.9). You can virtualize the last two calls in order to get the token and to check if you have starred the mountebank repo, with simple `is` responses. You can't virtualize the first call, to actually authorize, with an `is` response. in order to authorize. The fact that it has to call back into the system under test requires you to move beyond simple stubbing approaches. You'll use an `inject` response to do the callback with an easily identifiable test code.

Using easily identifiable names (like TEST-CODE and TEST-ACCESS-TOKEN) for the test data that the imposter creates is a useful tip to make it easier to spot in a complex workflow.

---

[5]  Don't worry—I removed this toy app before you had a chance to read these words. You'll have to register your own app to fully follow the source code in question, although you can use the same code located at https://github.com/bbyars/mountebank-in-action

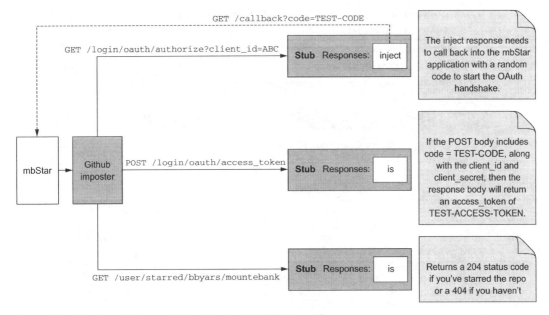

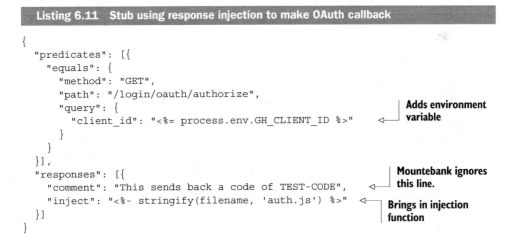

**Figure 6.9** **The three stubs needed to virtualize this GitHub workflow**

### STARTING THE OAUTH HANDSHAKE

The first endpoint (/login/oauth/authorize) starts the OAuth handshake by sending the random code (TEST-CODE) to your web app. It's also the most complicated response, involving calling back to the system under test, which you cannot solve using an `is` or a `proxy` response. Conceptually, the stub looks like the following listing.

**Listing 6.11  Stub using response injection to make OAuth callback**

```
{
  "predicates": [{
    "equals": {
      "method": "GET",
      "path": "/login/oauth/authorize",
      "query": {
        "client_id": "<%= process.env.GH_CLIENT_ID %>"    ⟵  Adds environment
      }                                                        variable
    }
  }],
  "responses": [{
    "comment": "This sends back a code of TEST-CODE",    ⟵  Mountebank ignores
    "inject": "<%- stringify(filename, 'auth.js') %>"    ⟵  this line.
  }]                                                         Brings in injection
}                                                            function
```

Both the tests and the example web app use environment variables for the `client_id` and the `client_secret`, and you will use EJS templating to interpolate them into your configuration file. Notice also the added `comment` field in the response. Mountebank ignores any fields it doesn't recognize, so you can always add more metadata. For complicated workflows like this one, such comments can help you follow along more easily.

The following listing shows the injection function in `auth.js`.

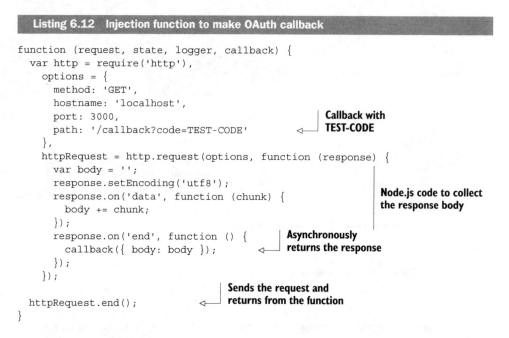

**Listing 6.12   Injection function to make OAuth callback**

```
function (request, state, logger, callback) {
  var http = require('http'),
    options = {
      method: 'GET',
      hostname: 'localhost',
      port: 3000,
      path: '/callback?code=TEST-CODE'          ← Callback with TEST-CODE
    },
    httpRequest = http.request(options, function (response) {
      var body = '';
      response.setEncoding('utf8');
      response.on('data', function (chunk) {
        body += chunk;                          Node.js code to collect the response body
      });
      response.on('end', function () {
        callback({ body: body });               ← Asynchronously returns the response
      });
    });

  httpRequest.end();                            ← Sends the request and returns from the function
}
```

Much of the code is manipulating the Node.js `http` module to make the call to http://localhost:3000/callback?code=TEST-CODE. Because the HTTP call involves network I/O, the function returns immediately after the call to `httpRequest.end()`. When the network call returns, Node.js invokes the function passed as a parameter to the `http.request()` call. Node's `http` library streams the HTTP response back, so you may receive multiple `data` events and have to collect the response body as you go. When you have received the entire response, Node triggers the `end` event, at which point you can create the response you want. In your case, you'll return the same body the callback URL provided. Passing that to the `callback` function parameter ends your response injection, returning the parameter as the response to mountebank.

For example, if your call to http://localhost:3000/callback?code=TEST-CODE returns a body of "You have already starred the mountebank repo," then the end result of the injection function would be equivalent to the following `is` response:

```
{
  "is": {
    "body": "You have already starred the mountebank repo"
  }
}
```

Remember, a key goal of mountebank is to make simple things easy to do and to make hard things possible. Virtualizing an OAuth flow is hard. This is about as complicated a workflow as you will see in most tests involving service virtualization. It's certainly a lot to walk through, but you were able to do the hard bits of it with about 20 lines of JavaScript, and when you run into similar problems, you will be thankful that solving them is at least possible with mountebank.

#### VALIDATING THE OAUTH AUTHORIZATION

Let's look at the next stub, for the /login/oauth/access_token endpoint. This one should only match if the app reflected back the TEST-CODE in its request body and correctly sent the preconfigured client_id and client_secret. You can use predicates and a simple is response to send back a test access token, as shown in the following listing.

##### Listing 6.13  The stub to get an access token

```
{
  "predicates": [
    {
      "equals": {
        "method": "POST",
        "path": "/login/oauth/access_token"
      }
    },
    {
      "contains": {
        "body":
  "client_id=<%= process.env.GH_CLIENT_ID %>"          ⟵  Requires client_id
      }                                                       from environment
    },
    {
      "contains": {
        "body":
  "client_secret=<%= process.env.GH_CLIENT_SECRET %>"  ⟵  Requires client_secret
      }                                                       from environment
    },
    {
      "contains": {                            TEST-CODE comes from
        "body": "code=TEST-CODE"          ⟵   injection in previous stub
      }
    }
  ],
  "responses": [{
    "is": {
      "body": {                                        Returns a test
        "access_token": "TEST-ACCESS-TOKEN",     ⟵     access token
        "token_type": "bearer",
        "scope": "user:email"
      }
    }
  }]
}
```

Once your web app retrieves the `access_token`, it has successfully navigated the OAuth flow.

### CHECKING IF YOU'VE STARRED MOUNTEBANK

At this point, the app should be armed with an access token and should make the GitHub call to check if you've starred the mountebank repo or not. Your predicate needs to validate the token, and, once again, you can use a simple `is` response, as shown in the following listing.

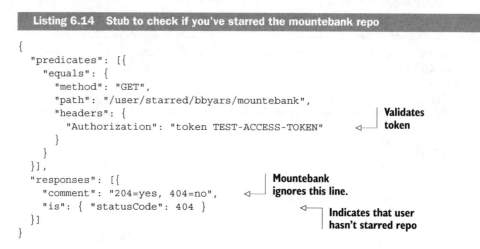

Listing 6.14  Stub to check if you've starred the mountebank repo

```
{
  "predicates": [{
    "equals": {
      "method": "GET",
      "path": "/user/starred/bbyars/mountebank",
      "headers": {
        "Authorization": "token TEST-ACCESS-TOKEN"          ←┘ Validates
      }                                                          token
    }
  }],
  "responses": [{
    "comment": "204=yes, 404=no",          ←┘ Mountebank
    "is": { "statusCode": 404 }                 ignores this line.
  }]                                          ←┐ Indicates that user
}                                              │ hasn't starred repo
```

With OAuth now virtualized, any other API endpoints should be quite easy to stub out. All you have to do is check for the `Authorization` header as shown in listing 6.14.

### 6.2.3 *Deciding between response vs. predicate injection*

Mountebank passes the `request` object to both predicate and response injection functions, so you could put conditional logic based on the request in either location. Compared to response injection, predicate injection is relatively easy to use. If you need to send a static response back based on a dynamic condition, programming your own predicate and using an `is` response stays true to the intention of predicates in mountebank. But response injection is considerably more capable, and you won't hurt my feelings if you move your conditional logic to a response function so you can take advantage of state or async support.

A predicate injection function takes only two parameters:

- `request`—The protocol-specific request object (HTTP in all of the examples)
- `logger`—Used to write debugging information to the mountebank logs

The response injection function includes those parameters and adds two more:

- `state`—An initially empty object that you can add state to; will be passed into subsequent calls for the same imposter
- `callback`—A callback function to support asynchronous operations

Response functions always have the option of synchronously returning a response object. You only need the `callback` if you use nonblocking I/O and need to return the response object asynchronously.

## 6.3 A word of caution: security matters

JavaScript injection is disabled by default when you start mountebank, and for good reason. With injection enabled, mountebank becomes a potential remote execution engine accessible to anyone on the network. When mountebank is run naively, an attacker can take advantage of that fact to do evil things on the network while spoofing your identity (figure 6.10).

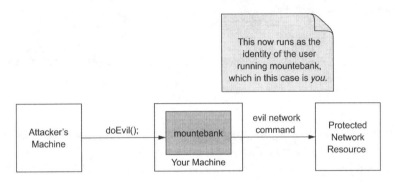

**Figure 6.10  Using mountebank to spoof your identity during a network attack**

Injection is an enormously useful feature, but you have to use it with an understanding of the security implications. This is why mountebank shows a warning message in the logs every time you start it with the `--allowInjection` flag. You can take some precautions to protect yourself.

The first precaution is to not run `mb` under your user account. Starting mountebank as an unprivileged user, ideally one without domain credentials on your network, goes a long way toward protecting yourself. You should always use the least privileged user you can get away with, adding in network access only when your tests require it.

The next layer of security is to restrict which machines can access the mountebank web server. We've used the `--localOnly` flag throughout this chapter, which restricts access to processes running on the same machine. This option is perfect when your tests run on the same machine as mountebank, and it should be the default choice most of the time. When you do require remote tests (during extensive load testing, for example), you can still restrict which machines can access mountebank's web server with the `--ipWhitelist` flag, which captures a pipe-delimited set of IP addresses. For example:

```
mb --allowInjection --ipWhitelist "10.22.57.137|10.22.57.138"
```

In this example, the only remote IP addresses allowed access to mountebank are 10.22.57.137 and 10.22.57.138.

## 6.4   *Debugging tips*

Writing injection functions has all the same complexity as writing any code, except that it's much harder to debug them through an IDE because they run in a remote process. I often resort to what, back in my college days when we coded in C, we called `printf` debugging. In JavaScript, it looks something like this:

```
function (request) {
  // Function definition...

  var rows = csvToObjects(request.body),
    humidities = rows.map(function (row) {
      return parseInt(row.Humidity.replace('%', ''));
    });

console.log(JSON.stringify(humidities));                    ◁――――| Shows full
                                                                   object structure

  return {};                                ◁――| I'll figure this out later....
}
```

The `console.log` function in JavaScript prints the parameter to the standard output of the running process, which in this case is `mb`. The `JSON.stringify` function converts an object to a JSON string, allowing you to inspect the full object graph. This code is quite ugly—I outdented the `console.log` function to not lose sight of it, and I returned an empty object for the response, relying on the standard default response. If you've written code for longer than a few seconds, you'll likely recognize the pattern. Most code starts out ugly before you figure out how to communicate your intent to a ruthlessly precise computer.

To make the output a little easier to spot in the logs, mountebank passes another parameter to both predicate and response injection: the logger itself. In typical logging fashion, the logger has four functions: `debug`, `info`, `warn`, and `error`. The `debug` messages are usually not shown to the console (unless you start `mb` with the `--loglevel` `debug` flag). To make your debugging messages stand out, use the `warn` or `error` functions, which will print your debugging output to the console in a different color:

```
function (request, state, logger) {
  // Function definition...

  var rows = csvToObjects(request.body),
    humidities = rows.map(function (row) {
      return parseInt(row.Humidity.replace('%', ''));
    });

logger.warn(JSON.stringify(humidities));              ◁――| Prints to the console
                                                           as yellow text

  return {};
}
```

The code above shows logging for response injection. Predicate injections pass in the `logger` as the second parameter as well.

## Summary

- You can create your own predicates with a JavaScript function that accepts the `request` object and returns a Boolean representing whether the predicate matched or not.
- You also can create your own response with a JavaScript function that accepts the `request` object and returns an object representing the response.
- If you need to remember state between requests, mountebank passes an initially empty `state` object to the response function. Any fields you set on the object will persist between calls.
- Because JavaScript and node.js use nonblocking I/O, most response functions that need to access data outside the process will have to return asynchronously. Instead of returning an object, you can pass the response object to the `callback` parameter.
- Injection is powerful, but it also creates a remote execution engine running on your machine. Anytime you run mountebank with injection enabled, you should limit remote connections and use an unprivileged identity.

# Adding behaviors

**This chapter covers**

- Programmatically postprocessing a response
- Adding latency to a response
- Repeating a response multiple times
- Copying input from the request into the response
- Looking up data from a CSV file to plug into a response

The basic `is` response is easy to understand but limited in functionality. Proxy responses provide high-fidelity mimicry, but each saved response represents a snapshot in time. Response injection provides significant flexibility but comes with high complexity. Sometimes, you want the simplicity of `is` and `proxy` responses with a touch of dynamism, all without the complexity of `inject`.

Software engineers who hail from the object-oriented school of thought use the term *decorate* to mean intercepting a plain message and augmenting it in some way before forwarding it on to the recipient. It's like what the postal service does when it applies a postmark to your letter after sorting it. The original letter you sent is still intact, but the postal workers have *decorated* it to postprocess it with a bit of dynamic information. In mountebank, *behaviors* represent a way of decorating responses before the imposter sends them over the wire.

Because of their flexibility and utility, behaviors also represent one of the most rapidly evolving parts of mountebank itself. We'll look at all of the behaviors available as of this writing (representing v1.13), but expect more to come in the future.

## 7.1 Understanding behaviors

If you ignore the complexity of interacting with the network and different protocols, mountebank has only three core concepts:

- *Predicates* help route requests on the way in.
- *Responses* generate the responses on the way out.
- *Behaviors* postprocess the responses before shipping them over the wire (figure 7.1).

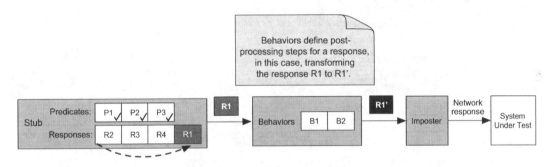

**Figure 7.1** Behaviors can transform a response from a stub before it goes out via the imposter.

Although nothing prevents you from using behaviors with `inject` responses, most behaviors exist to allow you to reduce the amount of complexity inherent in using JavaScript to craft the response. Behaviors are a way of avoiding the complexity of `inject` responses in favor of simpler `is` responses, while still being able to provide appropriate dynamism to your response.

Behaviors sit alongside the type of response in the stub definition, as shown in listing 7.1. You can combine multiple behaviors together, but only one of each type. No behavior should depend on the order of execution of other behaviors. That is an implementation detail subject to change without notice.

**Listing 7.1  Adding behaviors to a stub definition**

```
{
  "responses": [{
    "is": { "statusCode": 500 },
```

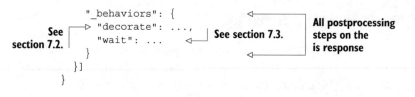

```
    "_behaviors": {
      "decorate": ...,
      "wait": ...
    }
  }]
}
```

See section 7.2.

See section 7.3.

All postprocessing steps on the is response

In this example, the is response will first merge the 500 status code into the default response, then it will pass the generated response object to both the decorate and wait behaviors. Each behavior will postprocess the response in a specific way, which we'll look at shortly.

Some behaviors still rely on programmatic control of the postprocessing, which requires the --allowInjection flag to be set when starting mb. This carries with it all the same security considerations we examined in the last chapter. We look at those behaviors next.

## 7.2    Decorating a response

The bluntest instruments in the behavior toolbox are the decorate and shellTransform behaviors, which accept the response object as input and transform it in some way, sending a new response object as output (figure 7.2).

They're quite similar to response injection, except they provide more focused injection (in the case of decorate), or more flexibility (shellTransform).

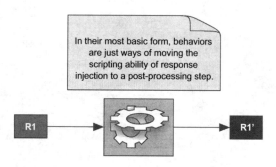

In their most basic form, behaviors are just ways of moving the scripting ability of response injection to a post-processing step.

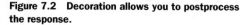

R1    R1'

**Figure 7.2   Decoration allows you to postprocess the response.**

### 7.2.1    Using the decorate function

Without behaviors, you'd be forced to use an inject response if only one field of the response were dynamic. For example, assume you want to send the following response body back:

```
{
  "timestamp": "2017-07-22T14:49:21.485Z",
  "givenName": "Stubby",
  "surname": "McStubble",
  "birthDate": "1980-01-01"
}
```

You could capture this body in an is response, setting the body field to the JSON, but that would assume that an outdated timestamp is irrelevant to the test case at hand. That isn't always a valid assumption. Unfortunately, translating that to an inject response hides the intent, as shown in the following listing.

---

**Listing 7.2  Using an `inject` response to send a dynamic timestamp**

```
{
  "responses": [{
    "inject": "function () { return { body: { timestamp: new Date(),
➥ givenName: 'Stubby', surname: 'McStubble', birthDate:
➥ '1980-01-01' } } }"
  }]
}
```

To make sense of what the response is doing, you have to extract the JavaScript function and stare at it. Compare that to combining an `is` response with a `decorate`
response, which sends the same JSON over the wire without awkward translation, as
you can see in the following listing.[1]

---

**Listing 7.3  Combining an `is` response with a `decorate` behavior**

```
{
  "responses": [{
    "is": {
      "body": {
        "givenName": "Stubby",          Return this...
        "surname": "McStubble",
        "birthDate": "1980-01-01"
      }
    },
    "_behaviors": {
      "decorate": "function (request, response, logger) {      ...but add a current
➥ response.body.timestamp = new Date(); }"                     timestamp.
    }
  }]
}
```

As noted, this is like the post office adding a postmark to your envelope. You provide
the core content with an `is` response, and the `decorate` behavior adds the current
timestamp to the message. The end response is the same as with the `inject`
approach, but separating the static part of the response from the dynamic part often
makes the code easier to maintain.

The `decorate` function isn't as capable as a full `inject` response. Behaviors don't
have access to any user-controlled state like response injection. They don't allow asynchronous responses, which eliminates a large class of JavaScript I/O operations, as discussed in chapter 6. That said, the `decorate` behavior does allow the majority of the
response message to be visible in a static `is` response, which simplifies maintenance of
your test data.

---

[1]  As always, you can follow along with the book's source code at https://github.com/bbyars/mountebank-in-
action.

### 7.2.2    *Adding decoration to saved proxy responses*

Behaviors are agnostic to the type of response they are applied to, which means you can decorate a `proxy` response as well. But by default, the decoration applies only to the `proxy` response itself, not to the `is` response it saves. (See figure 7.3.)

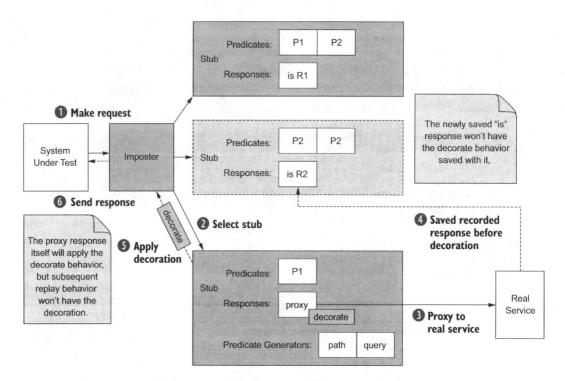

**Figure 7.3    Behaviors applied to proxies don't transfer to the saved responses.**

You *can* add a couple of behaviors to the saved `is` responses, including `decorate`. You have to configure the proxy with the `decorate` behavior. We'll work with a more complicated example than updating a timestamp to show how proxying and decoration work hand in glove.

Most industrial APIs include some sort of rate limiting to prevent denial of service. The Twitter API represents a standard approach, where Twitter sends back an `x-rate-limit-remaining` header in the response to let the user know how many requests the API user has left for a certain time frame. Once those requests are spent, Twitter will send a 429 HTTP status code (Too Many Requests) until the time period is up.[2]

---

[2]  You can read the full details at https://dev.twitter.com/rest/public/rate-limiting.

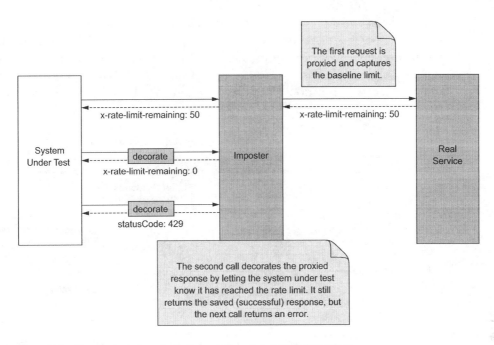

**Figure 7.4  Manufacturing a rate limit exception on a recorded response**

At times you may want to test the consumer's response when it triggers rate limit errors midstream through a workflow. One option is to proxy all requests to the downstream rate-limited service (using the `proxyAlways` mode described in chapter 5). But it may be difficult to capture a rate limit scenario through proxying real traffic. Another option is to capture the first response and use decoration to trigger a rate limit error after a few requests (figure 7.4).

Setting up this scenario requires you to proxy to the downstream server to save the response but add a decorate behavior on the *saved* response, as in the following listing. The original proxy response will be undecorated, returning the response captured from the downstream service.

**Listing 7.4  Adding a decorate behavior to recorded responses**

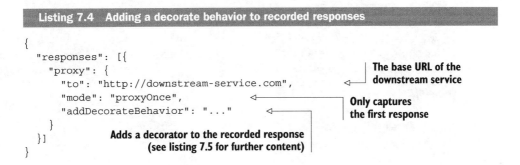

```
{
  "responses": [{
    "proxy": {
      "to": "http://downstream-service.com",
      "mode": "proxyOnce",
      "addDecorateBehavior": "..."
    }
  }]
}
```

The base URL of the downstream service

Only captures the first response

Adds a decorator to the recorded response (see listing 7.5 for further content)

The decorator function will have access to the saved response and can change the x-rate-limit-remaining header or return an error as desired by the test case. In the code below, you will decrement the header 25 requests at a time to accelerate reaching a rate limit error, but you can tweak that value according to your test scenario. Because decorate functions don't have access to the same ability to save state that inject responses do, you have to use a file to store the last value sent for the x-rate-limit-remaining header, as shown in the following listing.

> **Listing 7.5  Decorator function to accelerate a rate limit exception**

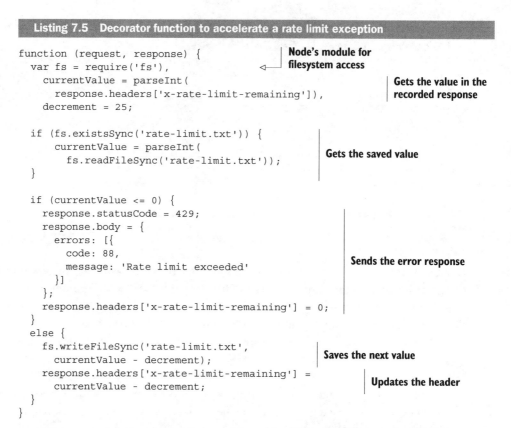

```
function (request, response) {
  var fs = require('fs'),                                    Node's module for
    currentValue = parseInt(                                 filesystem access
      response.headers['x-rate-limit-remaining']),          Gets the value in the
    decrement = 25;                                          recorded response

  if (fs.existsSync('rate-limit.txt')) {
    currentValue = parseInt(                                 Gets the saved value
      fs.readFileSync('rate-limit.txt'));
  }

  if (currentValue <= 0) {
    response.statusCode = 429;
    response.body = {
      errors: [{
        code: 88,
        message: 'Rate limit exceeded'                       Sends the error response
      }]
    };
    response.headers['x-rate-limit-remaining'] = 0;
  }
  else {
    fs.writeFileSync('rate-limit.txt',
      currentValue - decrement);                             Saves the next value
    response.headers['x-rate-limit-remaining'] =
      currentValue - decrement;                              Updates the header
  }
}
```

### What happened to nonblocking I/O?

In the last chapter, I described how JavaScript and Node.js use nonblocking I/O, which required adding asynchronous support to response injection. That is still true, but Node.js has added a small number of blocking, synchronous calls for common filesystem operations. Notice how the function names used in listing 7.5 end in Sync (fs.existsSync, fs.readFileSync, and fs.writeFileSync). These are special convenience functions that break out of the standard nonblocking I/O model. To the best of my knowledge, no such convenience functions exist for I/O that has to traverse the network.

You were forced to use the filesystem to save state because decorators cannot save state directly, and you were forced to use the `Sync` functions because decorators do not support asynchronous operations. Both of these are supported in response injection, as described in chapter 6. Future versions of mountebank may support them in decorators as well. The next behavior, `shellTransform`, suffers from neither of these limitations.

### 7.2.3   *Adding middleware through shellTransform*

The next behavior is both the most general purpose and the most powerful, and both of those aspects come with added complexity. Like `decorate`, `shellTransform` allows you programmatic postprocessing of the response. But it doesn't require the use of JavaScript, and it allows you to chain together a series of postprocessing transformations (figure 7.5).

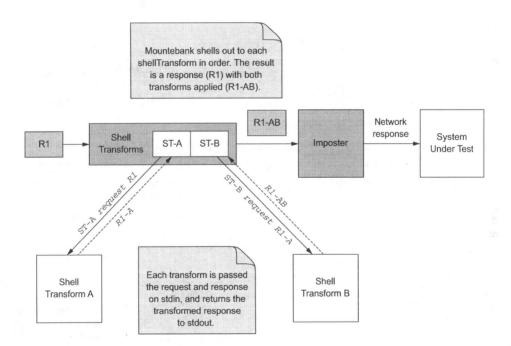

**Figure 7.5   The `shellTransform` behavior allows you to combine multiple transformations piped through the shell.**

To see how it works, let's take the two transformations you've already seen (adding a timestamp and triggering a rate limit exception) and convert them to shell-Transform behaviors. You implement each transformation as a command line application that accepts the JSON-encoded request and JSON-encoded response as parameters passed in on standard input and returns the transformed JSON-encoded response on standard output. You'll start by wiring up the imposter configuration, as shown in the following listing.

**Listing 7.6  Imposter configuration for `shellTransform`**

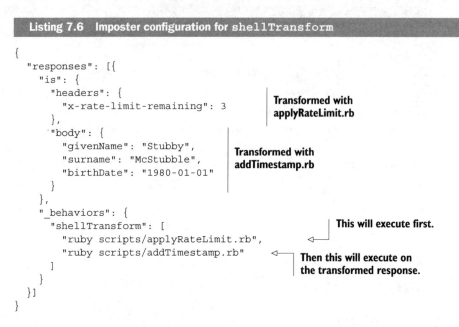

```
{
  "responses": [{
    "is": {
      "headers": {
        "x-rate-limit-remaining": 3          Transformed with
      },                                      applyRateLimit.rb
      "body": {
        "givenName": "Stubby",               Transformed with
        "surname": "McStubble",              addTimestamp.rb
        "birthDate": "1980-01-01"
      }
    },
    "_behaviors": {
      "shellTransform": [                     This will execute first.
        "ruby scripts/applyRateLimit.rb",
        "ruby scripts/addTimestamp.rb"        Then this will execute on
      ]                                        the transformed response.
    }
  }]
}
```

In this example, you have chosen to pipe the transformations through Ruby scripts, but it could've been any language. The code in applyRateLimit.rb is a simple Ruby conversion of the code in listing 7.5. Mountebank passes two parameters on standard input—the request and the response. Here you only need the response, as shown in the following listing.

**Listing 7.7  Ruby script to transform the response to trigger a rate limit error**

```
require 'json'                               Ruby module imported
                                             for JSON handling
response = JSON.parse(ARGV[1])
headers = response['headers']                The second command-
current_value = headers['x-rate-limit-remaining'].to_i   line parameter is the
                                                          current JSON response.

if File.exists?('rate-limit.txt')
  current_value = File.read('rate-limit.txt').to_i
end

if current_value <= 0
  response['statusCode'] = 429
  response['body'] = {
    'errors' => [{
      'code' => 88, 'message' => 'Rate limit exceeded'
```

```
    }]
  }
  response['headers']['x-rate-limit-remaining'] = 0
else
  File.write('rate-limit.txt', current_value - 25)
  headers['x-rate-limit-remaining'] = current_value - 25
end

puts response.to_json
```

◁── **Prints the transformed response to stdout**

Some syntax changes are obvious from the JavaScript code to the Ruby code (primarily a different hash syntax) and they use some different functions (`to_i` instead of `parseInt`), but most of the code looks like a Ruby decorator. The key differences are the input (parsing the response from the command line) and the output (printing the transformed response to stdout). In the following listing, you do the same thing with addTimestamp.rb.

**Listing 7.8   Ruby script to add a timestamp to the response JSON**

```
require 'json'

response = JSON.parse(ARGV[1])
response['body']['timestamp'] = Time.now.getutc
puts response.to_json
```

By chaining together transformations, `shellTransform` acts as a way of adding a transformation pipeline to your response handling, allowing as much complexity as you require. My standard advice still applies: it's good to have such power for when you absolutely need it, but try not to need it.

## 7.3   Adding latency to a response

The next behavior we'll look at is a whole lot simpler and doesn't require you to set the `--allowInjection` command line flag. Sometimes you need to simulate latency in responses, and the `wait` behavior tells mountebank to take a nap before returning the response. You pass it the number of milliseconds to sleep as follows.

**Listing 7.9   Using a `wait` behavior to add latency**

```
{
  "is": {
    "body": {
      "name": "Sleepy"
    }
  },
  "_behaviors": {
    "wait": 3000
  }
}
```

◁── **Adds 3 seconds of latency**

Like the decorate behavior, you can add the wait behavior to saved responses that proxies generate. When you set the addWaitBehavior to true on a proxy, mountebank will automatically fill in the generated wait behavior based on how long the real downstream call took. I show how to use that to create robust performance tests in chapter 10.

## 7.4    *Repeating a response multiple times*

Sometimes you need to send the same response multiple times before moving on to the next response. You can copy the same response multiple times in the responses array, but that practice is generally frowned on by the software community, as it hurts maintainability. It's an important enough concept that it even has its own acronym: DRY (Don't Repeat Yourself).

The repeat behavior lets the computer do the repeating for you (figure 7.6). It accepts the number of times you want to repeat the response, and mountebank helps you avoid those snooty software engineers looking down their noses at you for not being DRY enough.

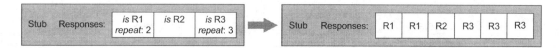

Figure 7.6    **Repeating a response multiple times**

A common use case involves triggering an error response after a set number of happy path responses. An example I already used a couple of times in this book involves querying an inventory service. In chapters 3 and 4, I showed how you can use a list of responses to show the inventory for a product running out over time:[3]

```
{
  "responses": [
    { "is": { "body": "54" } },
    { "is": { "body": "21" } },
    { "is": { "body": "0" } }
  ]
}
```

Most test cases don't require this level of specificity. In slightly oversimplified terms, a consumer of an inventory service only cares about two scenarios:

- The inventory is greater than zero (or greater than or equal to the quantity being ordered).
- The inventory is zero (or less than the quantity being ordered).

---

[3]   As we did earlier, we are returning an overly simplistic body to focus on only the point of the example.

Simplifying even further, the only two scenarios that matter for this test case are

- A happy path
- An out-of-inventory error

The only slightly complicated factor is that you might want to return a few happy path responses before returning an out-of-inventory error. You can do that with only two responses and a `repeat` behavior, as shown in the following listing.

**Listing 7.10  Using a `repeat` behavior to return an error after a small number of successes**

```
{
  "responses": [
    {
      "is": { "body": "9999" },          ← Return the
      "_behaviors": { "repeat": 3 }          happy path...
    },                                        ← ...three times.
    {
      "is": { "body": "0" }              ← Then return the
    }                                        error path.
  ]
}
```

**Test case construction**

We have looked at some advanced mountebank capabilities over the course of this book. Sometimes those capabilities are indispensable for solving complicated test problems. But you can simplify most test cases to a small essential core of what you're trying to test, and removing the noise in the test data setup helps keep the focus on that core. The `repeat` example we just looked at shows how the thought process of simplifying your test case has knock-on benefits to your test data management.

## 7.5 Replacing content in the response

You can always add dynamic data to a response through an `inject` response, or through the `decorate` and `shellTransform` behaviors. But two additional behaviors support inserting certain types of dynamic data into the response without the overhead of programmatic control.

### 7.5.1 Copying request data to the response

The `copy` behavior allows you to capture some part of the request and insert it into the response. Imagine that the system under test depended on a service reflecting the account ID from the request URL back in the response body, so that (for example) when you send a GET request to /accounts/8731, you get a response that reflects that ID and otherwise resembles my account profile in various online forums I participate in:

```
{
  "id": "8731",                          ◁─────────────   This has to match
  "name": "Brandon Byars",                              the ID in the path.
  "description": "Devilishly handsome",
  "height": "Lots of it",
  "relationshipStatus": "Available upon request"
}
```

This response has two core aspects:

- The `id`, which has to match the one provided on the request URL
- The test data you need for your scenario

A standard `is` response supports managing scenario-specific test data, and the `copy` behavior allows you to insert the `id` from the request. Copying the `id` from the request to the response requires you to reserve a slot in the response that you can replace and to be able to select only the data you want from the request. The first part is easier—you add any token you choose to the response, as shown in the following listing.

> **Listing 7.11  Specifying a token in the response to replace with a value from the request**

```
{
  "is": {
    "body": {
      "id": "$ID",                              ◁─┐   A placeholder that the copy behavior
      "name": "Brandon Byars",                    └─  will replace with the value
      "description": "Devilishly handsome",
      "height": "Lots of it",
      "relationshipStatus": "Available upon request"
    }
  }
}
```

The first section of the `copy` behavior requires that you specify the request field you're copying from and the response token you need to replace:

```
{
  "from": "path",
  "into": "$ID",
  ...
}
```

The only part you need to fill in is the part that selects the `id`. The `copy` behavior (and the `lookup` behavior, which we look at next) uses some of the same predicate matching capabilities we looked at in chapter 4, specifically regular expressions, XPath, and JSONPath. Recall that each predicate applies a matching operation against a request field. Whereas a predicate tells you whether or not the match was successful, the `copy` and `lookup` behaviors are able to grab the specific text in the request field that matched.

For this example, a regular expression will do the trick. You need to capture a string of digits at the end of the request path. You can use some of the regex primitives we looked at in chapter 4 to make that selection:

- \d — A digit, 0–9 (you have to double-escape the backslash in JSON)
- + — One or more times
- $ — The end of the string

Putting it all together, the stub would look like the following listing.

**Listing 7.12  Using a copy behavior to insert the ID from the URL into the response body**

```
{
  "responses": [{
    "is": {
      "body": {
        "id": "$ID",                                    The token
        "name": "Brandon Byars",                        to replace
        "description": "Devilishly handsome",
        "height": "Lots of it",
        "relationshipStatus": "Available upon request"
      }
    },
    "_behaviors": {                  An array—multiple
      "copy": [{                     replacements are allowed    The request field
        "from": "path",                                          to copy from
        "into": "$ID",
        "using": {
          "method": "regex",                 The selection criteria to
          "selector": "\\d+$"                act on the request path
        }
      }]
    }
  }]
}
```

The token to replace

There's a lot more to this behavior, but before we get too far, I should point out a couple of aspects that you may have already noticed. First, the copy behavior accepts an array, which means you can make multiple replacements in the response. Each replacement should use a different token, and each one can select from a different part of the request.

The other thing to notice is that you never specify *where* the token is in the response. That's by design. You could have put the token in the headers or even the status-Code, and mountebank would replace it. If the token is listed multiple times, mountebank will replace each instance, regardless of where it's located in the response.

#### USING A GROUPED MATCH

The previous example made an assumption that you could define a regular expression that entirely matched the value you needed to grab *and nothing else*. That's a pretty weak assumption.

Many services use some form of a globally unique identifier (GUID) as an `id`, and the `path` often extends beyond the part containing the `id`. For example, the `path` might be /accounts/5ea4d2b5/profile, where "5ea4d2b5" is the `id` you need to copy. You can no longer rely on \\d+ as a selector because the `id` contains more than digits. You certainly can rely on other mechanisms to match—for instance, by recognizing that the `id` follows the word "accounts" in the path:

```
accounts/\\w+
```

That selector uses the "\w" regular expression metacharacter to capture a *word* character (letters and digits) and adds the "+" to ensure that you capture one or more of them. Then it prefixes the "accounts/" to ensure you're grabbing the right portion of the path. With this expression, you do successfully grab the `id`. Unfortunately, you grab the "accounts/" literal string as well, and the replaced `body` would look like:

```
{
  "id": "accounts/5ea4d2b5",
  ...
}
```

Regular expressions support grouped matches to allow you to grab only the data you need from a match. Every regular expression has a default first group that's the entire match. Every time you surround a portion of the selector with parentheses, you describe another group. You will adjust your selector to add a group around the `id` portion of the `path`, while leaving the literal string "accounts/" to make sure you are grabbing the right portion of the `path`:

```
accounts/(\\w+)
```

When you match this regular expression against the string "/accounts/5ea4d2b5/profile", you get an array of match groups that looks like

```
[
  "accounts/5ea4d2b5",
  "5ea4d2b5"
]
```

The first group is the entire match, and the second is the first parenthetical group. If you place an unadorned token in the response, as you did in the previous section, mountebank will replace it with the first index of the array, which corresponds to the entire match. But you can add an index to the token corresponding to the index of the match group array, as shown in the following listing, which allows you to pinpoint the part of the `path` you want to copy with laser precision.

> **Listing 7.13   Using a grouped match to copy a portion of the request `path`**

```
{
  "is": {
    "body": {
```

```
      "id": "$ID[1]",           ◁──┐ Specifies the index in
      ...                          │ the response token
    }
  },
  "_behaviors": {
    "copy": [{
      "from": "path",
      "into": "$ID",           ◁──┐ Specifies the base
      "using": {                  │ token in the behavior
        "method": "regex",
        "selector": "accounts/(\\w+)"   ◁──┐ Uses a grouped match
      }                                      │ for more precision
    }]
  }
}
```

You can always use indexed tokens in the response. Assuming you specify a token of $ID like you did in listing 7.13, then putting $ID in the response is equivalent to putting $ID[0]. I doubt that matters much for regular expressions, as I suspect most real-world use cases will have to use groups to grab the exact value they want. That isn't necessarily true for the other selection approaches that the copy behavior supports: xpath and jsonpath.

### USING AN XPATH SELECTOR

Although a regular expression elegantly supports grabbing a value out of *any* request field, xpath and jsonpath selectors can be useful to match values inside an incoming request body. They work similarly to how xpath and jsonpath predicates work, as described in chapter 4. The key difference is that predicate XPath and JSONPath selectors are used with a matching operator (like equals) to test whether the request matches, whereas using those selectors with behaviors helps grab the matching text in the request to change the response.

Take the following request body from the system under test, representing a list of accounts:

```
<accounts xmlns="https://www.example.com/accounts">
  <account id="d0a7b1b8" />
  <account id="5ea4d2b5" />
  <account id="774d4feb" />
</accounts>
```

Your virtual response needs to reflect back details of the second account in the request. Those details are specific to your test scenario, but the ID has to match what was sent in the request body. You can use an XPath selector to grab the id attribute of the second account attribute, as shown in the following listing.

**Listing 7.14  Using an XPath selector to copy a value from the request to the response**

```
{
  "responses": [{
    "is": {                                              ┐ Tokenizes the
      "body": "<account><id>$ID</id>...</account>"   ◁──┘ response body
```

```
        },
      "_behaviors": {
        "copy": [{
          "from": "body",
          "into": "$ID",              ⊲———  Defines a token in
          "using": {                        the copy behavior
            "method": "xpath",
            "selector": "//a:account[2]/@id",
            "ns": {                          Selects the value from
              "a": "https://www.example.com/accounts"   the XML request body
            }
          }
        }
      }]
    }
  }]
}
```

The `xpath` selector and namespace support work identically to `xpath` predicates
(chapter 4) and predicate generators (chapter 5). As you saw with predicates, mountebank also supports JSONPath. We will look at an example with the `lookup` behavior
shortly.

### VIRTUALIZING A CORS PREFLIGHT RESPONSE

Cross-origin resource sharing, or CORS, is a standard that allows browsers to make
cross-domain requests. In the olden days, a browser would only execute JavaScript
calls to the same domain as the one that served up the hosting web page. This *same-origin policy* is the bedrock of browser security, as it helps prevent a host of malicious
JavaScript injection attacks. But as websites became more dynamic and needed to pull
behavior from disparate resources spread across multiple domains, it also proved to
be too restrictive. Creative developers found creative hacks to bypass the same-origin
policy, like JSONP, which manipulates the `script` element in an HTML document to
pass JavaScript from a different domain to a callback function already defined. JSONP
is confusing and hard to understand because it works around the browser's built-in
security mechanism.

The CORS standard evolves the browser's security model to allow the browser and
server to both weigh in on whether a cross-domain request is valid or not. The standard requires a *preflight* request for certain types of cross-domain requests to determine whether the request is valid. A preflight request is an HTTP OPTIONS call with a
few special headers that commonly trip up testers when creating virtual services[4]
(figure 7.7).

The browser is set to automatically send these preflight requests for some types of
cross-origin requests. If you want to virtualize the cross-origin service so you can test
the browser application, your virtual service needs to know how to respond to a

---

[4]  Future versions of mountebank likely will make virtualizing CORS preflight requests easier.

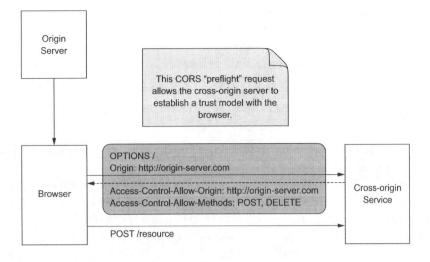

**Figure 7.7  A CORS preflight request to establish trust**

preflight request in a way that enables the browser to make the *actual* cross-origin request (for example, the call to POST /resource in figure 7.7). Copying the Origin header value from the request header into the response header, as shown in the following listing, is a great example of using the copy behavior and demonstrates tokenizing something other than the HTTP body.

**Listing 7.15  Virtualizing a CORS preflight request**

```
{
  "predicates": [{
    "equals": { "method": "OPTIONS" }          Looks for a preflight
  }],                                           request signature
  "responses": [{
    "is": {
      "headers": {
        "Access-Control-Allow-Origin": "${ORIGIN}",      Tokenizes the
        "Access-Control-Allow-Methods": "PUT, DELETE"    response header
      }
    },
    "_behaviors": {
      "copy": [{                                Looks in the request
        "from": { "headers": "Origin" },        Origin header
        "into": "${ORIGIN}",
        "using": { "method": "regex", "selector": ".+" }   ...with the entire
      }]                                                   request header value.
    }
  }]
}
```

Replaces the response header token...

The regular expression ".+" means "one or more characters" and effectively captures the entire request header. Because you don't need to use a grouped match, you can use the token in the response without an array index. You can do a lot more with CORS configuration, but the copy approach satisfies the need for creating a flexible virtual service that reflects the client requests in a way that enables the client to make subsequent requests.

### 7.5.2   *Looking up data from an external data source*

Service virtualization is great for testing error flows, which are often difficult to reproduce on demand in real systems but happen enough in live systems that you still need to test for them. The challenge is creating a set of test data that captures all the error flows in a visible and maintainable way. Take account creation, for example. Using predicates, you could set up a virtual *account* service that responds with different error conditions based on the name of the account you are trying to create. Let's say the first error flow you need to test is what happens when the account already exists. The following configuration would ensure your virtual service returns an error for a duplicate user when the name is "Kip Brady," assuming that's passed in as a JSON name field in the request:

```
{
  "stubs": [{
    "predicates": [{
      "equals": { "body": "Kip Brady" },
      "jsonpath": { "selector": "$..name" }
    }],
    "responses": [{
      "is": {
        "statusCode": 400,
        "body": {
          "errors": [{
            "code": "duplicateEntry",
            "message": "User already exists"
          }]
        }
      }
    }]
  }]
}
```

If you want "Mary Reynolds" to represent a user too young to register, you can use the same JSONPath selector to look for a different value:

```
{
  "stubs": [
    {
      "predicates": [{
        "equals": { "body": "Kip Brady" },
        "jsonpath": { "selector": "$..name" }
      }],
      "responses": [{
```

```
          "is": {
            "statusCode": 400,
            "body": {
              "errors": [{
                "code": "duplicateEntry",
                "message": "User already exists"
              }]
            }
          }
        }]
      },
      {
        "predicates": [{
          "equals": { "body": "Mary Reynolds" },
          "jsonpath": { "selector": "$..name" }
        }],
        "responses": [{
          "is": {
            "statusCode": 400,
            "body": {
              "errors": [{
                "code": "tooYoung",
                "message": "You must be 18 years old to register"
              }]
            }
          }
        }]
      }
    ]
}
```

"Tom Larsen" can represent a 500 server error, and "Harry Smith" can represent an overloaded server. Both require new stubs.

This is obviously an unsustainable approach to managing test data. The JSONPath selector is the same among all the stubs, as is the structure of the JSON body. You'd like to be able to centralize the test data in a CSV file, as shown in the following listing.

**Listing 7.16  Centralizing error conditions in a CSV file**

```
name,statusCode,errorCode,errorMessage
Tom Larsen,500,serverError,An unexpected error occurred
Kip Brady,400,duplicateEntry,User already exists
Mary Reynolds,400,tooYoung,You must be 18 years old to register
Harry Smith,503,serverBusy,Server currently unavailable
```

The lookup behavior, a close cousin of the copy behavior, allows you to do this. Like the copy behavior, it replaces tokens in the response with dynamic data. The key difference is where that dynamic data comes from. For the copy behavior, it's the request. For the lookup behavior, it's an external data source. As of this writing, the only data source mountebank supports is a CSV file (figure 7.8). That likely will change by the time you are reading this.

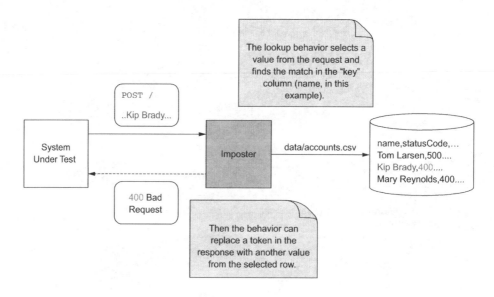

**Figure 7.8   Looking up a value from a CSV file**

Before we get to how the replacement happens, let's look at the lookup operation itself. As you can see in figure 7.8, a successful lookup requires three values:

- A key selected from the request (Kip Brady)
- The connection to the external data source (data/accounts.csv)
- The key column in the external data source (name)

Those three values are sufficient to capture a row of values you can use in the replacement. You represent them in a way that closely resembles the `copy` behavior, as shown in the following listing.

**Listing 7.17   Using a lookup behavior to retrieve external test data**

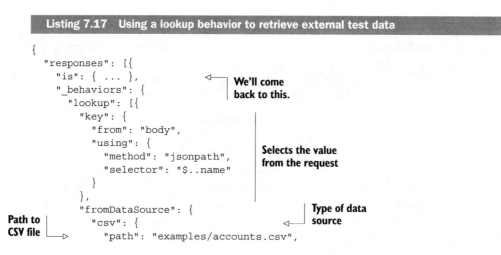

```
            "keyColumn": "name"        ◄────┐ Column name to
        }                                   │ match request value
    },
    "into": "${row}"          ◄────┐ Response
}]                                  │ token name
    }
}]
}
```

The `key` part of the `lookup` behavior is similar to the `copy` behavior we looked at earlier. It allows you to use a `regex`, `xpath`, or `jsonpath` selector to look in a request field and grab a value. You can add an `index` field to use a grouped regular expression match.

The `into` field is also the same as what you saw with `copy`. Here you used `${row}` as the token name. It can be anything you like. As far as mountebank is concerned, it it's a string. The addition is what you see in the `fromDataSource` field. For CSV data sources, you specify the path to the file (relative to the running `mb` process) and the name of the key column.

If you pass `"Kip Brady"` in as the name, your token (`${row}`) matches an entire row of values from the CSV file. In JSON format, it would look like this:

```
{
  "name": "Kip Brady",
  "statusCode": "400",
  "errorCode": "duplicateEntry",
  "errorMessage": "User already exists"
}
```

This highlights a secondary difference between `copy` and `lookup`: with a `lookup` behavior, your token represents an entire row of values, meaning each individual replacement has to be indexed with the column name. Let's look at the `is` response for your example, which tokenizes the responses you previously had to copy into multiple stubs, in the following listing.

---

**Listing 7.18   Using tokens to create a single response for all error conditions**

```
{
  "is": {
    "statusCode": "${row}['statusCode']",        ◄────┐
    "body": {                                          │ Looks up the
      "errors": [{                                     │ appropriate field in
        "code": "${row}['errorCode']",        ◄────────┤ the row you looked up
        "message": "${row}['errorMessage']"   ◄────────┘
      }]
    }
  },
  "_behaviors": {
    "lookup": [{ ... }]        ◄────┐ See
  }                                 │ listing 7.17.
}
```

The `lookup` behavior treats the token like a JSON object that you can key by the column name. This allows you to retrieve an entire row of data in the `lookup` behavior and use fields within the row to populate the response.

## 7.6    *A complete list of behaviors*

For reference, table 7.1 provides a complete list of behaviors that mountebank supports, including whether they support affecting saved proxy responses and whether they require the `--allowInjection` command-line flag.

**Table 7.1    All behaviors that mountebank supports**

| Behavior | Works on saved proxy responses? | Requires injection support? | Description |
|---|---|---|---|
| decorate | yes | yes | Uses a JavaScript function to postprocess the response |
| shellTransform | no | yes | Sends the response through a command-line pipeline for postprocessing |
| wait | yes | no | Adds latency to a response |
| repeat | no | no | Repeats a response multiple times |
| copy | no | no | Copies a value from the request into the response |
| lookup | no | no | Replaces data in the response with data from an external data source based on a key from the request |

Behaviors are powerful additions to mountebank, and we covered a lot of ground in this chapter. We will round out mountebank's core capabilities in the next chapter when we look at protocols.

## *Summary*

- The `decorate` and `shellTransform` behaviors are similar to response injection in that they allow programmatic transformation of the response. But they apply postprocessing transformation, and the `shellTransform` allows multiple transformations.
- The `wait` behavior allows you to add latency to a response by passing in the number of milliseconds to delay it.
- The `repeat` behavior supports sending the same response multiple times.
- The `copy` behavior accepts an array of configurations, each of which selects a value from the request and replaces a response token with that value. You can use regular expressions, JSONPath, and XPath to select the request value.
- The `lookup` behavior also accepts an array of configurations, each of which looks up a row of data from an external data source based on the value selected from the request using regular expressions, JSONPath, and XPath. The token in the response is indexed by the field name.

# *Protocols*

**This chapter covers**

- How protocols work in mountebank
- An in-depth look at the TCP protocol
- How to stub a bespoke text-based TCP protocol
- How to stub a binary .NET Remoting service

Let's get real: faking it only gets you so far. At some point, even the best virtual services have to lay down some real bits on the wire.

The functionality we have explored so far—responses, predicates, and behaviors—is largely the realm of stubbing and mocking tools. Those stubbing and mocking tools were created for creating test doubles in process, allowing you to perform focused tests by methodically manipulating dependencies. Responses correspond to what stub functions return, and predicates exist to provide different results based on the way the function is called (for example, returning a different result based on a request parameter). I'm not aware of any in-process mocking tools that have the concept of behaviors per se, but there's nothing preventing them. Behaviors are transformations on the result.

But there is one thing that virtual services do that traditional stubs don't: they respond over the network. All the responses so far have been HTTP, but mountebank supports other ways of responding. Enterprise integration is often messy, and sometimes you'll need to virtualize non-HTTP services. Whether you have custom remote procedure calls or a mail server as part of your stack, service virtualization can help. And now, at long last, it's time to explore mountebank's support for network protocols.

## 8.1    How protocols work in mountebank

Protocols are where the rubber meets the road in mountebank. The core role of the protocol is to translate the incoming network request into a JSON representation for predicates to operate on, and to translate the JSON mountebank response structure into the wire format expected by the system under test (figure 8.1).

All of the mountebank imposters that we've seen so far are full-featured HTTP servers, and the bits they put on the wire conform to the HTTP protocol. That's the secret sauce that allows you to repoint the system under test to mountebank with no changes: it sends out an HTTP request and gets an HTTP response back. It has no need to know that an imposter formed the response by employing a secret cabal of stubs to match the

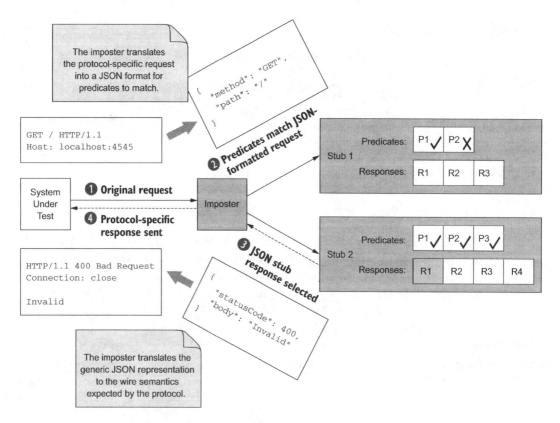

**Figure 8.1   The flow of a mountebank-generated HTTP response**

request with predicates, form a JSON response, and postprocess it with behaviors. All the system under test cares about is that mountebank accepts an HTTP request and returns a bunch of bits over the wire that look like an HTTP response.

Mountebank, unique in the open source service virtualization world, is multiprotocol. The clean separation of concepts allows the stubbing functionality to work regardless of what protocol your system under test expects. We'll explore that in the context of older remote procedure call (RPC) protocols, but before we get there, let's start with a primer on a foundational building block of network communication.

## 8.2 A TCP primer

Mountebank supports the TCP protocol, but TCP isn't on equal footing with HTTP/S. It's more accurate to say that mountebank supports a range of custom application protocols built on top of TCP. Most conceptual networking models show protocols in layers, and it takes a whole suite of protocols to make something as complex as the internet work. (See figure 8.2.)

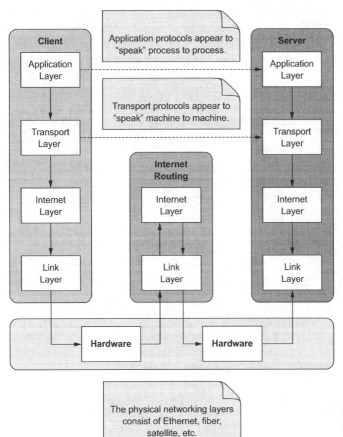

Figure 8.2   A client application talking to a server application over the internet

The genius of the TCP/IP stack is that clients and server processes can act as if they're talking directly to each other, even when they're on remote machines. When you visit the mountebank website (http://www.mbtest.org), your browser can act as if it's speaking directly with the web server on the other end. The same is true when your system under test makes an HTTP call. Regardless of whether the service it's accessing is real or virtualized, the client code can operate as if there's a direct connection to the server.

The reality is more complicated. HTTP is an *application protocol* and depends on TCP as the *transport protocol* to deliver to the remote host. TCP in turn relies on downstream protocols to route between networks (the IP protocol) and to interface with the routers on the same network (the network is often referred to as the "link," which is why the lowest layer is called the *link layer* in figure 8.2).

What your web browser is doing is forming an HTTP request and passing it to the local operating system, which hands off the request to the TCP protocol implementation. TCP lovingly wraps the HTTP message in an envelope that adds a bunch of delivery guarantees and performance optimizations. Then it hands control over to the IP protocol, which once again wraps the whole message and adds addressing information that the core infrastructure of the internet knows how to use to route to the correct remote machine. Finally, the doubly wrapped HTTP message is handed off to the device driver for the network interface on your computer, which yet again wraps the message with some Ethernet or Wi-Fi information needed to transmit the whole package to your router, which happily forwards it to the next network. (See figure 8.3.) The process works in reverse once it reaches the right server machine.[1]

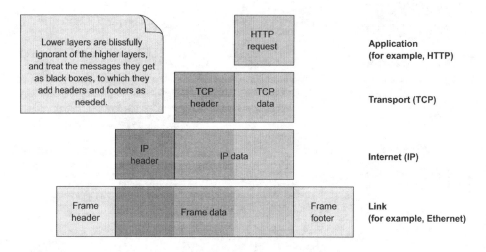

**Figure 8.3   Transforming an HTTP request to route across the network**

---

[1]  Figure 8.3 is inspired by a similar image on the Wikipedia page describing the internet protocol suite, which has a more comprehensive explanation of how layering works: https://en.wikipedia.org/wiki/Internet _protocol_suite.

TCP enables host-to-host communication, but it's the application protocols on top that allow a client process to talk to a server process. HTTP is the most famous application protocol but far from the only one. Mountebank aspires to treat well-known application protocols like HTTP as first class citizens, but a host of niche or custom application protocols exist in the archaeological substratum of enterprise integration, and mountebank's support of the TCP protocol also provides a way to virtualize them.

## 8.3　*Stubbing text-based TCP-based RPC*

For those of you who grew up in a world where distributed programming was commonplace, it can be a bit bewildering to look at some of the ways applications used to integrate. Imagine you are a C++ programmer in a bygone era being paid to integrate two applications over the network. The challenges of distributed programming aren't commonly understood yet. Early attempts at formalizing RPC using standards like CORBA may have happened, but they seem overly complicated. It seems much simpler to pass a function name and a few parameters to a remote socket and expect it to return a status code indicating whether the function succeeded and a return value. If you take out the networking, it looks similar to how in-process function calls work.

Now, 20 or 30 years later, younger generations are still adding capabilities to your custom RPC code because it's so central to keeping the lights on that it's cheaper to keep it than to rip it out. They may not like it, but none of them have ever written code that's stayed in production for decades. Like it or not, this is a common scenario in many long-standing enterprises.

Let's imagine that the remote server manages core inventory. The payload of a TCP packet making an RPC request to change the inventory may look like this, for example:

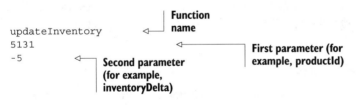

And the response may look like this:

In this example, new lines separate parameters, and the schema is implicit rather than defined by something like JSON or XML. Mountebank won't be able to understand the semantics of the RPC, so it encapsulates the payload in a single `data` field.

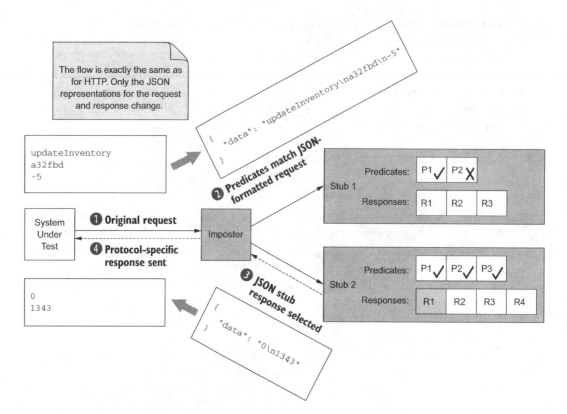

**Figure 8.4   Virtualizing a custom TCP protocol**

The flow of data, as shown in figure 8.4, looks similar to the flow of data in a virtual HTTP service (figure 8.1). The only difference is the format for the request and response.

### 8.3.1   *Creating a basic TCP imposter*

Creating the TCP imposter is as simple as changing the `protocol` field to `tcp`:

```
{
  "protocol": "tcp",
  "port": 3000
}
```

That configuration is sufficient for mountebank to spin up a TCP server listening on port 3000. It'll accept the request, but the response will be blank. If you want to virtualize the call to `updateInventory`, you do so with the same predicates and response capability that you've seen for HTTP, as shown in the following listing. The only difference is the JSON structure for requests and responses. For `tcp`, both the request and response contain a single `data` field.

**Listing 8.1  Virtualizing a TCP `updateInventory` call**

```
{
  "protocol": "tcp",
  "port": 3000,
  "stubs": [{
    "predicates": [{                              Looks for the
      "startsWith": { "data": "updateInventory" }   appropriate function
    }],
    "responses": [{
      "is": { "data": "0\n1343" }      Returns the protocol-specific
    }]                                  response format
  }]
}
```

You can test out your imposter using an application like telnet. Telnet opens an inter-active TCP connection to a server, which makes it tricky to script. Netcat (http://nc110.sourceforge.net/) is like a noninteractive telnet, which makes it ideally suited for testing TCP-based services. You can trigger your inventory RPC call response and test out your TCP imposter with netcat using the following command:

```
echo "updateInventory\na32fbd\n-5" | nc localhost 3000
```

You wrap the request message in a string and pipe it to netcat (nc), sending it to the correct socket. It'll send back the virtual response you configured to the terminal:

```
0
1343
```

### 8.3.2  Creating a TCP proxy

TCP imposters work with the other response types as well. You can record and replay using a proxy like you can with HTTP. For example, if the real service is listening on port 3333 of remoteservice.com, you could set up a record/replay imposter by point-ing the to field on the proxy configuration to the remote socket, as shown in the fol-lowing listing.

**Listing 8.2  Using a TCP record/replay `proxy`**

```
{
  "protocol": "tcp",
  "port": 3000,
  "stubs": [{
    "responses": [{
      "proxy": {                                   Destination of
        "to": "tcp://remoteservice.com:3333"         remote service
      }
    }]
  }]
}
```

The `proxy` behavior is identical to what you saw in chapter 5. In the default mode (`proxyOnce`), mountebank will save the response and serve it up on the next request without making the downstream call again. You can test this out with netcat:

```
echo "updateInventory\na32fbd\n-5" | nc -q 1 localhost 3000
```

Notice the added "-q 1" parameter. By default, when netcat makes a TCP request, it closes the client end of the connection immediately, which is appropriate for one-way fire-and-forget-style communication. It isn't appropriate for two-way request-response-style communication common in RPC. Because it takes a small amount of time for mountebank to make the downstream call to get the response, by the time mountebank tries to respond, it may discover that nobody is listening. The "-q 1" parameter tells netcat to wait one second before closing the connection, so you'll see the response on the terminal.

Unfortunately, the "-q" parameter isn't present on all versions of netcat, including the default version on Mac and Windows computers. If you leave it off, you won't get a response on the terminal and you'll see the error in the mountebank logs when it cannot send the response. But subsequent calls will still work, as mountebank now has a saved version of the response and can respond immediately.

You can use `predicateGenerators` with the TCP protocol as well, but it isn't very discriminatory because there's only one field. For example, the following configuration makes a new downstream call anytime *anything* in the RPC call is different.

**Listing 8.3  A TCP proxy with `predicateGenerators`**

```
{
  "protocol": "tcp",
  "port": 3000,
  "stubs": [{
    "responses": [{
      "proxy": {
        "to": "tcp://remoteservice.com:3333",
        "predicateGenerators": [{
          "matches": { "data": true }        ◁─┐  Generates a new stub
        }]                                       │  for each new payload
      }
    }]
  }]
}
```

Although it would be nice to generate predicates only on the function name, you can't. Mountebank has no way of knowing what the function name is, so any parameter that changes will force a new downstream call.

If you're lucky, the custom RPC protocol uses a payload format that mountebank understands: JSON or XML. If so, then you can get a bit more specific. We look at an example next.

### 8.3.3 *Matching and manipulating an XML payload*

I doubt you'll see many of these custom RPC protocols that use JSON, for the simple reason that by the time JSON was created, HTTP was already a predominant application integration approach. If you do see it, all of the JSONPath capability you've seen so far will work.

XML has been around a bit longer, and in fact one of the first attempts at using HTTP for integration was called POX over HTTP, where POX stood for Plain Ol' XML. Let's translate your `updateInventory` RPC payload to XML:

```
<functionCall>
  <functionName>updateInventory</functionName>
  <parameters>
    <parameter name="productId" value="5131" />
    <parameter name="amount" value="-5" />
  </parameters>
</functionCall>
```

You can easily imagine other function calls, for example, this one might be a call to get the inventory for product 5131:

```
<functionCall>
  <functionName>getInventory</functionName>
  <parameters>
    <parameter name="productId" value="5131" />
  </parameters>
</functionCall>
```

Now it becomes easier to build a more robust set of `predicateGenerators` for your proxy. If you want to save different responses for different combinations of function names and product IDs, you can do so, as shown in the following listing.

---

**Listing 8.4  Using XPath `predicateGenerators` with a TCP proxy**

```
{
  "responses": [{
    "proxy": {
      "to": "tcp://localhost:3333",
      "predicateGenerators": [
        {
          "matches": { "data": true },          The XML functionName
          "xpath": {                             must match.
            "selector": "//functionName"
          }
        },
        {
          "matches": { "data": true },
          "xpath": {                             The productId
            "selector":                          must match.
➥ "//parameter[@name='productId']/@value"
          }
        }
```

```
          ]
        }
      }]
    }
```

All of the behaviors work with the TCP protocol as well, including those like the `copy` behavior that can use XPath to select values from the request.

## 8.4    *Binary support*

Not all application protocols speak in plain text. Many of them instead pass a binary request/response stream, which makes them challenging to virtualize. Challenging, but not impossible—remember mountebank's mission statement: to keep the easy things easy while making the hard things possible.

Mountebank makes virtualizing binary protocols possible in two ways. First, it supports serializing request and response binary streams using Base64 encoding. Second, nearly all of the predicates work against a binary stream with exactly the same semantics they use against text.

### 8.4.1    *Using binary mode with Base64 encoding*

JSON—the *lingua franca* of mountebank—doesn't directly support binary data. The workaround is to encode a binary stream into a string field. Base64 reserves 64 characters—upper- and lowercase letters, digits, and two punctuation marks—and maps them to the binary equivalents. Having 64 options allows you to encode six bits at a time ($2^6 = 64$).

Any modern language library will support Base64 encoding. Here's an example in JavaScript (node.js):

```
var buffer = new Buffer("Hello, world!");          Prints out
console.log(buffer.toString("base64"));     ⟵    SGVsbG8sIHdvcmxkIQ==
```

Similarly, decoding from Base64 is done using the `Buffer` type as well, as in this Java-Script example:

```
                                            Base64 encoded
var buffer = new Buffer("SGVsbG8sIHdvcmxkIQ==");   ⟵   value
console.log(buffer.toString("utf8"));       ⟵    Prints out
                                                 Hello, world!
```

Having a TCP imposter return binary data requires letting mountebank know that you want a binary imposter and Base64 encoding the response, as shown in the following listing.

**Listing 8.5    Setting up a binary response from an imposter**

```
{
  "protocol": "tcp",
  "port": 3000,                         Switches to
  "mode": "binary",          ⟵         binary mode
```

```
  "stubs": [{
    "responses": [{                                    Returns binary equivalent
      "is": { "data": "SGVsbG8sIHdvcmxkIQ==" }   <⎯┘   of "Hello, world!"
    }]
  }]
}
```

Once you set the mode to binary, mountebank knows to do the following:

- Interpret all response data as Base64-encoded binary streams, which it will decode when it responds over the wire
- Save all proxy responses as Base-64-encoded versions of the wire response
- Interpret all predicates as Base-64-encoded binary streams, which it will decode to match against the raw wire request

That last bullet point requires more explanation.

## 8.4.2 Using predicates in binary mode

Binary data is a stream of bits. It might be, for example, 01001001 00010001. I have spaced the bits into two eight-bit combinations (octets) because, although a long string of zeros and ones can be poetry to a computer, it gets a little tricky for us human folk to read. Using two octets also allows you to encode them as two numbers from 0–255 ($2^8$). In this case, that would be 73 17, or, in hexadecimal, 0x49 0x11. Hexadecimal is nice because it lacks any ambiguity—each two-digit hexadecimal number has 256 possibilities ($16^2$), the same number of possibilities encoded in an eight-bit octet.

Let's say you wanted to create a predicate that contains that binary stream. To do so, you'd first need to encode it:

```
var buffer = new Buffer([0x49, 0x11]);            Prints out
console.log(buffer.toString('base64'));     <⎯┘   "SRE="
```

Now the predicate definition is conceptually the same as it is for text, as the following listing demonstrates.

---

**Listing 8.6 Using a binary `contains` predicate**

```
{
  "protocol": "tcp",
  "port": 3000,
  "mode": "binary",              Puts the imposter
  "stubs": [              <⎯┘    in binary mode
    {
      "predicates": [{                          0x49 0x11
        "contains": { "data": "SRE=" }    <⎯┘
      }],
      "responses": [{                           "Matched"
        "is": { "data": "TWF0Y2hlZAo=" }   <⎯┘
      }]
    },
    {
```

```
      "responses": [{
        "is": { "data": "RGlkIG5vdCBtYXRjaAo=" }
      }]
    }
  ]
}
```

"Didn't
match"

If we add an octet—say 0x10—to our binary stream, the `contains` predicate still matches. The binary stream 0x10 0x49 0x11 encodes to "EEkR," which clearly doesn't contain the text "SRE=". Had you not configured the imposter to be in binary mode, mountebank would've performed a simple string operation, and the predicate wouldn't match. By switching to binary mode, you're telling mountebank to instead decode the predicate (SRE=) to a binary array ([0x49, 0x11]) and to see if the incoming binary stream ([0x10, 0x49, 0x11]) contains those octets. It does, so the predicate matches. You can test on the command line by using the `base64` utility, which ships by default with most POSIX shells (for example, Mac and Linux):

```
echo EEkR | base64 --decode | nc localhost 3000
```

You get a response of "Matched," which corresponds to the first response.

Nearly all of the predicates work this way: by matching against a binary array. The one exception is `matches`. Regular expressions don't make sense in a binary world; the metacharacters don't translate. In practice, `contains` is probably the most useful binary predicate. It turns out that many binary RPC protocols encode a function name inside the request. The parameters may be serialized objects that are hard to match, but the function name is encoded text. We look at a real-world example next.

## 8.5    *Virtualizing a .NET Remoting service*

Back in the days of yore, a *town crier* often made public announcements. A crier would ring a handbell and shout "Hear ye! Hear ye!" to get everyone's attention before making the announcement. This neatly solved the problem of delivering a message to a public that was still largely illiterate.

Providing a town crier RPC service[2] may come off as a little antiquated, but it helps get your mindset into those halcyon days of yesteryear when we thought making remote function calls look like in-process function calls was a good thing.[3] .NET Remoting wasn't the first attempt at creating a largely transparently distributed RPC mechanism, but it did have a brief period of popularity and is representative of the broader class of RPC protocols you are likely to run across in the enterprise.

---

[2]  OK, the scenario may not be quite as real-world as advertised, but the protocol is....

[3]  Peter Deutsch wrote that nearly everyone who first builds a distributed application makes a key set of assumptions, all of which are false in the long run and inevitably cause big trouble. See https://en.wikipedia.org/wiki/Fallacies_of_distributed_computing.

### 8.5.1　*Creating a simple .NET Remoting client*

.NET Remoting allows you to call a remote method like you would a local method using the .NET framework. For example, let's assume that to make a pronouncement, you have to fill in an `AnnouncementTemplate`:

```
[Serializable]                                    Ensures that it can be
public class AnnouncementTemplate                 passed over the wire
{
    public AnnouncementTemplate(string greeting,
        string topic)                                     So you can change
    {                                                     "Hear ye!" to "Oyez!"
        Greeting = greeting;
        Topic = topic;                    The topic to be
    }                                     announced

    public string Greeting { get; }       Public getters
    public string Topic { get; }
}
```

Don't worry if you're not a C# expert. This code is as simple as it gets in most enterprise applications, which often are written in Java or C#. It creates a basic class that accepts the greeting and topic for the pronouncement and exposes them as read-only properties. The only interesting nuance is the `[Serializable]` attribute at the top. That's a bit of C# magic that allows the object to be passed between processes.

Once you create an `AnnouncementTemplate`, you'll pass it to the `Announce` method of the `Crier` class, as defined in the following listing.[4]

> **Listing 8.7　The `Crier` class definition**

```
public class Crier : MarshalByRefObject          Allows serialization
{                                                over the wire
    public AnnouncementLog Announce(
        AnnouncementTemplate template)                  Returns a log capturing
    {                                                   the announcement
        return new AnnouncementLog(
            $"{template.Greeting}! {template.Topic}");
    }
}
```

The `Crier` class inherits from `MarshalByRefObject`. Again, that is largely irrelevant to the example, except for the fact that it's the bit of magic that allows an instance of the `Crier` class to be called from a remote process. The `Announce` method formats the greeting and topic into a single string (that strange `$"{template.Greeting}!`

---

[4] The source code for this example is considerably more complicated than most other examples in this book. As always, you can download it at https://github.com/bbyars/mountebank-in-action. In addition, many of the command line examples in the book have shown a bit of a bias toward macOS and Linux. This example is geared toward Windows and will require additional effort to run on other operating systems.

{template.Topic}" line is C#'s string interpolation) and returns it wrapped inside
an AnnouncementLog object, which looks like this:

```
[Serializable]                                    ◁─┐  Makes it remotely
public class AnnouncementLog                        │  accessible
{
    public AnnouncementLog(string announcement)
    {                                                  ┐  Captures the time of
        When = DateTime.Now;                       ◁──┘  the announcement
        Announcement = announcement;
    }

    public DateTime When { get; }
    public string Announcement { get; }

    public override string ToString()
    {                                                  ┐  Formats a log entry for
        return $"({When}): {Announcement}";        ◁──┘  the announcement
    }
}
```

For our purposes, the AnnouncementTemplate, Crier, and AnnouncementLog
form the entirety of the domain model. You could've simplified it to the Crier class,
but we used to think that passing entire object graphs over the wire was a good idea,
and adding a couple of simple classes that the Crier uses—one as input, one as output—helps make the example ever so slightly more realistic.

You can call Crier locally, but that's kind of boring, and more in the realm of traditional mocking tools should you decide to test it. Instead, you will call a remote
Crier instance. The source repo for this book shows how to code a simple server that
listens on a TCP socket and acts as a remote Crier. We'll focus on the client, testing it
by virtualizing the server. To do that, your virtual service needs to respond like a .NET
TCP Remoting service would.

The following listing shows the client you'll test. It represents a gateway to a
remote Crier instance.

---

**Listing 8.8   A gateway to a remote `Crier`**

```
public class TownCrierGateway
{
    private readonly string url;

    public TownCrierGateway(int port)
    {                                                        ┐  URL to the
        url = $"tcp://localhost:{port}/TownCrierService";  ◁┘  remote service
    }

    public string AnnounceToServer(
        string greeting, string topic)
    {
        var template = new AnnouncementTemplate(
            greeting, topic);                               ┐  Gets a remote
        var crier = (Crier)Activator.GetObject(           ◁┘  object reference
            typeof(Crier), url);
```

```
        var response = crier.Announce(template);
        return $"Call Success!\n{response}";
    }
}
```

⟵ **Makes the (remote) method call**

⟵ **Adds metadata to the response**

Notice that the call to `crier.Announce` looks like a local method call. It's not. This is the magic of .NET Remoting. The line above retrieves a remote reference to the object based on the URL in the constructor. That desire to make remote function calls look like local function calls is highly representative of this era of distributed computing.

### 8.5.2 Virtualizing the .NET Remoting server

All the `TownCrierGateway` class does is add a success message to the response of the remote call. That's enough for you to write a test without getting lost in too much unnecessary complexity. You could write the test two ways, assuming you aim to virtualize the remote service.

The first way is to create a mountebank stub that proxies the remote service and captures the response. You could replay the response in your test.

The second way is much cooler. You could *create* the response (as in an instance of the `AnnouncementLog` class) in the test itself, as you would with traditional mocking tools, and have mountebank return it when the client calls the `Announce` method. *Much* cooler.

Fortunately, Matthew Herman has written an easy to use mountebank library for C# called MbDotNet.[5] Let's use it to create a test fixture. I like to write tests using the Law of Wishful Thinking, by which I mean I write the code I want to see and figure out how to implement it later. This allows my test code to clearly specify the intent without getting lost in the details. In this case, I want to create the object graph that mountebank will return inside the test itself and pass it off to a function that creates the imposter on port 3000 using a `contains` predicate for the remote method name. That's a lot to hope for, but I've wrapped it up in a function called `CreateImposter`, as shown in the following listing.

**Listing 8.9  Basic test fixture using MbDotNet**

```
[TestFixture]
public class TownCrierGatewayTest
{
    private readonly MountebankClient mb =
        new MountebankClient();

    [TearDown]
    public void TearDown()
    {
        mb.DeleteAllImposters();
    }
```

**MbDotNet's gateway to the mountebank REST API**

**Deletes all imposters after every test**

---

[5]  An entire ecosystem of these client bindings exists for mountebank. I do my best to maintain a list at http://www.mbtest.org/docs/clientLibraries, but you can always search GitHub for others. Feel free to add a pull request to add your own library to the mountebank website.

```
        [Test]
        public void ClientShouldAddSuccessMessage()
        {
            var stubResult = new AnnouncementLog("TEST");
            CreateImposter(3000, "Announce", stubResult);      Arrange
            var gateway = new TownCrierGateway(3000);

            var result = gateway.AnnounceToServer(
                "ignore", "ignore");                            Act

            Assert.That(result, Is.EqualTo(
                $"Call Success!\n{stubResult}"));               Assert
        }
    }
```

This fixture uses NUnit annotations[6] to define a test. NUnit ensures that the Tear-Down method will be called after every test, which allows you to elegantly clean up after yourself. When you create your test fixture, you create an instance of the mountebank client (which assumes mb is already running on port 2525) and remove all imposters after every test. This is the typical pattern when you use mountebank's API for functional testing.

The test itself uses the standard Arrange-Act-Assert pattern of writing tests introduced back in chapter 1. Conceptually, the *Arrange* stage sets up the system under test, creating the TownCrierGateway and ensuring that when it connects to a virtual service (on port 3000), the virtual service responds with the wire format for the object graph represented by stubResult. The *Act* stage calls the system under test, and the *Assert* stage verifies the results. This is nearly identical to what you would do with traditional mocking tools.

Wishful thinking only gets you so far. MbDotNet simplifies the process of wiring up your imposter using C#. You'll delay only the serialization format for the response under a wishfully-thought-of method I have named Serialize:

```
    private void CreateImposter(int port,
        string methodName, AnnouncementLog result)
    {
        var imposter = mb.CreateTcpImposter(
            port, "TownCrierService", TcpMode.Binary);
        imposter.AddStub()                                Adds
            .On(ContainsMethodName(methodName))        ←  predicate
Adds        .ReturnsData(Serialize(result));
response
        mb.Submit(imposter);              ←             Calls the REST API (We'll get
    }                                                   to the Serialize method soon.)

    private ContainsPredicate<TcpPredicateFields> ContainsMethodName(
        string methodName)
    {
        var predicateFields = new TcpPredicateFields
        {
```

---

[6]  A popular C# testing framework; see http://nunit.org/.

```
            Data = ToBase64(methodName)
    };
    return new ContainsPredicate<TcpPredicateFields>(
        predicateFields);
}

private string ToBase64(string plaintext)
{
    return Convert.ToBase64String(
        Encoding.UTF8.GetBytes(plaintext));
}
```

The `CreateImposter` and `ContainsMethodName` methods uses the MbDotNet API, which is a simple wrapper around the mountebank REST API. The REST call is made when you call `mb.Submit`. The `ToBase64` method uses the standard .NET library calls to encode a string in Base64 format.

All that's left is to fill in the `Serialize` method. This is the method that has to accept the object graph you want your virtual service to return and transform it into the stream of bytes that looks like a .NET Remoting response. That means understanding the wire format of .NET Remoting.

That's hard.

The good news is that, with many popular RPC protocols, someone else has usually done the hard work for you. For .NET Remoting, that someone else is Xu Huang, who has created .NET Remoting parsers for .NET, Java, and JavaScript.[7] You'll use the .NET implementation to create the `Serialize` function.

The code appears in listing 8.10. Don't try too hard to understand it all. The point isn't to teach you the wire format for .NET Remoting. Instead, it's to show that, with a little bit of work, you can usually create a generalized mechanism for serializing a stub response into the wire format for real-world RPC protocols. Once you have done the hard work, you can reuse it throughout your test suite to make writing tests as easy as creating the object graph you want the virtual service to respond with and letting your serialization function do the work of converting it to an RPC-specific format.

**Listing 8.10 Serializing a stub response for .NET Remoting**

```
public string Serialize(Object obj)
{
    var messageRequest = new MethodCall(new[] {          ◁──┐ Request
        new Header(MessageHeader.Uri,                        │ metadata
            "tcp://localhost:3000/TownCrier"),
        new Header(MessageHeader.MethodName,
            "Announce"),
        new Header(MessageHeader.MethodSignature,
            SignatureFor("Announce")),
        new Header(MessageHeader.TypeName,
            typeof(Crier).AssemblyQualifiedName),
```

---

[7] See https://github.com/wsky/RemotingProtocolParser.

```
        new Header(MessageHeader.Args,
            ArgsFor("Announce"))
    });
    var responseMessage = new MethodResponse(new[]        ◁┐ Wraps
    {                                                         │ response
        new Header(MessageHeader.Return, obj)
    }, messageRequest);

    var responseStream = BinaryFormatterHelper.SerializeObject(
        responseMessage);
    using (var stream = new MemoryStream())
    {
        var handle = new TcpProtocolHandle(stream);
        handle.WritePreamble();
        handle.WriteMajorVersion();
        handle.WriteMinorVersion();
        handle.WriteOperation(TcpOperations.Reply);    Writes response
        handle.WriteContentDelimiter(                  metadata
            TcpContentDelimiter.ContentLength);
        handle.WriteContentLength(
            responseStream.Length);
        handle.WriteTransportHeaders(null);
        handle.WriteContent(responseStream);           ◁┐ Writes response (with
        return Convert.ToBase64String(      ◁┐            │ request metadata)
            stream.ToArray());                │
    }                                      Converts
}                                          to Base64

private Type[] SignatureFor(string methodName)    ◁
{
    return typeof(Crier)
        .GetMethod(methodName)
        .GetParameters()
        .Select(p => p.ParameterType)              Supports RPC methods
        .ToArray();                                other than Announce
}

private Object[] ArgsFor(string methodName)    ◁┘
{
    var length = SignatureFor(methodName).Length;
    return Enumerable.Repeat(new Object(), length).ToArray();
}
```

The SignatureFor and ArgsFor methods are simple helper methods that use .NET reflection (which lets you inspect types at runtime) to make the Serialize method general purpose. The request metadata expects some information about the remote function signature, and those two methods allow you to dynamically define enough information to satisfy the format. The rest of the Serialize method uses Xu Huang's library to wrap your stub response object with the appropriate metadata, so when mountebank returns it over the wire, your .NET Remoting client will see it as a legitimate RPC response.

Remember the key goal of mountebank: to make easy things easy and hard things possible. The fact that, with a little bit of underlying serialization code, you can elegantly stub out binary .NET Remoting (and some of its cousins) over the wire is a killer feature.

In case you have forgotten how cool that is, I suggest you look back at listing 8.9 and see how simple the test is.

### 8.5.3 How to tell mountebank where the message ends

There's one other bit of complexity you have to deal with to fully virtualize an application protocol using mountebank's TCP protocol. We hinted at it back in chapter 3, when we looked at how an HTTP server knows when an HTTP request is complete. You may recall a figure that looked like figure 8.5.

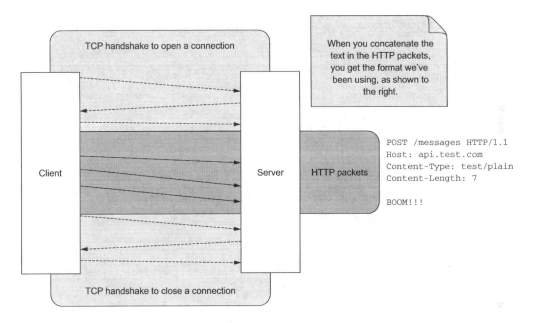

**Figure 8.5** Using `Content-Length` to wrap multiple packets into one HTTP request

As a transport protocol, TCP opens and closes a new connection using a *handshake*. That handshake is transparent to application protocols. TCP then takes the application request and chunks it into a series of packets, sending each packet over the wire. A packet will range between 1,500 and around 64,000 bytes, though smaller sizes are possible. You'll get the larger packet size when you test on your local machine (using what's called the *loopback* network interface), whereas lower level protocols like Ethernet use smaller packet sizes when passing data over the network.

Because a logical application request may span multiple packets, the application protocol needs to know when the logical request ends. HTTP often uses the `Content-Length` header to provide that information. Because this header occurs early in the HTTP request, the server can wait until it receives enough bytes to satisfy the given length, regardless of how many packets it takes to deliver the full request.

Every application protocol must have a strategy for determining when the logical request ends. Mountebank uses two strategies:

- The default strategy, which assumes a one-to-one relationship between a packet and a request
- Receiving enough information to know when the request ends

The examples have worked so far because you've only tested with short requests. You will change that with a simple proxy, saved as remoteCrierProxy.json, as shown in the following listing.

---

**Listing 8.11  Creating a TCP proxy to a .NET Remoting server**

```
{
  "protocol": "tcp",
  "port": 3000,
  "mode": "binary",
  "stubs": [{
    "responses": [{
      "proxy": { "to": "tcp://localhost:3333" }
    }]
  }]
}
```

The source code for this book includes the executable for the .NET Remoting server. You give it the port to listen to when you start it up:

```
Server.exe 3333
```

You start the mountebank server in the usual way:

```
mb --configfile remoteCrierProxy.json
```

Finally, if you start the .NET Remoting client on port 3000, it's configured by default to send a request greeting and topic that'll exceed the size of a single packet:

```
Client.exe 3000
```

You can see in the mountebank logs that it tried to proxy, but the server didn't respond, and the client threw an error. By default, mountebank grabs the first packet and assumes it's the entire request. It passes it to the server—a real, bona fide .NET Remoting server—which looks inside the packet and sees that it should expect more packets to come for the request, so it continues to wait. Mountebank, thinking it has seen the entire request, tries to respond. The whole process blows up (figure 8.6).

Once your request reaches a certain size, you have to opt for the second strategy: telling mountebank when the request ends. The imposter will keep an internal buffer. Every time it receives a new packet, it adds the packet data to the buffer and passes the

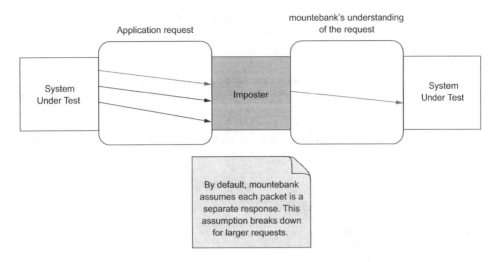

**Figure 8.6  Mismatched expectations around when the request ends**

entire buffer to a JavaScript function that you define, which returns `true` if the request is complete or `false` otherwise.

You pass in the function as the `endOfRequestResolver`. For this example, you'll add it using a template to include the function in a separate file called resolver.js, as shown in the following listing.

**Listing 8.12  Adding an `endOfRequestResolver`**

```
{
  "protocol": "tcp",
  "port": 3000,
  "mode": "binary",
  "endOfRequestResolver": {
"inject": "<%- stringify(filename, 'resolver.js') %>"
  },
  "stubs": [{
"responses": [{
    "proxy": { "to": "tcp://localhost:3333" }
    }]
  }]
}
```

.NET Remoting embeds a content length in the metadata for the request. You can use that in your function to determine if you've collected all the packets for the request or not. You'll once again rely on Xu Huang's parsing library, which includes a Node.js implementation, to do the heavy lifting. As before, the intention isn't to learn everything about .NET Remoting; it's to show how you would virtualize a real-world application protocol. Don't worry too much about the details of the message format. The essential part is that you grab the content length from the message and test it against the length of the buffer mountebank passes you to see whether you've received the entire request, as shown in the following listing.

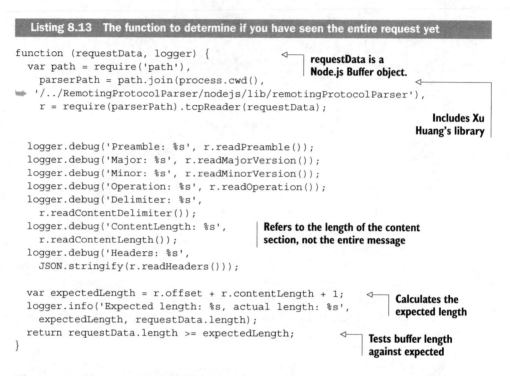

**Listing 8.13   The function to determine if you have seen the entire request yet**

```
function (requestData, logger) {                    ┌─ requestData is a
  var path = require('path'),                        │  Node.js Buffer object.
    parserPath = path.join(process.cwd(),            ◄─────────────
    '/../RemotingProtocolParser/nodejs/lib/remotingProtocolParser'),
    r = require(parserPath).tcpReader(requestData);
                                                    ┌─ Includes Xu
                                                    │  Huang's library
  logger.debug('Preamble: %s', r.readPreamble());
  logger.debug('Major: %s', r.readMajorVersion());
  logger.debug('Minor: %s', r.readMinorVersion());
  logger.debug('Operation: %s', r.readOperation());
  logger.debug('Delimiter: %s',
    r.readContentDelimiter());
  logger.debug('ContentLength: %s',      ┌─ Refers to the length of the content
    r.readContentLength());              │  section, not the entire message
  logger.debug('Headers: %s',
    JSON.stringify(r.readHeaders()));

  var expectedLength = r.offset + r.contentLength + 1;   ◄─┐ Calculates the
  logger.info('Expected length: %s, actual length: %s',    │ expected length
    expectedLength, requestData.length);
  return requestData.length >= expectedLength;   ◄─┐ Tests buffer length
}                                                   │ against expected
```

The parsing library isn't published as an npm module. If it was, you could install     it locally and include it without referencing a specific file path. In your case, you cloned Huang's repository according to the path expected in the second line of the function.[8]

The parsing library doesn't support random access, so you can't ask it the content length and compare that against your request buffer. Instead, it maintains a stateful offset and expects that you read all the metadata fields in order. To help you debug, I wrapped those metadata fields in a logger.debug function. You'll be able to see them in the mountebank logs if you run with the --loglevel debug command-line flag.

Now that you've written your function, you can try the proxy again. This time, because you're using a JavaScript function, you have to pass the --allowInjection flag:

```
mb --configfile imposter.json --allowInjection
```

---

[8]  I've done this in the source code repo for this book, including a complete copy of the library.

Restart the server on port 3333 and run the client again, pointing to the mountebank proxy:

```
Client.exe 3000
```

This time, everything works. You now have a fully functional virtual server for .NET Remoting. Congratulations! You've completed the hardest example in the entire book.

Hard, but possible.

And with that, you've now completed your tour of mountebank. But knowing how to use a tool isn't the same as knowing *when* you should use it. That's what the next chapter is about.

---

### Another example: Java serialization over a Mule ESB

In late 2013, I was working at a major airline company. Several years earlier, the website had been rewritten to communicate with a service tier over a Mule enterprise service bus (ESB). The ESB connector communicated over TCP and returned a serialized Java object graph. Unfortunately, passing raw objects over the wire created a tight coupling between the web tier and the service tier. It also ran a multibillion-dollar website for most of a decade. Production-hardened enterprise software rarely looks like the beautiful architectures you read about.

I was on a team creating REST APIs for a new mobile app that needed to go out before the website could be replaced, so our APIs had to integrate with the service tier. Although we had a top-notch team comfortable with automated testing, the friction of testing without also breaking the web tier was so painful that we gave up. We wrote automated tests when we could, but usually it was too hard, and bugs started creeping in.

Most of this book has described mountebank for HTTP, but HTTP wasn't the first protocol mountebank supported. I created mountebank to test a binary Mule ESB TCP connector, serving up Java objects in our tests in much the same way we looked at for .NET Remoting. At the time, a number of quality open source virtualization tools were available for HTTP, but none could stub out a binary TCP protocol. That's largely still true today.

---

## Summary

- In mountebank, protocols are responsible for transforming a network request into a JSON request for predicate matching, as well as taking a mountebank JSON response and transforming it into a network response.
- Mountebank supports adding an application protocol on top of its TCP protocol. All predicates, response types, and behaviors continue to work with the TCP protocol; only the JSON structure for requests and responses differs.
- Mountebank supports binary payloads by Base64 encoding the data. You have to switch the imposter `mode` to `binary` for mountebank to correctly handle the encoding.

- Once you figure out how to serialize an object graph into the wire format expected by an RPC protocol, you can write tests that look similar to ones that use traditional stubbing tools.
- By default, mountebank assumes each incoming packet represents an entire request when using the TCP protocol. To let mountebank know when the request ends, you can pass in an `endOfRequestResolver` JavaScript function.

# Part 3

# Closing the Loop

Now that you have the full breadth of mountebank functionality under your belt, part 3 puts its usage in context.

Service virtualization is a powerful tool, but, like any tool, it has its limits. In chapter 9, we explore it in the context of continuous delivery. We'll build a test pipeline from start to finish for some of the microservices we've looked at previously in this book and discuss where service virtualization fits and where it doesn't. We'll also look at how to gain additional confidence in your test suite with contract tests that give you lightweight validation that play together well with your services without going down the path toward full end-to-end testing.

We close out the book by looking at performance testing, always a difficult subject and one made even more so by microservices. The need to understand your service's performance characteristics in a networked environment is challenged by the cost and complexity of securing an end-to-end environment for testing. Service virtualization is a natural fit for performance testing and combines many of the features we've looked at previously, including proxies and behaviors.

# Mountebank and
# continuous delivery

**This chapter covers**

- A basic refresher on continuous delivery
- Testing strategy for continuous delivery and microservices
- Where service virtualization applies inside a broader testing strategy

A sysadmin, a DBA, and a developer walk into a bar. The sysadmin orders a light lager to maximize uptime, the DBA orders a 30-year-aged single malt to avoid undue adulteration, and the developer orders a Pan Galactic Gargle Blaster because it hasn't been invented yet. An hour later, the DBA has gone home already, the developer has moved on to a more modern bar, and the slightly wobbly and heavily overutilized sysadmin is holding down the fort, while also holding a lager in one hand, a single malt in another hand, and a Pan Galactic in another hand.[1]

---

[1] In *The Hitchhikers Guide to the Galaxy,* Douglas Adams describes the Pan Galactic Gargle Blaster as the alcoholic equivalent of a mugging—expensive and bad for the head.

Traditional siloed organizational structure forces a complicated dance to get anything done. It's no surprise that, in large enterprises, IT and the business rarely have a healthy relationship. Historically, the common approach to improving the situation was to add more process discipline, which further complicated the dance, making it harder to release code into production (and, by consequence, reduced value to customers). Having increasingly well-defined handoffs between a developer, a DBA, and a sysadmin exemplifies process discipline. Every time you fill out a database schema change request form or an operational handoff document, you have seen process discipline in action.

Continuous delivery changes the equation by emphasizing *engineering discipline* over *process discipline*. It's about automating the steps required to build confidence so that the business can release new code on demand. Although engineering discipline encompasses a wide spectrum of practices, testing plays a central role. In this chapter, we look at a sample testing strategy for a microservices world and show where service virtualization does and doesn't fit.

## 9.1    *A continuous delivery refresher*

Jez Humble and Dave Farley wrote *Continuous Delivery* to capture the key practices they saw enabling the rapid delivery of software. In chapter 1, I showed you how the traditional process discipline of centralized release management and toll gates increases congestion and slows delivery. The emphasis is on safety, providing additional checks to increase confidence that the software being delivered will work.

In contrast, continuous delivery (CD) focuses on automation, emphasizing safety, speed, *and* sustainability of delivering software. It requires the code to be in a deployable state at all times, forcing you to abandon the ideas of *dev complete, feature complete,* and *hardening iterations.* Those concepts are holdovers from the world of yesteryear, in which we papered over a lack of engineering discipline by adding more layers of process.

> ### A glossary of terms surrounding continuous delivery
>
> I introduce several important terms in this chapter:
>
> - *Continuous integration*—Although continuous integration (CI) is often confused with running an automated build after every commit through a tool like Jenkins, it's actually the practice of ensuring that your code is merged with and works with everyone else's on a continual basis (at least once a day).
> - *Continuous delivery*—The set of software development practices that ensures code is always releasable. The full spectrum of CD practices ranges from developer-facing techniques like feature toggles, which provide a way of hiding code that's still a work in progress, to production-facing approaches like monitoring and canary testing, which scales up a release to a customer base over time. In between comes testing, the focus of this book.

- *Deployment pipeline*—The path code takes from the time it's committed to the time it reaches production.
- *Continuous deployment*—An advanced type of continuous delivery that removes all manual interventions from the deployment pipeline.

In CD, every commit of the code either fails the build or can be released to production. There's no need to decide up front which commit represents the release version. Although still common, that approach encourages sloppy engineering practices. It enables you to commit code that cannot be released to production, with the expectation that you'll fix it later. That attitude requires IT to own the timing of software delivery, taking control out of the hands of the business and the product manager.

The core organizing concept that makes CD possible is the *deployment pipeline*. It represents the value stream of the code's journey from commit to production and is often directly represented in continuous integration (CI) tools (figure 9.1).

Every code commit automatically triggers a build, which usually includes compilation, running unit tests, and static analysis. A successful build saves off a package in an

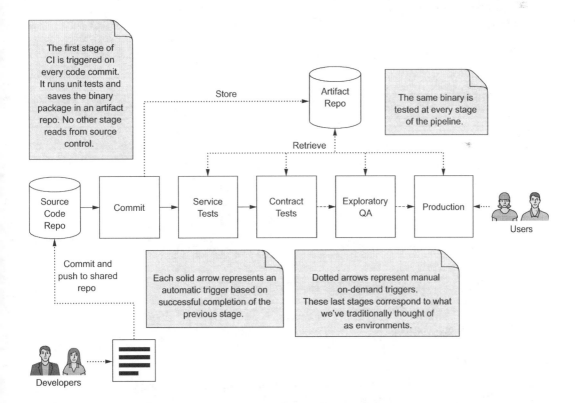

**Figure 9.1** A deployment pipeline defines the path from commit to production.

artifact repository—usually a binary artifact, even if it's just a tarball of source code for interpreted languages like Ruby and JavaScript. Every set of verifications downstream runs against a deployed instance of that package, until it ultimately reaches production.

The path that code takes on its way to providing value to real users varies from organization to organization and even between teams within the same organization. Much of it is defined by how you decide to test your application.

### 9.1.1   Testing strategy for CD with microservices

> *Testing in a very large-scale distributed setting is a major challenge.*
>
> — Werner Vogels, Amazon CTO

A common approach to visualizing testing strategy comes in the form of a pyramid. The visual works because it acknowledges that confidence comes from testing at multiple layers. It also shows that there's value in pushing as much of the testing as possible into the lower levels, where tests are both easier to maintain and faster to run. As you move to higher levels, the tests become harder to write, to maintain, and to troubleshoot when they break. They're also more comprehensive and often better at catching difficult bugs. Each team will need to customize a test pyramid to its needs, but you can think of a template for microservices that looks like figure 9.2.[2]

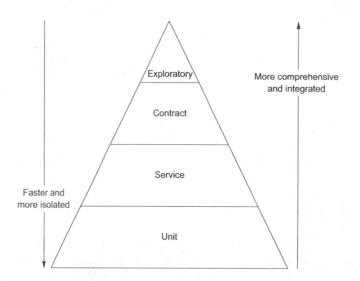

**Figure 9.2   Simplified test pyramid for microservices**

---

[2]  You also may be interested in Toby Clemson's description of the types of testing for microservices at http://martinfowler.com/articles/microservice-testing/.

People have argued endlessly over what makes a unit test different from higher level tests, but for the purposes of this diagram, the key difference is that you should be able to run a unit test without deploying your service into a runtime. That makes unit tests in-process and independent of anything from the environment (see figure 9.3).

Though there's some different terminology out there, I've used the term *service test* to describe a black-box test that validates your service's behavior over the wire. Such tests do require a deployment, but you use service virtualization to maintain isolation from your runtime dependencies. This layer allows you to do out-of-process, black-box testing while maintaining determinism. Service virtualization enables you to remove nondeterminism from your tests by allowing each test to control the environment it runs in, as shown in figure 9.3.

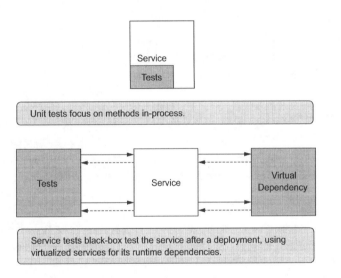

**Figure 9.3   The basic structure for unit and service tests**

You should be able to test the bulk of the behavior of your service through a combination of unit tests and service tests. They let you know that your service behaves correctly, assuming certain responses from its dependencies, but they don't guarantee that those stubbed responses are appropriate. Contract tests give you validation that breaking-contract-level changes haven't occurred (see figure 9.4). Service tests say, in effect, that *if* the service gets these responses from its dependencies, *then* it behaves correctly. Contract tests validate that the service does, in fact, get those responses. Good contract tests avoid deep behavioral testing of the dependencies—you should test them independently—but give you confidence in your stubs.

I've included exploratory testing as part of the test pyramid because most organizations find some value in manual testing. Good exploratory testers follow their nose to

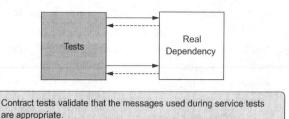

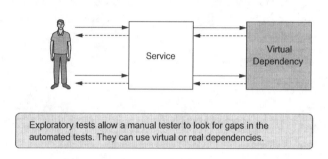

Figure 9.4    **The basic structure for contract and exploratory tests**

find gaps in an automated test suite. Such tests can be integrated or rely on service virtualization to test certain edge cases. Figure 9.4 shows exploratory testing using service virtualization.

Other types of testing exist that don't fit as well in the test pyramid metaphor. Cross-functional requirements like security, performance, and failover for availability often require specialized testing and are less about the behavior of the system than about its resiliency. Performance testing is an area where service virtualization shines, as it allows you to replicate the performance of your dependencies without requiring a fully integrated, production-like environment to run in. In chapter 10, we explore how service virtualization enables performance and load testing.

Finally, you should never forget that error prevention is only one piece of testing strategy. The rapid release cycles of microservices encourage you to invest heavily in error detection and remediation as well as prevention, as they contribute to your overall confidence in releasing software. Although error detection and remediation are not the focus of this book, companies that have used microservices effectively generally stage their releases, such that only a small percentage of users can see the new release at first. Robust monitoring detects whether the users experience any problem, and rolling back is as easy as switching those users to the code everyone else is using. If no problems are detected, the release system will switch more and more users to the new code over time until 100% of users are using the release, at which time you can remove the previous release.[3] Advanced monitoring allows you to detect errors before your users do. Although your testing strategy is a key component of continuous delivery, engineering discipline significantly increases the scope of automation.

### 9.1.2 *Mapping your testing strategy to a deployment pipeline*

Whatever your particular test pyramid looks like, mapping it to your deployment pipeline is generally pretty straightforward (figure 9.5).

I like to think of boundary conditions moving from one stage to the next. In figure 9.5, I've shown the following boundaries:

- The boundary of *deployment* represents the first time you've deployed the application (or service). All tests to the left are run in-process; all tests to the right are run out-of-process and implicitly test the deployment process itself, as well as the application.

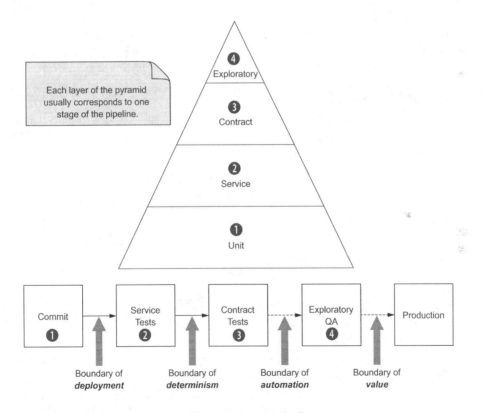

**Figure 9.5  Mapping your test pyramid to a deployment pipeline**

---

[3] This is called canary testing. You can read more about it at https://martinfowler.com/bliki/Canary Release.html.

- The boundary of *determinism* represents the first time you've integrated your application into other applications. Tests to the right of this boundary may fail because of environmental conditions. Tests to the left of this boundary should fail only for reasons entirely under the application team's control.
- The boundary of *automation* represents where you switch to manual, exploratory testing. (Note that the deployment itself is still automated, but the trigger to deploy requires a human pressing a button.) Some companies, for some products, have managed to eliminate this boundary altogether, automatically releasing code to production without any manual verifications. This is an advanced form of continuous delivery called *continuous deployment* and is clearly not appropriate in all environments. The software that helps keep an airplane in the air requires a much higher degree of confidence than your favorite social media platform.
- The boundary of *value* is the point at which real users have access to the new software.

Because this book is about testing, we only tackle the *test pipeline*, those early stages of the pipeline that give you confidence that you can ship to production. The full deployment pipeline would include the production deployment as well.

## 9.2    Creating a test pipeline

It has been a while since we looked at the example pet store website in chapter 2. We used it as a small-scale simulacrum of a microservices-backed e-commerce application and focused on the web façade service, which aggregated results from two other services (figure 9.6):

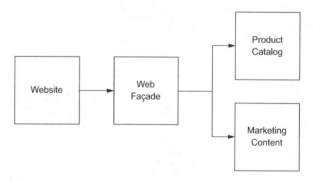

**Figure 9.6    An example set of microservices**

- The product catalog service, responsible for sending product information
- The content service, responsible for sending marketing copy about a product

For demonstration purposes, we'll take the perspective of the team writing the web façade code that aggregates product and marketing data to present to the website. The example is simple enough to digest in short order and complicated enough to require meaningful testing. The code is a simple Express app (a popular node.js web application framework). The following listing shows what you need to initialize the service.[4]

---

[4]    See the full source code at https://github.com/bbyars/mountebank-in-action.

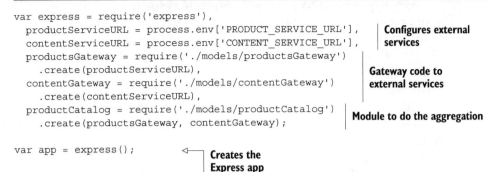

**Listing 9.1  Web façade initialization code**

```
var express = require('express'),
  productServiceURL = process.env['PRODUCT_SERVICE_URL'],
  contentServiceURL = process.env['CONTENT_SERVICE_URL'],
  productsGateway = require('./models/productsGateway')
    .create(productServiceURL),
  contentGateway = require('./models/contentGateway')
    .create(contentServiceURL),
  productCatalog = require('./models/productCatalog')
    .create(productsGateway, contentGateway);

var app = express();
```

**Configures external services**

**Gateway code to external services**

**Module to do the aggregation**

**Creates the Express app**

Using environment variables for configuration is a common approach and will allow you to use different URLs in different environments (and to use service virtualization for service tests). The two gateway objects are simple wrappers over the HTTP calls, allowing you to centralize error handling and logging around external service calls.

The code that responds to an HTTP request and returns the aggregated results of the product and content services is quite straightforward, delegating the complex logic to the productCatalog object, as shown in the following listing.

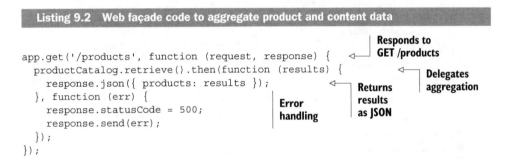

**Listing 9.2  Web façade code to aggregate product and content data**

```
app.get('/products', function (request, response) {
  productCatalog.retrieve().then(function (results) {
    response.json({ products: results });
  }, function (err) {
    response.statusCode = 500;
    response.send(err);
  });
});
```

**Responds to GET /products**

**Delegates aggregation**

**Returns results as JSON**

**Error handling**

You could've left the aggregation logic directly in the function that handles the HTTP request. You didn't, in part, because that would've made it harder to unit test.

### 9.2.1  Creating unit tests

Test-driven development (TDD) is often also called test-driven design because the act of writing unit tests helps enforce loose coupling and high cohesion in your production code.[5] Bundling all the aggregation logic into your HTTP handling code would have required a significant amount of setup to test it—exactly the type of friction that reduces your motivation to write tests to begin with. It also would've been a worse

---

[5] TDD is more than writing unit tests. It's a practice that involves writing a small test before the code exists and building just enough code to make the test pass. Those small iterations with refactoring in between help grow the design of the codebase organically.

design, coupling HTTP handling logic with aggregation logic. The drive to make unit testing your code as easy as possible is one of the best influences for keeping your codebase modular. Unit tests are as much about helping you design your application as they are about finding bugs.

Unit tests should be in-process to the application under test, and each unit test should focus on a small piece of code. Consequently, you should never use service virtualization in your unit tests. This is the realm of traditional mocks and stubs.

Let's look at the `productCatalog` code. We'll start with the wrapper logic needed to create an instance, as shown in the following listing, and export it to another Java-Script file.

**Listing 9.3   The shell of the `productCatalog` module**

```
function create(productsGateway, contentGateway) {        Creates an instance
    function retrieve () { ... }                           using dependency injection

    return {                                    See listing 9.4.
        retrieve: retrieve         Returns the instance
    };                             with one function
}

module.exports = {
    create: create          Exports the creation
};                          method to other files
```

Much of this is JavaScript and node.js plumbing. The creation function[6] accepts the two gateway objects as parameters. This pattern—dependency injection—is another area where good unit testing practices intersect with good design. If you created the gateways at the exact spot you needed them, you wouldn't be able to swap out the gateway instances with another object for testing. That would mean you would be forced to test the full end-to-end flow each time because the gateways are responsible for making the HTTP calls to the external services. It also would've created a tight coupling, preventing higher order code from adding decorators around the gateways for added functionality.

The `retrieve` function uses those gateways to retrieve and aggregate the data from the product and content services, as shown in the following listing.

**Listing 9.4   The code that retrieves and aggregates downstream services**

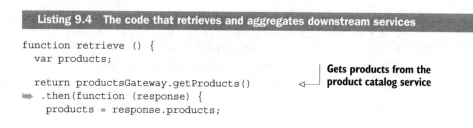

```
function retrieve () {
    var products;
                                                Gets products from the
    return productsGateway.getProducts()        product catalog service
    .then(function (response) {
        products = response.products;
```

---

[6]  You could've also used JavaScript constructors, but they add a bit more magic than a simple creation function.

```
    var productIds = products.map(function (product) {
      return product.id;
    });
    return contentGateway.getContent(productIds);
  }).then(function (response) {
    var contentEntries = response.content;

    products.forEach(function (product) {
      var contentEntry = contentEntries.find(
        function (entry) {
          return entry.id === product.id;
        });
      product.copy = contentEntry.copy;
      product.image = contentEntry.image;
    });

    return products;
  });
}
```

**Maps to the IDs only**

**Gets content for those products**

**Matches the content entry to the product by ID**

**Adds marketing content data**

Clearly, the bulk of the web façade complexity lies in this function, making it a great place to focus your unit testing efforts. To keep the unit test in-process, you will have to stub out the two gateways.[7] You'll use a common JavaScript mocking library called Sinon to help.[8] Sinon allows you to tell the gateways what to return, which supports a very readable test setup (the Arrange step of the standard test pattern of Arrange-Act-Assert), as shown in the following listing.

**Listing 9.5 The test setup, using dependency injection and stubs**

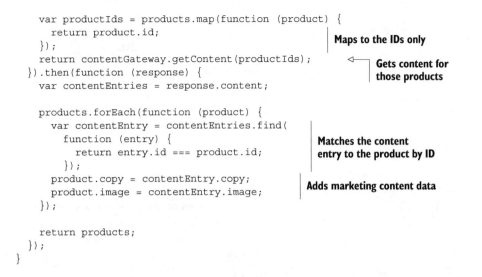

```
it('should merge results', function (done) {
  var productsResult = {
      products: [
          { id: 1, name: 'PRODUCT-1' },
          { id: 2, name: 'PRODUCT-2' }
      ]
    },
    productsGateway = {
      getProducts: sinon
                    .stub()
                    .returns(Q(productsResult))
    },
    contentResults = {
      content: [
          { id: 1, copy: 'COPY-1', image: 'IMAGE-1' },
          { id: 2, copy: 'COPY-2', image: 'IMAGE-2' }
      ]
    },
```

**Stages the product catalog service results**

**Sets up the product stub**

**Stages the content service results**

---

[7] I haven't shown the gateway code because it's not relevant to the example. See the GitHub repo for details.

[8] See http://sinonjs.org/, although it's not hard to write your own stubs if you'd rather avoid using an external library.

```
contentGateway = {
    getContent: sinon
                 .stub()
                 .withArgs([1, 2])
                 .returns(Q(contentResults))
  },
  catalog = productCatalog.create(
     productsGateway, contentGateway);

// ACT
// ASSERT
});
```

> Sets up the content stub

> Passes the stubs into the catalog

> See listing 9.6.

Most of the code is setting up the JSON responses that the gateways are responsible for returning. As you have seen in previous examples, I recommend using test data that's easy to spot to make the assertions easy to read, which is why I have opted for strings like "COPY-1." You stub out the two gateway functions—getProducts on the productsGateway and getContent on the contentGateway—using Sinon's stub() function and chain on the result you want with the returns function. Notice that when you create the stub for the contentGateway, you add a withArgs ([1, 2]) function call. This is like using predicates in mountebank. You're telling Sinon to return the given result if the arguments match what you specify.

The only other nuance to the test code is the mysterious use of the Q function, which is used in the stub responses. Q is a promise library that helps contain the complexity of using asynchronous code in JavaScript. The real gateways have to reach across the network to retrieve results, and because JavaScript uses nonblocking I/O for network calls, using promises helps make the asynchronous code easier to understand. If you look back to the retrieve function in listing 9.4, you'll see that you call a then function after each gateway call and pass in the code to execute when the I/O is finished. Wrapping the objects inside the Q function adds the then function to your stub results, so the production code works on the stubs as expected.

Let's close off the example by looking at the Act and Assert stages of the test in the following listing.

---

#### Listing 9.6   The unit test assertion

```
it('should merge results', function (done) {
  // ARRANGE                                          ◁— See listing 9.5.

  catalog.retrieve().done(function (result) {        ◁— Act
    assert.deepEqual(result, [
      { id: 1, name: 'PRODUCT-1',
        copy: 'COPY-1', image: 'IMAGE-1' },
      { id: 2, name: 'PRODUCT-2',
        copy: 'COPY-2', image: 'IMAGE-2' },
    ]);

    done();                    ◁— Tells the test runner
  });                                that the test has finished
});
```

> Assert

Anytime you're using asynchronous code, you have to tell the test runner that the test is complete. The assertion verifies that you merged the results of the two gateways correctly. The done test parameter is a function that you call after your assertion to signify the end of the test execution.

You could, and should, write many more unit tests on the `retrieve` function. For example, you could write unit tests to specify what happens in each of these scenarios:

- There's no marketing copy for a product.
- A downstream service times out (resulting in a gateway error).
- You get missing JSON fields from the marketing content service.
- The marketing content service returns products in a different order than the product catalog service.

It's much easier to write the code to support these scenarios in a suite of unit tests than it is to validate them with higher level tests. Unit tests should be numerous and run quickly, which is why they form the base of the testing pyramid.

You can create a build script that runs the unit tests and wire that into the first stage of your continuous integration tool. Once you have done so, you have automated the first stage of your test pipeline.

### 9.2.2 *Creating service tests*

Service tests should exercise your application over the wire, which rules out in-process stubs. This is where service virtualization shines, as service virtualization is the out-of-process equivalent of stubbing.

Although you can always set up your imposters using a config file, I recommend using mountebank's API when possible for service tests. The API allows you to create the test data for each test separately rather than having to depend on an implicit linkage between a magic key in your test setup and the scenario you're testing. You used mountebank's API in chapter 2.

I've modified the example slightly to highlight the point about keeping the test data as simple as possible. Let's take a fresh look at the test first in the following listing; we look at the helper functions again shortly.

**Listing 9.7 A service test that validates web façade aggregation**

```
it('aggregates data', function (done) {
  createProductImposter(['1', '2']).then(function () {     Arrange
    return createContentImposter(['1', '2']);
  }).then(function () {
    return request(webFacadeURL + '/products');     <— Act
  }).then(function (body) {
    var products = JSON.parse(body).products;

    assert.deepEqual(products, [     <— Assert
      {
        "id": "ID-1",
        "name": "NAME-1",
```

```
        "description": "DESCRIPTION-1",
        "copy": "COPY-1",
        "image": "IMAGE-1"
      },
      {
        "id": "ID-2",
        "name": "NAME-2",
        "description": "DESCRIPTION-2",
        "copy": "COPY-2",
        "image": "IMAGE-2"
      }
    ]);
    return imposter().destroyAll();      ◁─── Cleanup
  }).done(function () {
    done();                  ◁─┐  Tells the test
  });                          └  runner you're done
});
```

The createProductImposter and createContentImposter functions are similar. They use mountebank's API to create the virtual services. Both functions accept an
array of suffixes, which they use to append to the test data within each field name. You
can see what that results in by looking at the assertion in listing 9.7. The code to do
that does a simple string append to each field name:

```
function addSuffixToObjects (suffixes, fields) {
  return suffixes.map(function (suffix) {
    var result = {};
    fields.forEach(function (field) {
      result[field] = field.toUpperCase() + '-' + suffix;
    });
    return result;
  });
}
```

With that helper function, the imposter creation uses the same fluent API you built in
chapter 2 that wraps mountebank's RESTful API, as shown in the following listing.

**Listing 9.8  The imposter creation functions**

```
var imposter = require('./imposter'),      ◁─── See listing 2.5.
  productPort = 3000;

function createProductImposter (suffixes) {
  var products = addSuffixToObjects(suffixes,
    ['id', 'name', 'description']);

  return imposter({
    port: productPort,
    protocol: "http",
    name: "Product Catalog Service"
  })
    .withStub()
    .matchingRequest({equals: {path: "/products"}})
```

```
    .respondingWith({
      statusCode: 200,
      headers: {"Content-Type": "application/json"},
      body: { products: products }
    })
    .create();
}

var contentPort = 4000;

function createContentImposter(suffixes) {
  var contentEntries = addSuffixToObjects(suffixes,
    ['id', 'copy', 'image']);

  return imposter({
    port: contentPort,
    protocol: "http",
    name: "Marketing Content Service"
  })
    .withStub()
    .matchingRequest({
      equals: {
        path: "/content",
        query: {ids: "ID-1,ID-2"}
      }
    })
    .respondingWith({
      statusCode: 200,
      headers: {"Content-Type": "application/json"},
      body: { content: contentEntries }
    })
    .create();
}
```

Arguably, the hardest part of managing a suite of service tests is maintaining the test data. Test data management is a complicated subject, and many vendors are willing to sell you solutions that promise to ease the pain. Although such tools may help in complex integrated test scenarios, I believe you should use them sparingly. Too often, they're used as a way of avoiding shifting the tests *to the left*, where left refers to the left side of the deployment pipeline (close to development).

Creating test cases with appropriate isolation via service virtualization is key. The example in listing 9.7 virtualizes a couple of simple service schemas. Real world schemas are often much more complex. In such cases, you will want to save off the responses in separate files and use string interpolation to add in any dynamic data needed. You can reference the specific scenario directly in your test using a key that identifies the scenario. For example, if you wanted to test what happens when the product catalog service returns a product but there's no marketing content for it, use a product ID of NO-CONTENT. Leaving breadcrumb trails in your test data will make maintaining it much easier.

**The team writing tests needs to own the configuration
for the virtualized service**

Generally, two types of service virtualization tools are available.

The first type comes from the open source community. They almost always support HTTP/S. Although most of them support record-playback through proxying, they often expect the team writing the tests—the client team—to define the data that the virtual service returns.

The second type represents the commercial virtualization tools. They usually are more feature-rich and support a more complete set of protocols. But because of the licensing model, they typically expect a central team to own the virtual service definitions. For automated service tests, that's exactly backwards from how it should be.

Automated testing requires fine-grained control over the testing scenarios. Those scenarios will require a different set of test data than another team's automated tests, even if both test suites have a shared dependency that requires virtualizing. Having to go through a central team to set up your test data adds unnecessary friction, which has the unfortunate side effect of discouraging your developers from writing the tests. The complexity of the configuration will also become unwieldy to understand and maintain if your test data is comingled with that of other teams, adding more friction.

At this stage of the deployment pipeline, your team needs to be in complete control of its test data. That means your team needs to write the configuration for the virtual services. Relying on a central team or the team producing the service that you depend on to write the configuration for you will always result in a deficient test suite.

Throughout much of this book, I have described mountebank's mission statement as keeping things that should be easy actually easy while making hard things possible. Rephrasing that as a competitive product strategy, my goal with mountebank is to provide the power of commercial service virtualization tools with the CD-friendliness of the open source tools.

### 9.2.3   *Balancing service virtualization with contract tests*

Unit tests help you design your application and catch simple bugs created while refactoring. Service tests treat your application as a black box and help catch bugs from a consumer's point of view. Adding service virtualization keeps service tests deterministic, sealing your test scenarios in a pristine laboratory environment.

Production is more like a war zone than a lab. Although service tests give you confidence that your application works with certain assumptions about your runtime dependencies, they do nothing to validate those assumptions. Like it or not, your runtime dependencies change over time, as they have their own release cycle, so you need some dynamic way of detecting breaking changes in services that you depend on (for example, checking that the marketing content service returns the marketing copy in a top-level JSON field called `copy`). That's the responsibility of the next stage of the test pipeline: where you run your contract tests.

Contract tests move you into the realm of integration, and any time you integrate to the outside world (code written by another team or another company), you're no longer in a friendly, deterministic environment. Your tests may fail because your code has a bug, because *their* code has a bug, because of configuration bugs in the environment itself, or because the network hiccupped. Consequently, you test as much as you can in the friendly confines of unit and service tests. Contract tests shouldn't be deep behavioral tests; they should be lightweight validations of your assumptions about your runtime dependencies. In effect, they validate that your stub definitions are compatible with the real service (figure 9.7).

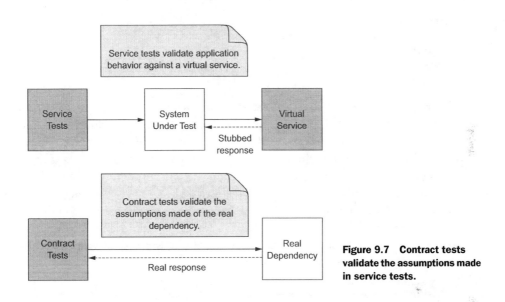

**Figure 9.7  Contract tests validate the assumptions made in service tests.**

You generally want to avoid behavioral testing of your dependencies—that's the job of the team building those dependencies. Except in dysfunctional situations, you are better off treating them no differently than you would a software as a service (SaaS) application that you'd pay to use, or an API from a third party like Google. Aside from the obvious cost of behavioral testing of your dependencies, it also increases the fragility of the environment configuration, as behaviorally testing your dependency requires *its* dependencies to also be functional. This leads you back down the path of end-to-end integration testing, creating exactly the kind of traffic jams on the path to production that you're trying to avoid by using service virtualization.

### A CONTRACT TEST EXAMPLE

The example we've been looking at is a bit too simplistic to show the value of contract testing, in large part because we asserted only that the marketing content gets correctly merged into the product data. The tests haven't put too much emphasis on what that product data is, but the website would depend on a certain set of fields to display the data appropriately. That means that the web façade service must expect a certain set of fields coming out of the product catalog service. Contract testing helps verify that those expectations remain true as the product service changes.

Let's say you expect a name, description, and availability dates for a product. You expect the dates to be in ISO format (YYYY-MM-DD) to ensure that you're parsing it correctly. A contract test validates that those fields exist in the place and format where you expect them. Let's start by showing the helpers to validate the type and format of data you get back, which use a regular expression to validate the date format:

```
function assertString (obj) {
  assert.ok(obj !== null && typeof obj === 'string');
}

function assertISODate (obj) {
  assertString(obj);
  assert.ok(/201\d-[01]\d-[0123]\d/.test(obj), 'not ISO date');
}
```

The regular expression uses the same \d metacharacter you have seen previously, which represents a digit. The rest of the regular expression matches either literal numbers (for example, to ensure that the year starts with the decade this book was written in—201x), or a limited set of numbers represented in brackets (for example, the month must start with 0 or 1, and the day with 0 through 3). This isn't a perfect test—it allows 2019-19-39, for example—but it's probably good enough. If you need more confidence, you can add more advanced date parsing to the test code.

You can use the assertString and assertISODate helpers to write the test, which validates that the fields exist in the location and format you expect them, as shown in the following listing.

> **Listing 9.9   A contract test validating the placing and format of fields from a real dependency**

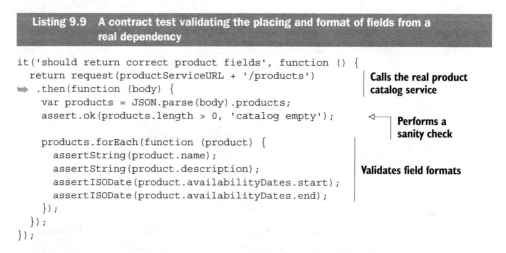

```
it('should return correct product fields', function () {
  return request(productServiceURL + '/products')          Calls the real product
    .then(function (body) {                                 catalog service
      var products = JSON.parse(body).products;
      assert.ok(products.length > 0, 'catalog empty');       Performs a
                                                             sanity check
      products.forEach(function (product) {
        assertString(product.name);
        assertString(product.description);                  Validates field formats
        assertISODate(product.availabilityDates.start);
        assertISODate(product.availabilityDates.end);
      });
    });
});
```

Before we get into what this function is testing, let's take a step back to think about what it's *not* testing. It's not testing the full breadth of the product catalog service. The product catalog service may return dozens of fields that aren't relevant to your service (the web façade), so you don't test them. Remember, you are testing your assumptions about the product catalog service, not the product catalog service itself.

What you *are* testing is that the format of the data you get back corresponds to what you expect. You're doing that for every product returned, but you also could've done it for only the first product in the array. It's a time versus comprehensiveness tradeoff, and you'll have to face that tradeoff on a case-by-case basis. It's generally a safe assumption that a well-behaved service will return the same schema for all elements in an array.

### MANAGING TEST DATA

The hardest part—by far—of contract testing is managing test data. Our example more or less avoids the problem by testing a read-only endpoint, although we still added a sanity check in the test to ensure that at least one product was returned. Contract testing services that allow you to change state are possible but require some support from the service.

The cleanest method is to have your test create the data before reading it. For example, you may submit an order by sending a POST to /orders and retrieve it by sending a GET to /orders/123, where 123 is the order ID in the response to the first call. With this approach, every test execution creates new data, which ensures that the data is isolated from every other test execution. However, it does require the ability to create test data. That's a reasonable enough assumption for the orders service, but the product catalog service is unlikely to provide APIs to create new products, as that is generally a back-office process.

An alternative is to coordinate with the provider team on a set of data you can rely on for testing purposes. The provider team is then responsible for maintaining a set of golden test data and ensuring that it's available with each release of the software into the test environment. Any such golden data should be nonmutable by your tests, so they can run repeatedly on the same data.

### WHERE SERVICE VIRTUALIZATION FITS

It's possible to use contract testing without any virtual services. This assumes that the dependencies are deployed in a shared environment with all of *their* dependencies also available, on down the stack to the systems of record. Some organizations are either small enough or have invested heavily enough in shared infrastructure to make this possible.

An alternative strategy is for the team that manages the dependency to deploy a test instance available for contract testing and stub out its dependency through service virtualization. This is likely to increase the availability and determinism of the test instance, as it's now less subject to the whims of environmental hiccups.

As a client of a service that another team provides, you have the right to set some expectations of that service. An expectation that a test instance is available is both reasonable and common. You're better off if you can treat that test instance as a black box and have the provider team decide whether they run their test instance integrated or with virtual dependencies.

### 9.2.4   *Exploratory testing*

Historically, tests were divided into scripted and unscripted, where the script referred to a documented set of steps and expectations a manual tester executed. The heyday of meticulously cataloging test cases in commercial tools so that unskilled QA testers (remote from the application team) could execute them without any system context is gone. You still do scripted tests, but you automate them nowadays. Test design occurs as you write the test, and test execution occurs every time you run the test.

Exploratory testing combines test design and test execution into one activity, bringing discipline to unscripted testing. The ability to follow their nose is one of the defining characteristics of great QA testers. Exploratory testing allows them to investigate the software with an attitude of curiosity, unearthing its sharp edges through creativity rather than through predefined scripts.

The pendulum has swung quite far from the days of yesteryear, when all scripted tests were executed manually, to the point where I occasionally perceive a stigma associated with manual testing altogether. This is unfortunate. Exploratory testing is a fine art, worthy of its own study.[9] Whereas exhaustive automated testing mechanizes the toil of scripted test execution, exploratory testing puts the ghost back in the machine. It relies on human ingenuity to find gaps in your automation. Despite the widely held perception that microservices are too technical to manually test, there's a great deal of similarity between how you manually test an API[10] and how you test a traditional GUI.

I've seen people fall into two traps, both of which hurt their ability to gain confidence in your service. The first is treating the service as an implementation detail, a cog in a larger value chain, such that the only meaningful test is of the overall end user delivery (where "end users" might be customers or business users). The second trap is believing that the service is too technical to test on its own.

#### MANUALLY TESTING APIs

Overcoming the first trap requires a mindset shift. The more your organization thinks of the API exposed by your microservice as a product, the more likely you are to gain the scaling benefits of microservices. Amazon provides an easy to spot example: Amazon Web Services (AWS). AWS started off as a simple object store (S3), with an API to store and retrieve files. In short order, Amazon released EC2, which allowed programmatic access to managing virtual machines. Both S3 and EC2 are products, as are the hundreds of other products in the AWS suite. They have teams that manage them, they have customers, they provide self-service capabilities, and they hide the underlying complexity of those capabilities.

AWS represents a collection of public APIs, but the same principle applies for APIs you build for your enterprise. The trick is realizing that your internal development

---

[9] James Bach gives a good introductory overview at http://www.satisfice.com/articles/what_is_et.shtml.

[10] Services and APIs are often used interchangeably. Here I use "service" (or "microservice") as the implementation and "API" as the interface. The users of a service only see the API. In fact, they have no way of knowing if the API is implemented with one service or multiple, because you could use a reverse proxy to route requests to different services under the hood.

teams *are* customers. They have needs and use your service to fulfill those needs, saving them time and reducing the complexity of their overall solution. Understanding their needs helps focus exploratory testing.

Once you recognize that your API is a black box to your customers, you are free to test whether the black box behaves correctly. A good exploratory testing session would start by trying to solve an end-to-end customer problem with your APIs and adjusting the path from one API call to the next based on what you learn as you go. Do the errors make sense? Does the response provide hints as to what happens next? Sometimes you might discover that, although your API is functionally stable, it has significant usability gaps.

Another way to look at the second trap is thinking that, because there's no UI, manual testing of APIs doesn't make sense. Once you treat your API as a product, this argument disappears. Anytime you have customers (developers), you have a user interface. For APIs, that UI happens to be JSON over HTTP (or equivalent).

In fact, you have been manually testing an API throughout this entire book. Every time you use `curl` (or Postman, a graphical equivalent) to send an HTTP request to mountebank, you're using mountebank's developer-facing UI to test it.

## WHERE SERVICE VIRTUALIZATION FITS

You certainly can do exploratory testing without service virtualization. Indeed, at least some of the time, you should. It helps gain full system context and understand the types of data that downstream systems emit.

But exploratory testing requires QA testers to get creative. A large part of the exploration is finding out what they *should* test, which requires playing with some unusual setups. Virtualizing the dependencies can help provide additional knobs to tune during the exploration.

A real-world scenario may help make that advice concrete. In chapter 8, I described how we used mountebank to help test APIs that powered the consumer-facing mobile application for a large airline. Our team was blessed with a couple of superbly capable QA testers who, through exploratory testing, unearthed several problems with our APIs before we released them to the public.

Although some of their testing was manual, they used mountebank to test flows under certain scenarios. Going to the downstream integration points for those scenarios was quite onerous, so when they wanted to follow a flow involving a canceled flight (or a rerouted flight, overbooked flight, delayed flight, and so on), they used a set of mountebank imposters to facilitate the testing experience. The first time they tested a flow within a given scenario, like a canceled flight, they did so fully integrated so they could see real data. Once they had the data, they used mountebank imposters on subsequent test explorations.

Exploratory testing completes our whirlwind tour of the role of testing in a continuous delivery world, including where service virtualization fits and where it doesn't. We'll round out the next chapter by using mountebank to help us with performance testing.

## *Summary*

- A CD deployment pipeline includes automation that extends beyond the realm of testing, but testing is central to providing the confidence needed to release software frequently. The testing portion of the pipeline requires validations at multiple layers.

- Unit testing is as much a design activity as it's a bug-catching activity. Unit testing is in-process and, as such, uses traditional stubbing approaches instead of service virtualization.

- Service tests are postdeployment black-box tests of your application. Service virtualization ensures appropriate determinism.

- Contract tests help validate the assumptions that your application and your service tests make. They should focus on testing your assumptions rather than behaviorally testing the dependent service.

- Exploratory testing unleashes human creativity to find flaws in your software. Service virtualization may play a role in validating testers' hunches, or you may avoid it in favor of deeper integration testing.

# Performance testing with mountebank

The final type of testing we'll look at in this book is performance testing, which covers a range of use cases. The simplest type of performance test is a *load test*, which uncovers the system behavior under a certain expected load. Other types of performance tests include *stress tests*, which show system behavior when the load exceeds available capacity, and *soak tests*, which show what happens to the system as it endures load over an extended amount of time.

All of the tests we've looked at up to this point have attempted to prove system correctness, but with performance tests, the goal is to understand system behavior more than to prove its correctness. The understanding gained from performance testing does help to improve correctness through unearthing bugs (such as memory leaks) in the application, and it helps to ensure that the operational environment of the application is capable of supporting expected loads. But no application can support infinite load, and stress testing in particular is designed to break the application by finding the upper limits of capacity. While that's happening, a certain degree of errors is expected in many kinds of performance testing. The goal is to verify system behavior in aggregate rather than verify each service call independently. Performance tests often help define service level objectives—for instance, that a service responds within 500 milliseconds 99% of the time under expected load.

Performance testing can be difficult. Fortunately, mountebank is there to help.

## 10.1   *Why service virtualization enables performance testing*

One of the first difficulties organizations run into when putting together a performance test plan is finding an environment in which to run it. Sometimes, that environment is production.

Believe it or not, production can be a natural place to performance test under certain conditions. The first time you deploy a new application to production, it's usually before users are able to use it. That gives you an opportunity to validate the capacity of the system, as long as you are careful with the data. In more advanced scenarios, with new features in existing applications, you may even want to validate performance by synthetically manufacturing load in production before users are aware of the new feature. Facebook calls this dark launching, and did it for two weeks prior to allowing customers to set their own username. The functionality existed in production but was hidden, and a subset of user queries was routed to the new feature to verify it held up under load.[1] Facebook's scale may be unique—imagine generating load from 1.5 billion people—but approaches like dark launching can be valuable anytime you want to have additional confidence that a feature scales before releasing it to the public.

Most performance testing happens prior to production, with the unfortunate corollary that it rarely happens with integrations scaled to support production load. An all-too-common scenario is that, when performance testing outside of production, the application dependencies crash well before the application, making it impossible to verify service-level objectives (figure 10.1). When performance testing the application, you are implicitly making the assumption that *the application* is the weak link in the system. If it isn't, then you aren't really testing the application and will be unable to discover the load it can support with the hardware it's using.

Although those runtime dependencies are stable enough to handle production load in production, creating that level of stability isn't always economically feasible in lower environments. Supporting additional load requires additional hardware, and doubling the cost of production hardware for testing purposes is generally a hard sell. Many other reasons exist, some reasonable and some unfortunate, preventing nonproduction runtime dependencies from supporting the load you need to make your application the weak link. For example, it's often difficult and expensive to scale

---

[1]  See   https://www.facebook.com/notes/facebook-engineering/hammering-usernames/96390263919/   for more information.

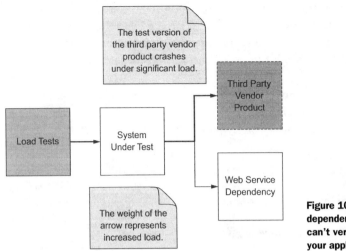

**Figure 10.1   When runtime dependencies are unstable, you can't verify the performance of your application.**

COTS (custom off-the-shelf software), especially when that COTS package runs on a mainframe.

Figure 10.1 looks like many other diagrams you have seen already, and for good reason. Performance testing sits within a class of problems that requires a more deterministic approach to testing an application with nondeterministic runtime dependencies. I hope by now you can spot exactly the class of problems that service virtualization aims to help. It's a problem that says "*if* the rest of the runtime ecosystem is more stable than my application, *then* I can determine the performance characteristics of my application." Service virtualization helps ensure that the application is the weakest link in the runtime ecosystem.

At some scale, you run into another problem: the virtualization tool itself becomes a weaker link than the application (figure 10.2). It's in effect a hidden dependency that exposes itself when the application's capacity exceeds that of the virtualization tool.

This problem exists with mountebank no differently from any other tool. The solution involves horizontally scaling the virtualization tool—running multiple instances with shared test data and using

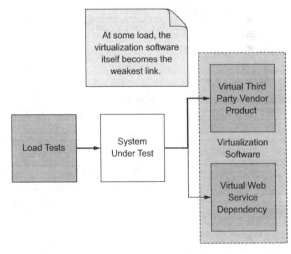

**Figure 10.2   At a certain scale, the virtualization tool itself becomes the problem.**

a load balancer to spread the load over the multiple instances. This is where mounte-bank stands apart from the crowd. Scaling commercial tooling is expensive, requiring additional licensing. Although a single instance of mountebank won't perform as well as a single instance of most of the commercial tools in the space, mountebank scales for free.

Capital One went through performance testing pain as it moved its mobile servic-ing platform to the cloud. Jason Valentino wrote about the cloud migration and acknowledged that they never anticipated the difficulty of challenges like perfor-mance testing.[2]

> *In fact, halfway through we discovered our corporate mocking software couldn't handle the sheer amount of performance testing we were running as part of this effort (**we completely crushed some pretty industrial enterprise software in the process**). As a result, we made the call to move the entire program over to a Mountebank OSS-based solution with a custom provision to give us the ability to expand/shrink our mocking needs on demand.*
>
> — Jason Valentino (emphasis his)

In the remainder of this chapter, we will stress test a sample service, finding its capac-ity. In doing so, we will follow a four-step process:[3]

- Define your scenarios.
- Capture the test data for each scenario.
- Create the tests for a scenario.
- Scale mountebank as needed.

Let's look at each of these steps in turn.

## 10.2   *Defining your scenarios*

Performance tests are all about figuring out common paths users will likely take, then calling those paths a *lot*.

For example, let's return to our favorite online pet store, but add a new compo-nent to make a more realistic performance testing scenario. You'll add a new adop-tion service that provides the pet adoption information, helping connect potential owners with rescue pets. (See figure 10.3.)

The service integrates with a public API from RescueGroups.org,[4] which makes it a perfect place to use service virtualization. Although you'd like to test the adoption ser-vice to make sure it can handle load, slamming a public API providing animal adop-tion information free of charge seems rude, especially when it's only for testing purposes. Every time you run your performance tests connected to a free public pet adoption service, your unintentional denial of service attack kills a kitten.

---

[2]  See   https://medium.com/capital-one-developers/moving-one-of-capital-ones-largest-customer-facing-apps-to-aws-668d797af6fc.

[3]  The steps are largely the same for other types of performance tests.

[4]  See https://userguide.rescuegroups.org/display/APIDG/HTTP+API for API details.

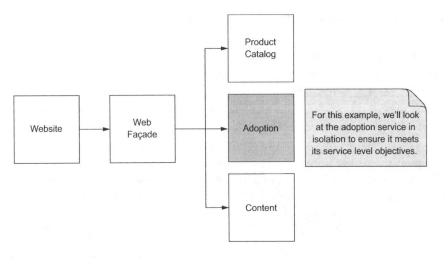

**Figure 10.3   Adding the adoption service to your pet store microservices**

A scenario is a multistep flow that captures user intent. The trick is to put yourself in the mind of a user and imagine a common sequence of activities the user would want to complete. In this case, because the adoption service is an API, the direct users will be other developers, but it will be in support of users on a website or mobile device, and their intent will be reflected in the sequence of API calls. You'd expect the end customers to search for nearby pets, maybe change the search parameters a few times, then click on a few pets. Let's formalize that into a performance test scenario:

- User searches for pets within a 20-mile radius of zip code 75228.
- User searches for pets within a 50-mile radius of zip code 75228.
- User gets details on the first three pets returned.

That scenario requires two APIs and five API calls in the process of completing two searches and providing three sets of details. The sequence of API calls with the adoption service would look like this:[5]

- GET /nearbyAnimals?postalCode=75228&maxDistance=20
- GET /nearbyAnimals?postalCode=75228&maxDistance=50
- GET /animals/10677691
- GET /animals/10837552
- GET /animals/11618347

The animal IDs may vary from run to run, as the data that the searches return changes over time. A robust test scenario would support dynamically pulling the IDs from the search, but you'll keep it simple to focus on the essentials.

   Now that you have a multistep scenario defined, it's time to capture the test data.

---

[5]  The GitHub repo for this book has the source code: https://github.com/bbyars/mountebank-in-action.

## 10.3   *Capturing the test data*

Accurately simulating a runtime environment for load tests requires that virtual services both respond similarly to how real services respond and *perform* like real services perform *in production*. A proxy can capture both bits of information, and for performance testing you'll almost always want to use `proxyAlways` mode. The default `proxyOnce` mode is convenient in situations when you want the saved responses to respond after the first call to the downstream service, but it's natural to separate the test data capture from the test execution in performance testing. Also, the richer set of data you are able to capture with `proxyAlways` often comes in handy. Recall from chapter 5 that `proxyAlways` mode means that every call will be proxied to the downstream system, allowing you to record multiple responses for the same request (where the request is defined by the `predicateGenerators`) (figure 10.4).

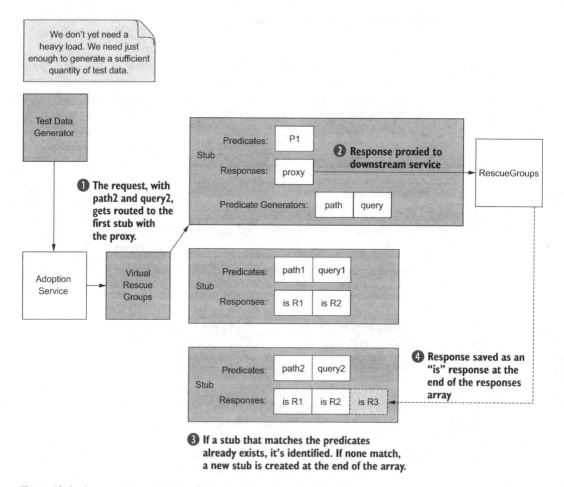

**Figure 10.4   A** `proxyAlways` **proxy allows capturing complex test data.**

Notice that the leftmost box in figure 10.4 isn't the performance tests themselves. You aren't ready for those yet; they come after you shut down the connection to the real RescueGroups API. At this stage, you want just enough load to capture meaningful test data. Anything more than that is an unnecessary load on downstream services.

### 10.3.1 *Capturing the responses*

This scenario is simple enough that you can capture data for the five API calls and replay it over and over again during the performance test run. Technically, this means you don't need `proxyAlways` mode for your proxy, but it's generally a good idea to use it anyway when you are doing anything mildly complicated with test data capture. The proxy stub looks like the following listing.

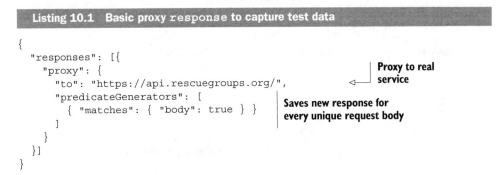

**Listing 10.1   Basic proxy `response` to capture test data**

```
{
  "responses": [{
    "proxy": {
      "to": "https://api.rescuegroups.org/",          Proxy to real
      "predicateGenerators": [                          service
        { "matches": { "body": true } }
      ]                                      Saves new response for
    }                                        every unique request body
  }]
}
```

The adoption service uses different URLs and query parameters for each of the five API calls, but behind the curtain, they route to the same URL in the RescueGroups.org API. RescueGroups.org uses a super-generic API in which every call is an HTTP POST to the same path (/http/v2.json). The JSON in the request body defines the intention of the call, any filters used, and so on. Recall from chapter 5 that you use a proxy's `predicateGenerators` to define the predicates for the saved response. Because each of your five API calls will send a unique request body to the RescueGroups .org API, differentiating requests by `body` makes sense. If you wanted to be more specific, you could use a JSONPath predicate generator to split on the exact fields within the `body` that are different, but that's overkill for this example. Once you have the proxy configured, you have to run your test scenario and save the test data (figure 10.5).

Anytime you use service virtualization, you have to be able to swap out the URL of the downstream dependency in the system under test. The adoption service

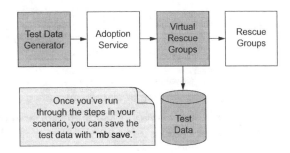

**Figure 10.5   Using a proxy to capture test data**

in the GitHub repo for this chapter supports using an environment variable to change the URL of the downstream service. Assuming you run your proxy imposter on port 3000, you could configure the adoption service like this:

```
export RESCUE_URL=http://localhost:3000/
```

With the proxy running and the adoption service pointed to it instead of the real service, you can capture the data for your five API calls with whatever HTTP engine you want, including `curl`. Assuming the adoption service is running on port 5000, that might look like

```
curl http://localhost:5000/nearbyAnimals?postalCode=75228&maxDistance=20
curl http://localhost:5000/nearbyAnimals?postalCode=75228&maxDistance=50
curl http://localhost:5000/animals/10677691
curl http://localhost:5000/animals/10837552
curl http://localhost:5000/animals/11618347
```

Once you have done that, you can save the test data:

```
mb save --removeProxies --savefile mb.json
```

With that, you have your responses. However, you need one more thing.

### 10.3.2  Capturing the actual latencies

To get an accurate performance test, you'll want to simulate the actual latency from the downstream service. In chapter 7, we looked at the `wait` behavior, which allows you to tack on latency to each response. You can capture it from the downstream system by setting the `addWaitBehavior` attribute of the proxy to `true`, as shown in the following listing.

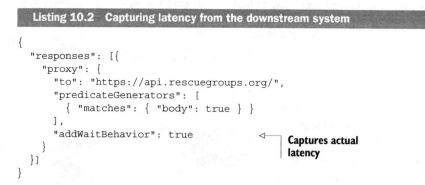

Listing 10.2   Capturing latency from the downstream system

```
{
  "responses": [{
    "proxy": {
      "to": "https://api.rescuegroups.org/",
      "predicateGenerators": [
        { "matches": { "body": true } }
      ],
      "addWaitBehavior": true            ⊲─┐ Captures actual
    }                                      │ latency
  }]
}
```

If you capture your test data again by making the five API calls to the adoption service and saving the data with `mb save`, the proxy will have automatically added the wait behavior to each of the saved responses. For example, in my test run, here's a trimmed down version of a saved response:

```
{
  "is": {
```

```
    "statusCode": 200,
    "headers": { ... },
    "body": "...",
    "_mode": "text"
  },
  "_behaviors": {
    "wait": 777
  }
}
```

**Omitted for clarity**

◁── **Wait 777 ms
before responding**

The two searches in the test run used to prepare this sample took 777 and 667 milliseconds, respectively, and the three requests for animal details took 292, 322, and 290 milliseconds. Those wait times were saved with each response to be replayed during the performance test run. The more data you capture during proxying, the more variability you'll have with your latencies.

### 10.3.3  Simulating wild latency swings

Our example assumes that the downstream system behaves correctly. That's a perfectly valid assumption to make when you want to see what happens when the system under test is the weakest link in the chain, but sometimes you also want to expose cascading errors that happen when downstream systems become overloaded, returning a higher percentage of errors and (even worse) responding increasingly slowly. If the environment supports recording proxy data under load, you may be able to capture the data from a downstream test system. If not, you'll have to simulate it.

The `wait` behavior supports an advanced configuration for this use case. Instead of passing the number of milliseconds to wait before returning a response, you can pass it a JavaScript function. Assuming you have started mb with the `--allow-Injection` command-line flag, you can simulate a wild latency swing with the following function. It usually responds within a second, but roughly every 10 times it takes an order of magnitude longer.

**Listing 10.3  Adding random latency swings with JavaScript injection**

```
function () {
  var slowdown = Math.random() > 0.9,
    multiplier = slowdown ? 10000 : 1000;
  return Math.floor(Math.random() * multiplier);
}
```

Instead of passing an integer representing a number of milliseconds, you'd pass the entire JavaScript function to the `wait` behavior. Assuming you saved the previous function in a file called randomLatency.js, you could use EJS templating:

```
{
  "is": { ... },
  "_behaviors": {
    "wait": "<%- stringify(filename, 'randomLatency.js') %>"
  }
}
```

The downside is that this doesn't work naturally with proxying, which captures actual latency.

## 10.4 Running the performance tests

You can write all of the tests up to this point in the book with traditional unit testing tools from the JUnit family. Performance testing requires more specialized tools that provide a few key features the JUnit-style tools don't:

- Scenario recording, usually by configuring the tool as a proxy between your HTTP executor (generally a browser) and the application you are testing
- Domain-specific languages (DSLs) for adding pauses, simulating the think time for users in between actions, and ramping up users
- The ability to use multiple threads to simulate multiple users sending concurrent requests
- Reporting capability to give you the performance characteristics of your application after a test run

Although many commercial options exist, some excellent open source performance testing tools are available that don't require you to open your checkbook. JMeter (http://jmeter.apache.org/) and a newer offshoot called Gatling (https://gatling.io/) are popular choices. You'll use a Gatling script simple enough to allow you to keep the focus on service virtualization without having to learn a whole new tool.

The Gatling download is a simple zip file, which you can unpack in any directory you desire. Set the GATLING_HOME environment variable to that directory to make the example easier to follow. For example, if you have unpacked it on your home directory in Linux or macOS, type this in your terminal (assuming you downloaded the same version used for this example):

```
export GATLING_HOME=~/gatling-charts-highcharts-bundle-2.3.0
```

The next step is to create a Gatling script that represents your scenario using its Scala-based DSL. I copied the sample scenario that ships with Gatling and adjusted it as shown in listing 10.4. As someone who has never programmed in Scala before, I found myself able to read and write most of the script quite fluently thanks to the expressive DSL. It executes your five API calls with pauses in between, representing the think time in seconds that the end users likely will take to process the results.

#### Listing 10.4  A Gatling script for your test scenario

```scala
class SearchForPetSimulation extends Simulation {
  val httpProtocol = http                               Base URL of
    .baseURL("http://localhost:5000")                   adoption service

  val searchScenario = scenario("SearchForPetSimulation")
    .exec(http("first search")                          Searches, with
      .get("/nearbyAnimals?postalCode=75228&maxDistance=20"))   think time
```

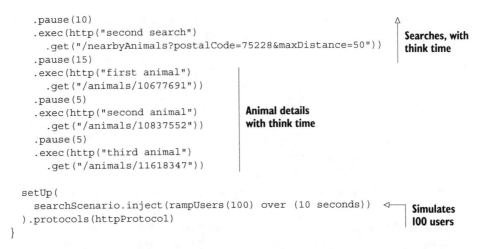

```
  .pause(10)
  .exec(http("second search")
    .get("/nearbyAnimals?postalCode=75228&maxDistance=50"))
  .pause(15)
  .exec(http("first animal")
    .get("/animals/10677691"))
  .pause(5)
  .exec(http("second animal")
    .get("/animals/10837552"))
  .pause(5)
  .exec(http("third animal")
    .get("/animals/11618347"))

setUp(
    searchScenario.inject(rampUsers(100) over (10 seconds))
).protocols(httpProtocol)
}
```

Searches, with think time

Animal details with think time

Simulates 100 users

The most interesting bit is near the bottom, which describes how many concurrent users you want to simulate and how long to ramp them up. It's fairly unrealistic to expect that, at max load, all users start at the same time, so most performance test scenarios account for a ramp-up period. Although 100 users isn't much, it helps you test out your scenario.

To run Gatling, navigate to the code for chapter 10 in the GitHub repo for this book and enter the following into your terminal.

**Listing 10.5  Testing your performance script**

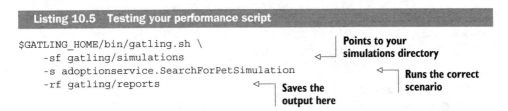

```
$GATLING_HOME/bin/gatling.sh \
    -sf gatling/simulations
    -s adoptionservice.SearchForPetSimulation
    -rf gatling/reports
```

Points to your simulations directory

Runs the correct scenario

Saves the output here

On my machine, running this scenario for 100 users takes a little under a minute, which is hardly enough to stress either the software or hardware but enough to validate the script. Once you're satisfied it's working, bump the users up an order of magnitude or two and rerun to see what happens:

```
setUp(
  searchScenario.inject(rampUsers(1000) over (10 seconds))
).protocols(httpProtocol)
```

On the MacBook Pro I'm using to create this example, the adoption service can handle 1,000 users with no problem but croaks pretty hard at 10,000 users. When I tried running with that many users, Google Chrome crashed, my editor froze, and I may have cried a little because of a failure to save work in progress, but, fortunately, no kittens died.

That's useful information—not just the kittens, but the number of users: the adoption service, when run on my laptop, has the capacity to support somewhere between

1,000 and 10,000 users concurrently. In addition to highlighting a horrific lack of error handling in the adoption service (subsequently improved), that information would help you determine the appropriate hardware to run in production based on the expected number of concurrent users trying to save a rescue animal from the pound.

I experimented a bit until I found a reasonable number of users that stressed the adoption service on my laptop without completely breaking it, which turned out to be 3,125 concurrent users. Understanding your application's behavior under stress is a useful activity for determining what happens at expected peak load and helps to validate your service-level objectives.

The test reports are saved in the "gatling/reports" directory you passed into the `-rf` parameter when you started Gatling. The HTML page gives you all kinds of information that helps you understand the performance characteristics of your application. The table shown in figure 10.6 comes from a report on one of my runs and shows the % KO (errors, with KO being both a common boxing abbreviation for knockout and a clever anagram of OK) and statistical information around response times for each request.

| STATISTICS | | | | | | | | | | | | | Expand all groups \| Collapse all groups |
|---|---|---|---|---|---|---|---|---|---|---|---|---|---|
| | ○ Executions | | | | | ⊙ Response Time (ms) | | | | | | | |
| Requests | Total | OK | KO | %KO | Req/s | Min | 50th pct | 75th pct | 95th pct | 99th pct | Max | Mean | Std Dev |
| Global Information | 15625 | 15591 | 34 | 0% | 318.878 | 8 | 447 | 906 | 1085 | 1386 | 1610 | 575 | 286 |
| first search | 3125 | 3125 | 0 | 0% | 63.776 | 905 | 912 | 919 | 1022 | 1152 | 1299 | 927 | 46 |
| second search | 3125 | 3125 | 0 | 0% | 63.776 | 625 | 636 | 644 | 673 | 714 | 729 | 641 | 15 |
| first animal | 3125 | 3113 | 12 | 0% | 63.776 | 11 | 314 | 333 | 440 | 471 | 501 | 329 | 45 |
| second animal | 3125 | 3107 | 18 | 1% | 63.776 | 12 | 347 | 380 | 1303 | 1408 | 1581 | 458 | 299 |
| third animal | 3125 | 3121 | 4 | 0% | 63.776 | 8 | 356 | 488 | 1335 | 1450 | 1610 | 519 | 332 |

Figure 10.6   Gatling saves error rates and response time data for each step of the scenario.

Service performance is often quoted as something to the effect of "99% of the time we promise to return in under 500 milliseconds at or below peak load." Clearly, you have some work in front of you before you can make that kind of guarantee.

## 10.5   Scaling mountebank

Given that the adoption service is a simple example, I was unable to get mountebank to crash under load before the service did. For production-quality services built by enterprises and deployed in a high-availability environment, that won't always be the case. When mountebank itself becomes the weakest link in your chain, you have some options.

The first and most obvious is to run multiple mountebank instances behind a load balancer (figure 10.7). This allows different requests to route to different mountebank instances, each configured with the same test data.

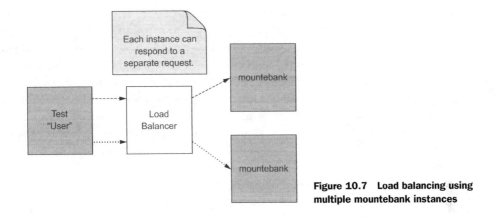

**Figure 10.7   Load balancing using multiple mountebank instances**

One situation requires additional thought. If the test data supports sending different responses for the same logical request, then you'll no longer be able to rely on a deterministic ordering of those responses. The diagram in figure 10.8 shows two calls to your virtualized instance of an inventory service, which should return 54 on the first call and 21 on the second. Instead, it returns 54 twice in a row.

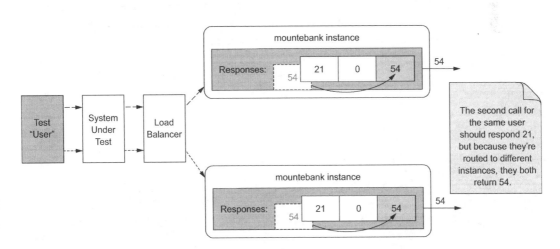

**Figure 10.8   Responses for the same request under load balancing yield unexpected results.**

There's no good way around this. Even if you use server affinity, a load balancer configuration that binds a client to the same mountebank instance for each request, you will likely still have the problem, because it's the system under test, not the test user, that's making the request to mountebank. In addition to load balancing, you should do a few things on each instance of mountebank to guarantee optimal performance.

First, avoid using the `--debug` and `--mock` command line options when running `mb`. These options capture additional information about the requests that the system under test makes to mountebank, which is useful both for debugging the imposter configuration and for verifying that the system under test made the correct requests. Although capturing that information during a behavioral test can be useful, performance tests require long-lived imposters. Computer programmers have a common phrase they use to describe the process by which a long-lived system remembers information without any mechanism of forgetting it: a memory leak.

Second, you will want to decrease the log output of mountebank. Mountebank uses a standard set of logging configuration levels—`debug`, `info`, `warn`, and `error`—and defaults to `info`. That sends some log output to the terminal and logging file on every request, which is unnecessary and unhelpful when you intend to send thousands of requests its way. I would recommend running with a `warn` level when you are writing and debugging performance scripts and with `error` during the test run. You do that by passing `--loglevel warn` or `--loglevel error` as a flag to the `mb` command.

Finally, you'll generally want to configure the responses mountebank sends back to use keep-alive connections, which avoid the TCP handshake on every new connection. Keep-alive connections are a *huge* performance increase, and the proxy will generally capture them because most HTTP servers use keep-alive connections by default. Unexpectedly, RescueGroups.org doesn't, at least in my test run, so the example avoids the use of keep-alive connections. This is probably appropriate because you're trying to accurately simulate the downstream system behavior. But it wouldn't be hard to write a simple script to postprocess your test data file and change the `Connection` headers to `keep-alive` in all of your saved responses, should you choose to do so.

Also remember that, if you're adding in simulated `is` or `inject` responses that you didn't capture through proxying, you'll have to manually set the `Connection` header to `keep-alive`, as mountebank defaults to `close` for historical reasons. The easiest way is to change the default response, as you saw in chapter 3:

```
{
  "protocol": "http",
  "port": 3000,
  "defaultResponse": {
    "headers": {
      "connection": "keep-alive"
    }
  },
  "stubs": [...]
}
```

And at long last, you have a complete performance testing environment that doesn't depend on any downstream system. And, best of all, no kittens were killed in the process.

Performance testing wraps up our tour of service virtualization. Although mountebank is clearly not the only tool you'll need in your tool belt, it makes many important contributions to allowing you to validate your application through a continuous delivery pipeline, even in a microservices world with a great deal of runtime complexity. Mountebank is always changing, and there's an active mailing list on the website, which I encourage you to use anytime you get stuck. Don't be a stranger!

## Summary

- Service virtualization enables performance testing by protecting downstream systems from load. It enables you to test your application as if it's the weakest link in the chain.
- Once you've determined your scenarios, you'll generally want to use a proxy in `proxyAlways` mode to capture test data. Set the `addWaitBehavior` to `true` to capture actual latencies.
- Tools like Gatling and JMeter support converting your test scenarios into robust performance scripts. Ensure you are running with virtual services if your goal is to find the capacity of your service without impacting downstream services.
- If mountebank itself becomes the constraint, scale through load balancing. Improve performance of each instance by decreasing logging and using keep-alive connections.

# index

## Symbols

& character  26
$ID token  145

## Numerics

3A pattern  13
400 Bad Request message  50
429 HTTP status code  134
500 status code  132, 149

## A

Abagnale service  66
Accept header  25
addWaitBehavior attribute  140, 208
allowInjection flag  110, 127, 132, 139, 152, 209
Amazon Web Services (AWS)  198
Announce method  165
AnnouncementLog class  167
AnnouncementTemplate  165
APIs (application program interfaces)
    manually testing  198–199
    test-by-test setup with  13–14
application protocol  156
ArgsFor method  170
Arrange-Act-Assert pattern  168, 189
assertISODate helper  196
assertString helper  196
asterisk character  69

asynchronous operations, adding  117–126
    starring mountebank repo  126
    starting OAuth handshakes  123–125
    validating OAuth authorizations  125–126
    virtualizing OAuth-backed GitHub clients  120–122
automated testing  194
automation, boundary of  186
AWS (Amazon Web Services)  198

## B

Base64 encoding  162–163
behaviors  130–152
    adding latency to responses  139–140
    complete list of  152
    decorating responses 132–139
        adding decoration to saved proxy responses 134–136
        adding middleware through shellTransform  137–139
        using decorate function  132–133
    overview of  131–132
    repeating responses  140–141
    replacing content in responses  141–152

copying request data to responses  141–148
looking up data from external data sources 148–152
binary mode
    predicates in  163–164
    with Base64 encoding 162–163
blocking I/O  119
boundary of automation  186
boundary of deployment  185
boundary of determinism  186
boundary of value  186

## C

callback function  124
canned responses
    cycling through  50–52
    default responses  46–49
        changing  49–50
        identifying complete HTTP messages  48–49
        reusing HTTP connections  47–48
    overview of  44–52, 105
    testing with  43–64
        HTTPS imposters  52–59
        saving responses in configuration files  59
capturing
    latencies  208–209
    responses  207–208
    test data  206–210

CAs (Certificate Authorities) 53, 106
caseSensitive parameter 81, 94
CD (continuous delivery) 179–200
  creating test pipelines 186–200
    balancing service virtualization with contract tests 194–197
    creating service tests 191–193
    creating unit tests 187–191
    exploratory testing 198–200
  overview of 180–186
  with microservices 182–185
Certbot 57
Certificate Authorities (CAs) 53, 106
CI (continuous integration) 180
circular buffer 19, 52
commercial virtualization tools 194
configfile command-line option 101
configuration files
  saving multiple imposters in 61–64
  saving responses in 59
configuring proxies 102–105
  adding custom headers 103–105
  mutual authentication 102–103
congestion 8
conjunctions with predicates 78–79
console.log function 128
contains predicate 71, 81
ContainsMethodName method 169
content in responses, replacing 141–152
  copying request data to responses 141–148
  looking up data from external data sources 148–152
Content-Length header 49, 171
continuous deployment 181
continuous integration (CI) 180
contract tests
  examples of 195–197
  managing test data 197
  overview of 184

service virtualization and 194, 197
convenience functions 136
copy behavior 142
copy field 194
CORS (Cross-Origin Resource Sharing) 146–148
COTS (custom off-the-shelf software) 203
create function 35
createContentImposter function 37, 192
CreateImposter function 167
createProductImposter function 37, 192
creation function 188
Crier class 165–166
csvToObjects function 112, 114
curl command 29–30, 45
custom off-the-shelf software (COTS) 203

**D**

-d@ command-line switch 45
data
  capturing test data 206–210
    capturing latencies 208–209
    capturing responses 207–208
    simulating wild latency swings 209–210
  from external data sources 148–152
  managing test data 197
debugging 128–129, 214
decorate function 132–133
decorating responses 132–139
  adding decoration to saved proxy responses 134–136
  adding middleware through shellTransform 137–139
  using decorate function 132–133
decryption 53
deepEquals predicate 75–76, 92
default responses 46–49
  changing 49–50
  identifying complete HTTP messages 48–49
  overview of 49
  reusing HTTP connections 47–48
default stub 46

DELETE command 38, 46
deployment pipelines 181, 185–186
describe function 37
deterministic tests 13, 186
dev complete 180
domain-specific languages (DSLs) 210
downstream capacity 9
DRY (Don't Repeat Yourself) 140
DSLs (domain-specific languages) 210

**E**

EcmaScript (ES) 35
EJS language 60
end-to-end testing 9–11
endOfRequestResolver function 173
endsWith predicate 72
engineering discipline 180
enterprise service bus (ESB) 175
equals operator 18
equals predicates 67, 72
ES (EcmaScript) 35
ESB (enterprise service bus) 175
escape characters 69
exists predicate 77–78, 85
exploratory testing 184, 198–200
  manually testing APIs 198–199
  service virtualization and 199–200
external data sources 148–152

**F**

fallback proxy 105
feature complete 180
File.readlines function 118
filename variable 60
fromDataSource field 151

**G**

GATLING_HOME variable 210
GET method 24, 99
GitHub clients 120–122
greaterThan predicate 110

grouped matches 143–145
GUID (globally unique
        identifier) 144

**H**

handshakes 123–125, 171
hardening iterations 180
hasThreeDaysOutOfRange
        function 114
headers 103–105
HTTP
    converting HTTPS to 106–107
    messages, identifying 48–49
    reusing connections 47–48
httpRequest.call() function 124
httpRequest.end() function 124
HTTPS
    converting to HTTP 106–107
    imposters 52–59
        trusted, setting up 56–58
        using mutual
            authentication 58–59

**I**

I/O operations 118
identifiers, matching on
        paths 73–74
imposters
    HTTPS 52–59
        trusted, setting up 56–58
        using mutual
            authentication 58–59
    multiple, saving in configura-
        tion files 61–64
    overview of 16, 28, 66
    TCP, creating 158–159
include function 61
inject response type 19, 109, 131
inventory checks 51
Invoke-RestMethod
        command 30
ipWhitelist flag 127
is response 19, 88–91, 97–101
ISO format 196

**J**

JSON format
    direct predicates 81–82
    values
        predicates with 81–83
        selecting with
            JSONPath 82–83

jsonpath parameter 80, 83
jsonpath predicateGenerator 94
JSONPath tool
    capturing multiple values 96
    generating predicates 94–95
    selecting JSON values
        with 82–83

**K**

keep-alive connections 48
keys 53

**L**

latencies
    adding to responses 139–140
    capturing 208–209
    simulating swings 209–210
Let's Encrypt 56
link layer 156
localOnly flag 127
loglevel debug flag 128
lookup behavior 142

**M**

MarshalByRefObject 165
matches predicate 68–71
matching
    grouped matches 143–145
    identifiers on paths 73–74
    multivalued fields 76–77
    object request fields 74–75
    XML payloads 161–162
matchingRequest function 34
mb protocol 28
mb replay command 101
mb save command 101, 103
metacharacters 69, 73
microservices
    CD with, testing strategy
        for 182–185
    evolution of 5–7
    organizational structure
        and 7–9
    overview of 4–9
    testing 3–21
        end-to-end testing, chal-
            lenges of 9–11
        mountebank, overview
            of 16–20
        service virtualization 11–16
        service virtualization tool
            ecosystem 20–21

middleware, adding 137–139
mock option 214
monoliths 4
mountebank
    HTTP and 24–27
    overview of 16–20
    starring repo 126
Mule ESB 175
multivalued fields,
        matching 76–77
mutual authentication 58–59,
        102–103
mutualAuth field 58, 102

**N**

namespaces, support for 85
.NET Remoting framework
    creating clients 165–167
    virtualizing servers 167–171
    virtualizing services
        indicating where messages
            end 171–176
        overview of 164–171
Netcat 159
nonblocking I/O 119, 136

**O**

OAuth protocol
    OAuth-backed GitHub clients,
        virtualizing 120–122
    starting handshakes 123–125
    validating
        authorizations 125–126
object request fields,
        matching 74–75
OS (operating system) 118

**P**

parameterizing predicates 80–81
parseInt function 139
paths, matching identifiers
        on 73–74
payloads, XML
    manipulating 161–162
    matching 161–162
PEM format 55
performance testing 201–215
    capturing test data 206–210
        capturing latencies 208–209
        capturing responses
            207–208

performance testing *(continued)*
  simulating wild latency
    swings 209–210
  defining scenarios 204–205
  running tests 210–212
  scaling mountebank 212–215
  service virtualization
    enabling 202–204
persistent data stores 14
pipelines
  deployment pipelines 185–186
  test pipelines 186–200
    balancing service virtualiza-
      tion with contract
      tests 194–197
    creating service tests
      191–193
    creating unit tests 187–191
    exploratory testing 198–200
Postman 32
predicate injection function 126
predicateGenerators 91–93, 160
predicates 65–86
  adding parameters 93–96
  case-sensitive 80–81
  conjunctions with 78–79
  creating 91–96, 109–114
    capturing multiple JSON-
      Path values 96
    capturing multiple XPath
      values 96
    for JSONPath 94–95
    for XPath 95–96
    with predicateGenerators
      91–93
  deepequals predicate 75–76
  exists predicate 77–78
  in binary mode 163–164
  matches predicate 68–70
  matching multivalued
    fields 76–77
  matching object request
    fields 74–75
  overview of 18, 31, 66–80
  parameterizing 80–81
  predicate injections vs
    responses 126–127
  replacing with regular
    expressions 71–72
  selecting XML values 83–86
  types of 68–74
    complete list 80
    matching any identifier on
      path 73–74
  with JSON values 81–83

direct JSON predicates
  81–82
selecting JSON values with
  JSONPath 82–83
preflight responses 146–148
printf debugging 128
private key 53
process discipline 180
product catalog services 27–32
productCatalog object 187
promises 39
protocols 153–176
  binary support 162–164
    binary mode with Base64
      encoding 162–163
    predicates in binary
      mode 163–164
  overview of 154–155
  virtualizing .NET Remoting
    service 164–176
    creating clients 165–167
    indicating where messages
      end 171–176
  virtualizing .NET Remoting
    servers 167–171
proxies
  adding decoration to saved
    proxy responses 134–136
  as fallbacks 105–106
  configuring 102–105
    adding custom
      headers 103–105
    mutual
      authentication 102–103
  replaying 100–101
  setting up 88–90
  TCP, creating 159–160
  use cases 105–107
proxy response type 19
proxyAlways mode 98, 206
proxyOnce mode 96, 206
proxyResponseTime field 90
public key 53
PUT command 63

**Q**

query parameter 26
querystring parameter 74
question mark character 69

**R**

rate limit exception 135
real imposter 66

record/replay behavior 14–16,
  87–107
  capturing multiple responses
    for same request 96–100
  configuring proxies 102–105
    adding custom
      headers 103–105
    mutual
      authentication 102–103
  generating correct
    predicates 91–96
    adding predicate
      parameters 93–96
    capturing multiple JSON-
      Path values 96
    capturing multiple XPath
      values 96
    creating predicates with
      predicateGenerators
      91–93
  proxy use cases 105–107
    converting HTTPS to
      HTTP 106–107
    using proxies as
      fallback 105–106
  replaying proxies 100–101
  setting up proxies 88–90
regex (regular expressions) 68,
  71–72
removeProxies flag 101
repeat behavior 140–141
repeating responses 140–141
replayable parameter 101
replaying proxies 100–101
request data, copying to
  responses 141–148
  using grouped matches
    143–145
  using XPath selectors
    145–146
  virtualizing CORS preflight
    responses 146–148
request library 39
requests, capturing responses
  for 96–100
respondingWith function 34
response injection function 123,
  126
responses
  adding latency to 139–140
  capturing
    multiple for same
      request 96–100
    overview of 207–208

copying request data to
141–148
using grouped
matches 143–145
using XPath selectors
145–146
virtualizing CORS preflight
responses 146–148
cycling through 50–52
decorating 132–139
adding decoration to saved
proxy responses
134–136
adding middleware through
shellTransform 137–139
using decorate
function 132–133
dynamic, creating 114–127
adding async 117–126
adding state 116–117
predicate injections vs
126–127
repeating 140–141
replacing content in
looking up data from
external data sources
148–152
overview of 141–148
saving in configuration
files 59, 61–64
retrieve function 188
RPCs (Remote Procedure Calls),
stubbing 157–162
creating TCP imposters
158–159
creating TCP proxies 159–160
manipulating XML
payloads 161–162
matching XML payloads
161–162
runtime dependencies 203

**S**

SaaS (software-as-a-service) 105,
195
same-origin policy 146
savefile argument 101
scaling 5, 212–215
scenarios, defining 204–205
security 127–128
Serialize method 169
servers, .Net Remoting 167–171
service test 183
service virtualization 11–16

contract tests and 194, 197
examples of 195–197
managing test data 197
enabling performance
testing 202–204
exploratory testing and
199–200
overview of 16, 194
persistent data stores 14
record and replay 14–16
test-by-test setup using
APIs 13–14
tool ecosystem of 20–21
shellTransform behaviors 21,
132, 137–139
SignatureFor method 170
simulating latency swings
209–210
soak tests 201
software-as-a-service (SaaS) 105,
195
spanned reports 116
starring mountebank repo 126
startsWith predicate 72
state parameter 116
state.humidities array 117
states, adding 116–117
stress tests 201
string escape character 69
stringify function 60–61, 112,
128
stub() function 190
stubs 18

**T**

TCP (Transmission Control
Protocol)
creating imposters 158–159
creating proxies 159–160
overview of 155–157
stubbing text-based TCP-
based RPCs 157–162
manipulating XML
payloads 161–162
matching XML
payloads 161–162
TDD (test-driven
development) 187
TearDown method 168
test case construction 141
test-driven development
(TDD) 187
testing
contract tests
examples of 195–197

managing test data 197
service virtualization
and 194, 197
creating test pipelines
186–200
end-to-end 9–11
exploratory testing 198–200
manually testing APIs
198–199
service virtualization
and 199–200
mapping strategy to deployment pipeline 185–186
microservices 3–21
mountebank, overview
of 16–20
service virtualization 11–16
service virtualization tool
ecosystem 20–21
performance testing 201–215
capturing test data 206–210
defining scenarios 204–205
running tests 210–212
scaling mountebank
212–215
service virtualization
enabling 202–204
service tests, creating 191–193
strategy for CD with
microservices 182–185
test-by-test setup using
APIs 13–14
unit tests, creating 187–191
with canned responses 43–64
HTTPS imposters 52–59
saving responses in configuration files 59
writing tests 33–40
then function 39
TLS (transport layer
security) 44
TownCrierGateway function 168
Transfer-Encoding header 49
transport layer security
(TLS) 44
transport protocol 156

**U**

unit testing pattern 13, 183
updateInventory function 158,
161
upstream capacity 9

**V**

validating OAuth
  authorizations 125–126
value, boundary of 186
virtual imposter 66
virtualization tools 194
virtualizing
  .NET Remoting servers
    167–171
  .NET Remoting services
    164–176
    creating .NET Remoting
      clients 165–167
    indicating where messages
      end 171–176
  CORS preflight
    responses 146–148

exploratory testing and service virtualization
  199–200
OAuth-backed GitHub
  clients 120–122
product catalog services 27–32

**W**

wait behavior 132, 139–140,
  208–209
wildcard certificates 58
withStub function 34

**X**

x-rate-limit-remaining
  header 134, 136

XML language
  payloads
    manipulating 161–162
    matching 161–162
  selecting values 83–86
XMLHttpRequest object 118
XPath language
  capturing multiple values
    96
  generating predicates
    95–96
  selectors 145–146
xpath parameter 80, 84
xpath predicate 95

**Z**

zero-character match 70

# How the book is Organized

*Story Building: Narrative Techniques for News and Feature Writers* is a guide to the use of narrative elements in news and feature stories. These specialized skills and practical approaches to journalistic storytelling are explained in 15 chapters. Taking into account the diversity of teaching and learning approaches, I have structured this book in such a way that journalism educators, students, newspaper editors, writing coaches, reporters and writers can adapt the contents to suit their specific needs. Each chapter can be read on its own or in conjunction with other chapters, or existing journalism books. The chapters are organized as follows:

1. *No News Is Hard News*
2. *Manic Curiosity: Gathering Information for the Narrative Story*
3. *Finding the Shoehorn: Aggressive Observation*
4. *Interviewing for Narrative: Why Interview when you can Chat?*
5. *Staying on Top of the Interview: Practical Tips*
6. *The Abuse and Use of Descriptive Detail*
7. *Language and Style*
8. *Stealing from the Novelist's Bag of Tricks*
9. *Laying out the Facts: How to Tell the Narrative Story*
10. *Leading to the End*
11. *Greed and Grit: Guided Tour of a Storyteller's Mind*
12. *Persuasive Storytelling: Not a Matter of Opinion*
13. *Between Typing and Writing: The Narrative Art of Reviewing Art*
14. *A Story about Getting Hired*
15. *Freelancing: Narrative for Hire*

Chapter 1, *No News Is Hard News,* situates narrative in the context of daily news reporting and writing, and provides a framework for the adaptation of narrative to daily journalistic assignments.

Chapter 2, *Manic Curiosity: Gathering Information for the Narrative Story,* emphasizes that narrative writing, and indeed all forms of journalistic writing, thrives on exhaustive reporting. It also offers a range of practical reporting techniques.

Chapter 3, *Finding the Shoehorn: Aggressive Observation,* provides instruction on effective observation and explains how to use aggressive journalistic observation to convert a routine occurrence into an engaging narrative. The chapter helps readers develop a higher level of curiosity.

Chapters 4, *Interviewing for Narrative: Why Interview when you can Chat?,* portrays the interview for narrative stories as an art of conversation, and uses real examples from working journalists to explain how to collect information for news, features and profiles.

Chapter 5, *Staying on Top of the Interview: Practical Tips,* provides guidelines on how to convince unwilling sources to speak to reporters, how to manage the trickiest interviews, and how to ask tough questions without upsetting sources or scuttling the interview.

Chapter 6, *The Abuse and Use of Descriptive Detail,* confronts one of the big criticisms of narrative: excessively colorful and detail-burdened writing. The section shows how to capture compelling details and use them judiciously and effectively.

Chapter 7, *Language and Style,* uses a jargon-free practical approach, to show you can energize your writing by applying key elements of good writing such as simplicity, portrayal of action, specification, imagery and bringing clichés to life.

Chapter 8, *Stealing from the Novelist's Bag of Tricks,* explains to readers how to adapt the key elements of fiction writing to daily news and feature writing.

Chapter 9, *Laying out the Facts: How to Tell the Narrative Story,* discusses the design and construction of the narrative story, and identifies and processes story elements that will be used to construct the story based on the Fat H model. The chapter offers a new concept of transition—as the story's inner intelligence and logic and the order of story details—as opposed to the traditional concept of transitional devices.

Chapter 10, *Leading to the End,* guides the reader through the construction of a journalistic story from the lead to the ending. The chapter introduces a fourth part of the story, the descent, to help writers set the stage for a resounding ending. The introduction of the descent is significant because the traditional story comprises the introduction (lead), body (middle) and ending.

In Chapter 11, *Greed and Grit: Guided Tour of a Storyteller's Mind,* the reader tags along with star writer and reporter Gary Tippet as he "vacuums up" details and explains how he turned those details into throbbing stories that won him awards.

Chapter 12, *Persuasive Storytelling: Not a Matter of Opinion,* applies narrative techniques to opinion writing.

Chapter 13, *Between Typing and Writing: The Narrative Art of Reviewing Art,* shows readers how to plan and write strong reviews using narrative techniques.

Chapter 14, *A Story about Getting Hired,* discusses the challenges of finding journalism jobs and offers practical and tested tips on how to use narrative techniques to captivate hiring editors around the world.

Chapter 15, *Freelancing: Narrative for Hire,* explores the freelancing market and shows readers how to write strong query letters using narrative techniques.

# Acknowledgements

*Story Building* is the outcome of a lifelong exposure to instruction, inspiration, motivation, guidance, love, patience, and a bit of growling, by people who care about life, journalism, storytelling and me. How else can I thank them except in a story? God has blessed me with a life and an abundance of stories and storytellers, and people to thank. I can trace the beginnings of my journey into storytelling to a childhood of peculiar privilege and opportunities, of youthful excitement, of a silly war, and afternoons in the woods. My little sister and I left home at seven, and ran the two miles to avoid being late and being made to run around the school soccer pitch five times. One beautiful day, I ducked into the woods, when the other kids were not looking, and spent time roaming the bushes reflecting on life, watching and scaring birds, eating wild berries that slapped my tongue, and swimming till my eyes turned red. I slid back into my elementary school uniform and into the stream of pupils marching home at about 2.50P.M. Then a war came to rescue me from school. Schools were instantly shut. Now I could discover the woods without having to play truant. When aerial bombardments intensified, families shifted in-country. We settled in an uncle's abandoned house in a tiny village. The living room had a piano, three cushion chairs, a rickety baby stroller, and two shelves filled with foreign magazines, including *Time* and *Newsweek*, and loads of books. My favorite was *The Abominable Showman*. I did sometimes wonder what a show man was doing on snow. My excitement about the book was probably unnerving Dad. One morning, without looking up from the 91st Psalm he was reading aloud in the King James Version, and saying, irritably I thought, "It's *The Abominable Snowman*." In the evenings we played moonlight games and listened to refurbished stories about the cleverness of the tortoise. African languages and stories have a distinct color, depth, warmth, wit and variety. The mixture of danger and boredom bred curiosity and adventure, and stories. War brought fun and freedom, and people from around the world: Germans, Dutchmen, Japanese, Austrians, Britons, Scandinavians and Americans. I befriended a bearded American Red Cross doctor named Steve Lerman, who let me play with his manual typewriter—picking one key at a time with a single finger, as I still do to day—when he was not preparing reports about starving children. I had it all: a war, freedom, an endless stream of stories, and Dr. Lerman's typewriter. Another American doctor, Phil Darney, lent me his books and spent all his spare time with me. A few years later, I produced my own newspaper and named it The Rocket. My journey into journalism had begun. To Steve and Phil who remain my friends; to my uncle, Etim Eno; who left his library; I am inextricably indebted.

I am grateful to both my parents for allowing me the freedom to discover the world and the word for myself. Dad taught me something else: how to die. In June 2003, as he entered his car to go to hospital, he flashed a radiant smile and, with calm and affection, said "Jesus", and passed away. And Mom taught me that, even though I looked like a chicken, I should always remember that I am an eagle—and fly.

Hundreds of people contributed to the conception, preparation, research, writing, editing and production of this book. I would like to thank everyone who offered assistance and advice.

Gene Roberts, a former editor of the New York Times and my professor and mentor at the Phillip Merrill College of Journalism, University of Maryland, College Park, deserves my gratitude for formally introducing me to narrative writing and continuing to provide strong support and inspiration. I am grateful to Mark Kramer, professor of journalism and Director of the Nieman Program on Narrative Journalism at Harvard University, for admitting me into the Nieman narrative fold and featuring me as speaker and panelist at Nieman Narrative Journalism conferences. I would like to thank Ted Conover, renowned author and narrative writer; Marc Lacey, *New York Times* correspondent and bureau chief; Doug Foster, professor at Northwestern University's Medill School of Journalism; and Liz Hart, head of the Journalism program at Monash University, Australia, for their insightful comments and for their endorsement. This book is also endorsed by British journalist and writer, Richard Dowden, who, as Africa Editor of *The Independent* (London), signed me on as the paper's stringer in West Africa.

I owe special thanks to Reese Cleghorn, professor of journalism and former dean of the Merrill College of Journalism, University of Maryland, for supporting my work and introducing me to then editor of the *San Jose Mercury News*, Jerry Ceppos. I hold fond memories of my time at the *Merc's* San Jose and Palo Alto newsrooms and the challenges and thrills of writing narrative op-eds and news stories for the paper. I owe my sustained passion for narrative largely to editors of newspapers around the world who, even in the days when hard news was the norm, took chances with my narrative efforts. Lowe Davies as executive editor of the Pulitzer-winning *Daily News* (St Thomas, US Virgin Islands) published and praised breaking news stories I wrote in the narrative for the newspaper that until then published only hard news.

My best friend, Ima, worked tirelessly with me through the night, to prepare and polish the manuscript for publication. I am deeply grateful to her. I am blessed to have Patti Belcher as Commissioning editor. Patti knows how to make things happen. Her enthusiasm, support, speed and efficiency accounted for the timely publication of this book.

I owe special gratitude to my colleagues in Australia, especially Gary Tippet, for sharing his narrative skills and letting us into his brilliant narrative mind. Patty Buchanan, journalist and teacher, who as a cub reporter interviewed one of the key players in the Watergate scandal that led to the impeachment of President Richard Nixon, agreed to share the details of that interview with us. Buchanan also copy-edited parts of this book. I am singularly indebted to Peter Pierce, writer and professor of Australian Literature at James Cook University, Australia, for his brilliant, sincere and humorous comments and suggestions.

# 1

## No News is Hard News

*In the Age of Information, the sheer amount of fact that is overcoming and over-whelming us day by day instills in us a need for stories to make sense of all the views of our lives.* —Brendan Cahill

Let's start with the labels. What type of story are you going to write? News features, same-day features, second-day features, backgrounders, color stories, profiles, seasonals, historicals, how-to-do-it features, lifestyle/trends, investigative pieces, human interest stories, first-person accounts, and new journalism pieces.[1] These are all types of feature articles.

Unfortunately, few readers know that what they are reading is a color story, a seasonal, or a how-to-do-it feature. Readers do not care whether they are reading a backgrounder or a first-person account. They want to be sure that the story is factual, meaningful, well researched, balanced and an easy and pleasurable read. Readers want stories that hold their interest, stories about people and things they can relate to.

For that reason, we will downplay the theoretical distinction between story types and formats. It will, instead, concentrate on the central techniques for writing good newspaper and magazine stories—of any kind. A story is a story, whether it comes in the form of news, feature, review, or opinion. The key role of the journalistic story is to serve the interest of the reader.

Anthropologist Barbara Myerhoff portrays the human species as *homo narrans,* or narrative beings (storytellers). We are by nature storytellers or narrative beings. Narratives define human life and identity in that they "structure the meanings by which [our] culture lives."[2] Key elements of our culture are based on storytelling. Kathleen Hanson and Nora Paul portray early human communication as great narrative and our forebears as narrative gurus:

> Early humans made elaborate cave paintings long before writing or printing were invented. Archaeologists think these paintings had several purposes—to catch and hold attention, to shock and frighten, to imprint information in memory . . . . Modern societies rely on stories told in a variety of ways to explain how the world works, why the established order prevails, and why things are the way they are.[3]

Today, our myths, news accounts, paintings, television and films all tell a story. Allan Bell calls journalists the "professional story-tellers of our age" who write stories, not articles.[4] Journalistic news is a form of storytelling that, like all forms of storytelling, uses selection, editing, condensation and exclusion to construct story elements that confer on occurrences a clear social significance. Cohan and Shires, affirming the narrativity of news, surmise that "a narrative recounts a story,"—a set of significant and meaningful events occurring "in a temporal sequence." The newspaper, the oldest and most enduring formal mass medium, reports and critically analyses newsworthy occurrences and issues of public interest. It invigorates democracy, sets the agenda for social change and public debate, and serves as a historical document of life and governance. The newspaper conveys information to the public in coherent narrative units of newsworthy and meaningful actions and perspectives. We call these units stories. Newspaper readers expect to read narrative accounts of what happened.

This narrative approach to news depicts the crucial social function of journalistic news: ordering and personalizing experiences, communicating and explaining the dramas and dilemmas of daily life. The very nature and strategy of storytelling places "the power of telling society's stories in the hands of journalists."[5] Dele Olojode, a 2005 Pulitzer Prize winner and former foreign editor of the New York *NewsDay* finds "no real difference between the narrative form and journalism, because journalism depends on the narrative in order to communicate powerfully with the audience."[6]

As Olojode put it, every journalistic story is a narrative:

> I do not think that there is really any other way of writing news except to do it in the narrative format. That is certainly how I have done it. Primarily because I saw myself, in all the years that I have been foreign correspondent and reporting from all corners of the globe, as a storyteller. I always imagined that there was a little old lady in Long Island, New York, picking up the 1,000 pages of *NewsDay* on Sunday morning, and relying on me to take her to places she will never be in her life . . . . Even when I deal with breaking news, this has never been a stylistic problem for me.[7]

Signaling their recognition of news as an essential narrative, media scholars studying narrative forms have identified elements that define narrative journalism. These elements include the conscious admission, omission or amplification of certain story details, the focus on people and a conscious effort to highlight narrative details that establish a connection with the reader or audience. Woodstock describes this relationship as the "communicative exchange between the narrator and the audience."[8] This exchange signals the difference between stories (narrative) and articles (hard news).

The inverted pyramid or hard news style produces articles and not stories. Technically, hard news is "anti story" because the writer "tells the story backwards and is at odds with the storytelling tradition that features a beginning, middle, and end."[9] Unlike stories, the punch line of the inverted pyramid comes at the beginning of the story and, as Bell put it, "finishes in mid-air".[10] The dismissal of the inverted pyramid or hard news style as an anti-story is apt because for a piece of writing to qualify as a story, it must have a beginning, a middle or body and an end.

To appreciate the nature, significance and struggles of the inverted pyramid as a predominant model, it is essential to place it in historical and contemporary context. The birth of newspaper journalism in England in the early 1600s triggered a current of social and political awareness that crept into the United States a century later. It is generally accepted that with the invention of the telegraph in 1844, journalism swept across the world delivering what journalists considered the key points of the previous day's local and international news to readers by the following morning. The inverted pyramid was born soon after the commercialization of the telegraph. The Mexican War in 1846, merely two years after the invention of the telegraph, gave the inverted pyramid style a boost. American war correspondents filing daily reports of the war triggered in the public "a large appetite for this new type of immediate news" dispatched instantly to their newspapers by telegraph.[11] However, filing stories was expensive. The telegraph often broke down while reporters' stories were being filed. To save costs and to ensure that the key points were relayed before a technical problem developed, editors instructed correspondents to go straight to the point, relaying the most important point quickly. The first few paragraphs, written to hurriedly answer the six crucial questions or the "5Ws and H" (what, who, where, when, why and how) were published. The key points that gave a summary of what happened became known as hard news. This method also allowed sub-editors the luxury of laziness. If a story was too long for the allocated space, sub-editors could cut the last paragraphs even with their eyes shut. More importantly, by giving readers the most critical bits of information quickly so they could move to other stories, the inverted pyramid was considered a time saver.

This arrangement of 'hard' news details in a descending order of significance came to be known as the inverted pyramid. Journalistic reports of what happened the previous day remained fresh the next day because there were no competing media such as radio, television and the internet at that time.

The writer's principal challenge was to rank information according to what the reporter considered important and interesting. The most important information came in the introduction or lead, which usually summarized the story. The second paragraph supported the lead, usually by explaining it or providing correlating or corroborating information or a direct quotation. The remaining paragraphs offered some additional information, and the final paragraphs contained background and context, which readers needed to be able to understand the story. The primary purpose of hard news writing, Hanson argues, "is to describe the event by recounting the 'who, what, when, and where,' and less frequently the 'why' and 'how' of the story."[12]

James Stovall defends the inverted pyramid structure, observing that "putting the most important information at the top allows the reader to decide quickly whether or not to stick with the story"[13]— a subtle indication that readers don't spend much time on of hard news articles. That is probably why some believe that the use of the inverted pyramid style guarantees that "the great majority of readers will not read the story to the end" and that, "many readers, in fact, will not get past the headline and the lead paragraph."

Narrative reporters and writers adopt a different approach and serve a different purpose. The Readership Institute distinguishes "a story type from a writing style," describing the featurized style as:

- More narrative, with a beginning, middle and end
- Often told through characters or using anecdotes to help illustrate points
- Likely to use more colorful language and a more playful writing style
- More engaging to the reader than a traditional news story. [15]

For Shah, narrative makes news meaningful to people.

In the . . . narrative model, the emphasis is on understanding how apparently discrete events fit into ongoing processes. Journalists interpret the meaning and significance of the "facts of the case" rather than letting the facts speak for themselves. To understand the subject upon which they are reporting, journalists rely not only on officials and experts but also on ordinary local people and their grounded knowledge about the situation. The purpose of their work is to provide an explanation of why the news is relevant and a cognitive "map" that attempts to illuminate the significance of the current historical moment. [16]

By buying a copy of the newspaper, readers are paying a premium, so to speak. They cannot readily travel to places where news is breaking. Even if they could afford the trip, few readers would want to travel from San Jose to San Francisco, from Seven Sisters to South Kensington, or from Venice to Vanuatu, just to witness a crime, a workers' strike, or the signing of a treaty. That is why they pay a premium that funds the reporter. The reporter is therefore expected to become the eyes, ears, noses, fingers, feet, knees, telescopes and microscopes of the public. Readers want to be put on the scene and given first-hand details of an occurrence. This enables them to grasp what happened and decide what to make of the occurrence. The 1993 standoff between U.S. law enforcement officers and the Waco, Texas, sect, the Branch Davidians, led by David Koresh, provides a good example of how reporters can engage readers. *The Philadelphia Inquirer* captured an element of the unfolding drama:

WACO, Texas: The end began with a phone call.
A few minutes before dawn, the phone that had been the vehicle for thousands of hours of fruitless negotiations rang one final time.
The FBI had a simple message: The time for talk is over; we are moving in with tear gas; surrender now.
The news was not well received inside the compound where David Koresh and his followers had held forth under siege for 51 days. The line abruptly went dead. [17]

Reporters are able to go where no camera could to bring readers rare glimpses and context. The sequencing of action and the fluid structure of narrative produce a climactic implication.

Narrative is not a style reserved for feature writing and other long-haul stories. It serves daily news reporters pursuing breaking stories. "It can be the most effective way to tell even a hard news story," notes Rick Bragg.[18] Bragg offers a snapshot of his experience covering hard news as narrative to a cruel deadline.

> In perhaps the hardest breaking news story I have ever worked on, the Oklahoma City bombing, The New York Times allowed me do a front-page [narrative] story on the scene. The story was written in less than two hours, because it had to be. [19]

To write the stories that turned into a series in the unfolding macabre drama, Bragg "borrowed a snippet, a snapshot, from every tale of great sadness" he had picked up in the course of reporting the story and painted this picture:

> After the explosion, people learned to write left-handed, to tie just one shoe. They learned to endure the pieces of metal and glass embedded in flesh, to smile with faces that made them want to cry, to cry with glass eyes . . . . They learned to sleep with pills, to sleep alone. Today, with the conviction of Timothy J. McVeigh in a Denver Federal court, with cheers and sobs of relief at the lot where a building once stood in downtown Oklahoma City the survivors and the families of the victims of the most deadly attack of domestic terrorism in United States history learned what they had suspected all along: That justice in a faraway courtroom is not satisfaction.[20]

Bragg used strong narrative elements to tell this breaking story. He said the rhythm of narrative made writing faster. For Bragg, narrative makes readers read a story they might merely have glanced at. Narrative seeks to give readers pleasure, a connection, and entertainment.

Let me share my own experience on the beat. An uncompleted building belonging to a real estate magnate in an American town was knocked down. By mid morning, the small town was abuzz with perplexed excitement and gossip. I was sent to cover the story that appeared quite insignificant.

The hard news was that one of the many buildings belonging to the town's major landlord was bulldozed at dawn. The landlord, by the way, had sold the land and building to someone who wanted to build the town's third department store.

I rushed to the site and kept vigil for three hours as tractors and earthmovers leveled the structure and excavated other areas. Reaching out beyond the hard facts, I asked the chief demolition man how long he had been demolishing houses, how many houses he has pulled down, what went through his mind as he was doing this particular demolition job, and whether he sometimes felt a pang of remorse or a rush of adrenalin when he was flattening houses. I ended up with a story that stated in the lead that [the name of the demolition man] has knocked down [total number of] houses with his bulldozer for [a specified number of] years, but this demolition has thrust him in the news. "Yesterday he rode his bulldozer like a deft horseman."

By this approach, I sought to widen the story's perspective and human appeal, generate interest and retain meaning and significance long after the event occurred, thus freeing the story from the constraints of time. The hard news version of the same story—Demolishers yesterday knocked down a building belonging to a property magnate—would have been, well, pedestrian, aloof and stale. Those hard details were broadcast on the radio and television on the morning of the occurrence, a full day ahead of my story. What is more, the event was already the talk of the town. I felt I needed to look beyond mundane hard news details and try to gather additional material to be able to tell a fresh and engaging story people can relate to.

A global study conducted for the British Broadcasting Corporation (BBC), the global news agency, Reuters; and the Media Centre, a U.S think tank, showed that television was the most trusted news source worldwide. Another significant study showed that readers found newspaper articles (the majority of which are written in the inverted pyramid), compared to television news, to be little significance to their lives.[21]

In a survey of newspaper readers commissioned by the American Society of Newspaper Editors (ASNE), the Readership Institute determined that a high proportion of stories written in the narrative style increased reader satisfaction by making newspapers easier to read and more appealing.

The writer who looks beyond the hard news provides the reader a richer reading experience, using perceptions, styles and techniques that include grace, humor and irony, without sacrificing meaning, immediacy and public interest. Narrative stories offer readers a multidimensional account of what happened and how and why the event should interest them. A good story balances matters of public concern and relevance with matters of light but vital interest, thus blurring the conceptual and stylistic distinction between hard news and feature. Identifying common characteristics of all journalistic writing should help us establish a kind of benchmark—and a framework—for good journalistic reporting and writing.

We shall now look at some of the key indices of a good journalistic story. A good story should explore as many dimensions of occurrences as possible. The story should be engaging and relevant to people and remain so for as long as possible, drawing readers into a sense of proximity to the story and the people or circumstances in it. Narrative establishes a connection between the elements and people of the story and the reader. Unlike disposable hard news articles, narrative offer details that reflect and enrich the values of the readers. It is not surprising that readers considered newspapers that ran narrative (non-inverted-pyramid) stories as "more honest, fun, neighborly, intelligent, in the know, and more in touch with the values of the readers."[22]

What determines good writing, therefore, is not the preset structure, but a devotion to enriching the reading experience: not structure but content. I am not essentially criticizing the existence of the inverted pyramid or hard news format, or any other news writing structure, but recognizing content over shape, and recommending a mind frame and professional procedures and practices that produce interesting and meaningful stories.

In the *Philadelphia Inquirer* story in Waco, Texas, the reporter chose content and a news writing approach that presented information in a natural and captivating way.

The structure of the featurized or narrative story is fluid. The lead, angle and structure of the story arise naturally from the nature and precision of data gathered on the subject. From all the information gathered, the writer determines the mood and the essence of the occurrence, which will determine the approach and shape of the story. The writer casts a wide net in the search for compelling details, sometimes pulling in and using information a hard news reporter may consider inconsequential, even frivolous. Those who swear by "hard facts" should pay attention to what Michelangelo, the great artist, said: "Great art which is not a trifle, consists of trifles." These trifles are known as "details: realistic detail, corroborative or circumstantial detail, concrete detail," notes Oakley Hall, a novelist and writing coach. The effective use of details is discussed in Chapter 6.

The journalistic storyteller builds the story with these implicative or corroborative details that make it easy for readers to relate to the people and the events in the story.

Good writing is the product of good reporting. Rare and insightful details that illuminate life, action, ideas and situational and human character often produce an arresting lead. The role of the writer shifts from the hard-news imperative of fitting information into a preset geometrical structure to that of weaving and connecting the story's components into an engaging reader-friendly story.

Matt Larney, my student at Australia's James Cook University, knew something about the elegance of realistic detail. When the class returned from our foreign news tour of duty in Thailand, Larney, who pursued a story on the conditions of Australian drug convicts in Bangkok, started his story this way:

> Peter Miles does not look out the window of his cell anymore. The last time he did he saw his best friend in Bangkwang Prison being led off to execution.
>
> Death comes with very little warning in Bangkwang. A bell will ring at 4.15 P.M. The prisoner to be executed will be dragged from his cell, across the yard and will be shot eight times. Sometimes eight shots are not enough and another eight shots will be fired. It is usually over by 4.30 P.M.
>
> Miles used to look out of the window of his cell when he heard the execution bell, to see who was going to die. The last time he did this was February of this year. He looked down and his friend looked up, knowing Miles would be watching. He smiled, waved at Miles and went to his death. "Since they took him, I can't look anymore," said Miles.

Larney's attention to corroborative detail brought the story to life and provided readers a rich and rewarding reading experience. It would be hard to find a story that cannot benefit from the storytelling elements used in narrative accounts. The big questions for newspaper reporters and editors are: Would something that happened yesterday afternoon be considered fresh or breaking news this morning? "Why should newspapers merely repeat what most readers already knew?"[23]

In the end, this is not about which writing style is superior. As Roy Peter Clark put it, pitting "narrative against traditional methods of news writing" is the "false dichotomy of the moment." This is about better reporting, and it's about better service to readers. This is about fulfilling what Clark calls the "journalist's primary duty", which includes "civic clarity" and "focusing on the needs of those we serve". Our journalistic, observes Clark, duty "leaves plenty of room for the telling of 'real' stories." That is why storytelling skills are a must for the 21st Century journalist.

# 2

## Manic Curiosity: Gathering Information for the Narrative Story

*The universe is made of stories, not atoms.* —Muriel Rukeyser

A good story is a reunion of nouns and verbs and not of adjectives and adjectives. That is to say that good writing is the accurate and committed depiction and explanation of action rather than the mere description of it. Narrative does not pose to journalists a "writing problem," notes Northwestern University journalism professor, Douglas Foster.[1] It's all in the reporting—keen journalistic observation and saturation research and interviewing. The journalistic storyteller is driven by manic curiosity and a passionate desire to discover and deliver action that will grab and retain the attention and excite the senses of readers. The astute journalistic storyteller does this by putting in motion meaningful actions that create in readers a ringing plausibility and a conspiratorial sense of being in the know. Narrative reporters provide a mental picture of the world. Every morning newspaper reporters help readers discover the meaning and significance of those life-defining moments, actions and decisions of the day before. Good writing is the piecing together of these actions into a coherent, meaningful and memorable account, while making readers see, smell, touch, feel and hear what is happening next door or thousands of miles away from them. The narrative story promises to "reveal the usually hidden, unidealized 'felt life' of individual people."[2] The next chapter will show you how to engage your senses so you can discover and communicate compelling details that would bring out the felt life. When our mind, eyes, ears are trained and our senses become alert and our antennae are up, we begin to attract the subtle but powerful details—those details that non-journalists and hard news reporters easily miss—that will make your story sing. We shall start with standard means of gathering details for the story.

With the explosion of Internet use among journalists, and the emergence of targeted courses, like computer assisted reporting and online journalism, finding documents has never been easier. First-year journalism study introduces students to paper trailing skills (phone books, court records, libraries, official records, and more). Internet search engines have become indispensable tools for background information and an avenue for local, national, regional and international angles to stories. The web provides reporters and editors verifiable story sources and story angles.

Google, Ask.com, and Altavista are among the most widely used search engines. At the turn of the 21st century, Google (www.google.com) surged ahead as the leading, comprehensive, user-friendly Internet information provider.

Do you want to know what color the governor of Nebraska's hair is? Do you want to find out the names of prominent witches in the United Kingdom, the pope's phone and fax numbers, or information about his family? Do you want to know which Australian brothels are trading on the Australian Stock Exchange? Simply type the key words into the dialogue box of Google and click the 'Google Search' button. Even then, search engines alone cannot meet all the research needs of the modern journalist. Internet databases, serving investigative reporters in computer-assisted reporting (CAR), are also great assets for general reporters and researchers.

In the United States, the National Press Club offers a database of excellent sources (http://npc.press.org/sources) searchable by keyword, category or organization. Christopher Callahan points to the PR Newswire's ProfNet (http://www2.profnet.com/login_prn.jsp?jsessionid=1431841109090092105).[3] Kitty Bennet provides a rich list for journalists looking for expert sources on deadline at (http://sunsite.unc.edu/slanews/internet/experts.html). Roland De Wolk lists a variety of sources including the "Reporter's Network" (www.reporters.net). He also recommends "A Journalist's Guide to the Internet" (http://reporter.umd.edu) and the "Reporters Internet Guide" [4] Reporters may, on finding the web site's search function, type the key words of the organization or topic they are researching. One of the numerous reporter-friendly web sites is http://assignmenteditor.com, which has useful links sites for such topics as breaking stories and in-depth and investigative reporting. Information on the use of the Internet designed for journalistic research is widely available, some of it tailor-made for specialized CAR or investigative reporting assignments.

Many journalists and students join listservs and other discussion groups. A listserv—an abbreviation for listserver—is a server and mailing list that drops a copy of each e-mail sent by a subscriber to the list in the mailboxes of all the subscribers on the list. Journalism listserv subscribers are reporters, editors, media teachers, and observers. Listserv subscribers join a list to contribute their expertise and to learn from experts in the field. Journalists may send a question or comment to the listers (members of the list), triggering a variety of answers from experts and people familiar with the subject. Say, you were working on a story about AIDS in California. You could ask the list for contacts in California, recent or old stories, background, anecdotes, figures, or studies.

A directory of listservs that are particularly useful to journalists can be found at a site called Liszt (www.liszt.com), on the web sites of American universities, particularly the University of Maryland (www.umd.edu), or on search engines like Google, Journet, Nicar-L, Carr-L, Jeanet, SPJ-L and Copyediting-L (the L standing for Listserv).

Discussion groups or newsgroups are issue-based Internet chat rooms. Many newsgroups are not moderated. Also, time zones can make international participation difficult. Unless saved, messages disappear after the discussion session. Unlike listservs, however, discussion groups allow for instant, if fleeting, conversation and feedback. It is also possible to use discussion groups as a story idea-generating and interviewing tool, using the archive function in such major newsgroup sites as http://groups-beta.google.com. Stephen Quinn offers a word of advice: "be specific. A search using the key word 'journalism' and selecting the 'all newsgroups' option produced 150,000 hits in May 2000."[5]

Because it is difficult to ascertain the veracity and authority of responses from news group subscribers, reporters need to cross-check and cross-reference information they receive from listservs.

# Web of Problems

The Internet—a melting pot of computer-linked information—is merely a host of information, not a type or content of information. People place information on the web. It would therefore be inaccurate to say that the web is inaccurate. Take a glass of water. The web is the glass and the information is the water. If the water is polluted, it would be wrong to blame the glass. Rather, we should check the source of the water. Likewise, journalists should investigate the reliability and authority of the authors of web articles before using such information. For journalists, information found on the web, just like information from other sources, is not gospel. It has to be checked out. Good reporters treat information from the web as a lead for further journalistic inquiry, and not as an end product.

The best journalistic use for the Internet is as a tool for recruiting sources. Reporters should look up the authors of the information they find on the web and make an effort to "interview" them (if not face-to-face, by telephone or e-mail) as well as other competent sources on the topic. Journalists need to confirm the authenticity, authority and plausibility of information posted on the web.

The Internet is just one of the many newsgathering tools. Interviewing, a major newsgathering tool is discussed in considerable detail in the next two chapters. Instead of duplicating general newsgathering techniques covered by many competent authors and teachers, this chapter will concentrate on the building of a framework for journalistic inquiry. This framework provides the basis and impetus for thorough newsgathering. Familiarity with tools alone does not produce good journalism. Almost anyone can rake up tools. The formulation of a mental map or framework that sets the stage for brilliant reporting is critical to good newsgathering. This framework, combined with keen observation, discussed in Chapter 3, and a right frame of mind, should prepare the reporter mentally for the challenges of effective and exhaustive interviewing that will be discussed in Chapters 4 and 5.

# Reporting for Story

The depiction of precise and concrete action, rather than colorful words, makes writing appealing. Good reporters and writers life to readers in strong nouns and verbs. This is because people act, people die, events happen, things change, and human life thrives on nouns and verbs.

The ability to collect ample detailed and relevant action is what we may call exhaustive reporting. With information obtained through exhaustive reporting—capturing ample, detailed, precise, corroborative and implicative action—a writer is equipped to create terse, dramatic sentences. Remember that it is not in the writing; it's in the reporting. Here is how *National's* Richard Meyer used the outcome of careful information gathering to create sentences capable of "pounding the reality of the disaster into your soul with specific images" in his news story.

> Hurricane Bertha smacked the Carolina coast Friday like the back of a devil's hand, hurling its 35-mile eye across Cape Fear, blinding the beachfront with rain, and wrecking homes and businesses with 105-mph winds that flung shards of glass through the streets.
> Skies darkened . . . . Riptides and 9-foot breakers crashed into boardwalks. A pleasure boat struck a major bridge and shut it down.[6]

The reporter captured the drama by gathering and animating strong nouns and verbs (Bertha smacked the Carolina coast; hurling, blinding, wrecking, at 105 mph, and flinging shards of grass through the streets). The conscious collection and articulation of action, and the absence of artificial colors of adjectives and adverbs, gave the story its dramatic force.

Remember that a story is as good as the variety, quality and implicative nature of the details the reporter captures. It follows that a reporter with an inquiring and attentive mind will report more effectively, and write better copy than a reporter with a truckload of clever phrases, but dull reflexes.

A narrative story is not just enjoyable or rich in detail; it serves the social function of journalism: giving people information that will enrich and secure their lives and the quality of their participation in democratic governance. Journalistic reporting requires a specific mental orientation. This orientation involves reflecting on the assignment beforehand and identifying conditions and frames of journalistic inquiry that serve journalism's civic function. In other words, we need to reflect on the outcome or function of our stories. The outcome of a story or the effect it will have on life will depend largely on the depth of the reporter's journalistic inquiry.

I shall use a plausible journalistic example of a fire in a small town library to explain the three models or levels of reporting that journalism and communication scholars have identified. We will call these three levels:

- Reactive reporting
- Perspective reporting
- Reflective reporting

Say, a fire guts the reference section of the Tuscaloosa public library in Alabama. I chose Tuscaloosa for no other reasons than the town's poetic name.

# Reactive Reporting

We could report the Tuscaloosa fire mechanically as hard news or spot news. This approach to newsgathering is called reactive because the reporter responds to and feeds on what people say about what happened. Such stories echo the subjective opinions of officials and witnesses.

At this level, the reporter gathers information relating to what happened and the immediate perceivable effects of the occurrence. The five W's and H— property damaged, time, cost, reasons, casualties, places and comments—power this level of reporting.

The sources of information for this story would normally be a press conference, the mayor, the chief librarian, a few eyewitnesses, the police, and other officials. The reporter pores through newspaper clippings, police logs, official reports, and court papers. Little observation is involved because the reporter is intent on giving the "objective" official position. Because the reporter bases the story on the sources' perceptions of what happened, the story will naturally be filled with attribution tags: "he said" and "she said."

The problem with mechanical reporting is that the reporter relies principally on sources that can be manipulative or easily manipulated. Usually, individuals who have a stake in the news event have their own agenda and considerable control over the information they give to reporters. The information they give is often self-serving. In addition, the story driven by this kind of reporting offers information for its own sake—just information, with no perceivable social context, meaning, or implications. The story leaves readers wondering why they needed to read the story, what the point of the story was.

Conceptually, reactive reporting is superficial and the story has little or no clearly defined significance. For this reason, the life span of the news is short. The fire goes out, the library is shut down, or someone gets fired. People express regret or other emotions, and the story drops dead.

# Perspective Reporting

Stories that touch our lives live and interact with us and help us answer some of life's questions raised by the story. At the perspective level, the reporter reaches beyond what happened—what, when, where, who and other superficial details— to delve into the hows and whys of the fire: it was caused by a faulty switch. The perspective reporter will look at the factors that made it happen and for answers to burning questions. Some of the questions would be:

- What guidelines govern fire safety at the library?
- Whether the guidelines were adhered to?

- Who was in charge?
- Who was to blame and who is to be praised?
- What preventive measures were taken or not taken?
- What were the real causes of the fire?
- How quickly did the fire department respond to the 911 call?
- How effectively did the fire department handle the fire?
- What specific books were lost and are they replaceable?
- What backup plans exist in this library?
- What are the practical implications of the fire on library users?
- Did the city council make provisions for safety and contingencies?

The perspective reporter will look at the immediate consequences of the event on specific individuals and on the community as a whole and the policies and procedures that govern safety. He or she will also look at individual and collective responses to and responsibility for the fire.

At this level of reporting the journalist goes beyond the immediate details of the occurrence to broader questions on the system that produced the event. In doing so, the reporter interviews more sources and scrutinizes more documents. The reporter also broadens and deepens the questions he or she asks officials, witnesses, and other members of the public. At this level, the public sees the cracks in the system and is equipped with the information to demand change, explanation and accountability. This approach offers a richer and more satisfying reading.

Even so, the solutions this story can produce would be cosmetic and ineffective—much like administering a painkiller for a broken bone: you find the symptoms, silence them or get rid of them, but you leave the initial problem intact. The fire started because of a faulty electrical connection caused by a shoddy job by the library's assistant electrician, Bob Firebrand. The library board may decide to fire Bob for his negligence. But does that solve the problem? Will a perfect electrician or electrical installation stop all related problems in this and other libraries and public places in the future? Is the library funded at a level that guarantees an end to such disruptions? These are some of the many questions that remain unanswered at the perspective level of reporting.

# Reflective Reporting

Reflective reporting focuses on the bigger picture or redemptive perspectives of an occurrence: the broader patterns and trends that relate to and actually explain the event and accord it social significance or meaning. For example, while official negligence might have contributed to the library fire, broader social, structural, and even political patterns might have contributed to or explained the incident. There could be socio-economic or political realities like reduced funding (for public services including the fire service, other public services or libraries), or a major domestic, or national policy shift. It could be the consequence of a national or international development—the same way the high cost of gas may be the result of global oil politics, even regional instability thousands of miles away—way beyond council ineptitude. It could also be a trend. For example, owing to the emergence of on-line libraries in the state of Alabama, the local council in Tuscaloosa decided to reduce funding or staff levels, resulting in a drastic drop in library use. Do people still visit or like to spend time in traditional libraries? Is there anyone we know or can relate to who visits the library regularly and who is distressed by the incident? What other types of libraries or arrangements are there? Are there any studies on these services? Are traditional library users heading elsewhere (say, to McDonalds, bars, or casinos)? Why?

At this level, the reporter's ears are on the ground, and not just on the lips of officials and witnesses. The reporter examines the minute details as well as the larger perspective. He or she will now use anecdotes and other narrative techniques to bring the story home to readers and pave the way for a deeper understanding of, and lasting and meaningful solutions to, the problems that brought about the fire at the Tuscaloosa library. Sources will include ordinary people.

After all, a story is an interaction of people and/or forces to produce conflict that the characters try to resolve. That is why reactive reporting, on which the hard news style is hinged, has become less attractive as a means of capturing and making sense of society's daily realities. The hard news mindset of reporters is a major reason many of the stories in many 21st Century newspapers linger on the reactive level.

By asking deeper and wider-ranging questions, and using a richer variety of details and sources, the reporter would need to gather material at more than one level to be able to write an engaging narrative story quickly and on deadline.

# 3

## Finding the Shoehorn: Aggressive Observation

*Talent is a long patience. It is a matter of considering long and attentively what you want to express, so that you may discover an aspect of it that has never before been noticed or reported. There is a part of everything that remains unexplored, for we have fallen into the habit of remembering whenever we use our eyes, what people before us have thought of the thing we are looking at. Even the slightest thing contains a little that is unknown. We must find it. —Flaubert*

Let me take you to an African village, the home of Chucky. There is a lot to learn from Chucky. It is 4.30 P.M., and Grandma is back from the Big Market with a brown four-month-old chicken. I name the chicken Chucky. Chucky's initial owner had trekked 14 miles to the local market. This makes it near impossible for Chucky to find her way back if she wanted to escape. Grandma tethers Chucky to a mango tree in front of the house to keep her from running away. After dinner the family goes to sleep, leaving poor Chucky still tied to the mango tree.

The next morning, I release Chucky and let her roam the 10-mile expanse of the unmapped village, pecking and tilling in an eternal scavenge for bugs. It is sunset and dinnertime, a sign for all chickens to start their uncharted journey back to their neighborhoods and homes. Chucky struts back to the yard, past dozens of houses and a maze of unnumbered village alleys and streets. She flies up the mango tree and nestles on the lowest branch. Night falls. Standing on one leg like a deft ballerina, Chucky falls asleep with her head tucked into her left wing.

## The Chucky Test

What has Chucky got to do with journalistic observation? She used the neatest form of journalistic observation to trace her way back to her new home after spending only one evening in the new surroundings before roaming a strange village in search of food. For Chucky to be able to navigate her way back, she had to activate all of her senses. Those tiny blood-shot eyes registered the smallest details of every tree and shrub and every house and shed. She observed that behind Grandma's auburn-colored detached house two mango trees caressed each other and a purple-leaved wild pineapple grew on the thatched roof. Every smell, every sound, every shape, every movement, every shade of color counted.

If you think Chucky's observation exercise was easy, here is a little test to help you see exactly what it was like for the chicken.

If you are in a room, have someone read the following paragraph out loud to you. Shut your eyes tight.

What's the color of the floor? And walls? How many light points are there? Is there a TV in the room? What brand is it? If there is anyone else in the room: what is the color of the eyes and hair, shoes, shirt or dress of the person nearest to you? What is the brand of your watch? What is the brand (label) of the shirt or dress you are wearing? Is there a poster or notice in the room? What does it say?

Now open your eyes. How did you perform in the Chucky test? If you could not answer all the questions correctly, do not be dismayed. Few students in my feature writing class could answer similar questions about the classmate beside them and about the classroom they had occupied for four semesters. In a certain class, not one student could say the brand of his or her own watch, clothing or shoes.

More than other people, journalists need to be aware of their environment. They must be able to observe, to notice things others ignore. They have to go to the Chucky School of Observation (CSO). Observation requires a conscious effort.

Now, observe in your environment things about yourself and others that would ordinarily escape your notice. Observation could be an enlightened application of our personality to an object or situation. It is a subjective enterprise; everyone has a unique way of seeing or feeling things. The fable of the blind men and the elephant is a good example of enlightened subjectivity. It goes like this:

> "God bless me, but the elephant is very like a wall!"
> "This wonder of an elephant is very like a spear!"
> "I see," quoth he, "the elephant is very like a snake!"
> "'Tis clear enough the elephant is very like a tree!"
> "This marvel of an elephant is very like a fan!"
> "I see," quoth he, "the elephant is very like a rope!"

We cannot rely on someone else's observation. No two people are identical, and two people rarely ever perceive things in an identical way. Our distinct personalities should produce dimensions or perspectives of objects that, like us, are personal and unique. Good observers remain before the object until that object becomes new and unique to them, and no longer resembles what others have seen. When a writer captures a new dimension of a familiar object, scene or event, the story earns greater appeal because it presents a fresh and challenging dimension of life – a dimension that would have remained unknown had that unique person not given it that peculiar interpretation.

Oakley Hall portrays the writer as an observer, but insists that "what the writer observes, and collects, are the details that show, that reveal, that imply, that specify, that build character and forward the story."

The reporter does not choose what to observe but takes in everything, and then determines what is significant in the context of the story. For instance, a minor occurrence in a courthouse may take on significance at a company's board meeting.

A seemingly insignificant detail may harbor powerful symbolism. When the Libyan leader Muammar Gadhaffi showed up at an Arab summit wearing a single glove, many reporters ignored the strange sight. A reporter from *The Guardian* (UK) asked questions. In a front-page story, *The Guardian* reported that Gadhaffi wore the lone glove to avoid direct physical contact with moderate Arab leaders who had shaken hands with Israeli leaders. That insight made it easier for readers to understand the atmosphere of distrust that in turn exposed the power play at the summit. The dynamics and outcome of that summit had serious implications for global peace and gas prices—a kind of psychological profile of the people who control the oil, the product that controls our lives in faraway North America.

Observation opens the way for further inquiry and therefore richer, fuller, more explanatory and more significant stories.

Some journalists insist that observation hurts the lofty ideals of hard news reporting. Well, they could very well have been one of those reporters who, along with Ernest Hemmingway, then a reporter, waited for the start of the press conference called by the almighty Italian leader Benito Mussolini. The story has it that the reporters were ushered into the conference room where Mussolini was already seated. While hard news twiddled their thumbs and waited idly for the start of the news conference, Hemmingway's eyes darted about. Hemmingway noticed that the Italian strongman was reading a book. He tiptoed up close and craned his neck to see what he was reading. His discovery: Mussolini was reading the French dictionary—upside down. The emerging insight revealed Mussolini's character, equipped the reporter with rich material for a captivating story, and offered readers illuminating insights.

# What observation offers a story

Observation can enrich a story by bringing to it:
1. Vitality
2. Precise Information
3. Filling gaps in a story
4. Human Drama
5. Making the Invisible Visible—finding the 'shoehorn'.

## 1. Vitality

A keen eye for detail can vitalize an ordinary occurrence. A few dozen army recruits snapping to attention to receive their commission is nothing out of the ordinary. That is, unless the reporter decides to pull in intricate and implicative detail to make the story explode with connotation, grace, and appeal. Helena Bachmann in the *TIME* story titled "Keepers of the faith" (June 3, 2002, p.49) captured the passing out parade of Vatican servicemen:

> Twenty-eight army recruits stood at attention at a swearing-in ceremony on May 6, each holding his weapon—a combination of spear and battleaxe called a halberd and listening intently to the boss' pep talk. "I hope that despite the heaviness of your service you will live this time of mission as a deepening of your faith," he said. Of course not many armies can boast that their commander is Pope John Paul II, the peace-loving head of the Roman Catholic Church.

By capturing precise details, including the fine physical and moral elements, the writer presented an energetic and meaningful account of a seemingly ordinary event.

## 2. Precise Information

Precise information tells a truer story than approximate or loose details.

- *Imprecise*:　　A woman graduated last week.
- *Precise*:　　Convicted serial killer, Maria Clintwood, received a law degree at Oxford University last week.

- *Imprecise*:　　A man was eating lunch.
- *Precise*:　　The lawyer tucked into his ham sandwich.

- *Imprecise*:　　Frank Spencer participated in a boxing tournament.
- *Precise*:　　Frank Spencer knocked out Sugar Ray in the third round.

Note how Gary Tippet, a reporter for the *Age* (Australia) used precise details to capture chilling details: April Spearing's skull is in the fridge.

> The fridge is in a cool room near the operating suites on the first floor of the Alfred Hospital and April's skull is on a rack inside, wrapped in gauze impregnated with the antibiotic Gentamicin, in a sterile plastic container, labelled and chilled to minus 70 degrees.
>
> It is not her entire skull of course, or April wouldn't be sitting up in bed in another hospital 15 kilometres away, smiling and saying how she can't wait to finally have it put back in her head tomorrow.
>
> In the package is April's frozen frontal bone: a glistening, grey-white, blood-speckled, ragged-edged, slightly ovoid bowl. Split roughly in half, a small jagged shard chipped out of each piece, it looks a little like a dessert dish

someone dropped and broke. Intact, it would be probably 115 or 120 square centimetres of bone—big enough to leave a hole the size of a middleweight's fist where April's forehead used to be.

Precision or specification, which will be explored in greater detail in Chapter 7, is one of the key attributes of good writing. Because reflective reporting sets the stage for good writing, specific and accurate portrayal reveals the dedication and competence of the writer as a thinking gatherer of information.

## 3 Filling the Gap

As a reporter for the *Daily News* in the U.S. Virgin Islands, I was sent to cover a fatal car crash. I used telling details to fill a factual and dramatic gap. The watch was what we may call the "eureka object"—telling the public (and police) the precise moment the accident happened. The details about what the driver was wearing (a red swimming trunk under his pants), and the music from an FM station (which was still playing) to which they were listening on the radio when death came calling, gave readers an idea of the mood, level of concentration, and state of mind of the driver. These details provided insights to the accident that witnesses and even the police missed.

## 4. Human Drama

The police and emergency services left the scene of the car accident. An ambulance carried the dead passenger to the morgue and the driver, who would later be charged for drunk driving and recklessness, to the emergency room at the general hospital. Only one person is left at the scene—this reporter. Like a demented detective I was combing the scene for clues, for details. Then, presto, I found the watch, the very object that would offer the readers a great insight, and provide the police with a critical clue to the exact timing of the accident. This detail would dance its way into my lead and turn what would otherwise have been a routine and boring accident or police story into a dramatic story with the unusual lead: "The irony of life and death: a wrist watch."[1]

Well, the watch of the dead passenger (yes, I inspected the watches on their wrists) was still ticking, but the driver's timepiece, a Citizen, smashed on an object and froze on impact at the time of the accident. The details of the story captured the human drama and brought a new dimension to the representation of road accidents.[2]

## 5. Making the Invisible Visible—Finding the Shoehorn

Our lives, our assignments, and the settings of the stories we report, are replete with telling evidence. Evidence remains invisible if we do not look for it. That bloodstain on the shirt collar, that syringe under the bed, that lipstick on the rim of the goblet, that smacking chew of the bubble gum, that strand of hair on the carpet, remain invisible unless reporters, like great detectives, find to them and, if possible, use them to build engaging and explanatory stories. The Citizen watch in my accident story, as well as its significance, was invisible to everyone except the reporter who rummaged for details. By finding the elusive but significant detail, the reporter can make the invisible details visible and unfelt emotions felt.

That elusive but critical detail is what I call the shoehorn. This imagery drew its inspiration and force from an unnamed 20th-century writer who, in describing a deserted village drew the reader's attention to "the banana station, with its dying mongrel and its shoehorn." You have to be a passionate observer to notice a shoehorn beside the shrub on the dirt road of a deserted village.

Every story a reporter pursues harbors a shoehorn. We must train and activate our senses and minds to find the shoehorn.

A good question is: what do we observe? The main details of interest to reporters are the:

- Shape
- Color
- Texture
- Dimensions
- Movements
- Condition
- Mood

## *Shape*

Is the person or thing round, triangular, or square? What does it/he/she look like, and what familiar thing or person does that thing or person resemble? What is the significance of this shape? Imagine that you are in the White House and you notice that the ashtray is shaped like a hammer and sickle. Or one of the former presidents had a moustache like that of Adolf Hitler.

Shapes are potent symbols. Take the hangman's noose. The shape can emerge in the most innocent of settings, even in the loop of a Christmas decoration. Whether the symbolism is intended or innocent it can establish a connection with readers.

## *Color*

An AFP wire story carried by Australia's national daily, The Australian, started with the following: "The black and white kefiyah draped over the chair was a stark symbol of Israel's determination to isolate Yasser Arafat, even in the face of international condemnation."

For the first time in seven years Mr. Arafat, then Palestinian president, could not attend the Christmas midnight Mass in Bethlehem, occupied by Israeli forces. The Israeli government blocked him. The chessboard colored *kefiyah* or scarf had become the symbol of Arafat. Draping the Arafat trademark colors on an empty chair held an explosive symbolism that words of defiance, rockets and anger alone could not express.

Color, perhaps more than shape, can harbor far-reaching ironies. In every culture, colors carry symbolism. Color blindness can be lethal. A news writer, failing to notice the flag and its color would be denying the reader crucial intelligence. He or she would be telling only a fraction of the story. If a soldier waving a white flag is gunned down, the incident has a deeper implication and emotive power than if that soldier were waving a red flag or no flag. Imagine a sailor who fails to notice that the approaching ship flies a black flag emblazoned with a white skull and bones. In the United States and other western countries, journalistic ethics demand that media writers make an effort to explore and give as many sides and dimensions of an event as possible. Journalists are also required to write accurate reports. Leaving critical detail out spells inaccuracy. Instead of injecting their opinion into stories, writers should find and deploy corroborative or implicative details that let readers into all the possible dimensions of a story and enable them to draw their own conclusions.

## Texture

Texture defines our sense of comfort, well-being and security. Sometimes, it reflects the nature of relationships. When rice is hard, we know it is uncooked. Millions around the world buy hand cream, fabric softeners, and hair conditioners. When you shake hands, do you pay attention to the texture of the hands you shake? A good reporter feels the texture of the chair he or she sits in. Or is the texture not important? Try eating tough beef, or driving on a soggy road, or diving onto a sofa made of nails.

Let's take the example of Pennsylvania Avenue in Washington, D.C. getting all soggy and pot-hole-ridden. The result would be a traffic jam on an important road in the country's capital. Viewing it in that context, would it not be wise to overlook the texture of that road?

## Dimension

The mere size of people or things may be unimportant but the contextual significance of size often offers compelling detail. This brings us to relativity. What may be big for us may be small for other people and vice versa. For example, on an American professional basketball team, a six-footer, considered to be tall on the street, is a dwarf in the NBA. The writer should not impose his or her subjectivity on readers. It is better to ascertain the exact dimensions instead. That is why writers are asked to show what happened in context rather than tell readers what they should believe. "Showing and telling" is discussed in some detail in Chapter 8.

Dimension also refers to figures. For example, one anti-debt advocacy group suggested that the amount of money used to organize the G-8 summit in Japan in 2000, could write off the debts several poor countries owed the eight super rich countries. Numbers and dimensions thrive better in context than in isolation. Idle citation of dimensions or figures, without focus or context, can be a distraction. However, dimension should be used to show the social, political or other significance or impact of events on the public and not to display the depth of the reporter's research or access to figures.

## Movement:

Movement is often considered as the sign of life and activity. Is the work or person sluggish or nimble, dead or alive? Road construction is slow or fast. Speech is slow (a drawl) or rapid fire, like Mohammed Ali in his hey day, or like a horse race commentator. In the event of an emergency, for example, movement and speed often determine survival.

For the writer, paying attention to movement is the first challenge. The other challenge is representing it in writing. Modifiers (such as adjectives and adverbs—fast, sluggishly, slow) do not define movement. We can best portray movement through strong verbs and specification, including actual measurement. Thus, a man does not walk unsteadily from left to right across the room; he *staggers*. You do not move fast, you run, sprint, bolt or dash. A car does not go too fast; it travels at 75 miles an hour in a 40 mph zone. Of course, context and significance should determine the inclusion of movement elements in the story.

## Condition

Condition is a wider, more inclusive, way of seeing things and people. Condition captures the sum total of characteristics of a person or thing. Let us say that the museum built a century ago is falling apart. To portray the condition, we must stick to specific detail (for example, the roof of the East Wing, not the entire museum, is caving in) rather than value judgment. We must show the condition through action rather than idle description, sweeping statements, or opinion. Condition is relative in the sense that it must be compared, if intrinsically, to something or to another state or condition people can relate to. In other words, journalists would compare the museum (in context) to other museums, decrepit or shining, to what a knowledgeable person expects a museum to be, or to what the museum had been or was designed to be.

## Mood

Observation captures the mood of a person, event, or circumstance. It announces the spirit of action. Mood, on the other hand, converts and links abstract feelings to concrete action in a symbolic context. Every occurrence comes with a mood. Writers don't need to create mood. They need to key into it by observing and depicting action, paying attention to the sounds, movements, and other accompanying natural elements. Precise depiction of action brings out the mood. So does pacing, including the use of punctuation (use of the colon, the comma, and ellipses for example). In my lead, "The irony of life and death: a wrist watch," I attempted to create a sense of expectancy with a colon. I used the colon deliberately to make readers pause and hold their breath for a surprise that is waiting for them at the end of the sentence. Writing the traditional sentence with the "correct" construction would have made the sentence bland, even idiotic: "The irony of life and death is a wrist watch."

Good writing shows rather than describes people. Happy people don't exist. Competent writers show people being happy: dancing, hooting (popular in Spain and Brazil), women strumming the tongue in a half-open mouth (in Palestine), singing, dancing, hugging people, clapping, laughing, throwing balloons into the air (many cultures) or pasting money on people's foreheads and buying drinks for everyone in the bar (in Nigeria). You must be able to consider the mood in context. Another Nigerian example shows some element of dramatic symbolism: When the military seizes power Nigerians drum, dance, hoot in the streets, and head for the bars, but when Nigerian military dictator General Abacha dropped dead in 1998 the country that venerates the dead exploded in jubilation, drumming, dancing, hooting, and buying strangers beer in the pubs. Any journalistic report that ignored the mood of the event would be incomplete and inaccurate.

The media are the barometers of public mood: how people react or relate to policies, events, and governance. Action captures mood better than emotional words and sweeping statements. Sometimes, reliable statistical figures depicting people's thoughts on certain issues—Should America attack North Korea? Is Michael Jackson the Christ? Should Australia let in the boatloads of asylum seekers?—are the best indicators of public mood.

In the *Daily News* auto crash story cited earlier, I offered readers details that revealed the pathos and emotive drama of the scene. The car was just one-year old and had clocked only 11,800 miles and had the air-conditioning on and the radio dial on FM 94 " Then came the sudden rhythmic thud of death made more touching, ironic and dramatic by the pulsation of the pop music on the lively FM 94. The story put the readers in the car, seated beside the fun-loving young men, sharing the caress of the air conditioner, the lilting rhythm of the music and the entire thrill that would end in a fatal crash. Now I am kicking myself. I should have called the station to find out what music was playing at 4:24PM that Sunday on FM 94. Who knows, it might have been a song about death, even life, a sad song, even a happy one—offering the event some symbolism or irony.

# Putting Observation to Work—Reporter Gary Tippet's Field Notes

Years ago I spent a week with a shearing crew at Dunkeld in Victoria's Western District and an entire day of that I spent learning exactly what the gun shearer did as he ran the blade over each sheep, watching carefully, getting the order of the whole repetitive business exactly right in my notebook. Asking one of the other blokes 'What's he doing now? Why?' and 'What's that bit called?' The resulting story started this way:

For the hundredth time today Ross Tua walks that strange bent-kneed, hunched-over slouch into the catching pen and drags out another mongrel big red-eye wether. For the hundredth time he tucks a foreleg behind his thigh, picks up the handpiece and— literally head down and arse up – goes to work.

"Shearing Kiwi-style: a couple of short blows down the first hock, then into the belly wool. Over the hind legs and crutch and into the undermine— three long sweeps of the wide comb over the rump and up the back—the dirty fleece falling away to unveil the whiteness beneath.

"The sweat wells up in tiny pearls on Tua's shaven head and drips steadily down his nose and onto the sheep. He shuffles forward, using his knees to muscle the animal into position. The hand piece buzzes over the neck, throat and head, following the body contours into the first shoulder.

"Wresting him onto his back now for the long blow, sweeping up the length of the spine. Now over the shoulder and down the last side, shuffling back all the while to the precise spot where, on the final blow, he can boot the struggling beat down the chute and out of the shed."

I was happy with a few elements. The momentum, the jargon the shearers use—mongrel big red-eye wether, long blow, undermine—and that tiny, tiny moment of the bead of sweat rolling down his nose and falling on to the sheep below. I think they're the sort of things that take the reader to the place and the moment and, hopefully make them want to stay for the rest of the journey.

Another section described the shed itself: a sprawling, ancient red-roofed thing that spends most of the years empty but for spiders, possums, the odd wandering feral cat.

But tonight its maze of blackwood pens is jammed solid with confused merinos, their bleating and their ammonia stink filling the place.

To put my readers on the scene, I needed to pick up the smell, the taste, the texture. I couldn't have written about the once-a-year bustle of that shed without noting the noise and especially the stink of sheep piss.

# Dealing with Distortions

Human perception is fallible. As important as observation may be, it can be subject to distortion. What we see or sense is constantly distorted by our habits, culture, social orientation, sentiments, moods, and even physical circumstances. Preferences, peculiarities, and the state of the mind or body can distort the information people receive (for example, color, shape of nose, size of body, sexual preferences). Here are some illustrations of this perfectly normal perceptual fluctuation. Pregnancy can distort some women's sense of smell and taste. Grief can distort our perception of life. So can culture. For example, in some parts of Africa, women used to be put in fattening rooms to make them rounder and therefore more appealing to men, while women in the United States and other Western countries spend thousands of dollars to become thinner. For Westerners, skinny is beautiful. The result of applying the indices of one culture or one writer's perception on aspects of another culture amounts to distortion of reality, if not outright misinformation.

Honest reporters acknowledged their limitations and biases that will impede accurate observation. When we recognize our biases, we can consciously disengage our emotions and prejudice and, at least momentarily, neutralize them ahead of our journalistic assignment. It is also our duty to research broadly to realize that there is a wide range of possibilities, perspectives and nuances our cultures and experiences have not exposed us to. To reduce bias and distortion of details, journalists should learn about their own surroundings and the outside world. More importantly, they should portray action, rather than rely on their own feelings and perceptions and interpretations.

# Using Detail: Selective Description

One of the biggest criticisms of journalistic storytelling is the abuse of detail— the mark of a poor writer, in any form. Enlightened storytellers are circumspect in their use of detail. While it is important to observe and gather detail, it is more important to use details judiciously. Just as journalists select only relevant bits of information from the heap they have gathered, they also use descriptive details sparingly and selectively, as we will see in Chapter 6. Good writing relies significantly on the writer's ability to gather significant information and use it selectively, discerningly, and strategically. What we leave out, more than what we include in our story, can be the true indicator of our journalistic pedigree.

# 4

---

## Interviewing for Narrative: Why Interview when you can Talk?

*Every person you meet—and everything you do in life—is an opportunity to learn something. That is important to all of us, but most of all to a writer because as a writer, you can use anything.* —Tom Clancy

I chat, therefore I am.

We were created to tell stories and to chat with each other. For the story-teller, the story process is built on conversation—conversation with sources, and conversation with readers. We chat with sources so we can chat with readers. Three levels of conversation make up the journalistic story.

1. Setting up the interview conversationally
2. Conducting the interview conversationally (limiting the use of questions and answers)
3. Telling the story conversationally (storytelling)

The outcome of a conversational interview is conversation with the reader. That is why it is important for reporters to gather details and write, simple, explanatory stories from the point of view of the readers. And that's why writing coaches advise writers to read their stories out. Do they sound like conversations? Conversation shows in a story.

The interview is journalistic jargon for a chat, a discussion, or a friendly exchange between two people, one of them representing a news organization. The purpose and context of the conversation—what the information supplied will be used for—distinguish a journalistic interview from idle chatter.

Journalistic storytellers rarely interview because the term *interview* has a bad name. When a journalist mentions the word, what comes to people's minds is a sadistic inquisitor swinging a microphone and other instruments of torture to extract blood and confessions. The term *interview* also reminds people of mobs of television reporters descending on attorneys, witnesses and public officials in Hollywood thrillers.

How, then, do we request interviews without mentioning the 'I' word? Well, consider phrases like: exchange ideas, discuss, confirm, check, cross-check, sound out, 'get your comments', 'learn from you,' 'pick your brain' or 'find out what you think about.' However, for the sake of brevity, and because it is frequently used in the newsroom, we will retain the term *interview* in this chapter.

# The limitation of questions

Traditional journalism overestimates the value of questions, viewing fact-gathering as a question and answer routine. Narrative news and feature writers need to determine whether questions will serve or frustrate their information gathering endeavor. Using the question and answer technique "may be of value in determining favored detergents, toothpaste, and deodorants, but not in the discovery of men and women," observe George Killenberg and Rob Anderson, who recommend "making conversation. And listening." Reporters would do well to acknowledge the problems of relying on the question and answer technique. Here are four key problems with questions:

1. Questions are often a quick fix—a bit like spanking a child.
2. Questions are narrow and limiting—they rarely elicit full and accurate answers.
   Question: Have you seen my little boy?
   Answer: No, I haven't.
   (Information the question might have suppressed: "Well, but I heard a kid scream this morning. The noise seemed to come from the trunk of an old black Toyota wagon.) A conversation would have engendered openness, rapport, and voluntary and inclusive responses.
3. Questions can indicate aloofness—a reporter just doing a job. It is an official engagement devoid of the kind of human connection that brings forth ringing anecdotes.
4. Questions create two levels of power imbalance.

   Level one—the interviewer as interrogator and parent figure.
   Level two—the interviewee, with a personal agenda, as the sole administrator of information and therefore the real controller of the interview.

   Question: What's a reporter without questions? Answer: Human being.

Chatting has taken New York Times correspondent, Marc Lacey, where interviews could not. Lacey's eyes lit up the first time he shared this insightful anecdote with me over coffee in Boston in November 2006:

> When I was a White House correspondent for The New York Times, I learned quickly that the best way to get President Clinton to talk was to keep my notebook in my pocket and chat. The kitchen on Air Force One is in the back of the plane, and the president would often walk past the reporters on the plane to

pick up snacks on long flights. If we jumped up and began firing off questions, he would retreat. But if we made a funny comment, remarking about the purple suit of the local official who introduced him, for instance, he would stop and chat. And chat. And chat. Bill Clinton loved to chat and he would talk to us so long on the back of the plane that his aides would get nervous and come back to see what he was saying. They would encourage him to return to the front of the plane, where he sits. He eventually would but after talking to us so long that we had learned some insights from the President of the United States.

# No Interviews, please; I'll Tell You Everything You Want to Know

Decades after the Nigerian civil war (1967 to 1970) my editors sent me to interview a retired general under whose orders military commanders fought to dislodge the rebel forces of the breakaway Republic of Biafra. The general was spending his retirement years as a magistrate in a country town called Calabar, a serene city on Nigeria's eastern coast. I showed up at the general's doorsteps unannounced one evening and told him I wanted to interview him about the planning and execution of the war under his command. His role was fascinating because it was the east—his part of the country—that had seceded. As a general in the federal army, he was effectively massing troops against his own people in the breakaway state. The general told me brusquely that he could not grant interviews on military operations without written clearance from Army Headquarters. Of course such a clearance, if it would be given at all, would take years. I had days, not years, to file my report. So I started talking about life, and war, and things normal people talk about. What did he end up as a magistrate? What is his typical day in court like, compared to his former life? What does he miss most? How did his people react to him when he returned? That way, I found the common ground: his surprising switch from soldier to magistrate—from the trench to the bench—and the effects of the war on him and his country. The general began to talk, and I took occasional notes to register sharp quotes. After about 40 minutes, he said. "Well, you have already got your interview." You bet.

Ken Metzler views the exchange between reporter and source as "just people talking, sometimes barefooted people". In other words, a good interview is one in which two fellow humans chat with little inhibition. Sometimes, however, good interviewers use the presence of a third or fourth person to explore the character (for example, relationships with or treatment of family, friends, challengers, subordinates, superiors, or coworkers) of the person being interviewed.

Although the interview is a form of research (obtaining specific facts and data from sources), its main goal is to offer explanations, motivations, and implications of actions—based on what the reporter had gleaned from other sources at different levels. Personal insights, comments and reactions—rather than simply an account of what happened—drive strong news and feature stories.

You do not wait for or expect a police chief to tell you in an interview that his area of jurisdiction has the highest level of car theft in the country. You get the information beforehand and now seek corroborative details, anecdotes and comments from the police chief: causes, implications or consequences, and what actions are planned. One possible plan of action could be that the police department is planning to increase patrols on the highway to reduce car theft.

A reporter is as good as the breadth and level of contacts he or she maintains. A good reporter has contacts from the street corners to the highest levels of government and in a variety of places and organizations, and relates to them at an equal level and obtains information from them promptly and accurately. Even junior officials and ordinary people—the receptionist, secretary, security guard or junior police officer—can offer a reporter a unique angle or dimension of a story, not to mention tip-offs and riveting first-person accounts. If reporters relied only on information volunteered by officials, the public would be left eternally in the dark. That is why preparation and the recruitment of sources are crucial to the interviewing process. And that is what makes the journalistic interview the cornerstone of reporting and writing.

# Why People Grant Interviews

Nobody speaks to reporters for purely altruistic reasons. People speak to journalists because they believe the story will be beneficial to them in some way. Finding out the real reasons people agree to be interviewed could serve reporters in a number of ways.

First, reporters would become aware of the interviewee's agenda, where the person is coming from. An awareness of the motivations of the sources should compel reporters to explore other dimensions of the story and seek further information and corroboration from other sources. Second, equipped with ready reasons—the benefits the person will derive from the story—reporters stand a greater chance of getting the interview. Consider telling the source what he or she stands to gain in speaking to you, and what the down sides of not talking to you are. In Metzler's view, people should jump at the chance of being interviewed because "there is only one thing worse than being interviewed and that's not being interviewed."

Metzler lists the benefits of speaking to journalists.

- Recognition and publicity
- A chance to give their side of the story or controversy
- An opportunity to educate the public
- A chance to influence or impress others
- An opportunity to clarify a position or reduce misunderstanding
- A boost of the subject's reputation or ego
- A touch of immortality of the subject's words captured in print
- Being identified with a novel approach or idea

- Sympathy and identification with a cause (enough to override the pain, example traumatic personal experiences)
- An opportunity to promote, such as actresses and authors.[1]

People usually cooperate when they realize that reporters can obtain elsewhere the same or new information that can be harmful to them.

# Public Relations

It is common practice in government and major organizations to direct reporters to the public relations department. While public relations officers are invaluable to reporting, they are trained to give out only information that favors their organizations and bosses.

We do not expect a true PR practitioner to draw our attention to a scandal, misdeed, or cover-up in his or her organization. Public relations officers are trained to distract or politely send away journalists seeking information or news angles that can hurt the organization's image.

Serious journalists do not rely solely on PR information, which serves better as background and leads (pointers). Ideally, PR officers should facilitate reporters' access to the people who are in the position to provide first-hand information. These include field officers, administrators and decision makers. A cabin crew member would offer you more useful information on an in-flight incident than the airline's spokesperson. Many chief executives will speak to knowledgeable, outgoing, and persistent reporters without the intervention of the PR people Building contacts within the organization opens wider doors, and generates more valuable information than the best-meaning PR managers can promise officially. PR people are often the last to be briefed on emerging events. Unless you can earn the confidence of a particular PR officer and get him or her to offer some tips or leak information, the PR officer will be of limited use in your pursuit for substantive information. With the Internet, the prominent role of the PR person is diminishing. The websites of companies list details and addresses of the right people to contact directly.

# Interviewing over and over

Multiple interview stories are invariably better than single-interview or no-interview stories because they offer depth and diverse dimensions. For some stories, reporters interview the subject once or twice. For others, such as profiles and investigative stories, they need to spend hours, days, or even months with them, interviewing them several times over in different circumstances, at different times and places, and for different reasons.

Preparing for her story on infidelity for *Esquire*, Lisa Grunwald interviewed a woman who admitted being a serial adulterer. Grunwald interviewed the woman on the telephone for five weeks, and these are her recollections before she started the series of face-to-face interviews in different settings:

> After five weeks, I had asked her every question I could think of, many of them more than once. She had told me about her father and mother, her years in high school and college; her favorite music, books, and movies.[2]

But she asked her more questions in the months to come and got illuminating insights into the world of this enthusiastic and resourceful double dealer.

# Planning the Interview

Interviews require two principal levels of planning: logistical and psychological.

## Logistical Planning

Logistical planning refers to determining what you need to know, areas you must explore, and sources and perspectives you need to write a rich, balanced, informative, and interesting story. Reporters also have to give thought to a suitable venue, access to the subject and appropriate dress, equipment, and follow-ups. A suitable venue is some in which the source would be at ease and a place that would bring out his or her unique character.

## Psychological Planning

One of the most important elements of psychological planning is acknowledging and neutralizing your biases or preconceptions against the person you plan to interview.

Everyone has biases, preferences, or prejudices. These can come across strongly in the conduct of the interview and in the slant and content of the story. As we saw in Chapter 3, it is important to identify these biases and push them aside to avoid imposing them on readers. For example, you may find it difficult to talk to people of another race, culture, religion, or vocation or people whose actions you consider despicable (e.g. serial rapists, notorious racists, or someone who hacked a child to death). On the flipside, you may have to talk to someone you admire exceedingly. You must tell yourself that the person is a fellow human being, an equal, and you must show interest and curiosity rather than judgment, disgust, or worshipful admiration. Bias is transparent in stories.

Psychological planning also entails realizing that some of the information sources provide might be upsetting. Be determined not to let the content and implications of the information sources provide shock you. You must be able to listen to the convicted murderer describe the gory details, or a serial lover reel out with gusto details of frequent love trysts, without giving away your moral indignation, anger, or judgment. Conversely, you must, without getting carried away, be able to watch a famous star recite his lines or replay his works, away from the delirious cheer of worshipful fans. Tips on interviewing difficult subjects are offered in the Chapter 5. Displaying strong emotions like indignation, rage, frustration, or awe could ruin your interview and your story.

Careful interviewers do not allow the subject to feel frustrated or angry enough to end the interview—and ruin the story. That is why reporters must prepare their mind and emotions ahead of time. Maintain an emotional distance from your subject. You cannot afford to be physically, ideologically, or emotionally attracted to or repelled by your sources. Involvement with a source could destroy your story, your sense of fairness and balance, and your reputation.

# Requesting an Interview

The ability to obtain an interview with a significant person or official will depend largely on your drive, your reputation as a reporter, the profile and reputation of your newspaper, the nature of the subject, the clarity of your request for an interview, the amount of research you have done, and your passion for the story and for your job. The lead up to the actual encounter will normally include the following steps:

## Contacting the prospective subject

Reporters contact sources by telephone and e-mail or simply show up. You may also get someone they know or respect to contact the person on your behalf. Top government functionaries and business executives may ask for a list of questions ahead of time. This can be tricky. If you send the full list of questions you may not get the interview. Consider sending a list of areas they want to cover rather than the actual questions you plan to ask. Controversial or ruthless questions can be asked as follow-up questions. In certain situations, providing some real questions in advance may be essential. Advance questions allow the sources to research or obtain accurate figures and facts from field managers. Even then the most valuable comments usually come when you ask follow-up questions.

## A Good Reason

The next challenge, discussed in greater detail earlier, is to articulate the purpose of the interview, the importance of the story, and why the source should talk to you. Remember that few sources speak to journalists simply to advance public discourse and freedom of expression. Sources may talk to you if they believe the story you are pursuing would bring them some form of gain, including psychological benefits. So, be prepared to appeal to the person's humanity and to articulate exactly what the person you are trying to interview stands to gain.

## *Sounding Out*

Another important step, especially if you are interviewing public officials, is to discuss some of the peripheral issues with lower ranked people in the organization, and even visitors. You could achieve this by checking out the venue of the interview a few days before to confirm the location, and perhaps to say hello to the boss' personal staff or other people who could be useful to you. With your foot in the door, you could ask a few questions or just listen to people. If there is a cafeteria on the premises, get a cup of coffee and say hello to people. If people know you will be speaking to the boss, they may have tips, insights, questions, or grievances for you. You can also garner some anecdotal information here—the day the boss threw up in the cafeteria, for example.

## *Appropriate Venue*

Give some thought to the time, duration, and venue of the interview. If possible meet the person in a variety of different surroundings. Go for an office interview—with the manic growls and twangs of telephones, and secretaries and associates stomping in and out—only if there are no better alternatives. Office interviews work if you need to capture the person in an office setting and if other venues cannot be worked into his or your schedule. Often, with an office interview, you can obtain documents and precise facts and figures. Officials tend, however, to give more time and to be more relaxed, more natural and more candid outside the work environment. Venues can bring out the character of a subject and give readers a sense of place. From my coverage of the US Virgin Islands senate for the *Daily News*, I remember the sound of gunshots and the screams of delight in the background as I spoke to a source on the telephone on a Sunday afternoon. The gentleman was Peter Burlingame, president of the U.S. Virgin Islands Shooting Association, described in my *Daily News* story as the "gun lover and firearm instructor [who] had just demobilized a legislative bill seeking to criminalize the possession of assault firearms," and "walked out of the Senate chamber with a smoking gun, so to speak, and a smug grin." The background sounds of gunshots from the police shooting range, where Burlingame spends his Sunday afternoons, provided a backdrop to our conversation and insights into the character of the source and the issues reported. I wrote:

> [H]e said amidst the sound of gunshots that he does not own an assault rifle 'by Department of Defense definition'. He portrayed the bill's expanded definition of an assault firearm as vague, saying it 'includes every firearm made in the last 150 years.'

# Preparing for the Interview

Like all good journalists, narrative writers are alert. They absorb details and the significance of daily news events. They observe the atmosphere in the city and people's reactions to events. They are in frequent touch with knowledgeable contacts or people (editors, contacts, acquaintances) who could hook them up with additional sources. Reporters constantly make mental notes of what they need to know. Working under pressure is no excuse for shutting off the senses and silencing human drama. Most interviews—whether they are with presidents or with hookers—involve elements of character. The resulting story should capture significant details (including details and quotes) that illuminate character.

The success of an interview-based story depends substantially on the preparation for the interview. Here are a few tips:

- Psyche yourself up for success. Believe you will get the interview. I usually tell myself that everyone I want to talk to will talk to me. Nobody I was determined to interview has ever really refused to talk to me.
- Study everything you can about your subject. Talk to other reporters who have interviewed the person. Look the person or issue up in the library and on the web for previous mentions. Typing the subject's name in the www.google.com search engine can be rewarding. Ask people about the person you are going to interview. *Radio Times* (UK) journalist Andrew Duncan's thorough research on then British Prime Minister Margaret Thatcher produced this memorable exchange during the interview:

  Duncan: "Why do you drink so much whiskey?"
  Thatcher: "What do you mean?"
  Duncan: "Alan Clark's diaries, page 67."[3]

- Sharpen your newsgathering skills (especially observation and curiosity).
- Note down areas you want to cover, including facts you already know and would like the subject to comment on.
- Confirm the working order of your journalistic tools including pens (yes, you need many, because pens can fail) and tape recorders. A word of caution on tape recorders: avoid the Napley Predicament (NP), my coinage, for failing to test new equipment ahead of an interview. Reporting a major kidnapping and espionage story at the London court, the Old Bailey, I was scheduled to interview Britain's famous solicitor Sir David Napley. He was the attorney for the Israelis—a high-flying doctor and a former intelligence officer—standing trial and later convicted for kidnapping and trying to spirit out an African ex-minister as cargo out of London's Stansted airport. On my way to Sir David's of-

fice, I stopped at an electronic shop to buy a sophisticated tape recorder. As the interview was about to start, I pressed the "record" button, and the recording light came on. Sir David blasted away about the very delicate and celebrated case he was handling. After the interview, I rushed to the newsroom to replay the tape. The tape was blank. The tape had not moved. It was all along on 'pause'. Fortunately I had paid full attention to the celebrated attorney and noted down sharp quotes and key points.

- Decide on appropriate clothing and appearance. Appropriate clothing means something that is comfortable and modest and does not draw too much attention to your appearance.

- If possible, find out beforehand what the person looks like, which goes back to research. By knowing ahead of time what the person looks like, you may be able to remove mental obstacles, such as stereotypes about the person speaking, including height, size, color, looks, disability, lifestyle and habits.

# Shush! Let Sleeping Lies Catch Them

"Truth" number one: To lie is human.

"Truth" number two: There is no truth in journalism. All reporters have been lied to. Journalists are not equipped to instantly recognize all lies at face value. People will always give reporters a version of the story that best suits or protects their own interests. They tell only one side of the story—theirs. That side of the story may be incomplete, embellished, slanted, and sometimes simply false. An incomplete "fact" can indeed amount to a falsehood. Take the fictitious example of Mark Hanson, a junior partner in a legal firm, tells you the firm is losing clients and clout because the managing partner, Tom Birch, promotes only his friends as partners. As proof, he offers that of the five people promoted the previous month, three were Birch's friends. Hanson fails to tell you, however, that the year before, five of Birch's outspoken critics, including Hanson, were promoted. Nor does Hanson volunteer that he and Birch were the best of friends, until the morning Birch found him in bed with Mrs. Birch. While it is true that some of the people Birch promoted were his own friends, the suggestion that those promotions were based on favoritism, and the statistical computation that led to that conclusion, were false and misleading.

For a statement to be considered true, it must in every detail and motive represent a full and faithful reflection of what happened in the context in which it happened. One slice of reality, even if accurate, does not constitute truth. For instance, saying that someone is a good father may be accurate. The same statement put in context, however, can be false and misleading. The one slice of truth does not reflect the man's true character as a serial killer. Because people often offer only the side of a story that favors them, reporters must search for as many slices of reality as possible, to attempt to construct the whole. Even then, the truth cannot always be guaranteed. That is why journalists should not be obsessed with the elusive concept of truth.

Even more shocking is "truth" number three: A lie can be a journalistic "truth." In 2001, the Australian government declared that travel weary Iranian boat people tried to manipulate the government into granting them refugee visas by throwing their children overboard. Pictures supported the government's "truth," which made front page news and became the subject of a raging debate around the country. It took a whistleblower and a senate inquiry to reveal that key people in government apparently knew that the boat people did not throw their children overboard. Pictures of life-jacket-clad children and adults floating in the sea seemed to corroborate the government's claims. It happened that the pictures in question represented a separate and older scene of asylum seekers trying to swim to safety. Yet, in context, the same photographs had suggested the contrary. The event had two opposing "truths:"

1. Boat people threw their children overboard; and
2. Boat people did not throw their children overboard.

Based on information from highly placed—authoritative—federal sources, both opposing bits of information were "truths."

Knowledgeable reporters are equipped with an inbuilt alarm system, or censor, that goes off when a questionable piece of information is given. Alarm trigger include:

- Could the source be self-serving?
- Does this source belong to a profession or system that relies on lies or inaccuracies?
- Is the source known to have lied previously?
- Does the source have something to gain from lying about certain issues?
- Is the source in the position to have or give accurate information?

Reporters must be seen to have made every effort to cross-check or verify and search beyond the isolated snippets of information they receive. They must also establish the authority and credibility of the source of that information. Reporters establish credibility by checking whether the source has perceptible reasons or motives to lie or misinform. Although reporters cannot always ascertain veracity, they can make an effort to capture as many nuances and perspectives of the story as possible. They should verify information by assessing the sources, weighing the information against relevant values, seeking background information and alternative views, cross-checking, and cross-referencing. The best guarantees against lies are thorough research, requests for backup documents, knowledge of the subject matter and procedures, reliance on competent sources rather than spokespeople (the systems engineer rather than the public relations officer), a healthy dose of journalistic cynicism (if your mother says she loves you, check it out), balanced reporting (using multiple sources), a high level of curiosity, a good grasp of body language, and maybe instinct.

# Surmounting Interview Problems

## 1. Reluctant Subjects

Every reporter encounters reluctant subjects: those who do not want to talk and those who are miserly with information. This is where persistence and persuasiveness come in. Also we must examine and deal with the person's excuses. We have already looked at one of the major reasons people are loath to speak to journalists: most people don't want to be interviewed; they would much rather chat.

## 2. Fear of Being Misquoted

This is a genuine fear. We have to admit that journalists around the world misquote people or quote them out of context. We even misquote fellow journalists. Some reporters put words into sources' mouths, relying on their own assumptions and using their own sentence structure and turns of phrase in direct quotations. Sometimes quotes are amended (embellished or toned down and therefore distorted) by editors or subeditors.

While journalists do misrepresent facts, public servants and even private people are known to fraudulently disown information they had given journalists. Sometimes what appears in print—although a replica of what was said—assumes greater potency than what was spoken. These words are judged, interpreted, and sometimes amplified by the public, the government, and the interviewee's bosses and colleagues. Because these words, accurately quoted, may hurt the interests of the interviewee, denial becomes a real temptation. Because journalists already have a bad reputation for misquoting people, defense against claims of misquotation is often fragile. We must address legitimate concerns. I often tell sources, who decline to speak to me because another journalist had misquoted them, that I cannot refuse to see a doctor because one doctor had misdiagnosed my hay fever. I add that journalists are not all the same and that I am sufficiently trained and educated to report accurately the information I am given. My most successful method is to offer to recap the main points with the subject to confirm their accuracy. I recommend the strategy because it reassures sources. Sources often offer additional information or insights at this point. The negligible disadvantage of this exercise is that some will deny telling you what they told you. I have had people recant what they had told me in a recorded conversation.

Some sources request that the completed story be sent to them for vetting before publication. Their reason is often that they need to ensure that they are quoted accurately and in context. In reality, they may only anxious to check what the words they said look like in print and how people might react to their views. Chances are that such people would unreasonably request the relegation, amendment or removal of important elements of the story at this point. Reporters should address this request tactfully, saying that it is editors and not reporters who decide what gets printed. Reporters should never allow an interview subject to edit their story, well, except if the editor rules otherwise.

Young journalists, to their peril, often ignore this important rule of engagement. A week after I stressed this rule in class, one second-year journalism major sauntered into my office to request an extension on his news writing assignment. He said the council official he interviewed was vetting his story had not returned it on time for an early submission. Imagine having to tell an editor that.

## 3. Fear of Reprisals

News hurts. News can cost people their jobs, relationships, reputation, even their life. Often people are afraid to talk to the media because they fear the information they give may be misrepresented or misconstrued. Some fear that the story, when published, will come back to bite them. There is no quick-fix solution to this problem, and no instant and sincere assurance we can offer sources who get jittery about the repercussions of a story. Our civic duty and professional responsibility as reporters are to provide the intelligence citizens need and to animate democracy. Journalistic responsibility should guide our responses to this fear.

We should use all the skills we can acquire to draw out the information that society needs to protect and preserve its civilization. If police officers dwelled on the impending loneliness or even the fatherlessness of pretty Samantha, then her serial killer and child rapist father, Eric "The Dragon" Hamster, would never be arrested, let alone charged. Public interest and our call to serve society are superior to our personal fears. The example is, of course, hypothetical.

On the brighter side, for felons who want a book contract about their exploits, talking to reporters can be a great incentive. Sometimes a criminal who speaks frankly to good reporters will reveal some fascinating human angles to their lives, and factors that would invite society's understanding, even empathy.

We should explain to our contacts the importance of the information and our commitment as journalists to be fair and balanced and to tell all sides of the story. It often helps to tell edgy sources that it is better for them to tell their own side of the story than to be denied that right.

However, at the editor's discretion, sometimes the information is more valuable than the source or people's names. In certain circumstances (usually ethical and legal considerations), editors accept exceptional information in exchange for the maintenance of the anonymity of the source or certain people in the story.

## 4. Inexperience

Many people balk at talking to the media because they lack the confidence, exposure or education, to deal with journalists. They may be unsure of their language and social skills, or just be afraid of the journalist's intimidating tools—tape recorder, microphone, cameras, lap top, notebooks and pens.

The general rule is not to thrust your equipment at people who have not had much direct contact with the media. You should also make the interview as informal as possible. Dress informally, curtail note taking, smile, and reassure the inexperienced subject. Of all these stealth techniques, curtailing note taking is the trickiest. There is a high risk of losing what you heard: the intricate points, the good quotes. In such circumstances, I often go to the bathroom to jot down sharp quotes in private before they evaporate. I sometimes get the person out of the way by requesting a glass of water or a tissue, or asking to see a family memorabilia. You may also just say that the point the person made was excellently put and that you need to write it down. Obtaining information while walking and talking does relax people, too.

## 5. Playing Hard to Get

People play hard to get if they fear the information they give, or merely talking to a journalist, might expose them and jeopardize their interests. Sometimes they feel they have a lot to lose and little or nothing to gain from granting the interview. Knowing what motivates people to talk to the media could turn the encounter with the hard-to-get person into one of the greatest thrills of interviewing.

Most people who hesitate to grant interviews can be persuaded to change their minds if the reporter explains the benefits of speaking to the media. The reporter may:

- ask to have a conversation people, thus probably making them feel like an anti-social person for refusing to exchange ideas, or be sounded out.
- appeal to their vanity by reminding them that they would be contributing to public discourse and displaying expertise.
- explain that the conversation offers them the opportunity to state their side of the story and protect their interests. Say that a mere "no comment" can be construed by the public to mean they are hiding something
- call their bluff by saying the story would be printed anyway or that other people, including those who might not agree with or who might be critical of him or her, would be speaking on the matter.
- offer reasons why it is in the public interest and, above all, in their own interest to give their views or tell their own story because you could get the information elsewhere.
- illustrate your journalistic competence and integrity to the person, for example, by showing an example of an article you had written that showed fairness and balance. If the person is important, you may drop the name of another important person you have interviewed. Ask him or her to call that person.

- if all else fails, and granting that the person's comments are crucial to the story, some reporters would tell the person some of the damning information they have gathered or just go ahead and ask the questions.

# Door Locked? Try the window

Nora Villagran who did celebrity stories for the *San Jose Mercury News* knew how to be persistent. "If the front door is locked, try the back door," she says, "If the back door is locked, try the window."[4] The front door was the PR department and the backdoor, the actor's agent. The windows were friends, associates and members of the actor's family. Villagran would even call a celebrity's mother because "they like to talk about their kids, and you can talk about their childhood". Sometimes celebrities grant interviews to find out what their mothers or other said about them, Villagran observes. There are some, however, who would grant an interview simply because the reporter showed evidence of thoroughness.

In the comic movie, *Ace Ventura: Pet Detective*, Ventura (Jim Carey) sets out to track down an elusive football star. The sports star's gun-wielding father sticks out a gun ready to blast Ventura's brains out. The athlete's mother, overhearing Ventura's accurate account of the athlete's exploits and career history, rebukes her husband and invites Ventura in. Talk about research. He is led to the room the star athlete occupied as a child. Here Ventura finds the key elements of the athlete's childhood, career and pain, and his scoop.

In real life, a passion for detail and accuracy served Lisa McCormack, a reporter based in the state of Washington, well. She called estate magnate Marshall Coyne to verify the veracity of information she received from another source. "You are the first damned reporter who ever called to verify a quote," the realtor said, "I like you."[5] McCormack got the interview.

Metzler advises reporters seeking to interview difficult people to try to meet them informally at a speech, press conference or social occasion. I took that advice. This was a classic test of how to enter a house when case of front doors and windows locked.

For a magazine cover story on how military coups are planned in Nigeria, I had to talk to Joe Garba, a retired general who had been involved in stopping and then plotting military coups. By this time, he was Nigeria's United Nations Permanent Representative, It was at the launch of his book, *Diplomatic Soldiering*, which examined foreign policy under military rule when he was foreign minister. Now, General Garba was an admirably arrogant and sharp-witted man. When I told him I wanted to pick his brains on military coups—in which he had been a prominent participant—he sniggered and said he had no time. The following conversation ensued.

> "I am very busy. I am expected at a dinner in the next few minutes."
> "Guess what, General, I can go along and then we can start talking on the way."
> "Who invited you?"

"It is important that I talk with you. I understand you are very knowledgeable in the matter. I have followed your career".

"Look, I have to go." He signals to his chauffeur.

"Then can I speak to you after the dinner?"

"No. After that, I am heading to my home town."

His home town, Langtang, was a one-hour, three times-a-week flight followed by a three-hour rough and tumble taxi ride.

I caught the earliest flight out of Lagos the following afternoon, and
checked into a hotel in Langtang. At dusk I hired a bicycle for reconnaissance.
The next morning at 6:45, I knocked on the massive front door of his fortress.
General Garba, in pajamas, opened the door. "You are not serious. Is this how
you journalists work?" he growled. "Why are you so interested in military
coups? Are you planning one?" After this rumble, the intimidating general invited me in and talked with me for two days, offering alarmingly frank insights
into military coup plotting. It is important to note that I had told him that a serving top general and head of the navy had spoken to me. I got him to comment on
my prized quote from the country's naval chief, an admiral who—ridiculing the
drunken coup plotter who declared a dawn-to-dusk curfew in an aborted 1975
coup—told me: "The coup is a holy, holy thing."

# The Profile of a Profile

For feature writers, the most important interview is the profile interview, which
many call the personality interview. The profile—a people-based interview-
driven story—is sometimes erroneously referred to as the personality interview.
Some of the best profiles are stories of very ordinary people, not personalities.

To explain what a profile is, let me start with what it is not. A profile is not
the life story of a celebrity or a personality. It is not the life history of an important person. It is anything but history. The profile is not the story of a personality
but a revelatory story of anyone, big or small, whose life "touches" society. To
do a profile of a Catholic priest, the writer needs to become familiar with the
issues, doctrines and practices of the Catholic Church in Rome and at the parish
level. Above all, the profile must tell the reader something new.

A profile is a journalistic story that answers the reader's questions ("so
what?" and "who cares?"). A profile uses a subject (the person profiled) to explain life and human experiences in the context of the society's social, moral,
intellectual, political and spiritual status or expectations. It is a story in which an
identifiable central thread in the subject's character or nature is used to tell a
story readers can identify with or relate to. It is the story of a fellow human passing through the forest of our collective consciousness, expectations, challenges,
triumphs and other human dramas. It is the story of a truck smashing through a
high school classroom. Surely, that is not just the story of the truck. It is the
story of the truck (and its driver), the story of the students and teachers, of the
police, of pandemonium, of relatives, of a hospital bed, and the story of the interplay of these details and characters.

The profile relies on extensive interviewing, research and observation. It uses the central techniques of narrative news and feature writing, such as an enticing lead, a nut graph or hook, a central thread or running theme, careful use of quotes, dialogue, anecdotes and transitions. It has a riveting or sobering ending. The quality and appeal of the story will depend on the acute mental vision of the interviewer. It is easy to produce a drab story from an interview with a colorful character. The primary challenge is to unravel the unique and surprising character of every person you interview. Such interviews require, on the part of the interviewer, an infectious humanity that triggers and draws out the humanity of the interview subject. It is the tale of two humanities. The reporter's humanity unfolds the mystery of the source's character, activates trust, and unravels the source's humanity—fallibility, insecurity and all shades of ugliness and undiscovered beauty.

You are Bill Clinton. You are human, fallible. Editors advise reporters to relate to the subject and not to be judgmental. Thus, if you interviewed Osama bin Laden, Adolf Hitler, a serial rapist, a pedophile priest, a mass murderer, a wife beater, or a bank robber, you could not be the star interrogator. You would want to uncover their humanity, not condemn their inhumanity. You would be a fellow fallible human tugging at the humanity of the subject. If you are a good interviewer, you will see yourself as human, sinful, fallible. You are not Billy Graham or Mother Theresa.

The interviewer's greatest challenge is to discover and relate to the humanity of the person being interviewed, whether the person is perceived as a saint or a felon. As we will see in Chapter 5, relating to the person's humanity may involve giving a little of yourself. This is how an interview becomes an informal conversation between two people.

The profile interview derives its vigor and appeal from the little things about big people, the big things about little people, the ordinary things about extraordinary people, and the extraordinary things about ordinary people. The writer is able to discover the saintly things about villains, and the naughty things about holy or saintly people The profile thrives on the journalist's ability to discover and communicate the frail ordinariness and commonness of demigods and the heroism and nobility of common people. It is stories about ordinary people that tend to captivate readers and writing judges most.

Rick Bragg's story, "All She Has, $150,000, is Going to a University", which appeared in the *New York Times* on August 13, 1995, was about a poor, barely educated black woman, Oseola McCarty. Part of this story, which won Bragg the 1996 Pulitzer Prize for Feature Writing, read:

> She had quit school in the sixth grade to go to work, never married, never had children and never learned to drive because there was never any place in particular she wanted to go.
>
> She spent almost nothing, living in her old family home, cutting the toes out of shoes if they did not fit right and binding her ragged Bible with Scotch tape to keep Corinthians from falling out. Over the decades, her pay—mostly dollar bills and change—grew to more than $150,000.

This ordinary person had done something extraordinary, but it took an exceptionally attentive reporter to use a well honed humanity, careful interviewing, observation and research to draw out this hidden but fascinating persona. This barely literate African-American woman donated all her life's savings to a university, to offer other poor black women in Mississippi the opportunity she did not have—to go to school.

People-centered interviews usually succeed if the reporter learns enough about the person, puts him or her at ease, and establishes trust, using a combination of childlike curiosity and the love and respect of people. Sincerity, trust, informality and a shared humanity facilitate and vitalize conversation. It helps the writer to establish the subject's essential character, to find out what the person is really like. The reporter searches for splinters of the person's life and tries to reassemble these pieces like a jigsaw puzzle. The story will strive to illustrate character by portraying the personality in action as a living, breathing, thinking, feeling and doing fellow human. This can be achieved through aggressive listening and using anecdotes to explore the person's essence and motivations.

Good writers portray character the way an actor interprets a role on stage. Good acting (according to the Stanilavsky Method cited by Metzler) rests on the ability to capture three aspects of a character.

1. Who is this person and why is he or she here (on earth, in this country, town or office)?
2. Where did the person come from, and how he or she get here?
3. Where is the person going?

A profile should bring out the subject's essential character—as a person and as a player in the complex drama of life in a given social context. It should also explore the subject's beginnings, struggles and crossroads. The crossroads is the point at which tough decisions must be made, a turning point. The story should also look at where people are heading: are they heading for the stars, the junkyard or prison?

# Profile Tips

- Find big things about little people and little things about big people.
- Find the dark side of the most honorable characters and the bright side of the darkest or most despicable characters.
- Take note of things like physical traits, voice, mannerisms, dress, grooming, and the setting: walls, what is written in or around the room and on the desk, books and magazines, even trophies.
- Interview for beginnings: How did it all begin: childhood, early days? I know a multimillionaire who started his working life as a servant. If you asked King Saul in the Bible his royal beginnings he would tell you he had gone out searching for a donkey. He returned home still looking ordinary but as an anointed king.

- Interview for crossroads: Did the notorious robber find it difficult to decide whether to rob a bank or an art gallery, or whether to rob Citibank or Lloyds Bank.? Ask about the steps, counter arguments, conflicts, and sleepless nights and fights that preceded an action or decision. This helps create suspense and reveal character. Even mundane decisions like what to cook for dinner or what present to buy can reveal a person's character.

- Interview for sympathy, empathy and identification: fiction writers use sympathy to generate pity for the misfortune of characters, for example, strong characters. Sympathy, empathy and identification with people also provide variety and balance to subjects' character or personality. Things that generate sympathy include poverty, abuse, degradation, ignorance and sickness. It is important to ask about the character's misfortunes, especially in early life. Empathy is the audience's identification with the condition or action of the character. For example, a woman who shoots the man who killed her child and was about to rape his husband may earn readers' understanding or empathy. Usually a cycle of inquiry that explores the motives and the frame of mind and fears of the person interviewed could produce reader empathy or shared feelings for the subject. Identification occurs when readers sympathize with the reader's circumstances but at the same time support the actions or goals of the subject and want the subject to succeed. The interviewer must explore the goals, projects and challenges of the subject by fishing for anecdotes.

- Hold their horses: If the subject tells you something interesting, slow him or her down and ask for details: what were you doing at that point? What were you wearing? Were you shaved? Had you brushed your teeth? Who was with you? Guide the person into reliving the events and relating them to their life and to the present or future. *Seattle Times* reporter Eric Nalder urges reporters to ask questions about past occurrences and experiences in the present tense: What are you doing now? What is your friend saying? That way you accompany the interview subject back to the scene and relive it together. In addition to sharpening memory, present tense confers on the account drama and immediacy.

- Judge not: What do you do or say if someone tells you he strangled his wife the previous night? Do you show righteous indignation and ask to use the telephone (to call the police who should take up the investigation from there) or do you stay calm, and try to understand this person? You should be fishing for anecdotes by asking questions like: "Hmm, Mr. Bottoms. How did it happen? Tell me how it all started? What did you use? Can I see the room where this took place? OK, now she enters the room, what are you doing? What does she say? And then what?" The only certified judge in the story process is the reader. No matter how distasteful a person or action is, you must not show indignation or endorsement, just plain interest and curiosity. Establish your neutrality.

If someone tells you something bright and wonderful, however, a show of excitement can help.

- Smile. Smiles put people at ease and make you look sincere, pleasant and trustworthy.
- Read good stories and try to figure out what action—observation, questions, research—produced such fascinating detail, insight and quotes.
- Beware of the Yemo principle. I have named long-winding, sleep-inducing questions after a colleague who interviewed several presidents and prime ministers around the world and got the story published in a question-and-answer format. The questions were often framed to display the interviewer's knowledge and make the celebrity dizzy. His standard question was something like this:

Mrs. Margaret Thatcher, you are the daughter of a greengrocer, which for non-British people is a shopkeeper, yet you broke away from that lowly preoccupation and studied chemistry at Oxford, biology at Cambridge and history at Eton. Mrs. Thatcher, you are known as the Iron Lady by friends and the Milk Snatcher among foes, in a country that is dominated politically, educationally, socially and anthropologically by men. You proved to the world your mettle as an economic reformer and a good leader in the time of war. My question, Mrs. Thatcher, MP, Prime Minister of Great Britain and Ireland, is: when are you going to reshuffle your cabinet?

# Aggressive Listening

- Remove obstacles, e.g. mental stereotypes about the person speaking (size, color, looks, mannerisms, language) and don't let emotional triggers go off in your head. Words like abortion, mother, sex, bomb, terrorism, and AIDS can trigger strong emotions.
- Watch your body language and eye and body movements.
- Listen for major points, and crosscheck meanings. This helps you and it helps the subject affirm that you are interested. "As I understand it, you are saying that . . . ." "What's the moral of your story?" "What do you mean by?" "Why is that?"
- Listen for supporting evidence. Once you get the point and how it connects to the main theme, seek evidence including anecdotes, documents, reference to corroborating sources, and specific details such as time, number of signatories, and names.
- Listen for counterpoints. Other sources may challenge the views and claims of your source.
- Listen for inner voices, what is not said or half-expressed ideas. For example, perhaps you ask a woman about her future and she blushes, smiles, and rolls her eyes. Maybe you have hit upon something significant. You wonder why she smiled and acted that way.

# Observation

Look for everything that could be significant, especially in a symbolic way. The book on the table or shelf, the painting, the color of the room, what the person considers humorous (jokes, cartoons on the bulletin board, the person's fantasies), may be revealing or instructive.

# Staple Questions

Some questions work in most profile interviews. They are known as stock questions—questions you ask almost every subject. Compile and update your stock questions. Use them in context because questions asked in isolation have limited power. Use follow-up questions to dig for details, anecdotes. Here are some examples of stock questions:

- *What is the most memorable thing that happened on your job or in your life?* Within my first few days at the *San Jose Mercury News* (San Jose, California), I went on patrol with a San Jose Police sergeant. I asked about his most memorable day on the beat. Sergeant Ryan said he helped an Asian woman deliver a baby on the street. The baby boy was named Ryan—after him.
- Metzler used excerpts (2–5 below) of reporter Susan Kissir's celebrity interviews to illustrate the power of stock questions.
- What one word describes you best?
- Steve Guttenberg: Dangerous
- Q: Oh, really! Why?
- A: Because I am unpredictable – and dangerous.
- Q: What's your biggest weakness as a person?
- A: I don't say "no" enough.
- What do you think the public would be amazed to learn about you?
- Actress Annie Potts: "People would be surprised at the lack of glamour in my life."
- What's your biggest fear?
- Richard Simmons: "That there will be no gymnasium in heaven."
- To a very powerful person or someone in a dangerous job you may ask: *Have you ever been frightened?*
- To a famous person: *Have you ever met someone who did not recognize your name or reputation?* That was a question I asked renowned Nigerian novelist Chinua Achebe. His response: 'Actually, yes. Someone I was talking to once introduced me this way: "This is Chinua Achebe, you know, the brother of the footballer."' And his brother was not even in the state, let alone national, team.
- *What do you like best about yourself? And what do you hate most?* (I once asked an extremely attractive woman famous for what many

called "drop-dead good looks" these questions. Her response: "What I like, em, nothing; what I hate, yeah, I hate my boobs, they are too big and my back side is too small."

- What do you do in your leisure time?
- Who are your heroes?
- And you villains?
- What is the craziest thing you have done (and/or what was your most embarrassing moment)?
- What makes you laugh, smile, and cry?
- What are your ambitions now?
- What was your ambition as a child?
- What and who do you fantasize about?
- What events and persons have had the greatest effect on your life and personality?
- What is your typical day like (at home, at work)?
- What is your life's motto?
- What are your beliefs? How do you relate to religion? What strengthens/motivates you?
- How do others see you?
- What is your most valued possession?
- If you weren't a politician [singer, teacher, actress], what would you have been?
- *How would you describe yourself?* (Or, as Kissir, put it: *If you had just one word to describe yourself, what would it be?*) I asked Miss British Virgin Islands (2000) how she would describe herself when she was little. Her response: "Mute."

# 5

## Staying on Top of the Interview: Practical Tips

*We all want to talk about ourselves; we want to talk about ourselves with people we think will understand us.* —Gay Talese

Most interviews contain what some call bombshells—the tough and sometimes embarrassing questions, such as: "Mrs. Simons, have you ever cheated on your husband?" We shall call these tough questions grenades because, like grenades, you—not your target—will be blown to pieces if you pull the pin at the wrong time. The name implies three principles that govern grenade use: strategy, carefulness and timing.

## Managing the Grenade

At the start of the interview, the source probably considers you a complete stranger. Once a rapport is established, the source becomes more accommodating and more open. You must be sensitive to the feelings of our subjects and the interest of your story.

Toward the end of a very smooth and frank interview, I asked Colonel Godwin Abbe, a Nigerian military governor, whether he had ever stolen anything. The governor observed a minute of eerie silence and then intoned, "Actually, yes." As a military cadet, he and his friends would sneak out at night to steal mangoes, making sure the sergeant majors did not catch them.

Carole Rich relates the experience of Barbara Walsh, a reporter for the *Lawrence Eagle Tribune*, who pulled the pin at the wrong time. The first question Walsh asked Willie Horton, a man convicted for killing a man and raping his wife while on furlough, was: "How the heck did you get out on furlough?" Horton exploded, and wanted to terminate the interview.

Walsh called her question the "stupidest thing" she had ever done. It was not so much the question that was stupid; it was the atrocious timing and her righteousness. That disaster teaches us the following invaluable lessons: save the tough questions for an appropriate time, and judge no one.

Not everyone explodes when asked an ill-timed, tough or embarrassing question. Some disintegrate into tears. We can prevent emotional outbursts or discomfort by introducing the questions gently—no sweat if you have ever asked someone out on a date or been asked out. Few men would walk up to a woman they just met and say, "Hello, I want to take you to bed." Instead, they would probably start by talking about the weather, maybe paying a neutral compliment, discussing other general issues, inviting the woman for a coffee, and maybe the movies, and then dinner. So it is with deeply personal or embarrassing questions, such as: have you ever cheated on your spouse, been arrested for driving under the influence, had an abortion, or killed someone? The reporter may start with harmless but focused chitchat that sets the stage for the eventual lob of the grenade. Ideally, the source should not know where the reporter is headed.

Here is a crude example of a focused question sequence:

1. Where do executives around here hang out after work? We journalists congregate at a small, cozy bar across the road from the newsroom.
2. Is it a good place? Would you recommend it?
3. Oh really. The Bull's Head specializes in Italian cocktails. You should come along and try it. It is the best in the region. (Here or before now you would have learned what the person's favorite beverage is.)
4. The problem with going out for drinks is getting back home. The police. (Pause and do not fill this silence. The source is likely to comment.) My colleague was stopped the other day and had to pay a $500 fine. (Pause) Do you think the police are exaggerating?
5. (Depending on the response, you could ask) I doubt whether there is anyone who does not know someone the police have booked for drinking and driving. (He or she will either know or not know someone the police fined; whichever way, you may now pull the pin and fling the grenade.)
6. How about you? Have you ever been stopped for driving under the influence?

Grenade management differs from story to story. Topics and sources present different challenges. While sources, interviewing styles and grenade types may differ, the following principles serve as a rough guide for reporters who have a tough question up their sleeves.

- Set the scene by introducing a harmless subject or angle with a "hook."
- Follow up with a general observation related to reality.
- Offer an anecdote about yourself or someone else.
- Remove the sting with phrases such as "It happens." "Normal people do it." "People have different opinions about this." "I am open."
- Ask the person's general view, experience or example.
- Watch for body language.

- Prepare the person for the shot, saying, for example, that it is a question you are afraid you have to ask. (If possible, ask the question in a context the source can relate to.)
- Smile and, very casually, pull the pin.
- Apply a balm. Talk about something flattering or uplifting afterwards, to help the person recover and to retain the cordiality. Keep a transitional question handy that will draw the conversation back to the original thread, show the significance of the grenade to the interview and story, or link the grenade to the remaining issues of the interview.

Here is how Australian national TV talk show host, David Denton, lobbed his grenade at President Bill Clinton:

Denton (after asking a very easy question about Clinton's opinion on Australian politics): "You remind me of a character in the book, "A Hitchhiker's Guide to the Universe," who is described as a man who has the brain the size of a planet. You have an enormous appetite for world affairs. Yet, when I spoke to people on the street today, I just asked them, 'When you hear the name, Bill Clinton, what do you think?' Almost all of them said 'Monica Lewinsky.' It must occur to you that for many people, that's how your presidency is recalled."

After two follow-up questions, Denton tried to help the blustered Clinton to regain his composure and get on with the interview.

Denton (starting to apply the balm): "You were raised to be an optimistic man raised by your mother to be so. Do you have as much faith in humanity now as when you took office?"

Clinton (smiling broadly and bright-eyed): "More. Oh, more. How can I not?" (A chirpy Clinton gives a long, bright answer.)

Denton then made reference to the bracelet that Clinton wore and loved to talk about. He got it on a trip to Columbia, a bright-eyed Clinton said with pride.

It was clear that Denton was not judgmental (Denton was Clinton, not Mother Theresa). The interview ended on a light and friendly note.

In the case of misdemeanors—driving under the influence (DUI), cheating on a spouse, or the like—it is useful to express your humanity or relate to the weaknesses or those of people close to you. That is one way of building trust. If you have no personal errors in your past, do not play saint or chief judge. Lisa Grunwald was interviewing the married woman who admitted she was having a series of affairs. Unexpectedly, the woman asked if the reporter had ever cheated on her husband. "I answered her in ways that would elicit more trust and confessions," Grunwald recalls. She replied that she had never had an affair, but afraid of sounding too holy and thus making the subject feel dirty and judged, Grunwald adds, "But of course I've only been married a year."[1]

# Giving a Piece of Yourself

From Grunwald and other accomplished interviewers, we can see that sharing a piece of our lives can be a great investment. The dividends include a boost in the source's confidence, openness, trust, and dramatic or sobering insights. This approach reminds me of what the Research Methods instructor told us at graduate school in the U.K. The lesson went like this: While interviewing a man who beats his wife, do not show shock or disgust. Instead, spur the informant on with words like "Really? So you punched her left eye! Why the left and not the right? What was the color of those eyes? Blue, oh interesting. Yeah, I understand, Mr. Spank, we all beat our wives!" Ok, we don't. But you get the point.

This approach is based on the reasoning that people will feel more comfortable sharing intimacies with fellow fallible humans.

# The Kissir Approach

We will name the principle of sacrificially sharing one's personal life with the interview subject after celebrity reporter Susan Kissir, whose work I cited in Chapter 4. While interviewing Hollywood star Danny DeVito, Kissir gave away a whole lot of herself.

> Kissir: If you had just one word to describe yourself, what would it be?
> DeVito: That's very difficult. I don't know. How about you?
> SK: Driven
> DV: Are you talking about me?
> SK: No, me. I don't know you well enough.
> DV: Are you driven?
> SK: Yeah.
> DV: What are you driven by?
> SK: Ambition.
> DV: A desire to get ahead?
> SK: Or passion, I don't know.
> DV: Do you have a boyfriend?
> SK: Uh, four.
> DV: Four boyfriends! You are a driven sex maniac! [Laughs uproariously].[2]

Kissir succeeded in demolishing the barrier between reporter and celebrity. It was one ordinary person speaking to another. When she eventually wrested control from DeVito, she had a very frank interview. The actor revealed a lot about himself. We saw the feisty, capricious, teasing Danny DeVito. The problem with Kissir's interview, however, was that she seemed to lose control. This fear of losing control has pushed some journalists to avoid sharing any part of their life.

Sally Adams, a freelance reporter, advises reporters to lie, if necessary, to keep sources from prying into their personal lives. For her, no interviewer must fall for the ploy of the interviewee's question. Her advice: "deflect them immediately" or lie, as Lynn Barber did when actress Julie Andrews wanted to know whether Barber had children. "She had two children but she said she had none," exclaims Adams, "because she knew Julie Andrews, being a pleasant woman, would ask about them and she didn't want to divert or break the flow of the interview.[3]

What some may see as diversions might just be one human being trying to connect with another. For the narrative writer, the interview is a flowing conversation. It does not require a rigid flight plan. The success of the interview and the story is predicated on flow, not on the reporter's coyness, preferences, or fears. Barber's interview could have progressed better if she volunteered the information herself. We would have had two mothers chatting away. Andrews might have reeled out illuminating and more intimate anecdotes that could have elevated Barber's story. We would have seen confidence building and more intimate and revealing information about Andrews' life and motherhood emerging.

A lie shows the interviewer's untrustworthy and disrupts the atmosphere of dialogue and trust with Andrews, whom Adams describes as a pleasant woman. By lying, the reporter only succeeded in truncating the human link, disrupting the rapport she needed to build with her source. Rapport generates freedom and frankness.

While reporters spilling out excessive, intimate details about their lives might constitute a distraction, failing to share any part of their life would be an error in judgment. Lying to a source is a breach of ethics and confidence.

Let us look at a fairly personal detail like sexual orientation. Say you are a gay reporter interviewing gay rock star Elton John. John asks you whether you are gay. Rather than lie to deflect further attention, the conscientious reporter may use his or her sexual orientation to establish empathy and confidence with the star. If you have friends or know people who are gay, you should mention them to establish a common ground. The person you are interviewing only wants to know whether the two of you understand the same language, whether you are a fellow human or some nasty interrogator from the morality police department.

There are, of course, certain questions a reporter may decide not to answer. Adams offers one good example: "What is your opinion?" An interviewee who asks this question is trying to turn the tables. In an interview, as in news and feature stories, it is the opinion of the source that matters, not the reporter's. Even when the reporter's opinion is sought, he or she does not have to lie or attempt to deflect it brusquely. Rather, the reporter may tell the source that in a news organization there are people who are better trained and qualified to give opinions (op-ed writers, members of the editorial board, and critics). I sometimes say that it would be presumptuous of me as a reporter to attempt to impose my opinion on people. Another approach is: "I want to be as neutral and balanced as possible. I want facts, your opinion—not my opinion—to come through in this story".

Researching, finding a common ground and persisting help reporters destroy the defenses of reluctant or guarded sources. Eric Nalder notes that finding the common ground, such as the interests the reporter shares with the interviewee opens doors. His example: "By the way, I notice you've got a poodle. I've got a poodle." People may talk to you, notes Nalder, if you let them know you already know a lot about the subject. That makes the exchange an informal conversation, not an interview.

# Handling Problem Subjects

In the last chapter, we learned how to get reluctant sources to talk to us. Getting an interview is only one of challenge. Some sources have no problem granting interviews, but troublesome sources make interviewing a harrowing experience for reporters. A troublesome source is an interviewee who deliberately frustrates the reporter or derails the interview. In particular, some sources use a variety of tactics to distract the reporter's quest for specific facts. Some of these tricks are:

- Rambling
- Hostility
- Steamrolling
- Evasiveness
- Restricting the use of information supplied

## Rambling

Just about every reporter encounters the non-stop talker who switches from one inane subject to another. Understanding ramblers may help the reporter contain them. The following people make great ramblers: publicity seekers, idle, nervous or disgruntled people, or people with a low self-esteem. Yet, ramblers may be custodians of a wide range of useful information. Reporters must handle ramblers with tact and think and act strategically—scavenging respectfully for precious stones from this swirling pool of junk. Here are some tips:

- Make an effort to listen for three to five minutes, even if the subject is talking in circles, before you intervene. That gives you time to assess the source and the symptoms of his rambling. Interrupting the ramble at this stage might hurt the source's already low self esteem. Reporters who don't listen and rather try to force focused information out of ramblers, often insult, alienate or harden ramblers. If you listen, you might be able to redirect the rambler. "Your unique economic policy is an interesting point I would like to return to. But tell me what you plan to do with the 300 dockworkers protesting outside the port."
- Longsuffering pays. So, listen for anecdotes and details. The rambling can provide telling details that could enrich your story.
- Throw in questions that can bring the conversation back on track (a reason to be attentive) and illuminate the story with anecdotes and detail in action. Say, you are investigating a homicide, and the victim's neighbor is busy telling you about how wonderful the weather has been lately. Instead of despairing, you may ask what the murder victim did when it was so sunny, what she was wearing, where she liked to go, and in whose company.

- Pretend to be taking notes (to whip the rambler's enthusiasm). Then say that the source was offering a unique perspective to which you would like to return, time and deadline permitting (a hint for the subject to be considerate).
- Yawn or look out the window or at anything that catches your eye. The person might believe you are not interested in those inane details they are reeling out.
- Ask the person if he or she minds giving you straight answers in a few sentences on some quick issues before a fuller, more general chat (perhaps over coffee sometime?). For good measure, tell the subject you needed to exhaust this *brief* issue in, say 10 minutes. If the rambling continues, you could look as frequently as possible at your watch to drive home the point.
- You could also intermittently ask: "May I quickly take you back to X issue before it escapes us. I really want your view or comment on (now state the issue or ask the question with precision) what Ann May was doing on the roof."
- Do not waste your tape recorder on frivolous information. Play the adult for a moment. Turn on the recorder or take notes only when the subject provides relevant or useful information. Stop the note taking or turn pf the recorder when he or she starts rambling again. By doing this, you reward good behavior and punish wayward actions. This approach may be used only as a last resort.

# Hostility

There are two broad categories of hostile subjects: those still feeling the sting of a previous encounter with journalists, and those seeking to dominate and intimidate the interviewer.

In the first category, the subject might be uptight because a previous interviewer had written an unfavorable story about him or her or because the subject has a personal problem unrelated to journalism—a fight with a colleague or family member, perhaps. By asking the source if anything is wrong, you may be able to "defuse it or set it aside," as Metzler puts it. Getting blamed for the sins of another reporter or of all journalists is fairly easy to handle. You may tell the aggrieved source that it would be an error for you to blame him or her for the wrongs of her colleagues or profession.

The second category of hostility is harder to contain. The interviewee feels he or she is smarter and more important than you. Some try to show that they know more about reporting than the interviewer. Others threaten to report interviewers to their managing editor. The hostile source could be a professor, a former top journalist, an author, or other celebrity. It could be that they hold journalists and journalism in low esteem. Sometimes, hostility occurs because the reporter was not prepared for the interview. Some subjects get hostile, however, because the reporter's questions are hitting too close to home. Reporters must psyche themselves up and be determined not to be intimidated and beaten down by the encounter with colossal reputations and tantrums. Have a ready smile, and make sure you keep the conversation on track. Let me share my experience on the beat.

Chinua Achebe is one of the world's biggest novelists. His book, *Things Fall Apart,* has been translated into some 50 languages worldwide and is read in high schools and universities on all continents. In addition, he was voted, along with William Shakespeare, as one of the 100 most influential novelists. It was this same Achebe that I, a mere reporter, had to interview. For the first interview I showed up at the writer's doorstep ill prepared and naive, knowing very little about him and his books beyond the little of *Things Fall Apart* I grudgingly learned in high school. In answer to one of my feeble questions, Achebe, eminent professor of literature, said calmly, "You know, you have no idea how it feels to be interviewed by someone who knows absolutely nothing about you." And often he would retort. "That is a stupid question." I felt stupid and little.

Years later, I was sent back well researched to interview Achebe, not about his books this time, but about his politics. By now I had read his books. I had prepared questions I believed nobody had ever asked him. I was going to bring the great Achebe to my turf, and make him human.

To the question, "Was the Nigerian civil war really necessary?" Achebe, who led a section of the breakaway republic's propaganda machinery barked, "That is a stupid question." I smiled and said meekly: "It is not stupid, professor, it is simple. Was the war necessary?" He now reflected, and answered the question calmly.

I asked another question, which he labeled as hypothetical and refused to answer. But he knew that refusal would come back and haunt him when the story got published. So, a week later, the day the story was published, a hand-written letter from Achebe arrived in the mail. He has reconsidered the question and thought it was a good one. He now offered a written answer—too late.

Foreknowledge of the source's character helped me evade some of the bullets. Another thing that helped was the deceptive simplicity of some of my questions, which offered new insights into the character of the source and teased out rare anecdotes. Those questions brought the giant off his high horse. Two key techniques of journalistic questioning are simplicity and novelty. The strategic use of "stupid questions" is discussed later in this chapter.

# Steamrolling

Like ramblers, steamrollers dominate the interview, carrying on with their speeches regardless of the reporter's questions, exasperation, and body language. To handle steamrollers effectively, reporters need to understand how they operate.

Steamrollers could be people in positions of authority or people who crave authority. They are usually people who care about their image or who are scared of being hurt by revelations. These are people who think highly of themselves and always demand to be heard. So, while they are bashful, they are also vulnerable. Here are some tips on how to handle them:

- Look for anecdotes. As they gush out information, ask them for specific instances and precise details. This will create a useful rule—that you can interrupt them.
- State up front the areas you wish to cover and the amount of time you have. Be flexible, however. They can reel out valuable information.
- Exploit their craving for publicity by insisting that, for the story to work, you do need to have a pattern. You may say the way you handle stories is to obtain precise information on a range of subjects and then (time and deadline permitting) you will look for wider comments.
- Consider the anti-rambling technique of pretending to take notes and looking distracted, although you must always pay attention to what is being said.
- Ask unexpected questions that get them thinking.

# Evasiveness

The evasive source considers himself or herself as an astute politician and a very smooth operator. This source has high self-esteem and sees the interview as an intellectual equal but as a lower being when it comes to maneuvering. To overcome evasiveness, we need to identify its symptoms. Some of the symptoms are:

- **Bridging**: The source discreetly switches to another topic or dimension. For example, the source deflects the question about his or her tax evasion by lecturing the interviewer on the obsession of the media with individuals instead of the corruption in the system. One possible solution to bridging is to smile and say that the new dimension is interesting but that you would like to begin with a specific issue, say, his or her tax evasion.
- **Tit for tat**: The source returns question for question. This art favored by subjects trying to be humorous or amiable was made famous by a bishop visiting New York from Rome. "Will you be visiting any night clubs in New York?" a mischievous reporter asked. As the story goes, the bishop quipped: "Are there any night clubs in New York?" Well, the next day, the papers carried a story with headlines saying the bishop's first question on arrival was whether there were any nightclubs in New York. Served him right. Variations to the tit for tat method are: "Did you kill your wife, Mr. Hacker?" And Mr. Hacker hits back: "Do I look like a wife killer?" (No, Mr. Hacker. Nobody looks like a wife killer. Did you kill your wife, Mr. Hacker?) Another: "What will be the fate of party members accused of corruption, Mr. President?" The president: "Corruption? What corruption?" The reporter may respond to this trick by asking the question again, slowly

and with a smile, or asking it another way. Consider a leading question, based on research.

- **Questioning the reporter's motive**: The interviewee accuses the reporter of asking questions with ulterior motives. A Nigerian federal minister once told me the question I asked him was scripted for me by his political opponents. The rule is to remain calm and smile. No, I said, the opposition did not formulate the question, but I would appreciate an answer. I went a step further and asked the politician to say what question he wanted me to ask his political opponent.

- **Pedantry or abstraction**: The subject may switch to complex terminology and jargon to show off, throw the reporter off the scent, or disguise ignorance. This is an intellectual mating strut, the signal of a juvenile seeking attention and approval. I sometimes compliment the subject's erudition and ask for the layman's equivalent of the terms he or she is using.

- **Amnesia**: Many sources pretend not to remember details that they fear may be used against them. Others cannot honestly remember the facts. This is the time to refresh the memory. Ask for sequence. Ask for people involved and for feelings. If someone forgot the year an event occurred, they might remember something else that occurred at the same time or period, such as the Queen's visit, a massive earthquake in San Francisco, the name of the U.S. president at the time, September 11, the hanging of Saddam Hussein, or other such memorable events.

One of the best cures for disruptive behavior is good preparation, and conversation. When the conversation moves smoothly and does not resemble an interrogation, interview subjects often drop their defenses and their stratagems.

# Restrictions on the Use of Information

Many interview subjects will ask you not to use crucial information they just gave you. This sounds really silly. In major newspapers in the United States and the United Kingdom, editors instruct their reporters to warn their sources not to say anything they do not want published. With a little effort, reporters often find people, including chief executives and public affairs heads, willing to give them the same information on the record or confirm or challenge the information.

The general rule is for reporters not to agree to suppress any information or source without the approval of the editor. The editor decides whether the information is valuable enough to be considered unattributable. As a newspaper editor I have, on occasion, had to go ahead and publish details the reporter had declared off-the-record, because I thought the anonymity deal lacked transparency and was a breach of public interest and of journalistic principles. To retain public confidence, we have the duty to disclose the sources of the information we publish.

# Questions and Anecdotes

## Questions

Good reporters strive to bring offer readers new perspectives, to discover something new and fresh. Chances are that other reporters have interviewed the same person you are about to interview probably on the same issues. Put yourself in the place of your interview subject. Would you like to answer the same routine questions from 10 different reporters? You have to show your subject your line of inquiry will generate new knowledge, a new way of understanding the issues. To achieve this, you need to set the stage for the interviewing by using clear and strategic questions to prepare the source and yourself for the interview. We shall look at two main types of questions reporters use to set the stage for the broader and deeper conversation.

### 1. Opening Questions

An icebreaker, the most popular type of opening question, is the interviewer's opening line—the easy-to-answer opening question or comment. It is the Novocain administered before the dentist starts pulling teeth. Introducing an ice breaker is akin to flipping the light switch on, or setting the table for an important dinner. It establishes the reporter's preparedness, affability and curiosity. It also establishes a pleasant atmosphere for free discussion. It puts both the interviewer and source at ease. Though opening questions put the source at ease, asking them is not an act of charity. They are a strategic questions used to coax the source out of his or her hole, so to speak. It is a give and take arrangement: the interviewer gives the subject a sense of importance and receives frankness and openness in return. An example: "I gather that you are a man of principles. What is the highest price you have paid for your beliefs in freedom of speech?"

The icebreaker could be the greetings from a mutual acquaintance, a comment on the wall painting or a question about it, if you are not knowledgeable in that area. Great icebreakers result from thorough research. Sometimes they are comments rather than questions, for example: "I understand that you represented your high school in badminton at the Helsinki College Games." The comment can generate good quotes and give insight to the character, for example, the business philosophy practices of the source. An icebreaking question posed to a bank chief executive helped me to understand why the bank was spending nearly $1 million on a deteriorating children's hospital: the bank's chief executive was born in that hospital, an orphan.

Talking to the wife of a prominent American figure, Kathleen Buchanan used an unexpected instrument to break the ice—a faulty tape recorder. She recalls:

> When I was a naïve young reporter in 1981, assigned to interview Gordon
> Liddy's wife, Frances, for the now defunct Sunday Press newspaper in Mel-

bourne, Australia, a male colleague mischievously suggested I take the office tape recorder that rarely worked.

As I recall, Liddy was visiting Australia after serving jail time for masterminding the notorious 1970's bugging of the Watergate Hotel, which contributed to the downfall of President Richard Nixon.

In those days, tape recorders were cumbersome, push-button-winding spool contraptions that could really take away from an interview if you let them, but when I mentioned, with a twinkle in my eye, mine wasn't operating properly, Liddy good naturedly took it from my hands, fiddled with it for a moment or two and, hey presto, it worked again! "No one has been able to fix that!" I remarked. Then Mrs. Liddy glided elegantly past and wryly commented. She said something like, "He's quite an electronics expert." And I had a great quote for my ensuing story.

Although Buchanan was assigned to interview Mrs. Liddy, the ice-breaker revealed the characters of both her subject and her newsworthy husband. Buchanan did not miss the symbolism of Mr. Liddy being portrayed by his wife as an expert in electronic devices. The ice-breaker opened the couple up for a free exchange. Buchanan recalls:

With the spools revolving on the table we sat around, we talked about all kinds of things—guns, prison sentences, presidents and Bob Woodward. The Liddys could have been any ordinary American family discussing events in their lives. Perhaps I unconsciously employed the type of casual conversant style, with a bit of comic relief that I have consciously tried to integrate into my interviews as a more mature journalist to create a relaxed atmosphere.

Back in the newsroom, my colleagues gathered around a desk to listen as the little tape recorder squeaked away on replay.

I remember some of my contemporaries questioning me later on the lighthearted nature of the copy. "Do you realize who you were interviewing?" one senior colleague asked.

We don't all have faulty tape recorders to thrust at our sources, but we can use what we got to make sources feel they are fellow humans rather than just interviewees.

## 2. Filter Questions

After breaking the ice, the reporter interviewing someone for the first time can now ask filter questions, for example: "How long have you been a surgeon?" "Where were you when the accident occurred?"

Filter questions, used frequently by cross-examining lawyers, researchers, psychologists, police officers, and journalists, establish the source's qualifications, reinforcing the credentials of known sources and introducing people with unknown credentials. Such questions can also weaken or screen out sources with poor qualifications. Filter questions can establish the reporter's knowledge and sophistication and improve conversational rapport with highly qualified sources. Some of the best filter questions are based on some element of research. That is why reporters must not ask filter questions in lieu of research: "What high school did you attend, President Bush?"

A good filter question is one used frequently by job interviewers and therapists: "Tell me about yourself." Sources' perceptions of themselves will reveal their character and provide information interviewers might not have considered requesting. Asking sources, especially known people, to tell you about themselves, could signal your incompetence. It would be better for reporters to ask sources to introduce themselves from their own perspectives, including what people need to know or don't know about them. For example, you could ask President Bush: "From your perspective, who is George W. Bush?" (Or "Tell me about the George W. Bush that you know.")

# The Interview as Negotiation

The principle of negotiation is that there is no free lunch, no fortuitous questions or moves. In his book, *Negotiation Skills* (John Whyte & Sons, 1994), Baden Eunson identifies questions as a major negotiating tool. We can deduce from Eunson's analysis of negotiators' questions that the interview is a process of negotiation. It is a give-and-take situation; what is said and unsaid come to light through careful inquiry. Interviewers negotiate for information, while interview subjects attempt to get across their own points and preserve their interests.

Journalists have a lot to learn from other professionals—negotiators, psychologists, lawyers, cops and counselors, for instance—whose work depends on the effective deployment and management of questions to elicit information and achieve their goals. It is important, therefore, for journalists to become familiar with the types and functions of negotiators' questions.

## Stupid Questions

Strategic stupid questions make the inquirer seem stupid because the answer to the question seems plainly obvious. What distinguishes a stupid question from a smart question disguised as a stupid one is the nature and purpose of the question. Was it a carefully thought out strategic question or one asked out of laziness or habit, even idiocy?

We shall concentrate on strategic "stupid questions." What may appear as a stupid question is often the most devastating. One of the greatest advantages of strategic stupid questions is that they give the source a false sense of confidence. The source underestimates the reporter's intelligence. The strategic stupid question, notes Eunson, could catch the source off guard and bring the discussion back to the basics.[4]

Here is an example: "Mr. President, what is your definition of racism, and apartheid? Is racism good or bad? Does your country practice racism? Is racism good or bad?" These sound like stupid questions. Even a donkey would know what racism and apartheid are! The reporter should get a dictionary or enroll in school, right? I asked then South African President F.W. De Klerk these questions at a London press conference in the twilight days of apartheid. Mr. de Klerk paused for 60 seconds and stuttered as he struggled to answer these deceptively simple questions. His painful answer (to the effect that racism was bad and his government frowned on it) made the front-page lead of the quality press in London the following day. The head of an apartheid regime defined racism negatively and distanced his racist government from it.

Questions are truly dumb if they reveal lack of reflection or research and if they have no strategic purpose. Such questions would normally be questions of habit such as "How do you feel?" How did you expect a man who just won a $50 million jackpot to feel? But if you had a hunch that the win could devastate him the question would be in order. If you have cause to suspect that the woman whose husband was killed in a car crash might actually be rejoicing at the death of the nasty man, then the medical question, "How do you feel?" would make sense.

# Open and Closed Questions

Open questions create some leeway for a variety of responses. They cannot be answered with a yes or no. An example: "Ms Boon, after seven broken marriages, what have you concluded about the institution of marriage?" Closed questions are specific, and call for specific answers. For example, Governor Vernon, do you plan to veto the abortion legislation?"

During cross examination, attorneys start with open questions to obtain information and opinions that will be used to extract an admission of guilt based on the attorney's devastating closed question. Preparing the grounds for the kill—a bit like circling the quarry—opening questions put sources at ease and massage their egos by showing that they and their opinions are valuable. (Open question: How would you describe your relationship with Michael Hanson?) When you want to establish a fact or extract a commitment, however, you narrow the inquiry down to a closed question: "Did you kill Mr. Hanson?" Closed questions can rope in an evasive source.

# Straightforward Probe

"What are your plans for retirement, Mr. Cassidy?" The straightforward probe seeks a direct answer—no rambling and no frills. It is a focused but open question that allows the source room to maneuver and even be creative. Straightforward probes sometimes elicit colorful quotes.

# Reflective Questions

"Could the pay increase you are proposing possibly give rise to inflation?" This type of question gets the source to reflect on the answer he or she gave, and to address the implications of that answer. Reflective questions reveal the reporter's preparedness and familiarity with the subject. They put the interviewer at par with the source. For instance, the answer of the labor leader who admits (or denies) that the pay rise the union is demanding could cause inflation could move the story to the other dimension of the issue—ramifications, and other sides of the issue.

# Softening Up Questions

"Would you say that last year was rougher than most?" Such questions, Eunson observes, are hard to say "no" to. Softening up questions condition or prepare the source to answer tougher questions, even grenades. These strategic questions reveal the interviewer's empathy and could give a hostile source a false sense of security, leading to guileless, implicating or revealing answers, and to tougher questions.

# Silent Probe

In human communication, silence is often an implicative answer. Silence can also be the best question and the deepest answer. Attorneys, negotiators, police interrogators, and psychologists, whose jobs thrive on their ability to extract delicate information from people, rely on silence as a tool of negotiation and coercion. Journalists seem to have the biggest problems with silence. Louise Ritchie, a journalist who holds a doctoral degree in clinical psychology, asked writers and journalists at the 1997 National Writers Workshop in Fort Lauderdale, Florida, what went through their minds when silence trailed an interview question. One participant answered: "I worry about whether I asked a stupid question." Others nodded in agreement.

A source's silence may not mean the interviewer asked a bad question. In fact, it could denote the opposite. The interviewer's question may have hit home. Silence could be the sign of an emerging expression of deep emotion (sobbing, show of remorse, defiance, anger or indifference) that would enrich a response and the general picture. As Ritchie put it:

> But instead of meaning that a reporter's question is awry, silences mean that the reporter has touched upon an important issue. In therapy, long silences ... occur before patients talk about things they have never revealed to another person; these even may be things so painful the patient had forgotten them.

Ritchie offers an example:

"Tell me about one of your turning points," a reporter asked a star line-backer. "I've been asked that question before, but I haven't had any turning points," the linebacker answered.

The reporter restated the question, mentioning that most people have turning points. Then the reporter waited in what began to seem like an interminable silence. Finally, slowly, and with tears in his eyes, the athlete described how when he was returning from a vacation at age 9, the van that he and his family were riding in flipped. His mother had almost died. His father and siblings were seriously injured.

"It was the first time as a family we felt so vulnerable . . . . God uses us for a reason," he said softly, adding that it had been years since he thought about that accident.[5]

Good interviewers crave silence. Silence before an answer often signals the possible existence of nuances to a situation or conflict not earlier made obvious. If someone answers the question, "How old are you?" and the source paused for 30 seconds before answering, the silence would trigger the alarms in the alert interviewer's mind. A bout of silence could also allow the source time to reflect in order to give a coherent, accurate and detailed response. When the void becomes obvious, even the most reticent source often tries to fill it. Silence confers more authority on the interviewer, especially if he or she can maintain polite eye contact with the interviewee. Silence could also afford the interviewer time to reflect, take notes, observe, or plan the next move. Do not be afraid of silence or be under any pressure to fill it with words.

# Anecdotes

An anecdote is a small narrative incident—a brief true story of a personal experience that illuminates human character or illustrates a point. It is the account of a sequence of events showing people in action—action that reveal character or explains what happened and how it happened. The way people react in specific instances explains their character. Anecdotes, therefore, bring out the ironies and quirks of life.

For example, Miss April Summers, a schoolteacher, tells you the crossroads of her life was the moment the chairman of the school board handed her a letter of dismissal. What did she do? She opened it, of course, and started reading. What was her reaction? She threw the letter in the air and started dancing and hugging and kissing the chairman on the cheeks. Well, that was an anecdotal detail that sets Miss Barley apart from other people, distinct from other schoolteachers just fired by the school board. She could equally have walked calmly home, dusted the Browning her grandmother gave her on her 30th birthday, walked back to school singing "We shall overcome," and shot the chairman on the right wrist, screaming, "You will never sign another dismissal letter with that wrist."

Anecdotes put readers on the scene, showing them what happened, rather than restricting them to the reporter's interpretation (she was angry, or she was surprisingly unperturbed) of a situation.

Anecdotes bring out color, entertainment, rare insight, credibility, life, and even humor to an occurrence or character. Anecdotes make stories fun to read, drawing out the humanity the subjects share with ordinary people. They put the reader in the eye socket of the reporter. They enliven dull interviews and sources and help build a rapport between the interviewer and the subject. Anecdotes make excellent material for leads, if they contain captivating detail and illuminate a situation or character.

The story by Nicholas Wapshott about the new mayor of New York, "Mayor tastes political life," started this way: "Michael Bloomberg is a self-made billionaire and Mayor of New York but he is still "a hotdog, hamburger, meatloaf, fried chicken kind of guy."[6]

*The Weekend Australian* magazine started the story titled "Mission Brown" about the "nation's most loved—and hated—environmentalist" this way:

"[Get lost], Bob Brown." It was a verbal hit-and-run; an aside rather than a shout. The man slid into the crowd in Hobart's Salamanca Place market, but Brown was after him like a shot: "What did you say? What was that you said?" In the space of a 20-minute stroll, it was just one snipe versus 13 separate hugs, congratulatory chats, handshakes, frenzied horn-tootings [sic] and thumps on the back, but Brown wasn't about to let go. It is a mantra now, not to let things go. Not to let jibes about his homosexuality slide, or the digs about eco-freaks and ferals, or the more measured criticism from the island's Establishment that he has blighted Tasmanian industry and cost Tasmanian jobs.[7]

If we ignore the unwieldy last sentence, we can see how the anecdote reveals the humanity and character of this powerful leader of the formidable Greens environmentalist movement in Australia. This anecdote establishes the thread of Mr. Brown's tenacity and self-consciousness, which will run through the story.

Anecdotes give authority to a story and, because they are not often attributed (he said, she said), they make stories flow. They also draw interviewees out because reflections on specific details often activate memory and associations.

Anecdotes flow when the inquirer uses human curiosity: You must wonder about things, people and situations. Gary Tippet used anecdotes to find out how a burglar's mind works, and to capture this felon's inner feelings and motivations in his *Sunday Age* crime story, "The big Steal":

He used to lie in bed some mornings and dream of houses just like this. Little white single-fronted cottage, picket fence, wrought iron around the veranda, pretty pocket-handkerchief garden. A laneway out the back, an extension in glass and timber bathing a sunroom in natural light. The sort of place that people had put a lot of work and pride and money into. And then he'd go and rob it.

Lie back, shut his eyes and he could picture the place perfectly: seeing the way in through the alley, the fence high enough for cover but not too high to climb, the very window he was going to pop. Imagining all the good gear inside. He'd lie there for half an hour or so, thinking it through, getting comfortable with it. Then he'd get up, get dressed - gloves in one pocket, screwdriver in the other - and walk straight out and do it.

The British press reported Margaret Thatcher, then prime minister of the United Kingdom, wore Marks & Spencer underpants. How did the reporter know? Curiosity, fishing for anecdotes.

I ask people about their most embarrassing moments. Everyone, including celebrities, has them. The answers are always fascinating and illuminating. Everyone has an illuminating little story. Remember the governor who used to steal mangoes.

If you are interviewing a great orator, surely you want to find out whether he or she ever gets stage fright, if a speech went bad, and you do want a lot of detail about the first public speech he or she made, about any mishaps.

Anecdotes helps set the mood of a story. An eminent professor, who cannot be named because of the embarrassment of the incident, was the keynote speaker at an international language and literature conference I attended in Canberra, Australia. After the glowing introduction from the moderator, the shiny-headed scholar mounted the podium, trundled toward the microphone, tripped on a wire, and disappeared behind the rostrum. Some delegates feared he had dropped dead. About two minutes later, two hefty men hauled the bald man up and hung him on the podium like a jacket. In that position he completed his brilliant speech and nodded to the riotous applause of the enraptured delegates.

Every human activity harbors an anecdote.

# Teasing out Anecdotes

Often the source does not know what information to give and what to leave out. It is the job of the interviewer to tease out details that will drive the story and make it compelling and relevant to the readers. Some of the standard prompts and questions include:

- Give me an example.
- Can you recall an instance . . . ?
- So what did you do?
- And what happened?
- And then what?
- Can you recall your exact words?
- Take me back there now.
- Let me see the room.
- Where are you in the room?
- What were you wearing?
- What can you smell?
- Who else is there?
- What are they doing and saying?
- What is going through your mind?
- What else can you remember?

# Fishing for Good Quotes

Few people you interview will lace their answers with elegant phrases, entrancing figures of speech, peculiar language, deep personal insights, human color or drama, or summarizing statements. What you invest in an interview is what you reap. In other words, incisive and insightful questions reap rich responses. Draw out quotable sentences and expressions. For example, you could get a merchant of drab sentences to use a figure of speech by seeking analogies, by asking questions such as: "What is it like?" or "How does it feel?"

In response to the question, "What is it like to be looking for your first job?" one source quipped, "It's like asking your wife for money."[8]

Metzler, with the following example, suggests that the metaphorical question will elicit a metaphorical answer. Asked whether his precarious position made him feel like "a man sitting on an iceberg in a storm-tossed sea," a commissioner replied: "No, it's more like lighting a cigar sitting on a barrel of high-octane gasoline."

One good image deserves another.

# 6

# The Abuse and Use of Descriptive Detail

*All you have to do is get a phony style and you can write any amount of words.*
—Ernest Hemmingway

Eliminating useless details is one of the writer's greatest difficulties. In any form, good writing consists of as much of what writers include as what they deliberately leave out.

Chapter 3 sharpened our reflexes and senses for a keener awareness of the diverse dimensions of our reporting environment, opening us up to unique perspectives and dimensions of things and people. We learned to pick up things that elude the untrained eye and mind. We called these otherwise invisible details "the shoehorn." In effect, we engaged our intrinsic power of observation and description. But we cannot throw all the details we collected into the story. This chapter will provide simple and clear guidelines on how to determine which descriptive detail to include in the story.

In his acclaimed book, *Writing for Story*, Jon Franklin reveals that the reader trusts the writer not to include anything that does not have meaning within the story. "This reader will assume that whatever you tell him will have some importance to the story," says Franklin, "and if that meaning is not immediately apparent, he'll be waiting, with part of his mind, for the other shoe to drop."[1] And it had better drop.

The mind of a storyteller is like a video camera. After observing a scene, with its many elements and actions, the mind plays back what it recorded. The details it captured constitute observation, but those details are merely raw stock. These raw shots will be reviewed in the editing suite. Only select clips will be used to prepare a program. The people for whom the video is meant trust the producer to select only clips that will enhance their understanding of the relevant message. Judicious selection of details promotes trust between reader and writer.

# Dropping the Excess Baggage

Selective use of details confers on every word, every person, every detail, every quote, every association, everything we put in a story an implication and meaning in the story. Adult communication hinges on the communicator's ability to select gold from debris, wheat from chaff, and sense from nonsense. If we reported everything we saw, heard or felt, we would be considered childish and dangerous. A pertinent question would be: If I'm not going to use all these details I observed, what is the point of keen observation? Answer: So that you have a wide range of material from which to select details that best serve the reader.

## Selective Description

Descriptive details are vital to good writing—as long as they promote a deeper understanding rather than constitute an obstacle, a distraction, or a decoration. The challenge, therefore, is to combine the excitement of our freedom of perception with the discipline of selectiveness.

Let us take a common example. Suppose you receive a phone call and learn your brother, Mick, whom you have traveled down to visit, fell suddenly ill and has been rushed to St John's Clinic. Your sister, Sally, communicates this development to you this way:

> Hi. It is a warm and beautiful day out there. The sky is bright and a golden eagle is gliding across the bright blue summer sky. Down below, the traffic flows fluently.

Do the details Sally has given you make it easy for you to get to get to Mick's sick bed or are they pointless, an annoying distraction? Idle description prevents readers from getting to the point of the story. They block the movement of the story and exasperate readers.

Let's try another description. This time Sally is giving you driving directions to St John's Clinic:

> St John's is 20 miles from Mick's house. Take I-95 South and take exit 23. Turn left at the third circle. Its main feature is the statue of President Lincoln. You will go past a string of six houses with yellow roofs. Turn right immediately after the sixth house onto Marx Avenue and drive for seven miles until you see a billboard advertising Nokia cell phones. Turn left onto Delaware Street. It is a narrow street with speed bumps. The clinic is on that street, on the left, opposite the Mobil gas station.

Would these details guide you to your destination? Would they help you navigate to a destination and made the journey easier? Then, they were useful and illuminating details.

Obviously, your guide left out a lot of interesting information. For example, colonies of red ants marched up and down the pavements of some of the side streets. A few swallows tumbled perilously out of the gray sky. A 40 year-old woman in a purple jump suit was breastfeeding her child in a red Chrysler parked beside the "no parking" sign. A pine tree was swaying in the gentle summer wind. However, none of these details would have helped you navigate your way to the clinic to see Mick.

The Bible is acknowledged as great literature. This story from John 4: 43 – 50 reveals the disciplined use of descriptive detail. Jesus has just done wonders and attracted followers in Samaria. Now he is going to his homeland, Galilee. The writer captures this activity, headlined as "Jesus Heals Official's Son" as follows:

> 43. After the two days he left for Galilee. 44. (Now Jesus himself had pointed out that a prophet has no honor in his own country.) 45. When he arrived in Galilee, the Galileans welcomed him. They had seen all he had done in Jerusalem at the Passover Feast for they had been there. 46. Once more he visited Cana in Galilee where he had turned water into wine. And there was a certain royal official whose son was sick at Capernaum. 47. When this man heard that Jesus had arrived in Galilee from Judea, he went to him and begged him to come and heal his son, who was close to death. 48. "Unless you people see miraculous signs and wonders," Jesus told him, "you will never believe." 49. The royal official said, "Sir, come down before my child dies." 50. Jesus replied, "You may go. Your son will live." The man took Jesus at his word and departed.

There is no doubt that much else happened in the town. The blazing sun was probably up and the temperature approaching 120 degrees. The cows mooed and the donkeys brayed. A child squealed. There might have been lovers promising to die for each other, as swallows streaked across the bright blue sky. The men, women and children of the town surely had heights and ages and wore different colors of clothing. However, those details would constitute a distraction so the writer kept them out of his story.

Jesus' frame of mind, explained in verse 43, is crucial in that it sets the scene for what is to happen eventually (Jesus being despised by his people). It reveals his prophetic qualities. In verse 45, the warm welcome heightens the irony and drama of the story: his people despise him yet they crave his miracles. The dramatic irony of this situation is that we—the readers and Jesus—know that these people will desire miracles while despising the miracle worker. The writer presents additional corroborative descriptive details. The flashback to Cana is strategic in the text. Even though Jesus effectively conjured enough wine for the villagers, he was to them just a miracle-dispensing machine.

The writer succeeds in transporting readers from A to B, indicating to them where they are being taken. The writer also provides a valid motion chart, the way a tour guide does, as the story cruises toward its destination, with essential details, without distractions.

Good writers, like ace cameramen, set the story in motion by establishing a shot, showing a setting. They now zoom in to the theme of the shoot, linking the facts and relevant background, and using panoramic shots sparingly to put the images in perspective. Good cameramen focus on images that establish and enhance context, meaning and understanding. The idea of focusing on a person is to portray that person in such a way that he cannot be mistaken for another person.

Good writers use apt, concrete description to set the scene, reveal ironies or symbolism, and kick-start or propel a story. Bad writers decorate their stories with descriptive details. For novelists, the use of non-implicative detail can sometimes be forgiven as a well-earned right to vanity. In novels, description sets the scene and often captures the spirit of the entire work, rather than the segment in which the description is featured. The journalist does not have such privileges, such space or such assurance of the reader's longsuffering and goodwill.

Some scenic and atmospheric details do provide a sensory footnote, the way a television camera does. Writers who imitate the camera, however, must also know how to focus on a central theme, even if they have to pan out with their mental camera now and then to sweep in on peripheral details that lend context and a sense of reality to their story.

# The Drama of Detail

No detail is innately idle. What makes a detail idle is its irrelevance or lack of implicative connection to the story or the characters. The writer needs to follow details home to see what those details can reveal and how energize (rather than adorn) the story. Reporters must pursue details, captured them, explore them and put them to work. Raw, undiscovered details are idle details. On its own, the purple stain on a man's shirt may be idle if it carries no revelation, and conveys no implication, no drama, and no deeper meaning of what happened. If captured in its state of being and thrust on the story, the detail would be idle. However, the same stain would turn into a telling detail if the reporter chases it. By asking questions, the reporter might find that the detail carries character elements. For example, it could be that the man was having an affair, that his hygiene was impeachable, or even that he was a wonderful father, whose toddler spewed the strawberry juice on his shirt as he was stepping out of the door, already late. These details come alive when the writer pursues the stain, by asking questions and giving it context, relevance and implication in the story.

Good descriptive details trigger questions and more questions, which will help reveal relevant and illuminating information. To use another illustration, suppose you notice that the senator has a strip of adhesive bandage on his chin. That detail in itself is idle. The reporter has to investigate, ask questions, and explore the significance of the bandage. The findings will only be valuable if they illuminate the context, reveal or enrich character, or if they harbor some symbolism or irony that can advance and enrich the story.

Description will either enhance or block the reader's enjoyment and understanding of the story. Focused and illuminating description draws in the reader. Good writers think of the reader and write to the reader. Bad writers heap pointless details on a story to display their descriptive prowess. Fortuitous, careless, pompous or habit-driven description impedes the flow of the story and frustrates the reader. Essential details are those that are so crucial that, without them, the reader would be bored, lost, confused or short-changed. We need to reread our stories to check the function that those descriptive details perform. The following detail filters should guide reporters and writers in selecting essential details. Vital descriptive details would normally:

1. move the story forward;
2. enhance understanding;
3. heighten the reading pleasure;
4. put the reader on the scene;
5. serve as a transition.

# 1. Detail in Motion: Moving the Story Forward

A good story never stops; it keeps moving, slowly but steadily. Sometimes, it slows down—tactically—to absorb significant detail that would provide illumination, unravel mysteries, heighten the reader's pleasure, or gather the energy to propel the story on.

Details should not be stagnant. Strong narrative details thrive in motion, revealing and interpreting action (activity, movement) on the move. The writer's challenge is to put detail in motion and motion in detail.

## Detail in Motion

The President arrived at the local university with a cigarette dangling from his lips (detail). The dangling on its own is idle. That dangling cigarette could, for example, propel readers toward a fuller appreciation of the President's speech announcing a $300 million incentive for the production of cheap cigarettes for college students. The detail propels the story toward the President's speech and sets the scene for a better grasp of the speech. The reader immediately sees the significance and indispensability of the details to the story.

## Motion in Detail

A black cat (detail) jumped (motion) over the altar at communion time. The cat described here is doing something, something that causes something else to happen, or explains what is happening. It is not a naughty cat (abstract, static) but an active, moving cat. Strong details capture action. Meredith Hall makes turns the killing of her old and tired hens that were no longer laying eggs into a motion picture in her story.

> I held her beak closed, covering that eye. Still she pushed, her reptile legs bracing against mine. I turned her head on her floppy neck again, and again, corkscrewing her breathing tube, struggling to end the gasping. The eye, turned around and around, blinked and studied me. The early spring sun flowed onto

us through a silver stream of dust, like a stage light, while we fought each other.[2]

Note the writer's deliberate use of motion in her details: *pushed, bracing, turned, again and again, corkscrewing, struggling, gasping, turned around and around, blinked, flowed, stream,* and *fought.*

# 2. Enhancing or Deepening Understanding

To explain how descriptive details heighten understanding, let us start with an analogy. I am your dinner guest and would now like to use your bathroom. You tell me to take the stairwell on the right. To get there, I should go past the first two doors on the left. The next is the bathroom door. It is purple. These details help me understand unmistakably how to get to the bathroom.

Surely, you would not tell me the temperature of the room, the ornaments on the mantelpiece, the color of the carpet and ceiling, the type of paintings, and the coffee stains on the living room wall, nor would you tell me that your old and demented Aunt Pamela, groaning from protracted dysentery and arthritis, is drinking Japanese tea in the pantry. All these details are factual, but they are irrelevant to my current needs. Those details, instead of helping me find the bathroom quickly and easily, would distract and frustrate me. Idle details inflict pain on the story and its readers.

If you were describing the scene of an accident, giving a description of the victim and the scene would be appropriate because these details add humanity to your story and to the victim. The details transport your readers to the scene and make them see and feel what happened. They convey to readers the humanity of characters in the story. Descriptive details matter to readers. Failing to identify and use significant and implicative detail is as bad as supplying idle detail.

# 3. Heightening the Reader's Pleasure

Have you ever wondered why people read novels, watch soap operas, go to Las Vegas, or travel abroad on holidays? Pleasure and escape. Stories offer the reader a new world, a different reality.

A newspaper story should offer readers vital details that facilitate the grasp and appreciation of the depth, diverse dimensions and implications of what happened. Social scientists tell us that the human mind thrives on five basic realities: time, place, character, subject, and mood. The accomplished writer supplies details that add a dimension of pleasure to the story, details that give the story a swagger, and the reader that deep smile of conspiratorial pleasure.

A good narrative will move readers from their own world into someone else's real world. It will make readers forget they are sitting on a sofa at home. The pleasure is brought about not by the sweetness of the circumstances portrayed—for it could be the portrayal of pain and gloom—but the accurate depiction of that mood transports readers from their own world to the world so deftly represented. I grew up believing that witches turned into bats, owls, or black cats after midnight. The smarter ones flew off to California for a nocturnal convention and dashed back into their sleeping bodies before dawn. How joyful the life of a witch must be! If all our stories, our depiction of the human drama, would give our readers wings like African village witches!

# 4. Putting the Reader on the Scene

Writers of hard news stories, clinging to "hard facts", usually only scrape the surface of an occurrence or activity. The reporter feeds readers only peripheral details that old-school reporters believe readers have the right to know. These are "what happened, to whom, where, when, why and how."

Focused, concrete descriptive details convey to the reader the mood, impact and taste of otherwise faraway stories or occurrences the way only a guided tour or a top grade television documentary would. The writer should transport readers to the scene of the story, making them feel, see, touch, and sometimes even do or experience what people in the story or affected by the story are doing or experiencing. In the *Weekend Australian* story, "Hate emerges from under the rubble" Catherine Taylor places readers on the scene of the devastation.

> Every few steps, objects from everyday life appear underfoot – a baby's knitted jumper, a drawer still filled with plastic cups, a child's mathematics homework. And then it became clear: the rubble was once a kitchen. Above it is the exposed interior of a house, the entire wall shaved off. A mirror still hangs above a couch. Jagged pieces of plaster and wood dangle over the street.[3]

The reporter draws readers' attention to the intimate signs of a shattered life. Lee Gutkind describes intimate details as "images that symbolize a memorable truth" about characters or occurrences, images "readers won't easily imagine". Using keen observation and precision, Taylor co-opted the witnesses to the devastation, rousing the implicative details—the baby's jumper, the schoolgirls' math homework, a dangling mirror, the plastic cups in the drawer and other self-expressing aspects of what was once a normal life—to speak for themselves. Here, readers are made to partake in the reality of the story's characters. You know you are reading a good story when you forget that you are still in your own house, find yourself instead on the scene of devastation, with the victims, and with the reporter as facilitator and tour guide.

Poorly written stories alienate or ignore readers, offering essentially the writer's way of seeing and feeling things. Such writers block readers from the action, forcing them to rely on a subjective account—the writer's narrow worldviews. They use vague or general terms to describe people or scenes. Without showing how they arrived at the judgment and what evidence is available to support their position, unskilled writers describe people abstractly as tall, fat, angry, sleepy, good, bad, ugly, or happy. For them, objects are expensive, large, or tiny, while ideas are wonderful, important, or useless.

The cover story of *TIME* titled "Inside Saddam's World" is a telling example of how idle description based on personal opinion and exacerbated by debilitating modifiers can sabotage a story and frustrate readers. Part of the lead of the story states:

> It's April 28, Saddam's 65th birthday. Crowds and military men with fat moustaches, sheikhs in flowing robes and farmers in shabby pants spill onto the expansive parade grounds Saddam has built for special occasions like this. High-ranking guests fill up chairs in large pseudohistorical reviewing stand where Mussolini would have felt at home.[4]

An enlightened reader would notice the vacuity of the descriptive words or modifiers—fat moustaches, expansive parade grounds, high-ranking guests, and large pseudohistorical reviewing stand. The writer forces his personal opinion and idle details on readers.

Descriptive details must be factual. Information is generally considered factual when it is precise, accurate, and devoid of bias and when it offers proof or presents an index to test or prove its accuracy. If I describe someone I dislike as stupid and ugly, especially when that person and a neutral and knowledgeable person cannot challenge or balance what I said, my statement is not factual. That means I have not offered any evidence to support my claim. I am merely expressing my bias. Because I did not test my notion of stupidity and ugliness against a collectively shared set of indices, that description lacks accuracy (precision), authority, fairness and balance.

In the *TIME* article, the static descriptive terms—fat, expansive, and large—do not offer a rational person any basis for belief or conviction, or reasonable insight, into the size (and the significance of size) or nature of what is being described. Take the fat moustache. If the moustache and its size were indeed a vital element of the story, the writer should have sought precise details and created associations. For example it could be the same shape and size as something Western readers were familiar with—a croissant, or a boomerang, for example. In any case, the photograph that illustrated the story showed a group of moustache-challenged men hoisting the framed photo of Saddam (with his trademark boomerang moustache).

Furthermore, saying "sheikhs in flowing robes" is like saying "soldiers in uniform," "a priest in habits or soutane" or "a doctor with a stethoscope." What else do sheiks in Arabia wear? Also, how do descriptive details like *shabby, expansive, large*, and *small* help readers relate to or better understand the story? Precision—dimensions, associations or analogies, or a picture—would have served the reader better. Similarly, filling up chairs is a stilted way of saying people sat on chairs. What else do people sit on, anyway? It is like saying people sleep on beds or walk on the ground. If they sat on donkeys, or on a particular type, shape or color of chair, or if the officials were extremely fat, each man filling two chairs, readers would understand why they had to be told Iraqi officials filled up chairs.

The sentence "High-ranking guests fill up chairs in large pseudohistorical reviewing stand where Mussolini would have felt at home" is uneconomical for other reasons, as well. The sentence makes a vague association between Mussolini (as a historical figure and possibly parade-reviewing buff), reviewing stands and Saddam. For that association to work, the writer must establish that readers know and care about Mussolini's preferences or about pseudohistorical reviewing stands. Even then, the writer should know enough about Mussolini to cite a specific, well-known reviewing stand on which Mussolini loved to perch.

Precision comes from hard work, from following details home. This requires research, careful interviewing, general curiosity, a serious commitment to the readers (including the determination not to lose their trust) and to good writing, and respect for facts and detail. Details you don't sweat for and what you cannot peel and check, you should not include in your story. For example, the details about officials would be essential in the story only if the reporter found out precisely who they were. The "minister of Political Propaganda" is more precise and more meaningful than "a high-ranking official," just like "a carpenter named John Doe" is better than a "hard-working tradesman." If you cannot give the reader an idea of what is big, small, high-ranking or shabby something, and if you cannot paint a picture that shows the relevance and use of the detail, leave it out.

Heavy and unwarranted use of descriptive details destroys the flow and rhythm of the text. Qualifying every verb and noun degrades the text, and makes it look like a joke. Try this:

"On a hot, damp morning, a little gray old man sat timidly on the elegant blue chair waiting anxiously for his slim and unhappy wife to walk slowly and daintily through the wide brown door and into his tanned muscular and hairy arms."

Unfocused or decorative description renders the story clumsy and impenetrable.

# 5. Description as Transition

Description can serve as a transition and as a foreshadowing (heralding) or flashback narrative element. Descriptive details help writers to connect the narrative to another strand of reality propelled by action. In the following example from the award-winning magazine story, "Like Something the Lord Made", Katie McCabe uses description as a heralding device. This means either shifting the scene, or shifting the reader's state of mind, or signaling a new but connectable strand of narrative. It is like setting the table as a sign that food is on its way.

> The book was the last work of Vivien Thomas's life, and probably the most difficult. It was the Old Hands' relentless campaign that finally convinced Vivien to turn his boxes of notes and files into an autobiography. He began writing just after his retirement in 1979, working through his illness with pancreatic cancer, indexing his book from his hospital bed following a surgery, and putting it to rest, just before his death, with a 1995 copyright date.
>
> Clara Thomas turns to the last page of the book, to a picture of Vivien standing with two young men, one a medical student, the other a cardiac surgeon. It was the surgeon whom Clara Thomas and her daughter asked to speak at Vivien's funeral.
>
> He is Dr Levi Watkins, and the diplomas on his office wall tell a story. Watkins was an honors graduate of Tennessee State, the first black graduate of

Vanderbilt University Medical School, and John Hopkins's first black cardiac resident. Levi Watkins Jr. is something Vivien Thomas might have been had he been born 40 years later.

That was what he and Thomas talked about the day they met in the hospital cafeteria, a few weeks after Watkins had come to Hopkins as an intern in 1971.[5]

The precise descriptive details in italics prepare the reader for the shift in story focus. They prepare set the reader's mind for the introduction of Watkins. It is not hard to see the point of Watkins' qualifications, which connect the Thomases to Watkins, whose angle of the story is about to unfold.

In this passage, description does not spring up from the writer's impulse. It serves a strategic purpose. Good description is not something you pick off a shelf. You dig for it like gold. You clean and define it and send it to readers as a precious gift.

# 7

## Language and Style

*Easy reading is damned hard writing.* —Nathaniel Hawthorne

## What is Style?

One of the harshest criticisms and most common misconceptions of narrative writing is that it is decorative and thrives on flowery language. In any form, decorative writing is bad writing. Good writing is focused, precise and concrete. Style, notes Peter Richardson, does not mean artificiality or ornamentation and is not the opposite of substance. It is not a "dress of thought" and is not the opposite of substance.[1] Novelist Evelyn Waugh says style was not a "seductive decoration added to a functional structure." For Ernest Hemmingway, good writing is architecture and not interior decoration.

James Stovall defines style in a wider sense as the "conventions and assumptions underlying writing and the generally accepted rules of writing and usage for a particular medium."[2] These include capitalization, punctuation, spellings, syntax as well as accuracy, clarity and brevity. We can also look at style in a different and more specific journalistic sense.

Style is the set of expectations that govern good writing. It is the product of who we are—how we think, how we see life, what we have read, where we have been—all defined by the distinct way we gather details and the way we animate these details and communicate them to our audience. Style is also the deliberate individuality and lucidity of perception, inquiry and expression. The individual way journalists view life (based on their unique cultural, social, intellectual and even biological orientation) will determine the kind of details they look for and the kinds of questions they ask. These in turn will determine the way they see things and communicate their findings. We are all imbued with a unique character, with fresh and fascinating personal perspectives. Each time we write, we are exposing our unique style. My trademark as a reporter is the way I see, record, and report events. That trademark must pass a quality test that sets the minimum standards of style acceptable to readers.

Style can be improved. In this chapter, we will explore ways of activating and elevating journalistic style. Besides the unique perception and reporting approach, the main indicator of a writer's style is that writer's unique selection and combination of words. The following are five of the major indices of a writer's success in selecting and combining words:

1. Simplicity
2. Portraying action (showing rather than telling)
3. Specification
4. Imagery
5. Refurbishing language (bringing clichés to life)

# 1. Simplicity

In 1996, a reporter asked Australian political party leader Pauline Hanson whether she was xenophobic. "Please explain," said Hanson, a former fish shop owner. The reporter had not learned about the power of simplicity.

Australian breakfast television host, Tracey Grimshaw, asked the Dalai Lama, the exiled Tibetan head of state, monk, and demigod whether good people went to heaven and bad people to hell. "Or is it just pot luck?" she added with a smile.

"What is that?" asked the Dalai Lama.

"Oh," said the presenter, still smiling, "that means 'luck'".

The monk knew what luck was. As for potluck, he didn't have a holy clue. "Potluck" was just the bombastic equivalent of "luck."

If you find it difficult to use simple words, consider the schoolteacher who, disturbed by his students' preference for long and complex words, gave the class this memorable piece of advice: "In promulgating your esoteric cogitations, and articulating your superficial sentimentalities, beware of platitudinous ponderosities."

At best, overblown writing generates humor—at the writer's expense. When I was a Sunday magazine editor, the copy of one freelance music reviewer gave me frequent heartaches. I was not exaggerating when I parodied the gentleman's overblown reviews this way:

> The seismological propensities and razzle-dazzle of apocalyptic proportions in this quasi-literary, if pseudo-literate, literati's cognitive cataclysm is a mere razzmatazz of the shenanigans of the neo-narcissistic idiosyncrasies in the dichotomy between the flotsam and jetsam of Nigeria's literati and the quixotization of the hoi polloi. This ostensibly is the repast for infinitesimal postulation and encapsulation of the raison d'etre of hoity-toity and higgledy-piggledy sociolambastic effluvia in our concatenated body politic.
>
> Translation: The books are well written, relevant to contemporary Nigeria, and a compulsive read.[3]

"When something can be read without great effort," Enrique Jardiel Poncela observes, "great effort must have gone into writing it." That conscious effort—

the activation of all the senses, discipline, simplicity and clarity—accompanies all good writing.

The list of writers who promote simplicity is endless. Here is a cool tip from Gerald Grow, journalism professor at the Florida A & M University. "The key to journalism is learning the difference between someone with only a ninth-grade vocabulary and a well-informed, intelligent writer using a ninth-grade vocabulary by choice."

Good writing makes good reading. For writing to be good, the writer must work hard to keep it simple and fresh.

The key elements of simplicity are:

- Short words
- Simple words
- Simple sentences
- Concrete words
- Doing words

## Short Words

Good journalism thrives on the writer's willingness to opt for the shortest, simplest and most representative words possible, without sacrificing precision or accuracy. Instead of saying "educational institution," the good writer would say "school" (or college or university) and in place of "relative," the good writer would say "brother," "sister," or "cousin."

In the English language, some of the words that convey the greatest emotional connections are short words of Anglo-Saxon origin: *home, friend, land, drunk,* and *dead.* These words should be used instead of their longer, more pedantic Latin-derived equivalents: *domicile, acquaintance, territorial integrity, inebriated,* and *deceased.*

Fred Fedler et al. observe that length does not confer power on words. In fact, many words gain power as their syllables shrink. *Communicate* is weaker than *discuss,* and *talk* is stronger than both words. Likewise, *stress* is better than *highlight.* However, in choosing between short and longer words, the writer must not sacrifice power, precision and accuracy for brevity. For example, *swagger,* used in context, is stronger than the shorter word, *walk.*

## Simple Words

People do not *purchase* books; they *buy* them. They do not *navigate an automobile* when they can *drive a car.* They should not bother to *respire* when they can *breathe* or perspire when they can *sweat.* People hardly ever *commence;* they *start.* They don't *congregate;* they *gather* or *meet.* The meeting does not *terminate;* it *ends.*

Short and simple words are more economical and, by extension, more forceful than long ones. Here are some examples:

- Commence (start)
- Purchase (buy)
- Emolument (pay)
- Construct (build)
- Tranquility (calm)
- Perspiration (sweat)
- Decapitate (behead)
- Incarcerate (imprison)
- Consume (eat, drink)

Walter Fox shares an example of the force a simple structure and simple words can confer on a sentence: "1992 began in Chicago the same way 1991 ended, with a hail of gunfire."[4]

Now, compare that sentence with this one: "Brockovitch failed to excel academically, hampered by dyslexia" ("Erin Brockovitch: the Sequel," in *The Weekend Australian* Magazine, January 12–13, 2002).

The big words are pretentious, and imprecise. What does "fail to excel academically" mean? Did she fail math, physics, law, psychology or English? What is dyslexia and how did it hamper the student? Dyslexia is a reading (and often speech) deficiency. The simpler, clearer and more elegant sentence would have stated the specific subject Brokovitch failed (American Literature?) because of her reading deficiency. The moral here: avoid, or explain, complex words and jargon.

## Simple Sentences

Brevity is power. The writer of the *Chicago Tribune* story used short words to construct a short and forceful sentence. One of the shortest and most forceful and evocative sentences ever written is this one from the Bible (John 11: 35): "Jesus wept."

One often-ignored reason the sentence is so powerful is that it obeyed one rule of good writing: keep the subject and verb close together. The subject is *Jesus* and the verb is *wept*. Jesus wept.

The sentence also owes its power to the intimacy between the subject and the verb and to the lean and concrete construction. There is a good reason to keep sentences simple. Sentences cluttered with many words and structural twists "contort the straightforward flow of thought," notes Bob Baker. Consider the construction of the loose and winding sentence in the story titled "We're Taking Him Out" (*TIME*, May 13), which only succeeded in obstructing the story flow and enjoyment of readers:

> While key allies in the Middle East, such as Saudi Arabia, Jordan and Egypt, would be *more than* happy to see Saddam go, they are *too busy* worrying about their *own* angry citizens—and *quietly* profiting from trade with Iraq—to help.

The italics signal redundant words. For sentences to be short, they must have few words. Before we kill the redundant words in the *TIME* sentence, let's figure out what the reporter was trying to say. To do this, we must identify the subject and the verb: Key allies in the Middle East (subject) are too busy (verb or verbal clause) to help.

This construction makes it difficult for readers to associate the elliptical "to help" with the "key allies." Too many clauses, twists, and turns alienate and block the action from the actor.

How can the congested sentence be made to communicate more effectively? We shall try to simplify the sentence, weed out redundant words and create from it short and meaningful sentences.

"Key U.S. allies in the Middle East—Saudi Arabia, Egypt and Jordan—want Saddam removed. But they cannot back their hopes with action because they do not want to endanger their trade with Iraq. They also fear angry reactions from their citizens."

Let us look at a few other examples. The story titled "Ex-MP's love child turns 18, but dad's still the real bastard" in the *Weekend Australian* (January 12–13, 2002, p. 11) begins as follows:

Sara Keays broke her 18-year silence yesterday to speak for the first time about the daughter she had after an affair with the former Conservative Party Chairman, Cecil Parkinson.

Taking out redundancies is one way of shortening, simplifying, and therefore invigorating sentences. Breaking silence to speak is tautological. Speaking implies the disruption or replacement of silence.

From another story on the same page ("HK court overturns itself and sends mainlanders home"), we learn:

Thousands of mainland Chinese living in Hong Kong yesterday began the heartbreaking process of packing up to leave what they had believed was home, after the highest court in the former colony ruled that they had no right to stay.

The decision by Hong Kong's Court of Final Appeal, that most Chinese citizens who sued to be allowed to live in Hong Kong must return to China, has cast doubt on the enduring autonomy of the territory's system of justice.

Most of those affected by the ruling, handed down on Thursday, are young adults.[5]

Because this chapter is not about news writing skills, we shall concentrate on simplicity. Leaving a country one calls home is heartbreaking—it is too obvious, rendering the term "the heartbreaking process" redundant. In addition, we learn that few will leave without "packing up." This too, is a redundant, opinion-driven detail. The phrase "what they believed was home" is sentimental and irrelevant. It should be replaced with either "the territory" or "the country." The sentence that ends with "the highest court in the former colony ruled that they had no right to stay," is long, sluggish and sentimental. The reporter probably meant to say that the litigants lost their case at the "Court of Final Appeal" (four, short, precise and implicative words, as opposed to "the highest court in the former colony"—seven weak words).

In the third paragraph, the judge "handed down a ruling." He should simply have *ruled*. Saying that people were affected by the ruling was stating the obvious. People are always "affected" by rulings. The reporter can, however, tell the readers the specific, newsworthy effect the ruling had on specific people.

Even then, stating obvious effects and consequences makes stories sluggish and can irritate readers. Examples include reporting that a mother mourned the death of her baby, that a man was disappointed that he failed an exam, or angry that his wife cheated on him. Here is a specific example from the same newspaper. In a story titled "French twist on right to be born" the paper reported: "When Xavier Mirabel's daughter, Anna, was born with Down syndrome in 1996 the diagnosis came as a shock to her French father."

How many fathers would celebrate the discovery that their daughter had Down syndrome or any other sickness, for that matter?

In a story on U.S. former Vice President Al Gore's tenure at Harvard, titled "How's He Doin'?" a *Newsweek* story (on www.msnbc.com, March 7, 2001) stated: "He entered the building with an entourage in tow, including daughter Karenna and several secret service agents."

The term *in tow* is redundant in the sentence. Its removal would not hurt the sentence. Rather it would make it flow. We can even go further and remove the term *entourage*. An entourage is a group that accompanies a dignitary. The word *several* is vague and useless. The reporter needed to ascertain the number of agents or leave the imprecise and confusing modifier out. Or did we expect Gore to be accompanied by just one secret service agent? If the number is important, give a precise figure.

Redundancies reporters frequently use include:

Strike *action* (strike): Strike is an action.
*Doleful* mourners (mourners): We don't have joyous mourners.
*Tall* skyscrapers (tall buildings or sky scrapers): There are no short skyscrapers.
*Old* adage (adage): It is age that makes a saying an adage.
*Happy* reunion (reunion): A meeting has to be happy to be called a reunion.
*Heavy* downpour (downpour or heavy rain): If it is a downpour, it's got to be heavy.
*Free* gift (gift): To qualify as a gift, it has to be free.
Free *of charge* (free). If there's a charge, it is not free.
*Added* bonus (bonus): If it is not added, it is not a bonus.
*Entirely* absent (absent): You cannot be partially absent.
Sink *down* (sink): You can't sink up.
Pace *up and down* (pace): You cannot pace on one spot.
*Heated* argument (argument): When an exchange gets hot, it becomes an argument.
*Actual* fact (fact): For something to be considered a fact, it has to be actual.
*Personal* friend (friend): An impersonal association is not a friendship.
*General* public (public): The public is usually general.

*New* dawn (dawn or new day): Dawn equals daybreak. You cannot have a new or old daybreak, just a dawn
*Complete* stop (stop): You cannot stop partially. You may slow down, but once you stop, you stop. Stopping is a completed action.
*Blindfolding* the eyes (blindfolding): You cannot blindfold eyes. You blindfold a person, not the eyes.
*Brutal* slaying (slaying): You cannot slay tenderly.
*Innocent* victim (victim): If you are guilty, you are a culprit, not a victim.
*Temporary* suspension (suspension): Suspension means temporary exclusion.
*Close* proximity (proximity): Proximity is another word for closeness.
*Ultimate* goal (goal): A goal is ultimate as it stands.
Stand *to your feet* (stand, rise): You cannot stand down or stand on your hands.
Part *and parcel* (part): Parcel is clichéd and redundant.
We must also shrink obese phrases and sentences. For example:
*On account of the fact that* (because): Avoid long and winding phrases.
The governor *gave his approval for* (The governor approved).

Some redundancies look so friendly that even major national western English-language newspapers unwittingly invite them into their pages. The lead regional story titled "Two die in Thai school bus shooting" started this way: "Armed gunmen opened fire yesterday on a school bus near western Thailand's troubled border with Burma, killing two teenagers" (*The Australian*, June 5, 2002, p. 10).

The writer should have chosen between "gunmen" and "armed men." People become gunmen when they carry guns for a nefarious purpose and open fire. Therefore, a gunman opening fire on a bus is both redundant and vague.

We learn in the third paragraph that there were "three unidentified gunmen with M-16 automatic rifles on the bus." The term *unidentified gunmen* is a redundancy. If you know the identity of the gunmen, tell us, otherwise delete the word *unidentified*.

With that information, the story in its barest form, and in its original structure, should have read something like: "Three men (description, if available) opened fire yesterday on a school bus . . . killing two teenagers." Or you could say, "Three gunmen, armed with M-16 automatic rifles, killed two teenagers on a school bus near Thailand's border with Burma yesterday".

We know they are gunmen, and we even know they are toting M-16 rifles. Saying they opened fire would be superfluous. A gunman kills with a gun—not with an arrow or a baseball bat.

Another common redundancy is the phrase *unknown assailant*. If the assailant were known, we would and should have given his or her name. The reporter should ask the police or witnesses for a description of the assailant.

Good writers make a conscious effort to construct simple, short words and sentences, or a measured combination of short and average-length sentences, to achieve pace and dramatic effect.

A good example is Craig McGregor's story in the *National Times* (May 9 – 14, 1977) titled "Inside Bob Hawke."

> [Bob] Hawke is listening to parliament on a trannie. It's question time, and Hawke has been in touch with [Gough] Whitlam about a question on the settlement of the oil drivers' dispute. Treasurer Lynch is talking. "Wind him up, wind him up!" Hawke says, sneering. Whitlam gets up to ask a question, but not on the oil dispute. "Gough's is in deep water; he's on economics," says Hawke. "He's superb in other areas, but this isn't one of them." He grins.[6]

The passage owes its drama to the lean and trim use of words and sentences.

### Quick Exercise

Edit the following extract from "The Guy thing." Extract the redundancies and attempt to rewrite the story in its original structure.

> Above gaunt cheek-bones and ill-mannered wisps of beard sit the perpetually wary eyes of a hardened jailbird. Prisoner Dale Twentyman's face is so hard-boiled it could be mistaken for breakfast . . . . The sometimes matinee idol effects a startling transformation into scam-bucket, albeit a strangely likeable one, in Australian comedy drama *The Hard Word* (*Weekend Australian Review*).

# 2. Portraying action – showing rather than telling

## a. Concrete and Abstract Words

The Latin roots of the terms *concrete* and *abstract* are instructive. *Concretus* (Latin for concrete) means to grow together, solidify. But *abstrahare* (abstract) means to move away from. Abstract terms alienate us from action and meaning. Abstract words state what writers think or feel about things. Abstractions are hard to grasp. They do not appeal to the sensual or mental experience of readers because they merely express the subjective impressions and biases of the writer. A dictatorial authorial voice tells the reader what to think or believe. Abstract words are based on the senses and judgment of the writer. Fraudulent prose deliberately blocks readers from experiencing life—smelling, touching, feeling, see and judging—for themselves. Abstract words describe (rather, guess or estimate) the state of things or people. For example, rooms can be large, tidy, or bright. A person might be angry or happy, rude or polite, beautiful or ugly. They do not offer concrete information.

**Abstract:** It was cold.

**Concrete:** The thermometer on the mantelpiece read 3 degrees Celsius (37.4 degrees Fahrenheit).

By providing concrete evidence, the writer is describing what he or she witnessed. You could also show gloved hands, three layers of sweaters, or other indicators of the cold. Concrete words measure and explain what happened, using familiar human indices and relying on experiences common to beings. A good writer will seek and use concrete evidence, dimensions, or illustrations to represent characteristics.

## b. Showing rather than Telling

Readers want to tag along with reporters, without having to leave their sofa or breakfast table. They want to be shown and made to feel what is happening as the events unravel. They do not want an approximate summary. Let us look at some examples.

**Telling:** John was angry when a policeman stopped him at the city center. He got into a fight with the cop.

**Showing:** John flung his red Ford Mustang on the curb, scrambled out, and walked toward the police car. He pulled the officer out of the car, kicked him in the groin, and yelled: "Do not ever stop me again."

Showing relies on nouns and verbs preferably with a subject doing something to an object. "Andrew kicked Mark" (subject/noun-verb-object/noun) is stronger than "Andrew is cruel". The principle of showing instead of telling is based on the rule of evidence. If you call someone a thief, that is slander. Show proof and evidence, including specific details of what the person stole, and when.

Our value judgments are abstract, narrow and faulty. Such values as beauty, strength, stupidity, intelligence, cruelty, kindness, trustworthiness, morality, and honesty are common examples of subjectivity. The wider audience rarely shares our perceptions and values. Writers have to step aside and let actions speak to readers. Readers want to see life and people in action to be able to make their own judgments. Often readers will see beyond the actions and descriptions. And they can see the writer's bias, apathy, or idiocy. Writers should be facilitators and guides, and not judges and despots.

Evelyn Waugh, praising Graham Greene's ability to show character and implicative detail had this to say about his work:

> It is the camera's eye which moves from the hotel balcony to the street below, picks out the policeman, follows him to his office, moves about the room from the handcuffs on the wall to the broken rosary in the drawer, recording significant detail. It is the modern way of telling a story.[7]

Greene was a witness, and rarely a judge. The role of the witness is to answer the question: What did you see and hear? That is showing. Poor writers give their own ruling and do not involve the reader in the process. Now, that is authoritarian. That is telling.

### c. To Do and Not to Be

The little sister of the "telling" habit is the "being word." A doing word captures motion or activity. A being word merely points to the existence of a thing or person in a stationary, inactive state.

**Being:** There is a bull in the china shop.

**Doing:** A bull is smashing plates, teacups and glasses in the china shop.

Nothing merely exists. Everyone and everything is doing something. Inactivity is activity for the good writer. When the air is stationary, it does not just exist, it stands still. Even corpses do something; they lie in a coffin or on a bed. Writing is about what happens, not what is.

# 3. Specification: Using Hairy Words

One of the biggest weaknesses of telling, a signal of the writer's failure to use measurements, is the lack of specificity. Good writing gives precise information. Let us review a part of Rick Bragg's Pulitzer-winning story we saw earlier. Miss McCarty, who donated her entire savings to a university, bound "her ragged Bible with Scotch tape to keep Corinthians from falling out." It was not just any book but the Bible, and not just any book of the Bible that threatened to fall out. It was Corinthians.

Bragg does not try to force or beg readers to see, say "abject poverty" or her "religiosity" (abstract)  but causes them to see Ms McCarty's poverty, using concrete and implicative details (her ragged Bible bound with Scotch tape..)

Noam Chomsky calls this precise, evocative and implicative language hairy. A Lamborghini is hairier than "a car". Likewise, Corinthians is hairier than "pages of her Bible." The Lamborghini connotes status or cost and evokes or implies the owner's taste, wealth, or pretensions. But it is up to the reader to make the connection and the judgment.

Precision or specification is the product of a writer's attention to detail and a commitment to fair and accurate reporting. Baker had this to say about specification:

> Details. Get them all. Not just black shoes. Black shoes with laces and little heels. Not just cigarettes. Lucky Strikes. Details. Details. Individually, they are very important. But taken all together they are more important still. They help convey your subject to your readers not just at the level of what can be seen and heard and smelled and tasted, but taken all together, they help you convey your subject at the level that Henry James called the "felt life."
>
> Which is to say, they give your readers feeling for your subject that they just can't get otherwise.[8]

Margaret Carlson captures presidential contender Senator John McCain in action: "Back in his office, McCain gobbles a tuna sandwich" (*TIME*). He did not just eat lunch or food.

Conversely, generalized words offer imprecise, even inaccurate information. Saying that a man ate a snack, when you should have said that President Bush choked on a pretzel, would be inaccurate and misleading.

The narrative writer must be wary of generic words with loose meanings. Take the hairless word *change*. He c*hanged* his behavior; she *changed* the salary of her deputy; the temperature is *changing*; we will *change* our visa status. These sentences are limp and vague. Changing a salary can mean increasing it or decreasing it. The salary could change from $40,000 a year to $800,000 a year. and the level of change can be insignificant or significant. A change of behavior can be for the better or the worse. Another word open to any interpretation is *affect*. It is one of the feeblest and most meaningless words in the English lexicon. For example, "The winter affected the people of Virginia." But how did it affect them?

Find one or more specific words for the following generalized words. For example: Say (whisper, shout, mumble, lisp, stammer, argue).

- Employee
- Relative
- Food
- Drink
- Moved
- Saw

A weapon is general and therefore weak. But an Uzzi submachine gun is specific. So is a kitchen knife. Clothing is general, but underpants, shirt, dress, or mini-skirt, are specific, and hairy. Likewise, the verb *attack* is general. Bite, kick, shoot, clobber, behead or slap are specific. A strong verb shows what happened and how it happened. For example, a bite shows that an attack took place as well as how it took place.

The word *touch* is fluid but *grab*, *grope*, and *caress,* are precise because they indicate how the touching was done. Terms such as *staring, ogling, spying,* or *glancing* are more specific than *looking*. A good writer makes searches for the term that most specifically represents what he or she is writing about, and that gives the reader an adequate mental picture of the thing or person.

Imagine if the film *Honey, I Shrunk the Kids* were called *Honey, I Changed the Size of the Kids.*

Modifiers sabotage specification.

## Modifiers

In the context of this chapter, we will describe modifiers as adjectives or adverbs that attempt to support weak verbs or nouns. To understand why Ezra Pound distrusted modifiers, think about a horse that is so weak you have to carry it. William Strunk, stylist and author of *The Elements of Style,* observes that the adjective "hasn't been built that can pull a weak or inaccurate noun out of a tight place." Modifiers are built on the telling principle.

Hemmingway credits Ezra Pound with teaching him to "distrust adjectives as I would later learn to distrust certain people in certain circumstances." Pound should have advised him to distrust adverbs, too. Mark Twain was even less tolerant of modifiers. "When you catch an adjective, kill it," he said.

Edith Hamilton rules that most modifiers are useless. They just occupy space and state the obvious and often replace facts with the reporter's opinion. An example:

It was not until 9 P.M. that the police were finally able to find the child.

**Translation:** Police found the child at 9 P.M.

Hamilton said the term *finally* suggests that the police had been negligent all along. The reporter gave no facts to support such a suggestion.

In the following sentence from *TIME* (May 20, 2002, p. 29), the modifier *easygoing* is idle: "Such easygoing popularity should seal Ahern's bid to return to office." The term *easygoing popularity* is confusing (which is easygoing: Ahern or popularity?) and the modifier redundant. The sentence lacks what novelist and critic Evelyn Waugh identified as the necessary elements of style: "lucidity, elegance, and individuality."

A sentence could be saved from detracting modifiers mainly by deleting the idle or burdensome modifiers and invigorating the verbs. Effective reporting (observation, concentration, measurement) invigorates verbs. Narrative reporters need to check what precise action took place.

The *TIME* (May 20, 2002, p. 33) story titled "Hostile Congregation" was another example of the use of a habit-driven redundancy. The story started this way: "For Christians, Palm Sunday is a day of quiet reflection that commemorates Christ's entry into Jerusalem."

The offending modifier *quiet* is redundant. Reflection connotes quietness. It finds itself in the league of such redundancies as: *loud bang, long epic, hot fire, gentle breeze,* and *angry outburst.*

Fedler et al. offer an example of how to trim and invigorate an obese sentence. The sentence "The fast-moving bullet went through the wall quickly" is flabby. Consider the taut version: "The bullet tore through the wall."

Merely removing a modifier does not always fix sentences. Take this tired sentence: "He walked heavily across the large patch of green grass." Removing the modifiers *heavily* and *large patch of* will make the sentence light—and bland. In this case, it is better to find a strong verb that shows what happened and how it happened, and a noun that is shorter, clearer and more precise than *a large patch of green grass.* Try: *He trundled across the field.*

Its economy, power and precision aside, the verb *trundled* disguises the writer's point of view. The writer considered the walk heavy and maybe even clumsy; that is why he said the person trundled.

The use of analogies can also help writers disguise their subjectivity while highlighting their competence as communicators. Carole Rich describes a good analogy as one that compares a vague concept to something readers are familiar with. In the *St Petersburg Times* (Florida), David Finkel used a reader-friendly analogy to convey the mental picture of the "World's Biggest Man," weighing 891 scale-blitzing pounds:

Now: 891 and climbing. That's more than twice as much as Sears' best refrigerator freezer—a 26-cubic-footer with automatic ice and water dispensers on side-by-side doors. That's almost as much as a Steinway grand piano.[9]

A lesser communicator would perhaps have described the man as huge or overweight. Such portrayal would not offer readers an idea of how big and heavy the man was, in practical, everyday, objects and terms.

Modifiers are not always evil. Sometimes they are essential. An essential modifier is one that would rob a sentence of meaning or force if it is removed. In Shakespeare's *Julius Caesar*, Mark Anthony portrayed Caesar as one who "bestrode the narrow world like a Colossus." The phrase *bestrode the narrow world* replaces the weak, modifier-ridden version: *stood legs astride across the narrow world*. The modifier *narrow* is crucial because it establishes an illuminating contrast with Caesar's colossal stature as a globally revered politician and warrior. It also implies that Caesar's powers made the world look small.

Writers can use modifiers *knowledgably* to invigorate scenes. This technique works when writers are not using modifiers to decorate or support feeble verbs and nouns. Note the use of the modifier *knowledgeably* in the sentence above. Would the sentence be weaker or less precise if we removed the modifier? That is one test of a modifier's admissibility. We can test the aptness of a modifier by deleting it. Does the sentence lose its punch, meaning or clarity? If it does, the modifier is welcome to stay. For example, in the phrase I used earlier, "weighing 891 *scale-blitzing* pounds," does the phrase lose anything if we remove the modifier in italics?

Sometimes, removing a functional modifier would make the sentence look stupid. In her article titled "Learning While Black" (*TIME* May 20, 2002, p. 42) Jodie Morse described Kenneth Russell as a high school junior "with a filthy mouth." If you remove the modifier (*filthy*), you are left with a totally idiotic idea: Russell is a high school junior with a mouth!

# 4. Imagery

Of all the signals of style, the use of imagery or rhetorical images—metaphors, similes, and figures of speech—is the most prominent symbol of a writer's presence and inner strength. It is a kind of mental fashion statement. Life grants every human being a unique collection of experiences which, when combined, form distinctive associations of symbols and representations that others can relate to. Imagery is the use of figurative illustration to engender the formation of a mental image of the situation or action portrayed in a story. Later in this section, we will see how writers draw strong images from their socio-cultural background.

Images are the vehicles of clarity, action, thought and meaning. Their principal purpose is to invigorate actions, thoughts, and a perceived reality by transporting the reader into a new experience using known symbols and cues. They energize known experiences to produce in readers a new dimension of apprecia-

tion and connection. An effective image serves readers by facilitating and enriching their reading experience. Images were not created to adorn writing.

Many mistake imagery for flowery language. In horticulture, imagery
would be an orange tree, not a rose bush. Images must have a practical use—to
initiate the reader into the real world of action, movement nouns and verbs. It is
a translation or reinforcement of a reality. The nursery rhyme "Twinkle, twinkle
little star," tells us that the star is like a diamond. If you stop by a jewelry store,
you will see how the scintillating wink of a diamond is much like a star gleam-
ing in the sky. The poet brought an object of the faraway constellation within
our reach. Look at an engagement ring, and you have a picture of the twinkling
star.

Good images are based on substance. They offer a better feel of the subject
and heighten the reader's participation and understanding. The best images are
concrete. Remember Richard Meyer's hurricane that "smacked the Carolina
coast like the back of a devil's hand." The hurricane is invisible, but its force is
compared to the backhand slap (concrete, physical, relating to action) of a cruel
being most people dread. My St. Thomas demolition man "rode his bulldozer
like a deft horseman." The image the story presented was that of a gleefully sadistic cowboy getting his horse to gallop, in full charge.

Writers of fiction and nonfiction use imagery to set the stage for the dramatic intentions of the story and of the scene and objects. While the plot is the
conceptual and material framework of the story, the image is the spiritual pro-
peller of action, which constitutes the force of the plot. All of this takes place at
the macro level of story building, which is used by narrative writers and novelists. This level relates to sequencing or unfolding the story in a logical and dynamic manner and establishing unity between scenes and between individual
actions and occurrences. The macro level, the level of the plot, will be discussed
in detail in the next chapter.

The constituents of the story—words, phrases, sentences and paragraphs—
also rely on imagery, which I will call internal or micro images, to convey
meaning. These images inhabit and thrive in the normal construction of individual phrases and sentences. At this macro level of expression, the image helps
convey (by simplifying, illustrating, practicalizing or explaining actions, concepts, situations, and character) the meaning and associations the writer conveys
to the audience. To put it another way, the details the writer has obtained
through observation, research and interviews need to step into the reader's
world, to talk to the reader (in the reader's own cognitive language) so that the
reader can recognize and relate to the objects, people and circumstances in the
story. A successful image will enable the writer to:

- illuminate an action, character or issue, providing a wider or deeper understanding and familiarity
- provide fresh perspectives or dimensions
- stretch the knowledge and experience of the reader
- offer the reader a personal experience
- simplify issues by associating the unknown to the known

- stretch the reader's knowledge and imagination by associating the known to the unknown or unfamiliar
- heighten the reader's emotional or intellectual experience

Writers who use imagery fall into two broad categories: those who use their own imagery and those who use imagery abandoned by others. Original images are more honest and more powerful. Previously owned expressions or images are weak. They reek of plagiarism. They are often called hackneyed expressions or clichés. For Jon Franklin, the biggest problem with clichés is not that they are tired but that they deny the writer the ability to be specific in his or her perception and communication.[10] A cliché denies the writer both voice and individuality.

Fresh imagery is not difficult to build because it is based on things we already know, experience or feel, or things we have observed. It is an extension of our personality. All we have to do is compare something, someone, or some situation with something we already know, to make the point clearer or to show the magnitude of the effect of the person, thing or situation on life or on people. To be able to build our own images, we shall try to dismantle familiar images built by their original owners. Let us look at a few examples.

*The tickets sold like hot cakes.* In the olden days, people rushed to buy cake while it was still hot. Cold cake was probably stale. That image is now dead because we have refrigerators and microwave ovens. People no longer form frantic lines just to buy cake that is fresh and hot.

*Tom broke Martha's heart.* Martha has a fragile heart (that too is an image, by the way), and what Tom did was the equivalent of smashing a glass (Martha's heart) with a rock.

*Emma is busy as a bee.* Whoever coined that image probably spent some time watching bees thrashing about the hive. Emma seems to be just as busy. Because few modern people have ever seen bees, let alone a beehive, the image is out of date. It is also not accurate to say bees are busy. It is beehives (or bees in a beehive) that are busy.

Some images have passed into everyday use. When we decide *to lie low*, or accuse someone of being *hard-hearted*, thus *entering their black book*; when we *bury our differences* or *our hatchet* when we *hang out with* everyone including *blue-collar workers*, and sometimes *buy their arguments*, especially if they *lay their cards on the table* if we want to *call a spade a spade*, we are using everyday images. We do not consciously insert them into our communication. They just flow. We do not look for the words; they are just there, like a pimple on an adolescent's face. Take the pimple simile—that is my own image, my own association. It is that simple. But some writers have hardly any sense of shame and fairness. How can we so comfortably reap what someone else has sown?

If we use the stale associations that already populate our tired language, we will contribute to the fatigue of the language and of our readers. No two actions are identical. An existing image is unlikely to survive the weight of the expectations of the modern reader's expectations and our increasingly complex and dramatic humanity.

Overused images are public images, flogged to death over the years. Imagery is part of everyday discourse. Each person sees life in his or her own peculiar ways and uses that inner picture to communicate a reality to a larger audience in an illuminating way. Writers are like hosts. They must present our readers (their guests) with fresh, warm food, not mildewed or rotten leftovers or something picked from the trash bin or the roadside.

## Image Making

Everyone can produce captivating images. Creating images does not require genius. It requires honesty, openness, childlike curiosity, and simplicity. We are capable of creating imaginative images by delving into our own experience and personality. No matter how boring or young a person is, that person has a range of perceptions and character that can produce crisp, fresh imagery. As a five-year-old, I used to describe lizard eggs as the eggs of the airplane. I believed that the plane, that hulking, roaring metal bird, probably crept behind our house to lay tiny gray eggs while I was asleep or away at school. And those eggs, I figured, would one day hatch into a fleet of giant birds roaring in the clouds.

To make new associations and comparisons, we only need to observe, reflect, absorb, and try to use communicate what we see, feel, hear or perceive to readers using readers' experience as cue.

Gary Tippet, the award-winning narrative writer for *The Age*, Melbourne, explains his image-building techniques:

You need imagery to take your reader to a scene. And similes can give them something they can relate to, painting a picture for them. For instance I wrote about Heath Brew, an Esso worker badly hurt in the Longford explosion, trying to get away from the fireball he knew was coming:

"He began dragging himself, going backwards, useless legs trailing behind, using both hands to push himself along, like a sculler on a pond. He went at it for maybe a minute and went nowhere."

Or in a story describing surgery on car accident victim April Spearing's skull, I laid them on. Three in one par:

"The fissure along her saggital suture is a short, fat lightning bolt. To its left is the bathplug of bone riveted back after her second blood clot was removed in December . . . the dark pink dura slightly overflows and sticks to the edges like a fallen soufflé."

In "Sudden Impact," a long narrative about another car crash victim Melinda Cole, I wrote:

"The car folded around her like ugly origami."

I came up with that one at home one night when I was searching for the lead, lying on the couch. I wanted some way to describe the shape of the car Melinda was trapped in. It seemed to me it was wrapped or folded around her. I thought: What sorts of things are folded? Origami. But origami is a beautiful, delicate creation. This was ugly origami. I liked that. I also liked the sound of the hard Gs banging up against each other in those two words when I read them out aloud.

Graham Greene's army officer stood in the sun like a question mark. The soldier's curved posture reminded Greene of a question mark. The soldier would remind me of a shrimp or a croissant.

The wrinkles on the face of the miner in Marion Castle's story looked like "tiny accordions".

Jan Herman in the travel story "Cuba Where Time Has Stopped," described an old Cuban looking out of the airplane. "Poquito! Poquito!" he said, grimacing sadly and *holding up his thumb and index finger like a pair of tweezers.*"[11]

The finger sign of *poquito* (Spanish for tiny) took the form of a pair of tweezers. Tweezers are a familiar object that the writer uses to connect the reader mentally, emotionally, and even physically to the theatrical action of an unfamiliar Cuban man. It is hard to resist the temptation of tweezing your fingers like the Cuban man. Try to say *a little*, holding your thumb and index fingers like Herman's pair of tweezers, and you can see the old man in the plane come alive. What a simple, honest, but forceful simile.

# 5. Refurbishing Language

The ability to use strong, fresh and original words and expressions is one of the indices of good writing. As the cliché goes, however, you cannot reinvent the wheel. Well, not always. There are many tired expressions, many turns of phrases and many exhausted images that lie dilapidated on the roadsides of our collective lexicon. By refurbishing these expressions, we could give them a new vigor.

For one of my narrative stories I borrowed the framework of Greene's image. Greene had the heat standing in a room like an enemy. Depicting the scene of the Pratunam market in Bangkok Thailand, I started my feature article this way: "Heat stood outside Bangkok's Pratunam market like a sentry."

## *Massaging Clichés Back to Life*

Mark Twain refurbished one of the very annoying aphorisms of all times, by adding two plain words. "Familiarity breeds contempt—and children," he said.

You probably know the Biblical tribute of King David to his fallen enemy, master and predecessor, King Saul: How are the mighty fallen! Change that to: "How are the fallen mighty," and by reshuffling the words, I created an image in a newspaper article about some "Pentecostal" church members who fell "under the anointing" as a mark of spiritual correctness. The fallen were the big stars of these miracle services—the fallen became the mighty.

Most of the images that have now become stale were constructed from the fresh experience and imagination of someone. Frequently the elements that constituted the image come together in front of us. A business story about tax concessions for oil companies in Australia (*The Australian*, June 24, 2002, p.32) was captivatingly titled: "Tax relief in the pipeline—is it enough?"

We all know the cliché about something in the pipeline (in the process of being executed or considered). Here, tax relief was going to be literally in the pipeline. This literal interpretation of a cliché gave the expression vigor and a new lease of originality.

During a visit to the offices of the *Wall Street Journal* newspaper in New York in 1998, I saw an actual rat race. Two rats streaked across the plush conference room, one at the tail of the other. Oh what a rat race!

Movie star and producer Woody Allen did something clever with a biblical cliché. He refreshed and empowered it by adding something to it. "The lion and the calf shall lie down together," Allen once wrote, "but the calf won't get much sleep."[12]

Good writing thrives on our ability to use ordinary words in an extraordinary way, by demonstrating what we write, while being plain, simple and therefore creative.

# 8

## Stealing from the Novelist's Bag of Tricks

*Literature is the art of writing something that will be read twice; journalism what will be grasped once.* —Cyril Connolly.

To establish the connection between fiction and journalistic (nonfiction) writing, and the reasons journalists need to acquire storytelling skills, we need to find out what a story is.

Steven Cohan and Linda Shires define a story as a series of events placed in a sequence of change or "the transformation of one event into another." They define an event as an action that depicts some sort of physical or mental activity, an occurrence in time, or "a state of existing in time." For an event to qualify as part of a story or narrative, action must take place. That action must have consequence or relevance. In the words of Tzvetan Todorov, a story begins "with a stable situation which is disturbed."[1]

In traditional journalism, we would say that conflict makes news. We would insist that readers need to know what happened, as well as where, when, how, and why it happened. Some of the key elements of newsworthiness are conflict, impact, consequence, and relevance.

Fiction and nonfiction (including journalistic stories) are propelled by the same motive force that Cohan and Shires call "narrativity." The narrative features of a story (characters, sequence or time frame, and thematic thread) tell a story more compellingly than words and images.

Written well, both fiction and nonfiction embody and transmit "humanity and warmth" and "create a virtual reality that plunges the reader into an adventure of spirit".[2]

Jon Franklin takes this argument further. For him, just as human beings have common features—a brain, a heart, a stomach, and a pancreas, for example—all stories have a common set of characteristics. "A story, any story, involves a special relationship between character, situation, and action," he notes. Once these relationships are faulty or inexistent, the story—like a person without a heart, a brain, or a stomach—dies.

If all stories have these critical universal similarities, then newspaper stories—features, news, opinion (see Chapter 12), reviews (discussed in Chapter

13), and the rest—have a lot in common with short stories and novels. Manoff and Schudson go so far as to say that journalism, "like any other storytelling activity, is a form of fiction." Journalists need to be familiar with the techniques of storytelling that make works of fiction retain their popularity, even after the incursion of film and television.

It is not surprising, therefore, that a number of great writers of fiction such as Ernest Hemmingway and Graham Greene were also journalists. While Hemmingway and Greene introduced their journalistic skills into fiction writing, journalists probably have more to learn from fiction writers. The only marked difference between fiction and nonfiction is where and whether the characters live. What they do have in common is the medium of telling, which is conveying action through words.

That is why Walter Fox challenges the narrative writer to dip into "the fiction writer's bag of tricks" to pull out such stylistic elements as "contrast, paradox, anecdotes, description and dialogue."

This chapter will look at key parts and elements of fictional writing and show how they can be applied to narrative writing.

# 1. Outline and Plan

Franklin maintains that "every writer of any merit at all during the last five hundred years of English history outlined virtually everything he wrote." The whole story process needs to start with a plan and an outline.

The outline allows writers to organize their thoughts and analyze the story before they begin to write. An outlined story has integrity. The individual components come together to form an "organic whole." If you refuse to outline, you are effectively telling yourself you do not want to think your story through before you start writing. It means that you want, instead, to pursue the story and all its nuances blindly and chaotically. Because you will have gathered three or four times more information than your story will need, you need a structure or central intelligence to guide the selection and processing the information. This information will include compelling tiny bits of information and atmospherics about people, places and issues. The story outline is discussed in greater depth in Chapter 9.

## *Walking Around the Story*

When you have collected the huge amount of material for the story, another charting process starts. You must now "walk around" your information. You must look at the whole body of information and chart its flow—including main strands, central thread, high points, gaps and question marks. This gives you a fair idea how the story will begin, progress and end. You preselect details, quotes or glimpses for your lead and ending. You feel the pulse of the story, and establish its direction and central thread. You may find some missing details, logic or links that require investigation. This is the time to clarify facts or quotations, to confirm that you have a full, balanced picture, and that there are no holes—or that, if indeed, there are unavoidable holes, they are acknowledged. At this stage, you also establish the story's turning points and the way the story could flow—how you will bind the story elements together to keep the story engaging, even suspenseful, from beginning to end. This order creates a natural transition. In Chapter 9, we will see that the ending, for example, has a special link with the body, and particularly the beginning of a story.

## 2. The Start

In fiction, the plot often starts with a "situation." It gives a wide sweep of scenes, relationships, and compulsive actions, often opposed by others, by society, or by nature or the supernatural. This situation produces conflict or instability. The journalistic story, like fictional writing, has a deliberate opening. The opening line is arresting. Unlike hard news, story openings rarely start with a statement that addresses the themes of the story, supplies facts that match the theme, or summarizes the story. For all of these and other reasons, hard news hardly qualifies as a story.

In stories, the beginning sets the scene for the reader to gain a deeper understanding of the story. The writer does this by introducing an atmosphere, a character, or the main issue in a way that teases the reader into a sense of expectancy. The beginning points the reader to the direction, meaning and circumstances of the story. The writer makes an effort not to reveal everything or to make the full story too obvious at this point. Otherwise, the reader will find no reason to continue reading the story. The narrative writer seeks instead to create suspense, even tension, using simple but implicative words. The lead, as we shall see in Chapter 10, must capture the essence of the story. It serves as a cue, an essential vehicle for narration. Living to its billing as the introduction, the narrative lead introduces the story and does not pretend to be the story. It's role is to make it easy for readers to understand and be involved with the story and its characters and scenes.

## 3. Complication

The next crucial element of the novel or short story is the complication. Franklin defines the complication as any problem human beings encounter: "an event that triggers" a situation that changes or complicates our lives.

A lot of things that complicate our lives would have elements of conflict or tension, impact, human interest, geographic, or cultural or emotional proximity. For these things to interest us, they would normally have to be both basic and significant to our human experience. In other words, they should be newsworthy.

Human character is replete with complications. Complications that are fundamental to the human condition include fear, love, hatred, pain and death. The story—fictional or journalistic—seeks to identify, explore, expose, analyze, explain these complications and situate them in everyday context, using standard everyday language.

Consider, for a moment, a former U.S. president making a living as a knife thrower at a circus in Colombia. That is a complication in his life. Consider, too, a beggar who sends half the alms he receives monthly to the children of Afghanistan. Or consider the village priest who sends money to revolutionary rebels in the jungle. Consider Graham Greene's Catholic whisky priest, an alcoholic fleeing persecution by a fascist Mexican regime and who, although sworn to celibacy, has a daughter. These events or actions trigger a set of reactions that will complicate the lives of the characters. Every story—short story, novel, or newspaper story—has a complication. For the journalistic story, the substance or thrust of the story is its complication.

Fiction writers and journalists face the same challenges: identifying, capturing, and unraveling the complication. Because actions define people's character, writers must unravel the central personality and the essential humanity of the story's characters, taking into account decisive factors and people that influence or disrupt their process of thought and action. Unraveling character is important because all action and ideas are powered by and are attributable to character. The writer must also decipher the effect of the key person's character on society (and even on the writer), and the influence of the society and other forces on the person's character. Writers must unleash their curiosity, asking why people do the things they do. This frame of inquiry propels writers to explore and explain, rather than judge, humanity.

# 4. Crisis

The crisis is that point in the story where things come to a head, a critical juncture at which a tough decision must be made. This stage further reveals individual character and recognizes strengths and weaknesses in people, in the system, and even in human nature.

The crisis, like the consequences of it, can be external or internal, or both. A war hero may have earned many medals for bravery (external), but may not be at peace with himself (internal). A multi-millionaire may be a lonely person, or may be despised by his associates. This often provides the surprise element that makes stories and characters interesting. A good reporter will explore both levels.

A story's crisis does not necessarily have to come after the complication. In fact, as a rule of thumb, writers generally "start as close to the climax as will allow for bringing in all pertinent information," observes Oakley Hall. This is one aspect of fiction that the journalistic storyteller must take seriously. The enticing lead needs to ease the reader into a climactic statement of the point of the story. It must answer the "so what?" question. Some call this paragraph that contains the peg of the story the nut graph (or nut graf). The peg is the hook (picture a coat rack) on which the story hangs.

The complication often presents its own crisis. That's the challenge. While interviewing and researching for a story, we have to look out for the crisis points and crossroads of the key people and circumstances of the story. In other words, we must think *narratively* about the interplay between the forces and people in the story. We are no longer collecting static facts. We are setting facts, actions and people in motion, with motives, goals, implications and consequences. Exigency rather than a structural requirement determines where the writer situates the crisis element in the early part of the story. You don't want to steal your own thunder.

# 5. Resolution

The resolution is the unraveling of the complication in the story, thereby reducing, resolving or removing the conflict or tension. It is a significant internal or external change of the character or situation that resolves the complication.

A man condemned to death may resolve his complication by fighting for his release, resisting the release (external), or blissfully resigning himself to his fate (internal). The complication is the problem, and the resolution is the solution to that problem. Let us take the example of Jerry Rawlings arrested and imprisoned on suspicion of plotting to overthrow the government of Ghana in a military coup. The arrest is the complication. While he was in prison, however, the resolution evolved. He escaped form prison, moving from prison to government house, from prisoner to president of Ghana. This resolution reveals Rawlings' character, puts the suspense to rest, sheds light on the political situation, and unravels a mystery. In addition, the plot—discussed in the next section—is simplified. (Rawlings became head of state, simple.)

While some complications may not have resolutions, every resolution has a complication for the newspaper story. That is one element that hard news shares with storytelling. A pop star decides to run for president (news and resolution). The journalistic storyteller fishes for complications such as the motivations, chronology, flashbacks, factors that led to the decision, the implications, the character traits, and the problems and reactions. Franklin advises reporters to "single-mindedly pursue" the complication until they find it.

Narrative writers have to crown their resolution with a revelation or illumination (of character perspectives and human possibilities) and a befitting ending. In fact, the anecdotal wisecrack or intimate observation that captures the essential character can make a brilliant ending. Chapter 10 will look at the main parts of a journalistic story from lead to ending.

# 6. Denouement

In fiction, the denouement (showdown) precedes the resolution, where the good live happily ever after, and the bad get disgraced, captured or killed. The journalistic storyteller has the choice of where to place the denouement. It can go in the lead, the ending, or deep in the body of the story. The nature of the action and the depth of material collected, rather than a set structure, determines the structure of a journalistic story.

# Elements of Fiction

In addition to structural components, works of fiction have what we may call content components. These elements are common to all fiction. They include the plot, characterization, dramatization, style, point of view and setting. Because Chapter 7 had already discussed style, this chapter will concentrate on plot, characterization, setting, point of view, and dramatization.

## The Plot

The plot is the alignment of progressively developed actions—conflict or instability, climax or crisis, resolution, showdown action—with the theme or focus of a story. It is the development of events and character. Hall calls it the dynamic element of the story, "a progressive system of compulsion toward some significant and satisfying end." The author, like a train driver, takes a normal route replete with conflicts, incidents, and tests that reveal the character of the train and the significant of targeted characters on the train. The train juggles for a right of way to leave the station, competes with cars, trucks and other road users at intersections, and travels—sometimes in inclement weather—on speed-limiting tracks. Inside the train, the character of passengers is put to the test. Travelers search for seats, adjust to the train environment, relate to other passengers, and grapple with human needs and comforts curtailed by the mobility, and the restrictions and dangers of rail travel. Character is not static; it adjusts to circumstances, challenges, and discomforts that drive the plot. Plot is propelled by character, character by action, and action by nouns and verbs.

Fiction writers create a plot (often based on real people or circumstances). Journalistic storytellers are trained to identify and pursue every thread of the existing plot or the human drama, using strong verbs and precise nouns to propel action and people in the direction of the ending.

## Character

Events do not happen in isolation; they require a vehicle of action and meaning. That vehicle of action and meaning is the character. Action plus meaning (nature, context, significance) of the action equals character.

Because characters are agents of action and meaning, their actions and characteristics become crucial to the exposition, interpretation, and symbolization of life. For that reason, the physical appearance and actions of a president delivering a national address (with a gash on his forehead and tears streaming down his cheeks, for example) are as important as, if not more important than, his words. A media report that concentrates only on the words people speak, and edits out the human drama and characterizing indices, would be considered as lacking in context and meaning.

Like all stories, journalistic reports should have more than one character. This requirement makes one-source stories bad stories. It is the duty of journalists to identify and examine significant characters and characters (influences) within a character. The unfolding of the plot in fiction depends on decisions and actions the characters take in response to a challenge. It is, therefore, essential for the reporter to grasp the motivations and the character's essential character (or unique way that character thinks and responds to his or her environment or challenges).

Some indices of character are habits, tastes, loves, hates, fears, desires, quirks, prejudices, strengths, weaknesses, even a person's moral and intellectual orientation. These are only indices. The real character of a person is the combination of these indices in a series of actions and in a set of defined conditions. In other words, character is dynamic. It consists of human characteristics in action under specific conditions. The condition of action is important because a person's action often depends on the scene or condition. For example, while Catholic priest Father Anthony may not use swear words during Mass, he may find himself shouting or tempted to shout obscenities at one of the notorious drivers in Rome or Boston. The change of scene, circumstances and roles has shed more light on what might otherwise remain a dormant element of Father Anthony's character. The writer's job is to relay to the reader what the character *does* in a variety of situations, not what the character *is*. Good writing draws out latent forces and lets action silence the thoughts and biases of the writer.

Novelists seek to persuade their readers that fictional characters are "real, alive, and worth responding to."[3] Journalists should use details to show that the characters in the story are alive and human. When the writer succeeds in unraveling the characters in the story and sets them in motion, these characters become real, even familiar. Readers relate to them. To succeed in creating real and credible characters, writers must be able to show readers the following:

- Actions: Show the character in action, including gestures and mannerisms—fiddling, walking, hesitating, screaming, gesturing, touching, cursing, crying, cooking, drinking, coughing, writing, gardening, fixing tape recorders, shooting hoops, or changing diapers.
- Settings: Capture the character in his or her settings or different environments—work, play, home, or other lives, for example.
- Interests and Tastes: Show the character's taste—where relevant—in books, movies, women or men, drinks, clothing, philosophies, and more.
- Reputation: Explore the person's achievements or notoriety, what others think and feel about him or her. This opinion will also reveal the character of the person giving the opinion

- Contradictions: Identify the contradictions and ironies that define the person's life.
- Words: The words characters write or speak (syntax, lexicon, grammar, vocabulary, and articulation, for example), especially in dialogue, reveal their character and motivations. Novelists also explore the character's thought. Journalists do not enjoy such luxuries. They derive the thoughts from the words and actions of the character. A good dialogue allows the reader to hear and see the emotional reactions of the people in the story.
- Select Features of the Character's Appearance: Include relevant and implicative details including weight, size, clothing, even the shape or thickness of their eyeglasses, gait and general grooming.

Fiction writers strive to create characters that are capable of pulling off convincing surprises. Journalists seek to unveil the surprising turns of mind and actions of the key person(s) in the story. This is brought about by patience, aggressive listening, careful questioning, and a constant process of self-humanization. Self-humanization is the state of mind that, in recognizing the whole spectrum of human behavior (from the vilest to the noblest) attempts to think, read, and listen for this humanity without judgment. Good writers use indices of their own imperfect humanity to explore the humanity of the people they are writing about.

The test of an interesting character in fiction and in journalism is the ability of the writer to show the character's ability to convincingly surprise readers. That is why the chief challenge of a reporter doing a profile is finding small and ordinary things about the extraordinary people, extraordinary things about ordinary people, and the mundane actions of a noble person.

Journalists can penetrate people's humanity by asking, for example, how those people reacted to a situation, what went through their minds, what options they wrestled with. At the interviewing and researching stage, journalists escort their subjects into the world of their fantasies, their inner selves, and their undressed true selves— the "gee whiz" dimension of their humanity.

I read a story about an American ambassador who hosted his British counterpart at his residence. The American went upstairs to get something. When he came back down, he froze midway down the stairs when he the British ambassador wagging his bare behind at the fireplace in what was apparently his country's tribal dance. I call it the British Bottom Boogie (BBB). All humans have their BBB. Search for it. Ask questions. Ask people about the silliest or funniest things they have done.

Ask the pope about his most embarrassing moments or actions. By the way, did you know Pope John Paul II used to be a boxer? From pugilist to pope. Can you beat that? Unleash your curiosity and naughtiness.

Characters emerge and thrive in a social context determined by the people and circumstances they encounter. The writer uses these encounters to explain or reveal the character.

# Exposition

Exposition means interpreting the character by revealing his or her attributes. This is one of the rare occasions that the writer can get away with telling rather than showing. Even then, however, showing, or putting attributes in motion, should follow the telling. Telling is like making an allegation. You have leveled an accusation in court. You must now give evidence (showing) to complete your testimony.

Although exposition is not the most effective device for character portrayal, writers use it principally to set the scene for the dramatization of character. Exposition helps the writer achieve word and space economy while unraveling character. The story and the characters within them are like trains leaving a station for a destination. They may slow down at intersections and traffic signals, even pause now and then in response to instructions or exigencies, but the journey does not stop until the trains pull in at the destination (the end).

Exposition works when writers use incisive, illuminating and implicative details to expose her character.

For journalists, the best exposition is the one offered by a third party (an acquaintance, a spouse, a friend, an enemy or better still the character himself). Otherwise the story will read like the writer's biased opinion.

# Description

One of the biggest functions of description is the revelation of character. This is why description is also known as indirect characterization.

Description fills gaps in our mental jigsaw. For a gap to be filled, however, it first has to be created. The writer creates the gap by teasing out implicative detail about the character, thus using suspense or foreshadowing to develop in the reader an eagerness for greater acquaintance.

The writer needs to focus on traits that explain character or recommend a character to the reader's attention (as someone unique, someone to watch). Even in hard news stories, an appropriate and revealing description could reveal and universalize the people, actions and context of the story.

The physical state of Pope John Paul II says a lot about his papacy and what the world can expect. In the *TIME* magazine story titled "The Man Behind the Pope," Jeff Israelly effortlessly connects the physical stature and actions of the pope to our communal interest and anxiety:

> With each of the Pope's excruciating appearances—from the shuffling steps and slurred sermons of last month's trip to Azerbaijan and Bulgaria to his abbreviated meeting at the Vatican last week with President George Bush – speculation has grown that John Paul II may be too enfeebled to continue leading the world's 1 billion Roman Catholics.

The descriptive elements of the story show cause, effect, consequence, context and relevance. Every descriptive element—from shuffling feet and slurred sermons, to the abbreviated meeting—is unique and plays a predetermined role of character and thematic revelation.

Physical description can be used to set the scene for the introduction of an impressive personality. I call it the MC method—in the same way that the master of ceremony (MC) would say, "Our next speaker graduated from Harvard. He holds ten doctoral degrees, walked from Cape Town to Timbuktu in two months. He has one eye and half a leg, yet he is the world's best golfer. Ladies and gentlemen, please welcome the one and only, the amazing, Don Mango!"

MC details work wonders when the details are engaging and suspenseful. Ron McIntosh is the master of the MC method of description. In his book *The Quest for Revival*, he recounts his colleagues' experience in a shopping mall:

> As they were walking toward the escalator, they saw a large black man walking ahead of them. The man was really "decked out" in an array of white. He had on white shoes, white socks, white pants, a white vest, a white shirt, a white coat, a white wide-rimmed hat, and white rimmed sunglasses.
>
> When he came to the top of the escalator, he tripped and fell. He did not just tumble, but tumbled head over heels down the escalator. Copeland and Savelle raced to the top of the escalator to see if they could help. They arrived just in time to see the man somersaulting off the foot of the escalator.
>
> When he hit the bottom, amazingly, he landed on his feet and caught his sunglasses flying off his head in midair.
>
> He paused for a moment, squared his shoulders, and exclaimed, "Well, all right!" and kept right on walking.[4]

What a literally moving character, unwrapped, and energized by grippingly revealing description. This is the sort of character we all want to meet.

The description, a precursor to the drama, was apt, engaging, and implicative. Imagine a large black man cascading in a storm of white. The description also prepares the reader for the rare display of physical and psychological acrobatic genius, which brings us to another method writers use to reveal character

# Action

We have seen how exposition and description reveal character. The most powerful device for character revelation is action. Fictional characters come to life when they are shown in action, doing things.

In *The Poetics*, Aristotle declared that "all human happiness and misery take the form of action." For him, "character gives us qualities but it is in actions—what we do—that we are happy in the reverse."

Jon Franklin's story, "Mrs. Kelly's Monster," which received the Pulitzer Prize for feature writing, started simply but was packed with explosive implicative action. In three sentences, we have a fairly rich psychological profile of the surgeon:

> In the cold hours of a winter morning Dr. Thomas Barnee Ducker, chief brain surgeon at the University of Maryland Hospital, rises before dawn. His wife serves him waffles but no coffee. Coffee makes his hands shake.

Here is how Jane Albert, reporting for The Australian, used action to capture the character of controversial Austrian opera director Barrie Kosky:

> Barry Kosky bursts through the café door in a cloud of cigarette smoke and cold air, disentangles himself from a jumble of scarves, beanies and gloves, plonks himself down and calls for coffee and cigarettes. The day can now begin. Outside it is a bright winter morning in Vienna, with the temperature a brisk minus 10C. But in the kaffeehaus there is a palpable blaze of energy as Kosky, barely drawing breath, launches enthusiastically into life post Australia.

Note Albert's use of vigorous verbs—*bursts, disentangles, plonks, launches.* Kosky's energetic activity depicts his energy, control and influence. The sentence, "The day can now begin," shows the authority of a director whose presence and force of character seem to decree the start of the day. The description of the weather is not idle. It implies a contrast between the climatic frigidity outside and Kosky's combustive energy inside.

In a story I did for a London magazine, I used action to introduce the colorful eccentricity of a senator in the United States Virgin Islands and to capture the glitz of the island's annual carnival of dance and decadence this way:

> The man in the green clown's outfit and a sombrero is acting like a car. From the graveyard he is bopping, shuffling and squinting down Main Street, dancing to ghetto-blasting peals of thunderous calypso and shouting: "Windshield wiper; windshield wiper, reverse, back up, back up."
> For those familiar with life on St Thomas, the prime island of the US Virgin Islands, the man has to be either crazy or a senator, or both. He is Senator Donald Ducks Cole . . . . "This particular senator is a carnival man", Cole . . . told *NewsAfrica.*
> And how do these senior officials view a senator parading himself before the people? 'They say, "That's Senator Cole doing his crazy thing'," said Cole, laughing.

Note how the elements of exposition (the part "telling" the reader that the senator is a crazy type) become stronger because someone other than the writer—in this case, the senator himself—gives the value judgment. As you can see, the words a character speaks and the way he communicates them, reveal character. This brings us to dialogue, another character-revealing method.

# Dialogue

Fiction writers use dialogue—the select direct speech between fictional characters—to reveal character, keep the story moving and the reader engaged. This technique is available to news and feature writers, as well.

Dialogue is not just any exchange of words between two people. It is the riveting and implicative portion of the exchange. The writer must learn to identify captivating, ringing dialogue from everyday discourse. Two dialogues rush to mind.

I have always known the question, "How are you?" to be an empty formality. One Monday morning a colleague from the newsroom popped the question.

"How are you, buddy?"

"Do you really want to know?" I asked.

"Actually, no," the colleague said as he disappeared into an office three doors away.

Just as in real life, we learn about a person's mood, character traits, and even background, by listening to them. The tone, choice of words, and manner of speech, can give away the person's background and psychology, even motives.

In the movie *Shrek*, the self-conscious Lord Farquaad, who wants to be king at all costs, orders his subjects to entertain him by playing a dangerous game. He gives them the assurance that some of them might die in the process but that he was willing to make that sacrifice. His subjects dying while entertaining him was a sacrifice he was ready to make. What does that tell us of the Lord's character?

The choice of words could give an indication of age, level of education, nationality, life experience or social class. Sometimes manner of speech give away a person's state of mind. Acting US Virgin Islands Fire Chief Ricardo Santos became very nervous when senators told him at a senate hearing that he had wasted their time by requesting that the House grant an amendment that had already been tabled. Afterwards, I decided to test his nervousness by asking him how many firemen were under his command. His answer: "200, maybe more, maybe less." Reporting the Senate deliberations of the day for the *Daily News*, I saw no better way of showing the Fire Chief's nervousness and his attempt to show that he was in control than the use of a dialogue. I ended the story this way:

> If the senators took Santos on a rough ride, they did not escape the fireman's treatment.
>
> [Senator] Petrus: "What is the standard procedure when a fire is reported?"
>
> Santos, with a smile: "It depends on what it is."

The dialogue is a good way of revealing character, explaining a scene, and specifying mood, intentions, and professional and personal attitude.

Dialogue gives a story a strong sense of reality, as if the characters pop out of the pages and confess to the reader their deepest thoughts and motivations.

Dialogue is also a great source of humor in stories. Humor inherent in a dialogue is instant and dramatic. It does not require an expatiation because it offers a universal, inclusive experience. Perhaps this is why stand-up comedians rely heavily on dialogue. Take this comedy routine that offers humor and a punchy dramatic irony:

> "Sir," said the young man, "I would like to marry your daughter".
>
> "Young man," said the father, "have you seen my wife?"
>
> "Yes sir . . . but I still prefer your daughter."[5]

# Scene Setting

Thus far, we have seen that details help the writer reveal character and explain occurrences. But detail, especially scenic description, must be strategic, purposeful, and in context. Like most writing tools and techniques, scene setting should serve as a vehicle transporting readers from their sofa to the scene of the action. Fiction writers frequently use the scene to set the tone and theme of their story, and to announce the impact of activity and the interplay of the various components of a situation. The scene also specifies the mood.

Graham Greene opens his novel *The Power and the Glory* with the ominous scene of parading vultures looking down the roof at Mr. Tench who wasn't a vulture's meal yet. The hapless humanity, death, persecution and the loss of Mexico's collective morality provide the thematic thread for Greene's narrative. This scene projects the foreboding mood of danger and death.

It would be almost criminal for the writer to overlook the thematic details—those symbolic elements that propel and amplify the theme and narrative thread and mood of a story. In capturing the scene, the narrative writer can reveal the atmosphere and physical elements or a scene that highlight the interactivity of objects, nature and people.

Only precise scenic details that have implication and meaning should be exposed. The elements of the scene must limit themselves to a statement of implicative, correlative and interactive relevance. If the scenic elements do not reveal relationships (emotional, moral, psychological, mental, cultural or physical) between the components or characters of the story, in a way that illuminates or advances the story, they should be left out.

As we saw in Chapter 6, not every scene or story needs atmospherics (the breeze in the leaves, the birds in the sky, and the steamy summer afternoon). To avoid stating the obvious and boring readers, the narrative writer must gauge the familiarity of the reader with the scene, and confirm that scenic description does indeed enhance both reader understanding and the writer's focused storytelling. Good writers do not use scenes to show off their observation skills; they report and write from the reader's point of view. The point of view as a narrative element is treated in greater detail later in this chapter.

Let us see what happens when writers adopt their own point of view in language and content rather than the point of view of the average reader. In the following *TIME* story, "Growing their own future" (August 27. 2001), the writer, flaunting her descriptive prowess and floral vocabulary, clogged the path of the story, and confounded the reader, with description:

> Just off the highway that roars through the outer Suva suburbs of Nakasi. On a dead-end street near a busy gas station, Laite Naivalu lives in an acre of Eden. Her family's small, simply-built house is surrounded by tropical opulence: harlequin-colored crotons, ginger plants, unfolding crimson fans, waxy pink authuriums like heart-shaped candle holder, spiky orange-plumed strelitzia, heliconias heavy with bunches of red-and-yellow claws, and beneath shady mango trees, white, cobra-hooded peace lilies and massed caladiums and dieffenbachia, their broad, soft leaves stippled purple, pink and cream.

Three years ago, Naivalu was living in a government flat in Suva, raising her four children and dreaming of a garden of her own.

Even if we ignore the unwieldy second sentence (57 words, if we count the many compound, double- and triple- barreled words as single words), and the excessive use of modifiers and futile imagery, the sentences are just a showcase of confounding names and characteristics of tropical flowers. The location of Naivalu's home in a suburb near a gas station, as well as the litany of botanical names, makes the story impenetrable. The writer made no effort to illustrate how the orgy of descriptive activity served readers. The next paragraph did not develop, elucidate, contextualize, or connect the lead. Instead it offered protracted personal detail of a woman most readers of *TIME* do not know or care about. The extensive use of gardening jargon and the botanical names of plants restricted the story's audience, appeal and meaning. The story failed to answer early enough the two great questions of journalism: Who cares? So what?

Scenes should heighten the reader's understanding and pleasure, and help the story glide forward. Scene setting is subject to standard good writing. Scenic elements do not tell great stories. Writers do.

There is no definitive list of what scenic elements the writer should include in a story. As long as the writer has readers and the mobility of the story in mind, he or she can portray any scenes, keeping in mind these two guiding principles:

- What the readers might like to know or experience
- What the reader ought to know and experience
- Some of the main instances in which scenic portrayal has been successfully used are:
- An unfamiliar or surprising situation
- A familiar situation that features an unfamiliar or ironic action
- A situation whose dramatic implication is as strong as or stronger than the event itself
- A scene whose beauty, ugliness, emotional or mental effect will aid a fuller grasp of the facts or mood
- A story that runs too fast and needs to be slowed down for readers to take in the environment that produced the scenes:

Here is an example of how a writer, adopting the reader's point of view, used a scene to slow down a story and, at the same time, enrich the reading experience. The *TIME* magazine story "Kim's Rackets (June 9, 2003) about North Korea's strongman Kim Jong Il takes the reader on a whirlwind tour of North Korea's alleged international drug dealing locations. Then on approaching Australia, the reporter Anthony Spaeth deliberately slows the story, using scenic elements to explain, situate and foreshadow crucial information:

Australia hadn't encountered North Korean drug smuggling before. Its police believe the heroin comes from South East Asia's Golden triangle—suggesting that Kim, or one of his minions, sent a 4,000-ton freighter to the southernmost edge of Down Under to deliver someone else's smack.

That's how far . . . he will go to keep his dirty dealings rolling. And to understand how Kim runs his business, you have to enter his weird world. There is no better place to start than at Bureau 39.

Central Committee Bureau 39 of the Korean Workers Party is housed in a corner of a six-story, rectangular concrete building within a stiffly guarded Party compound in the heart of Pyongyang, not far from the Koryo Hotel, where many of Korea's esteemed foreign guests stay. Kim Jong-Il's office is in a nearby building.

The details in the third paragraph help readers slow down and visualize this important building that in itself tells a story. We note the Bureau's geographical and bureaucratic proximity to the center of government. Its proximity to Koryo Hotel, for instance, is not idle. Foreign dignitaries connected to the regime stay there.

Other instances of successful scene portrayals are:

- A symbolic place or activity with a captivating history: A symbolic or exceedingly mundane newsworthy activity taking place at or near a historic spot lends itself to scenic portrayal
- Elements of the setting that re-echo the mood and feel of a scene in the reader's mind: This continuity device acts as an aide-mémoire to readers and provides a running scenic sub theme. Some symbolic and repetitive climatic or physical occurrences would also qualify.

Even then, narrative writers need to justify the inclusion of the scenic detail in their stories by establishing the relationship between the atmosphere and the story. In the *TIME* story "Musharraf on the Spot," Karl Greenfeld's inclusion of the temperature in his lead is obvious and justifiable:

The Urdu phrase is shaded garmi, extreme heat. It was 50θ C last week in Delhi, 45θ in Islamabad and over 40θ in Kashmir. For the Indian grenadiers of the J. K. Light Infantry regiment and the Pakistani troopers of the 15th Northern Division entrenched on opposite sides of Kashmir's Line of Control, the torrid weather made for the itchy fingers and an eagerness to join the battle— anything would be better than pointlessly sweltering in full battle gear. For Calcutta day laborers and Lahore rickshaw drivers, the unreasonably warm weather meant abandoning the bricklaying or cruising for fares and squatting in the shade . . . to chat and stoke suspicion and hatred of their neighboring nation.

It is not hard to see the role the high temperatures (and the heavy military outfits) played in the escalation of the Kashmir conflict between India and Pakistan. That Kashmir, which both countries are fighting for, has the sanest temperature, is also symbolic; they both seem to be craving a slightly cooler land: Kashmir with the lower temperature of 40θ. The scenic elements show that, while the leaders of both countries may be cooled by the central air-conditioning in their mansions, their anger and lethal hatred for the other side nearly matched those of their sun-scorched, heat-propelled citizens.

And *TIME* reporter Alex Perry positions a raging war "against the backdrop of idyllic beauty" in his story titled "Battlefields in the Garden of Eden." Alluding to the disturbing encroachment of violence on the sublime beauty of Kashmir, Perry offers an evocative scenario:

"Rebels today slaughtered 31 women and children in a savage attack beside a babbling brook in a meadow of wild irises, daisies and tiny pink anemones."

If we delete the superfluous "savage attack" (to qualify as a slaughter, the killing had to be savage, rather than affectionate), we could see the beauty and peace of the setting heightened the effect of the savagery of the slaughter of women and children. The scenic description accentuated the mood and drama of the occurrence.

# Point of View

In a work of fiction, the point of view is the central intelligence of a story. It announces the narrative direction or slant of the story. The story can be told by a servant or a sage, a writer or a waiter. For example, Osama bin Laden's account of the US war on terrorism would naturally have a different slant and set of facts than President George W. Bush's account. In fiction, the author can elect to have a third person tell the story. The author may choose to give or deny himself or herself access to the narrator's mind. The story can also be told by a first person, which is, at least in theory, not the writer. In fiction, the author can claim omnipresence.

It is tempting to believe that there would be major differences between fiction and journalism with respect to the point of view. In reality, the opposite is true.

Journalists cannot create people or scenes, nor can they inhabit the mind of anyone they choose. However, through creative interviewing, they can find out how and what people feel and think. The challenge is to establish a non-fictional point of view. The success and accuracy of the story depend on the journalist's ability to choose an appropriate point of view.

Christine Gorman, writing in *TIME*, determined that the best way to explain to readers the medical condition known as anxiety was to make readers stake part in the storytelling. She does this by addressing the handpicked reader directly and confronting this reader with commonplace occurrences this and other readers may have encountered. This reader is the representative sample of other readers.

> It is 4 a.m., and you are wide awake – palms sweaty, heart racing. You are worried about your kids. Your aging parents. Your retirement account. Your health. Your sex life. Breathing evenly beside you, your spouse is oblivious. Doesn't he—or she—see the dangers that lurk in every shadow? He must not. Otherwise, how could he, with all that's going on in the world, have talked so calmly at dinner last night about flying to Florida for a vacation?
>
> Are some of us just born more nervous than others? And if you are one of them, is there anything you can do about it?
>
> The key to these questions is the emotional response we call anxiety.

In this explanatory piece, the writer uses a reader-powered point of view. A writer who simplifies or explains story elements is one who has the reader in mind, who writes for the reader, not himself. Gorman's story sidesteps dizzying medical jargon. Although anxiety is a medical condition normally discussed by doctors in a barrage of multi-syllabic medical jargon, the writer uses familiar everyday circumstances and everyday people to explain anxiety to the ordinary reader, using everyday analogies. "Unlike hunger or thirst, which build[s] and dissipate[s] in the immediate present," she pursues, "anxiety is the sort of feeling that sneaks up on you the day after tomorrow."

Communicating to readers directly in the second person may have worked for this writer. It established a direct line of communication, on target. It is not a broadcast but a person-to-person chat with the reader. Yet, the direct address is frowned on by some editors. Beginning reporters should avoid "you" stories, and stick to the third person.

The reporter, as an uninvolved or uncommitted observer who has no stake in the evolving human drama cannot rely solely on his or her own point of view. So, Christopher Scanlan, a storytelling techniques instructor and director of the writing program at the Poynter Institute for Media Studies, asks journalists to make an effort to write their stories preferably using the eyes and heart of someone affected by the incident being reported. At worst, reporters could try to tell the story from the point of view of an eyewitness.

In the evolving world of journalistic storytelling, a point of view is, as Tom Wolfe put it, the writer's ability to shift "as quickly as possible into the eye sockets of the people in his story." But the point of view goes beyond the writer's ability to inhabit the eye sockets and minds of the characters and sources. It is the reader's ability to inhabit the entire humanity of the characters and of the people touched by the story. The writer has to assume the status of the victim, terrorist, priest, mother and villain to be able to think and to ask questions that capture the pain and thrills, the stratagems, and the flights of minds and fancy—in other words, the essential humanity of people in the story. Reporters should put themselves in the place of the victims and try to figure out what the people feel and want to communicate. Adopting a character's point of view makes it easier for writers to capture the spirit of the story and to reconstruct the events that led to the incident and the feelings and actions that erupted. To do this, the reporter needs to pay attention to people's verbal and nonverbal communication. It is a way of involving the reader in the storytelling.

Narrative writers should also make an effort to grasp and portray the different doses of the human spirit, including, for example hope and despair, pathos and bathos. By easing themselves into this universal humanity, writers become more curious, more interested, more connected, and less judgmental. This frame of mind helps to keep reporters unruffled when they encounter confronting details and characters. It puts them equally at ease with presidents and movie stars as they are with serial rapists and terrorists.

# Dramatization

The writer's goal is to engage the imagination of the reader. Writers are expected to show a three-dimensional movie on a flat sheet of paper, putting people in motion, making people act (talk, walk, fall, feel) before the eyes of the reader. This process is known as dramatization. Dramatization is also the technique of putting detail in motion through a careful choice of words and the rubbing of the words and the setting of scenes to generate life and human drama.

In a breaking news story for the *Daily News* (August 16, 1999), I attempted a reconstruction of events, capturing the drama of a fatal car crash:

> At about 4:24 Sunday, the red jeep roaring . . . down the eastbound side of Veteran Drive, overtook a small white car, banked to the left, leveled a fence and charged into a trailer parked nearly opposite the Frenchtown Post office, and smashed into a stationery ship container, its indicator still blinking.

As we saw earlier, dramatization does not just put detail in motion. It must also put motion in detail. The writer can bring out the drama of an otherwise simple or static action by capturing the telling details of the event and showing how the dynamic elements of the occurrence lead to a new reality. That is what we mean by putting details in motion. Auspicious details dramatize the story and transport the reader into the unfolding drama.

Writing about the resurgence of gangs in Los Angeles, *Newsweek* reporter Terry McCarthy drummed out the drama from a suburban bedroom by the clever use of symbolic contrast, simple narration, and non-emotive language:

> On a Sunday afternoon in July, 13-year-old Elizabeth Tomas was sitting at her bedroom window in the Boyle Heights section of Los Angeles. She was putting on her makeup when a bullet came through the window and hit her just above the left eye. Tomas, who had just started high school, was the innocent victim of a random gang shooting . . . . Los Angeles is in terrible shape—again.

# 9

## Laying Out the Facts: How to Tell the Narrative Story

*Gather your material around you, reorder and reshuffle it as you would a bunch of Scrabble tiles, and let the natural structure of a story emerge . . . naturally.*
—Peter Rubie

By now, we have developed and sustained the art of journalistic reporting, gathering information through observation, interviews, and rigorous document searches. We have given thought to the effectiveness of language and structure. We have also walked through our story and decided which of the nuggets of information we gathered will actually be included in our story and where. Now, we are almost ready to write the story.

We must now establish a framework, a kind of architectural design that will guide our story building task. The story design principle is that writing is a construction project and not creative art. The writer is not a painter or decorator, but a mason. The writer is also a worker on an automobile assembly line, laying metal on rubber, installing wires and switches, and working with a one-track mind to create from a collection of concrete and soft substances a vehicle that moves and transports people.

## Story Outline

Think of yourself as a basketball coach for a moment. You want to raise a team, so you pick a group of 20 kids with the potential to play great basketball. In the end, you will need a solid team of five, and another five players on the reserve. You will have to drop some of the players and may even invite good players from elsewhere to join the team. You finally pick the ten and beat them into shape, into your dream team. Everyone picked must have strong personal skills and be able to function as an effective team member. Let us relate this example to writing. Like members of your basketball team, each story detail must be strong on its own and capable of supporting other details and the entire story. The main goals of the team are to wow the audience, score great baskets and win the match. The writer's main goals are to keep readers, informed, challenged, engaged, fulfilled and refreshed, and to keep them glued to the story all the way to the end. Like the coach, the writer needs a game plan. That game plan is known in writing as outlining.

There are two levels of outlining. The group of twenty represents the tentative outline—a rough idea of what you think your story might be, or what you want to achieve. The final team represents material you have selected and checked along the narrow lines of your story—what you will present to the public. Likewise, you should start your story building project with a tentative outline, which guides your research, interviewing, content and direction. Out of carelessness or ignorance, and in some cases, professional persuasion, some writers refuse to design or outline their story before writing it. William Blundell, feature writer for the *Detroit Free Press* calls himself a "strong opponent of outlining." For him, outlining means predetermining what the story will be "and then just bolting the whole thing together like something out of a hardware store."[1]

There is a difference between an outlined story and a story with an outline. An outlined story is one with a preset, ironclad order of material. A story with an outline is one in which the reporter, showing respect for the dynamic nature of the people and details in the story, develops a sense of direction both in reporting and writing the story. Because no story has a mind of its own, it can go astray without the reporter's direction. However, the facts and texture of a story can persuade both the reporter and the editor to change direction.

The writer remains in control of the story and must determine how best to incorporate emerging details, detours and angles into the story. Sometimes an entirely new story emerges. The writer has to decide whether to persevere in finding material to support the original thesis or veer toward an emerging, more interesting, or significant piece of information or thread, which may be an offshoot of the original idea. Even then, the writer—equipped with a new or modified story chart—decides how the story will end. If the story is a car, then the writer is a driver. Sometimes the driver may change travel plans due to poor road conditions, mechanical problems, and other compelling factors.

At the first level, the outline merely guides the story. It does not drive it. The outline is tentative —a guide, not a blueprint. The second level of outlining occurs during newsgathering. At this stage the writer tries to make sense of the material at his or her disposal, and specifically pursues essential details that were not foreseen at the first level, and tries to give knock the details and the story into shape. The outline serves as a narrative map, which sorts out the different strands of narrative. The outline, designed by an alert writer, directs the plot of the story (which we defined in the previous chapter as the alignment of progressively developed actions, scenes, and events) with the theme and flow of the story. Because story details have no independent life or existence, they cannot thrive on their own. The story defines and realizes itself through an intellectual, moral, emotional, and contractual engagement with the journalist (and to some extent the expectant audience).

The story line, or flow and sequence of information that the writer decides on, becomes the story's focus. The essential flow and logic of a fact-driven focus is known as the theme. The theme must have a thread that runs through the story. Let us call that thread the Fat H.

# The Fat H

A story is like a train ride from New York to Boston. The journey consists of a station of departure and a train that moves on a track to the destination. The thematic thread connects the start to the end. The plot of the journey is a bit like an H, with an extended crossbar. The horizontal line represents the thread of the story, or the rail line. The two poles that support it represent the departure station and the point of arrival. The track itself is not one long slab of steel. It is a series of small pieces joined together to reduce bumps and enable the train to glide through to its destination. In writing, that connection of disparate pieces is the transition. Consider that train ride graphically. Once you arrive at the Grand Central Station, you go to the ticketing counter to buy a ticket, proceed to the correct boarding gate, and get on the train that travels on a track to the exit gate at the destination, Boston. The train moves unwaveringly from New York to Boston. If the train ventures off its track, it ends up in a derailment, and the premature termination of a journey. If it veers off onto another track, you end up in a destination other than the one you set out for. You wanted to go to Boston, but you end up in Philadelphia.

The story must have a focus, specific goals, and a destination. On the train from New York to Boston, you will see on the way interesting towns, bars, shopping malls, and countless attractions. Imagine a train conductor who decides to stop the express train to shop or join in a parade. Passengers would be upset. That is how readers feel when the story features irrelevant details.

We must keep this structure in mind as we write. It will save us from unnecessary digressions and gratuitous description. It will save the readers—and the writer—from getting lost. We have just looked at the framework of a story. Now let us look at how the pieces are joined together to form a story.

# Transition

A story is made up of words, scattered bits of information, sentences and paragraphs—just as a brick house is made up of pieces of concrete, wood, metals and a variety of fasteners.

A piece of writing would collapse if the components are not secured and connected. A story that is not bound with an inner transition is just a jumble, a collection of scraps of information.

Transitions have two function levels. The first level relates to the construction of the tiny pieces (connecting bricks with mortar, connecting brick and wood with nails, and laying the roofs and securing them with nails). The second level refers to the aesthetic and structural balance of the construction or the logic of the story or construction.

On the first level of transition, the writer must link words to words, sentence to sentence, idea to idea, and paragraph to paragraph in such a way that the story emerges as one whole and not disjointed pieces of information. Transitions are bridging details of the story (not just connecting words or devices such as: but, meanwhile, therefore, despite, however, in, after, while, etc. that apply to hard news). In other words, transitions are the connections, the interplay and the correlation, between individual actions and the theme of the story.

On the second level, a transition is a conscious sequencing of details to achieve coherence and meaning. In this way, the transition, as a factual bridge, is the mind, the meaning or inner intelligence and logical order of the story. It directs the path of the story by a conscious selection, organization and liaison of details and insights.

Let us illustrate this logic with a jumble of details:

1. John Henry drank five beers.
2. John Henry scored a touchdown.
3. John Henry is upset.
4. John Henry got a penalty flag.

Now have some fun arranging the four sentences in as many orders as you can. The connection between the sentences will determine the direction of the story and the message readers receive. The transition is that connection. If the order is 4,3,2,1, the story is that Mr. Henry was upset after he got the penalty flag. He went on to score a touchdown. Then he drank five beers in celebration. Arranging the facts differently, Mr. Henry could have wept after he scored a touchdown, or could have drunk the beers before the match, and so on. This little exercise restates the need to outline a story, and shakes off the notion that a story can manage itself.

We can deduce that the arrangement of details determines the meaning or central image of the story and, to a large extent, the character of the people in the story. It is the transition or the inner logic of the story that will bring out the true *story of the story*, its substance and meaning. The writer determines this story path at the outlining stage, and then uses sequenced action, which are essentially transitional details, to connect and direct the factual and stylistic elements that guide the story to its goal—a central, thematic image.

There is a significant difference between the artificial transitional devices, commonly used in hard news and traditional feature articles, and what we may call the substantial narrative transition. In hard news, the transitional device—an external and unrelated word, a group of words, or a sentence—is imported to connect ideas, sentences and paragraphs. These words are not story details; they are alien to the story—just repair or salvaging tools or connecting devices, like duct tape. Transitional devices include words like *meanwhile, perhaps, in another development, but, also, consequently*, and *unlike*. They are empty words, carrying no concrete story details, no action, no movement. They are foreign bodies, not based on newsgathering: observation, research or interviewing. In storytelling, transitions are internal components or the substance and actions of the story, which, when combined, create a coherent central image. And actions take place in nouns and verbs.

A story is coherent when it flows from the lead to its destination—retaining its main ingredients—without accidental cascades. The transition at the basic level of construction is the safeguard against distortion, disruptions, or disconnections.

Schoenfeld offers a good analogy for coherent writing. The writer, he says, should lead her reader "by the hand through the entire development," to avoid a disconnection. Leading the reader by the hand means guiding the reader and pointing to the direction of the story or, as he put it, "supplying the reader with a map, a compass . . . so he knows at all times where he is on the terrain." [2]

The story unravels itself in threads, strands, or correlated actions. Now think of a rope. It is one thick rope made up of several strands woven together into one solid rope with which you could tow a car or pull down a tree. The rope's strength comes from the combination of strands each of which would snap if left on its own.

To understanding the different strands of a story, picture a tree with many branches. Each of the branches contributes (with leaves and sub branches) to the entire parachute shape of the tree. From a distance, a tree looks like a parachute or an umbrella—one object. You cannot pick out the individual branches from a distance. If one branch sticks out or grows laterally (away from the tree), the gardener may chop it off so that the tree retains good health and shape.

In writing, internal cues or transitions sustain the threads or branches of the story. Let us take the story of a child who survived brain surgery only to die three years later when an aspirin entered his nasal passage. The story will have many threads: the doctors who conducted the surgery, details of the surgery, reaction of parents, the boy's character, his schooling, siblings and friends, his town, the new ailment, the administration of the aspirin, and other significant details. The story will move (transit) across time, events, space and psychological terrains.

Each motion or development of the actions relating to the boy breaks a thread of reality that must be instantly reestablished by a careful arrangement of actions and the filling of factual gaps that provide meaning and coherence. It is the duty of the writer to maintain the orientation of the reader through all those changes. That is another reason outlining and transitions are crucial to good journalistic writing.

We noted earlier that the transition also acts as a bridge, connecting the reader to the facts of the story and explaining and connecting the different points and twists of a story. Let us dwell on the bridge image for a moment. The bridge does not just connect strips of road. It makes the journey happen. Without a bridge, the roads—and the cars—end up in the river. Without the bridge there is, in effect, no road, and no journey. The driver cannot get to his or her destination. Transition points the story to its destination. As the story's central image, the transition controls the inner psychology of the story.

There is another way of viewing the transition. Transition is the biggest sign of the writer's presence in, and influence over, the story. Before the creation of a story, we have a jumble of information. The transition sorts these bits of information into threads, pointing the facts toward the direction they should go to become a story—the kind of thing you expect a conscientious author to do. Two writers are unlikely to write identical stories with the same details.

Let us see how a writer can use transitions to set the tone, propel the message, and establish the central image and thrust of a story. Patrick May's story "Society Pays Awful Price for Violence," published in the *Miami Herald*, explores the literal cost of violence to taxpayers in dollar terms. The transitional cues are set in italics.

> Derrick Hanna, 16, would-be car thief, pointed a .357 magnum at a kid in a driver's seat one night. "Get out," he screamed at Lazaro Guttierez, 17. Lazaro flinched. Derrick squeezed the trigger—five-eighths of an inch.
> The upshot:
> For Derrick 50 years in prison.
> For Lazaro, life in a wheel chair.
> For the rest of us, $661,554.83
> Forget, for the moment, the wasted lives. Forget the arguments about gun control.
> Think about the money.
> ...*There are costs of rescue*: $638 for the seven-minute helicopter flight to Jackson Memorial Hospital
> *Cost of respiration*: $56,996 for pumping oxygen into the victim for 10 weeks.
> . . . Cost of rehabilitation.
> . . . Cost of justice
> . . . Then there is the unresolved lawsuit.
> . . . Counting the dead is easy, counting the cost is not.
> . . . But the figure is shaky.
> . . . "Hospitals are growing." she says.
> . . . How high is the cost?

In another segment of the story titled "Victim's Costs," the transitional sentences are shorter. Stringed together, they capture the image of the story more compellingly

> A life is saved.
> . . . and the bill begins.
> Total ER, ECU, and recovery: $224,871.56
> The expenses never cease
> . . . even on Christmas.
> Rehab comes in tiny shapes.
> . . . help comes from many directions.
> Lazaro finally comes home.
> . . . and waits and waits.
> TOTAL TO DATE: $549,604.46.
> And there is no end in sight.[3]

Through the succession of details, May uses transitions to tell the story. By reading the transition alone, along with the lead, it is possible to draw out the facts, mood and emotional impact of the story

The performance and role of transitions are not always that awe inspiring. In its more modest role, the transition tells readers where they are, where they have or have not been and where they are going. It tells readers why they should bother reading the next paragraph and the rest of the story, and why the information and the story are important. The transition also establishes an emotional and mental connection between the reader and the characters and situations in the story. In a nutshell, the transition establishes:

- where readers are;
- where they have been;
- where they are going;
- why a given piece of information is important (context);
- the reader's emotional and mental response;
- the link between the abstract and concrete (human realities, people); and
- the context or background of the story, of people or a statement.

## Where Readers Are

By stating the status of things, the writer summarizes or briefly repeats what had been covered: Take May's transitions: *A life is saved . . . and the bill begins . . . . Total ER, ECU, and recovery: $224,871.56.*

Somewhere else, May announces impending action with a transition: "At the scene of the crime . . . ." That is where the story is, and that is where the writer has placed, and should place, his readers.

## Where Readers Have Been

There is no way a reporter can know exactly what readers know about a story. It is sometimes important to give readers a brief update, a background or context. And that is what Maryann Bird did in her story on Turkey's draconian media ownership laws in her *TIME* story entitled "Power of the Press Lord" (June 3, 2002, p. 48). Bird offered a playback on one such law:

> The same law was vetoed nearly a year ago by President Ahmet Necdet Sezer, a former judge, who listed 18 clauses he thought violated the constitution. Legally barred from vetoing it twice, Sezer reluctantly signed the law last week, while referring it for court review.

Schoenfeld advises writers to move from the known to the unknown; from the experienced to the new, informing readers where they are (situated in the story), not where the writer is. For example, toward the end of his story, May's transition announced: "And the bill keeps climbing."

## *Where Readers Are Going*

Writer often drop a hint about the idea, detail, subject, or person they are about to introduce into the story. The writer can also hint at the nature of information to come. The transition here serves as an itinerary, a timetable. Competent writers use this form of transition as a story question: an alluring foreshadowing device. It is called the story question because the information teases the reader into wondering what would or could happen next. Novelists use story questions to generate and retain the reader's attention. It is "the simplest and most direct way to create suspense." And it is a "tease," an attention-grabbing device to get readers curious about what would follow, notes James Frey.

Take May's sentence: "*The expenses never cease . . . . [Lazaro] waits and waits.*"

[Readers' questions: What are the other expenses to come? What is Lazaro waiting and waiting for?] The writer must supply the answer to the quiz immediately or as soon as possible. If the question is weak or trivial or is not reinforced, elaborated, or answered, the reader will lose interest in the story.

The writer of the story, "Quebec Adopts Same-Sex Union and Parents Rights," featured in Canada's *The Globe and Mail* (June 7, 2002), prepares the reader's mind and builds the reader's anticipation for the immediate future, consequence of these actions:

> When the law comes into effect in July, Ms Greenbaum can have a civil-union ceremony. She will also change the boy's name to Paquette-Greenbaum, adding the name of her partner, Nicole.

In the story based on an interview of Venus Williams (*Weekend Australian* June 22-23 2002), Neil Harman writes:

> The conversation about the joy of being the Wimbledon champion was in its infancy when Venus Williams started discussing the intimacy of centre court.
>
> "The people there are very nice and respectful, Williams said. "But I have never played an English woman there, and I don't know how they will react to that."
>
> She will soon find out.
>
> Venus plays 19-year-old Jane O'Donoghue from Lancaster in her opening match on Tuesday and may well be horrified at how one-eyed a Wimbledon crowd can be.

Here the writer connects the hook of the story (the point that Williams considers British fans polite) to the near certain development that will alter that British sweetness: Williams having to face a British opponent at Wimbledon and the wrath of British fans. The transitional sentence creates suspense and a twist in the story. It connects the known to the expected and makes the reader eager to know what will follow.

## *Why the Information is Important*

The hook is an indispensable transitional detail. Readers are enthralled by the narrative or anecdotal lead. Of course, the lead is not the story; it is the story's launch pad. The nut graph will connect the captivating lead to the sober realities of the story. It is a bit like marriage. The lead is the glitzy wedding ceremony, but married life does not take place in a church or ceremonial hall. The couple needs a vehicle (literally) to take them to their new home where they will experience the sobering realities of married life—actions, choices and circumstances that will build and test their character and their relationship. That vehicle is the transition. Let us look at an example in *TIME* ("Lean and Hungry," June 3, 2002, p. 53).

Lead:

> Like millions of less celebrated Americans, Carnie Wilson is not just fat. At 160 cm (5 feet 2 inches) and more than 136 kg (299 pounds), she was morbidly obese—more than 45 kg (99 pounds) above her ideal body weight" (and after getting her stomach sewed up in a gastric-bypass surgery, she dropped 150 pounds).

Transition (Nut Graph):

> Wilson's experience isn't all that unusual, and while doctors still aren't exactly sure what's going on, a report in last week's New England Journal of Medicine offers a tantalizing clue. The loss of appetite in bypass patients may be linked to a recently discovered gastric hormone called ghrelin.

The nut graph explains what the brow-raising anecdote was all about. It introduces a medical and social phenomenon. It helps the lead to humanize an academic and scientific discovery by relating the findings to ordinary people readers can relate to.

May's nut graph, "Forget, for the moment, the wasted lives. Forget the arguments about gun control. Think about the money," reassures readers and focuses their mind on the impending journey into a fresh new reality, away from the glitzy world of the lead. The writer is saying to readers: this is not another of those tear-inducing stories about crime in America, which we have all heard and read before. This is about money, your money.

The writer owes readers an explanation on why each detail relates to them—what has that got to do with me?—and what purpose it serves in the story.

## *Emotional and Mental Connection*

Transitions provide details that encourage the reader to feel something. The reader is not a cold, unconcerned bystander. In his story about the cost of crime on taxpayers, May quoted an official saying that the crime victim is "only half the equation" and that "we are also paying for the apprehension and incarceration of the shooter." And the next paragraph (one terse sentence) provides a pensive pause: "The key word there is 'we'." With that transitional sentence, May drags the reader's feeling into the story.

If your story's theme is the president's stubbornness, you must isolate circumstances and actual actions and scenes that illustrate this theme. This can be done in at least four ways, namely:

- using anecdotes;
- focusing on an individual;
- including detailed descriptions; and
- incorporating quotes.

The anecdote becomes the link between an observation or a statement and its implication or consequences. It is the illustrative statement, the "for example" statement.

The same applies to larger topics. If you are writing about the rise in drunkenness among teenagers, you would include details about a particular young person whose life and habits best illustrate the trend. As we could see from May's story, precise statistics also add substance to the story while at the same time establishing credibility and a link to the previous and subsequent parts of the story.

The reader feels the heartbeat of the characters in the story when the writer gives these characters a voice. The careful use of direct quotations and dialogue also allows for an excellent transition between different actions, issues, speakers and circumstances.

Anecdotes, examples, telling details, quotes, and dialogue make good transitions. They help readers connect with the people and circumstances of the story. For example, somewhere in the story, May shows the victim of the violent crime mentioned early in the story sitting "in a $3,400 electric wheelchair." As the victim views it, "That chair costs more than the car I was shot for."

## Linking Abstract to Concrete

A good story puts facts, figures, ideas, and other abstractions in the context of real life and real people. Writers can switch between, and thus link, the concrete and the abstract by means of a transition. Take this story from the *Weekend Australian* that measured the tempers of Palestinians following the Israeli military occupation of the Jenin refugee camp.

> Israel puts the number [of dead Palestinians] at about 50 and claims it killed only militants. Palestinians say hundreds are dead, but only 36 bodies have been brought to the hospital morgue. Thousands are unaccounted for, and if they are trapped under the rubble it is hard to imagine how they could have survived.
>
>     *Jihad Hassan did.*

> His tiny baby boy was born during the attack on the camp... Bleeding and in pain, Jihad, his wife and their new baby, Hadi—Arabic for "quiet"—lived for a week trapped in an air pocket in the rubble."

The short and evocative transitional sentence, "Jihad Hassan did," gives a concrete and human dimension to the remote and impersonal figures and postulations of the previous paragraph. The transitional sentence develops and contextualizes the story's personalized narrative details. It illustrates and liberates the information, giving it life, feeling, reality. It is an effective bridge between the professional act of reporting and human reality, between the collection of facts and figures and the faithful representation of a felt life and a shared humanity.

A similar transition could also precede a set of facts, figures, and abstract scenarios after the writer has set the scene with actual human experience. This type is common in anecdotal leads, which accord narrative stories universality, implication and relevance.

## Details, People, and Story in Context

One of the key roles of the transition is to explain complex or unfamiliar concepts and terms to readers. The transition also explains procedures, the implications and value of an action or development. In the story titled "Abu Sayyaf Leader Lost in Sea Battle" Kimina Lyall, (*The Weekend Australian*) provided context and meaning to the story and its protagonist this way:

> The cruel and ruthless reign of Abu Sabaya, a key commander of the Abu Sayyaf terror group, came to an end yesterday when the notorious kidnapper died in a gun battle at sea with Philippines marines.
> *Abu Sabaya was one of the top Abu Sayyaf leaders who has a US$5 million price tag put on his head by the US.*
> He was shot and wounded in a pre-dawn gun battle yesterday.

The writer gives meaning, direction and context to the story by showing the importance and relevance of the person who died. The world's chief of police, the United States of America, is hunting for him. The transition (in italics), acts as a link to the third paragraph. But it also elaborates and contextualizes the lead—and the story.

Poorly conceived transitional paragraphs can throw a story out of alignment. A good example of a disjointed and dysfunctional transition was published in the *Weekend Australian* (June 15-16, 2002), the story titled "Marriage, Babies . . . Nauru Life Goes On", began this way:

> One Iraqi-Afghan marriage and six new babies: proof that life goes on even in the detention camps in Nauru.
> *More than 1100 asylum seekers, mostly Afghans and Iraqis, have been interned in Nauru for months—most since October last year.*
> Despite the frustrating waiting game of life in the two hot and dusty detention camps, the asylum seekers on Nauru now go on supervised swimming and shopping trips.

Placed in the wrong place, the background gives the story an awkward bulge in the middle and breaks the flow of the story, leaving the reader confused.

# The Mechanics of Transition

Transition is an inbuilt mechanism of human communication. It is a natural order rather than a collection of linking words and phrases. The writer must activate that natural storytelling order by establishing sequential logic between story details.

The best transition, notes Carole Rich, is no transition. She means that the writer should master the transition so that the story flows so smoothly that the existence of transitions is unknown to the reader. The reader needs not look at sentences, phrases, or words, and say, "Wow, now that was a great transition." Transitions must be silent, stealthy. Transition, adds Jon Franklin, is meant to "move the reader's attention" rather than attract it. The transition becomes obtrusive if it is visible or external device such as connecting words. And it is obtrusive if it comprises long, complex, or exceedingly creative words or sentences. Engaging a transition is like changing gears in a stick shift car. If the passenger feels the car jerk when the driver shifts gears, we know we've got an inexperienced driver.

Each idea, thought, sentence and paragraph should flow quietly into the next. As we could see from May's story, it was hard to distinguish the transition from the main story because the transitional elements were actual story details (actions, facts, figures) and not add-ons. The writer's conversational tone gave the transitional elements their vigor, and silence.

# Constructing Transitions

It is not clear whether the transition is imbedded in the human subconscious or has to be deliberately created during conversation. But because life itself is a cycle of careful and sometimes accidental transitions (conception, birth, life, good times, bad times, death), one can safely say that our education and life experiences have conditioned our minds to expect an order and flow of story details. Whatever the case, the use of transition in writing requires a rehearsal and reflection. We will now look at mechanisms we can use to connect details in a story.

## *Associations*

Many objects and ideas hold within them inherent associations or cues. When you see clouds forming, you think of rain or water. When you think of smoke, you naturally think of fire. You are watching television and an advertisement on holiday destinations comes on. Then the penny drops. It is your second wedding anniversary, after all. One action, symbol, or occurrence results in another.

The narrative writer looks out for these associations. They are what we need to connect ideas, people, and situations. These associations serve as promise cues.

## Contrasts

Contrasting situations make excellent transitions. There is an interesting link between the dwarf and the sky-scraping NBA star, between the moron and the genius, the loser and the winner, the poor and the rich, the wicked and the righteous. The first chapter of the Book of Psalms in the Bible (New International Version) offers an excellent example of a transition built on contrast.

> Blessed is the man who does not walk in the counsel of the wicked...But [who delights] in the law of the Lord . . . . He is like a tree planted by the streams of water, which yields its fruit in season and whose leaf does not wither. Whatever he does prospers.
> Not so the wicked!
> They are like chaff that the wind blows away.
> The reader does not notice the switch because the opposites, the wicked and the righteous, have been brought into one module of judgment and outcome by a transitional element: "Not so the wicked."

## Questions

The reporter's job includes searching for answers to society's questions. Thus reporters are generally expected to supply answers, not questions. However, sometimes questions allow the writer to place a comment or answer in a context. Such questions carefully and purposefully chosen, can create a very subtle, effective and insightful anecdotal transition. A good example is this story published in *UVIsion*, the campus newspaper of the University of the Virgin Islands. It was about one of the university's students who happened to be the reigning Miss British Virgin Islands (BVI), and was preparing for a Miss Universe beauty pageant. She had told the reporter that as soon as she became a beauty queen all kinds of men came out of the "woodwork."

> Before she became Miss BVI she did not receive much male attention. "People thought I was a lesbian because I spent most of my time with my girlfriends," she said.
> But as queen, all types of men "came out of the woodwork" to seek her attention. She picked herself a man.
> "Out of the woodwork"?
> "Yes," she giggled in agreement.

Without the question, that sharp quotation would be hanging or lost on readers. Neutral questions, which appear almost rhetorical, also make good transitions. However, narrative writers should use question transitions with great care.

# The 5 Ws and H of the T

Although the hard news concept of the 5Ws and H can be a distraction to 21st Century reporters—well, because rote learning leads to rote writing—these letters can be useful in building the transition. It is in building transitions that the 5Ws and H reveal their true colors. Transitions use the *what, where, when, why, who* and *how* elements to relate one paragraph to the next, and one idea to another.

**What:** After using a creative lead (such as anecdotal, narrative, descriptive, and other types) to hook the reader into the story, the writer must say what happened or what the story is as quickly as possible. In the *TIME* story "The Flightless Kakapo Takes Off" (June 10, 2002), Lisa Clausen delves into the life and troubles of the New Zealand parrot this way:

> New Zealand's kakapo parrot can growl like a dog, lives to over 70 and has a booming mating call that can be heard kilometers away. It also has a habit of standing still when confronted—not always a good idea if you're a bird that waddles rather than flies. In the past that made the kakapo easy prey, pushing it so close to extinction that by 1995, just 50 of the world's only nocturnal parrots were known to survive. The kakapo seemed doomed.
>
> But the species that many dismissed as a lost cause is making a comeback. After six chicks were born in 1999, there were none for two years. This last breeding season was the best yet, producing 24 chicks, 15 of them female and some from birds that hadn't laid eggs in more than a decade.

The story is: the kakapo parrots that nearly went extinct are making a comeback. The story now smoothly switches to details of this comeback.

**Why:** The writer can pull the reader discreetly out of the fast lane to explain the reasons for an event, action, or state of being—the same way a sports commentator gives the background or statistical details of a player in motion. In the *International Herald Tribune* story titled "England beats Argentina," George Vecsey uses a transition to explain the significance and background of a soccer player's manic celebration of a goal:

> He ran directly to the Argentina stands here, containing all those celestial blue and white jerseys, and he tilted back his head . . . . David Beckham was releasing four years of emotion, four years of frustration . . . but there he was, spiky hair and all, showing his teeth, and flapping his red England jersey in front of Argentina.
>
> He had wanted this moment for four years, since the game in France four summers ago, when he had made a fool of himself in front of the world."
>
> He had been given a penalty kick in the 44th minute . . . and he had plunked the ball into the goal and now he let it out in a primal scream of release. After a second half of tenacious defense, England had the 1–0 victory that kept it very much alive in the World Cup.

Now we know why David Beckham would parade himself before the Argentineans and the world. But then the story continues, and few readers would have noticed the crossing of the bridge.

In the story about the death of John Gotti, the New York mafia kingpin, "Throat Cancer Claims Mafia Don Who Talked Too Much," Rodney Dalton (*The Australian*) uses a "why" transition (why Gotti got into trouble: his talking) to link the don's fashion statement to the method the FBI used to monitor him:

> Gotti was the quintessential spiv so beloved by Hollywood, strutting around New York in $4000 suits and sporting a hairstyle that required daily attention. His style made him the first media don.
>
> He also loved to talk, and that proved his undoing.
>
> In 1990, the FBI planted eavesdropping equipment in an apartment above the Ravenite Social Club in Manhattan's Little Italy, where Gotti received aides in secret.

**Where and When:** The *where* element does not feature frequently in transitions because, as in news stories, where things happens are not usually as important as what happened and why it happened. Occasionally the where element is important. For example, if a party was being organized for Saddam Hussein in New York in January 2000, the where element would be insignificant. But if the venue of the party were the White House in August 2006, now, that would be another matter.

The *when* element is equally not considered an urgent and most prominent dimension of a story or a transition except where the timing revealed some elements of irony or symbolism. For instance, the groom filed for divorce, 12 hours after the wedding.

**Who:** Before he became party leader, Mark Latham, attack dog of the Australian Labor Party, who had just bloodied a disabled former member from the Liberal Party, received the support of a former prime minister. This is how Matt Price, in his front-page story, "Labor's Attack Dog Bares Teeth" (*Weekend Australian*, June 8–9 2002) used a transition to create suspense and context and to introduce former Prime Minister Paul Keating into the parliamentary fray.

> A month ago Mark Latham received a phone call.
>
> "Don't worry, mate," said the distinctive voice, "You are doing the right thing."
>
> *It was Paul Keating*
>
> Latham, Labor's volatile frontbencher . . . had been dealing with the flak from Liberals offended by his description of ex-Fraser government minister Tony Staley—who requires calipers to walk—as "deformed".
>
> Don't listen to them, advised the former prime minister. "You're only making progress in politics when you've got the right enemies."

**How:** The transition explains the how of things—including people's perceptions, attitudes or frame of mind. In their long-running feature, "Return of the River", in *The Oregonian*, Doug Bates, Tom Hallman, and Mark O'Keefe present Captain Chris Satalitch in action. In the section sub-titled "Riding it out in Portland", the reporters use a block of brisk one-sentence transitional paragraphs (in italics) to explain the captain's attitude toward his work, and they channel this attitude (the "how") back into the story. Few readers would notice the switch:

Satalich began riding tugs when he was a boy. He's been working on them since he was 16—first as a deck hand and now as captain. His job is pushing grain barges and assisting ships.

*It's a job.*

*That's all.*

*When it comes to the river, Satalich is no romantic.*

And yet he senses that this Friday is special.

And in the *International Herald Tribune* World Cup story cited earlier, the writer used a 'how' transition to amplify and contextualize David Beckham, the English soccer player's World Cup goal and glory: *"Diego Maradona of Argentina had fallen on him, and leaned all his weight on him,"* we are told, *"Beckham had lashed back with a trivial little kick but the referee caught it and red-carded him out of the game."*

# Transitions in a Nutshell

The transition is the inner engine of every story. Transition is the careful arrangement of information and details—sentence merging into sentence, paragraph into paragraph—to produce a coherent story. Transitions create associations, correlations and implications, and summarize and project story elements—helping writers organize and pace information. Transitions order stories into thematic modules or sections, enabling writers to manage complex strands.

# 10

# Leading to the End

*The audience expects storytelling to take art and life to the limit—the depth and breadth of human experience. —Robert McKee*

Narrative stories are built with arresting leads, organic structure, vivid imagery, captivating quotations, and a powerful ending. While the lead of a hard news story jumps at the reader like an over-enthusiastic dog, the storyteller's lead socializes with the reader. It uses elements of a shared humanity to speak personally, and with sensitivity, to each reader. Narrative writers rely on an arresting lead to:

- entice the unsuspecting reader into reading the story;
- give the reader a personal feel of the story (the theme, importance and circumstances);
- establish a direct connection between writer, reader, characters and issues;
- lead the reader by the hand into the story (the kernel and development);
- announce the story and its slant.

This chapter will help you to think like a story builder, and walk you through the construction of narrative news and feature stories from the lead to the ending.

## The Lead

Most stories that touch our lives will not be, in their essence, hard-hitting and sensational. Sensational stories can satisfy our idle curiosity about our world without showing how the events touch our own lives. For example, the story of a 30-year-old woman killed in a car crash the day before will merely inform us of some event unrelated to our lives.

It takes a writer with a developed awareness, empathy and storytelling skills to convert a cold hard news occurrence into a story. The journalistic storyteller invites readers into the story and encourages them to stay till the end by presenting the story details in an engaging and meaningful way. Drawing the reader into the story connotes the conscious establishment of a link between writer and reader, and between reader and the people and circumstances of the story.

The reader-friendly story connects the reader to the story by establishing a focus based on reader interest (and relevance) and organizing the story in such a way that its flow or logic keeps the central theme (the promise to the reader) alive throughout the story. This happens when the writer introduces the story to the reader and shows what the reader stands to gain from the experience.

So what does the reader stand to gain? A reader-friendly story brings reading pleasure as well as connection or identification with the people and circumstances of the story. According to one saying, when diplomats tell you to go to hell, they say it so diplomatically that you look forward to the trip. Whether the story is about a husband lounging on the sofa, dead and purple, while the wife is entertaining guests, or about three brothers drowning in a frozen lake, the writer must make the story a fun, easy and memorable read, rather than a chore.

This awareness of the reporter's storytelling responsibility is particularly important because journalists are trained to think that bad news is good news. So, telling bad news in an engaging way—a bit like marketing bad news—is the challenge for the 21st Century reporter. Reporters owe the public the courtesy of breaking bad news gently and professionally. In many cultures, you don't call a person on the telephone to give her bad news this way: "Hello Maya, your mother is dead." Instead, a competent person with the sensitivity to handle such delicate information is appointed to communicate the sad news. The emissary would visit Maya if possible, set the scene, and prepare her psychologically for the devastating news. Often, the news bearer will ask about work, family, Maya's current life's circumstances, and other details, before gently steering the conversation toward the news of the death in the family.

Also, the successful story appeals to people who are removed physically, and sometimes emotionally, from the story. Good writers will use universal images based on a shared humanity to bring readers into the reality of a single member of a large, diverse or unknown public. Such universal images include the portrayal of grief, disappointments, pain, love, family, childhood, human foibles, and the little symbolisms and ironies of life. The writer picks out elements of these images and combines or associates them to produce, explain or present a powerful representation of a shared reality.

People read books and newspapers principally to gain enlightenment or pleasure, or both. Therefore, writers should design their stories not to fit a rigid structure but to establish a relationship between the reader and the information contained in the story.

# The Trust Factor

The relationship between readers and writers is based on trust—trust that the information the writer provides is rich and accurate, and trust that the writer respects readers and acknowledges their intelligence. Readers want to be sure that the journey on which the writer is taking them is memorable and worthwhile and, above all, that promises made in the beginning and throughout the story will be kept. Each sentence, each key detail, is a promise—a promise to elaborate, explain and to relate it to the story, and a promise that the story is fun and worth reading to the end. The reader should find a reward for reading each sentence, each paragraph and the story as a whole. This means that a colorful lead—any lead—becomes a good lead only when it is developed and equipped to lead the reader by the hand into interesting aspects of the story. A good lead has ready and satisfactory answers to the questions "so what?" or "who cares?" The lead is the writer's statement of intent.

Jon Franklin uses Chekhov's Law to explain the writer's promise principle. This law stipulates that if the opening scene or lead mentioned a shotgun hanging over the mantel, "then that shotgun had to be fired before the story ended."[1] Delivery on that promise is important, because people read a story trusting that the writer will not include any detail, no matter how captivating, that does not have meaning or significance. The lead is the car taking you to an airport. The drive is the lead up to the holiday. It is not the holiday resort you have booked into. If the journey ends at the airport, the drive was probably a waste of time.

At the reporting stage the writer need to preselect situations or words that look, feel or sound like lead materials. To accomplish this, they ask penetrating questions and seek details, through observation and careful research that would set the mood or scene of the story. They scan their notes and memory for details, quotes, anecdotes and situations that would whet readers' appetites. Obviously, not all information can make a good lead. Often, the weightiest information, the type used in hard news stories, if presented in the lead, will bring the story and the reader's interest to a premature end. Remember that the lead is not the main event. That is why it is called the introduction.

Because a good lead should generate reader interest in the story, the information scheduled for the lead must be thoughtfully chosen. For material to qualify as lead-worthy, it should generally set the scene (exposition), entice readers (appeal) and relate to the central story (direct of indirect connection).

## Exposition

The lead as an introduction to the story could explain the concept or substance of the story or set a scene for the optimal appreciation of the elements and circumstances of the story.

## Appeal

The lead could be an appetizer, a teaser to engage and draw readers into the story. The writer's chief challenge is to take readers to the scene of the story, showing implicative action, instead of telling the story from an abstract or "removed" position.

## Direct or Indirect Connection

The lead can capture actions that relate to the story and at the same time create a mental, emotional, psychological or other link between the reader and the people, facts, angles, and circumstances of the story. The lead writer has a one-track mind—to relate the contents of the lead to the focus of the story. Sometimes, the writer poses a problem to readers to involve them in the story and prepare them for the exposition. This technique also allows readers to applaud, deride or understand, the way people in the story acted or reacted.

From the rich collection of details the trained writer is likely to find choice elements that have the potential of engaging and intriguing readers and teasing out elements of humanity readers share with the character and situations in the story.

Iain Payten (*The Australian*) used elements of this shared humanity to engage the reader's attention and create suspense:

> Meet Ron Conway, one of Australia's most successful golfers. Chances are you wouldn't recognize him teeing up on the first at your local course.
>
> This is an athlete who won two world championships and five Australian titles, shared big galleries in the US and Japan with Greg Norman and Nick Faldo, and will trade putts with Sergio Garcia when he arrives in Perth next week for the Johnny walker Classic.
>
> Still no idea?
>
> Perhaps his handicap will make things clearer. At the moment it is 14, but it does get down to 12.
>
> Oh, and Conway is blind. He can't see a thing.

Facts alone do not make great leads. What makes a lead shine is the association of these facts—how they play against and consort with each other. The association of simple details makes a better lead than a parade of powerful details. The lead writer must establish association at two levels: between the key elements within the lead and between the lead and the rest of the story. In other words, the lead action must be linked to the focus of the story.

Let us see what happens when the lead fails to establish these connections. The following story, ("Precious Memories of City Under Attack," *Weekend Australian*), alienated readers with its lead:

> Marjorie Hancock was having a magic night dancing on The Showboat with her sailor boyfriend who had just come from the Coral Sea.
>
> "I was 19, it really was a wonderful night," the 79-year-old recalls.
>
> "Later that night someone woke me up, said the air sirens were going. I told them not to be silly and went back to bed."

By the second paragraph, the reader is bound to ask the questions: Who cares? So what? We do not know who Hancock is and do not care about her age, her wonderment, or her personal life. We cannot trust or relate to Ms. Hancock or her ruminations. Instead of the quotes, the writer might have provided a hook that unites the events—the memorable or captivating ones—and connects Hancock to our humanity, interest, even curiosity, or a collective sense of pleasure or pain. A creative lead that goes astray—failing to tell readers the point or importance of an anecdotal or scenic detail—is weak because it distracts and alienates readers. It has no human application. Above all, the lead above failed because the details the reporter supplied were not memorable. They were bland, with no ringing humanity. There is nothing intriguing or appealing, let alone memorable, about a 19-year-old having a boyfriend and telling people who disturbed her sleep to be quiet. Also, they were not memorable because they lacked precision and implication. It would be hard for us to relate to such abstract experiences as a magical night (what specific actions or details made it magical?). We cannot see, and therefore cannot connect or empathize with Marjorie and other characters in the story. We do not know what made the dancing night 50 years ago so magical and wonderful, and we cannot relate to the sleeping habits of this stranger.

Ernest Hemingway, on the other hand, considered as memorable an encounter in which Italian dictator Benito Mussolini was reading the French dictionary upside down. Readers knew Mussolini. He was an Italian demigod who constantly made international headlines. If readers didn't know Mussolini, the writer would have been bound to trigger an interest in him, perhaps by establishing the human connection with the readers. Reading a French dictionary upside down was memorable because it was a precise, surprising and revealing detail. Mussolini was not reading a book; he was reading a French dictionary, and reading it in a memorable way—up-side down. These implicative details revealed the curious character of this powerful man. It put us in the same room with him.

Note how the detail-powered lead of the following story that appeared in *UVIsion*, the student magazine of the University of the Virgin Islands, (St Thomas, April, 2000), used select everyday details students would identify with to and propel them to the point of the story:

> She looks like the girl in the next dorm. Long nails painted purple, hip-tugging black jeans, hair dyed auburn, a casual cap, a prolonged electronic giggle, and loads of smiles paved with a set of braces.
>
> She does not look like a queen. She looks and acts like any girl on campus. But Tausha Vanterpool, 22, is the reigning Miss British Virgin Islands, and, come May 12, Vanterpool will put on her best act, and with about 50 other national beauty champions around the world, contest for the glitzy title of Miss Universe in Cyprus.

By using specific detail to show that the subject "looks like the girl in the next dorm," the writer whets the appetite of readers to find out about someone out of the ordinary. Dropping hints along the way (she does not look like a queen), the writer goes on to show the college-dorm ordinariness of the intriguing woman, a college student heading for the Miss Universe contest.

# Building Narrative Leads

Having clarified the connection between lead and reader, and lead and the point of the story, let us go back to the techniques of lead building. There are precious few resources on how to construct a narrative lead. Journalism textbooks traditionally acquaint us with the different types and examples of story leads—more than 40 of them. Friedlander & Lee identify offer a dozen. These are: delayed, descriptive, direct address, expression, first-person, freak, prediction, question, quotation, relationship, surprise, and summary leads. A list such as this may provide the learner with some technical information about leads, especially how to identify and perhaps analyze leads that appear in newspapers and magazines.

In real life, each story will demand a lead that best presents and helps the writer (through outlining) to order the material in a coherent and logical form. It takes much more than the knowledge of nicknames to construct remarkable leads. What makes one piece of writing different from another is the combination and interplay of these words, phrases, sentences, or details. A good way to arrive at a combination that could produce a solid lead is to identify the key elements of the lead.

The primary elements of the storytelling lead are: action, suspense, surprise, and association—usually, but not necessarily, in that order. The writer must present action-based information in a way that makes the reader hunger for more.

Storytelling thrives on action and the progression of action. The most successful leads involve the depiction of activity, and preferably movement, change of scene or tempo, and progression. The lead is composed of—and propelled by—action, not static words. The lead should state what *happened*, and not just what *is*. It should portray action, not opinion or merely an abstraction or a state of being. For things to happen, one or more actors must engage in some activity—change, move, or stop moving. In other words they must interact with other elements. This goes back to the imperative of showing rather than telling.

Take the *TIME* story "One-Way Ticket," which starts with very ordinary action and progresses suspensefully toward the surprise element and the punch line.

> Klaus Eckstein hopes that he will never have to go to Zurich. Four years ago, the 70-year-old retired schoolteacher, who lives in Cambridge, England, was diagnosed with bladder cancer. The disease was successfully treated with chemotherapy and surgery, "but if it returns and can no longer be cured, I am determined to go to Switzerland," Eckstein says, "I don't want to suffer needlessly.
>
> Eckstein would not be traveling to Zurich to see its famous Bahnhofstrasse. He would be part of a small but growing number of non-Swiss known grimly as "death tourists," terminally ill people who come to Zurich to take their own lives.

The magazine's Zurich correspondent Helena Bachmann's portrayal of the familiar business of human hope and hopelessness is simple, but tantalizing. She then drops a hint that could make readers curious, then empathetic. Then she reveals the surprise and the point of the story, told from a very human perspective, a worrying trend brought home to us. In tragic stories, the effectiveness of the lead is often determined by the reporter's ability to engage the reader, by giving them pleasure or comfort, or sharing with the reader the pain or tragedy of an occurrence.

In his Pulitzer-nominated story on the death of three brothers in Missouri, Tad Bartemus used associations to animate a scene of death and elicit a strong emotional response from readers:

There is so little left.

A red cardboard valentine with torn paper lace, which proclaims, "I love you Mom." A carefully penned Thanksgiving essay in which the writer says he's grateful for his family "to have someone to love me." A child's "Love Story" book with extra pages left blank for future adventures.

Chad Gragg, 12, Aaron Gragg, 11, and Stephen Douglas Gragg, 8, died together at dusk on the cold afternoon of Feb. 4.

It was Aaron's 11th birthday. Despite admonishments from a teacher and a chum who rode home with him on the bus, he chose to celebrate it by sliding on the frozen surface of a farmer's pond.

The ice broke. Aaron fell into the frigid water. His big brother Chad, doing what his parents taught him to do, attempted to save him. He too fell in. Stevie, strong for his age, also tried to be his brother's keeper. His body plunged through the thin crust.

A horrified neighbor boy rang for help.2

What did the writer do to create such a moving lead? She selected telling details and combined them to create impact and emotional connection. She achieved this by picking sentimental but concrete details of action and affection—love notes and essays, gaping blank spaces that will never be filled, sibling devotion, and parental love and counsel. The association of concrete elements of serial love with the chilling deaths of the three boys produced the compelling beginning to a moving story. The writer made a bonfire out of several scraps of wood brought together and set on fire. This is the central truth of all great stories—using select, tiny, everyday human elements to build big stories. Note how even static objects are put into action. The cardboard valentine *proclaims,* the ice *breaks,* a body *plunged,* and the essay *was penned.*

In the front-page story, "City Bustle Broken by Blast," Sian Powell activated stationary objects to portray the horror and madness of a fatal car bomb that shook the Australian Embassy in Jakarta, Indonesia.

A single bloodied basketball sneaker lay on the pavement surrounded by shards of shattered glass. Behind a tin fence, a victim's head lay on the grass near a bulldozer in a building lot.

A scalp with long hair was smeared on the road and in front of the Australian embassy building an arm stuck out from under a yellow tarpaulin (*The Australian*, September 10, 2004).

The sneaker did something (lay on the pavement). The shards did not just exist; they surrounded the glass. Even a dead arm stuck out. Powell animated and associated seemingly minor objects to produce a powerful, moving story.

Now, let us examine how Robyn Chotzinoff constructed the cryptic but playful lead of the story "Life of the Party" published in the alternative weekly, *Westword* (February 12–20, 1999):

"If I had it do over again, I would use dry ice," Shaun Gothwaite says, "Louie began to turn a little purple without it."

Other than that, it was a perfect wake. No one who knew Louie Aran could imagine him filled with embalming fluid or laid out among waxy flowers in a funeral home. So they had an enormous party the day after he died of a heart attack, at home, at age fifty. Louie's wife, Shaun, stayed home to direct the revel, which stretched on into a week. Louie himself was in attendance, dead on the sofa.[3]

By paying attention to the freaky but simple details (including elements of color and texture) of a conversation, the reporter was able to create an explosive association with other details that take the reader by surprise. The surprise—driven by compelling and liberating details—propels the reader into the story. The reporter captures the widow's mindset and uses a careful exposition of mood and keeps the reader's eyes glued to the story, and proving that even a story about death can titillate the reader. The reader comes face to face with Louie Aran "who was in attendance, dead on the sofa" and his ingenious widow, Shaun. The writer captures simple, peculiar, but symbolic actions. The characters in this story, defined by their actions, highlight, explain and exemplify the infectious humanity on which the story is built.

# Leading Ingredients

The choice of material for the lead is largely subjective, much like a sense of humor. It depends on the writer's personal, professional, social and intellectual orientation and the ability to use universal images co-opt readers into the writer and of the characters. Certain types of information lend themselves easily and frequently to leads. Let us examine the following qualities of information that make a good lead:

- contrast
- conflict
- irony
- paradox
- the vagaries of human character: hubris, shame, and humanizing details
- word play

## Contrast

In my story about the carnival in the US Virgin Islands the man gyrating on the street near the cemetery, pretending to be a car, struck a contrast with his prestigious position as senator. To accentuate the contrast and surprise, I asked the senator what people would think if they saw him dancing that way. His answer: 'They'd say, "That's Senator Cole doing his own thing."'

## Conflict

Conflicting morals, statements, or interpretations and conflicts between people and ideas, especially within the same camp, make good leads.

## Irony

Irony presents itself in many shades. My favorite example of irony is the story of a man who had to be told by police and paramedical officers that he had been run over by a train.

> "John Lester awoke to some real bad news," began the *Philadelphia Inquirer* story. "Police and paramedics in beacon, N.Y., jostled him and told him he'd been run over by a train. Lester, 31, yawned." The train had "rumbled" over him while he was asleep—too drunk to notice.[4]

On the beat, I watch out for ironies. After months of wrangling with the Senate, government of the U.S. Virgin Islands finally presented its belated budget. The Senate invited a priest to open the day's budget deliberations with a prayer. Now, the whole budget affair was characterized by postponements, acrimony and confusion. Seventh Day Adventist pastor Sutton Brown, in his opening prayer, invited to the day's deliberations "the God who created order out of confusion." The man the Senate Finance Committee had called to bless the day's deliberations, unwittingly took a swipe at the senators and the governor.

## Paradox

A paradox is a statement or situation that defies generally held opinion. People's lives and public affairs are replete with paradoxes. Elements of a paradox make good material for leads. An example: One would have thought that if more people quit smoking, the number of people dying from tobacco-related illnesses would reduce. But the following Associated Press report brought out the paradox—an incredible or absurd statement or tenet contrary to received opinion or belief:

> "More Americans are quitting smoking, but more are dying from smoking-related illness . . . federal officials said yesterday."[5]

The explanation was that although more people are quitting smoking, those who had smoked for decades were coincidentally now paying the ultimate price for their indulgence.

## Human Character

Peculiar and revealing character is ready material for the lead. Take the case of the extremely confident official who had his boastful words come back to bite him in my narrative news story.

Acting Tourism Commissioner Michael Bornn, testifying Friday before the Senate Finance Committee, discovered that everything was against him—a miserly $3,6 budget, a failing economy and his extreme confidence. Especially his extreme confidence *(Daily News)*.

A senior official told the senate the commissioner had "publicly stated that if he did not receive a minimum of $20 million for advertising, he would not remain in office." The official was taking a swipe at the commissioner, who needed the job apparently, and daring him to keep his word, and resign.

## *Word play*

Statements or situations that offer a play on words or coincidence of terms or numbers can be selectively used in leads.

In the lead to the story about the meeting of an Australian movie star with the man who, as governor, was the subject of the star's topless protest, Ebru Yaman *(The Australian)* wrote:

There they are, our Rachel and that Jeff. Exchanging conspiratorial flirtatious whispers, and getting along famously—like a couple of bosom buddies, it could be said.

Of course . . . international movie star Rachel Griffiths and former Victorian premier Jeffrey Gibb Kennett have encountered one another before. They may not have exchanged words at the time, but Mr. Kennett could not have failed to notice Griffiths' spectacular bare-breasted protest at the opening of the new Crown Casino in May 1997.

# The Body of the Story

Some believe that the lead is the most important part of a story. "It doesn't make so much difference how to write the middle of the story," a teacher told his writing class earlier in the last century, "providing in the beginning and at the end you knock 'em dead."[6] I wish it were that easy.

Every paragraph of the story is important and dependent on other paragraphs for meaning, relevance, direction and function. The writer must generate and sustain interest, making the reader glide along carefully laid details of action to the story's graceful end. Much as the lead, which ushers readers into the story, and the ending, which bids them farewell, are important, the meat of any story is the body. The lead introduces the story and its characters to the reader. The body explains and develops this relationship.

In the inverted pyramid, preset indices called newsworthiness determine the weightiness or significance of the "facts." Values such as prominence, conflict, proximity and others guide all hard news stories. The body contains other significant information, in descending order of importance.

Stories are like athletes on a long distance race. The hard news is that athlete who shoots off like a meteor, runs hard, loses momentum, and collapses in exhaustion before the end of the race. The narrative story starts gracefully, accelerates, then slows down when necessary, to conserve energy or bring in an important element. It then picks up speed and breasts the tape at the finish line, then jogs around the stadium waving and blowing kisses at fans and absorbing the howling applause. Races are run in different conditions and each runner has his or her own unique running rhythm and style. Similarly, depending on the information available and the people involved, each story has its own unique flavor, rhythm, and sequence.

# Body Building

Different stories, by their character and varying levels of complexity, demand different approaches and structures. Most stories defy set structures. Content, the interplay of key elements and the quality of material gathered—much more than structural blueprints—dictate the story's structure or organization. This explains why the narrative structure is often described as organic. Another reason a narrative story is considered organic is that the components of the story move. The reader accompanies the writer, the characters, and the story to the different scenes and into the complex recesses of the human experience.

Therefore, we would probably not approach a story about a drunk who is unaware that he had been run over by a train the same way we would the story about the election of a new president or the sighting of a new planet. Except for the lead and the ending, and to some extent the nut graph (which must come as early in the story as possible), the shape of the story and the arrangement of information will be guided by the texture and strength of the details and quotes gathered and the storytelling skills or orientation of the reporter.

Stories cannot be forced to conform to a single, uniform structure. Writers can use diverse story components to portray the action and human drama. These story components include:

- justifier/nut graph
- anecdote
- narration
- exposition
- anecdote
- description
- dialogue/quotations
- paraphrasing
- exposition

# Justifier

The justifier is also instructively known as the engine paragraph. It is the point of the story, the story's reason for being or why the reader needs to read it. It gives the story a context. The nut graph is the liaison officer, linking the reader with the story. It also answers the questions: *So what? Who cares? Why should I spend my precious time on this story?*

Simon Robinson's *TIME* article starts with engaging details of human plight. It edges toward the point of the story—the deadly Ebola virus, a dreadful, immunity-ravaging disease that craves international attention.

> One of the first to die was Esther Owete. Sometime in early September, the 36-year-old from Kabedo-Opong, in Northern Uganda, began complaining of "a coldness in her body," remembers her brother Richard Oyet . . . . "Then she said she had pains in the muscle on her legs." Owete's chest began hurting. She became feverish and vomited blood. "We thought it was malaria," says a neighbor, Justine Okot. At a clinic in the nearby town of Gulu, Owete was injected with the antimalarial chloroquine and sent home. "She didn't even last 24 hours," says Okot. "We didn't understand that someone could die quickly. We began calling this thing gemo, which in [the local language] Luo is a type of ghost or evil spirit. No one knows about it, but it comes and takes you in the night.
>
> Uganda's health officials suspected, and tests in South
> Africa two weeks ago confirmed, that this ghost was real and goes by the name Ebola. A lethal virus . . . Ebola attacks almost everything in the body except bone, destroying the immune system in fast-forward and causing organs to melt down, hemorrhage and then bleed out through the body's orifices (30 October 2000).

# Anecdotes

The New Shorter Oxford English Dictionary defines the anecdote as an account of a small narrative incident, or a recollection of an amusing or striking personal incident or occurrence. People seem remote, and ideas appear abstract, until the reporter uses questions to fish out a recollection of a real occurrence. Some examples: What happened? And then what? What did you say? What did she say? What was the time? What were you doing when she called? Who was with you? What went through your mind? What were you wearing? Anecdotes move the story from the general to the specific, from the abstract to the concrete. For example, the closure of a university is a broad and unfocused topic. A good writer, telling the story from the anecdotal position of the person affected, humanizes the event and the people in the story. Anecdotes give the story freshness, vitality, and a sense of realness and proximity. Anecdotes are discussed in greater detail in Chapters 4 and 5.

# Narration

The bulk of writing involves narration: the presentation of the components of the story in an order or sequence (not necessarily chronological) that best connects and correlates actions and circumstances to create a coherent and meaningful story. The author uses narration to present, replay, or illustrate action and to let readers experience what happened. The writer puts people and details in motion. In the segment of Chotzinoff's story cited in the Quotations section that follows, we are told:

> On the night of January 26, in fact, Shaun and Louie discussed their marriage while walking their dogs. The talk ended peacefully. Shaun went to bed but Louie stayed up—he planned to sharpen knives and then make bullets for the next day's shooting. He had his fatal heart attack within the hour.
>
> That is an account of what happened, as seen or perceived and ordered by the narrator. Note how the anecdotal detail (he planned to sharpen knives and then makes bullets) brought clarity and reality to the narrative.

# Description

Description—a portrayal of action in nouns and verbs—conveys to the reader what the reporter or witnesses saw. It sets in motion people, places, things and events, and activates senses—smell, feel, taste, sight, and hearing. In Chapters 6 and 8, we discussed description and storytelling techniques in considerable detail.

# Quotation

Generally, writers use direct quotation when the source says something more interestingly than they could. That means that an attempt to paraphrase the statement would reduce its force and accuracy. Quotations permit the reader to assess directly the impact or significance of an event on people. Unschooled writers burden their writing with a string of quotes, making the quoted material tell, rather than merely support the story. Such practice transfers the control of the story from writer to source and veers the story off track.

To a large extent, it is the reporter's careful deployment of quotations (in their supporting role) that distinguishes a sales pitch or political manifesto from a journalistic story. In hard news writing, reporters often quote a person's words if, for example, those words:

- are said in a particularly punchy, colorful or unique way
- give specialized, direct information or details
- constitute or contain a peculiar expression or phraseology
- contain imagery.

At the story ending, some writers use punchy quotes to take away the reader's breath. The narrative writer can use the type of quotations that would be used in hard news, but in addition, the writer can quote statements that, among other things:

- permit the character, and therefore the writer, to tell the story vividly even if the words contain seemingly insignificant information
- provide insight into the character of subject, scene, or situation
- contain illuminating nuances and implication, thus capturing the essence of the story
- contain words that are memorable or implicative
- break the monotony of a narration.

Relating the pain that accompanied a terrorist bombing in Bali, Indonesia, in her story "Giggles, Fun Before Family Fell Apart," (*The Australian*, October 17, 2002), Jennifer Sexton wrote: 'Candace Buchan's last giggled words to her father Steve were about his "heaps embarrassing" dancing. "Oh dad, don't; I just want to be with the girls."'

The expression "heaps embarrassing" is not just colorful; it places Candace in a revealing sociolinguistic context. Although the direct quotation that follows is not that potent or colorful, it reveals the flavor of the father-daughter relationship.

As we can see from the quotations above, words the characters speak do not always have to be of substantial weight or news value in a narrative story. Quotations reveal character and expose the social or emotional framework in which the characters operate. This includes how the characters think, act, and see the world. It can also reveal the characters' educational, cultural or social orientation, peerage, political or spiritual persuasion, and even the character's preferences in books, movies, or people.

Conveying the revealing words of the character directly enables the reader to bypass the reporter's impressions, limitations, and biases. Beyond the basic techniques of capturing a character's words in print, however, the reporter must learn to achieve textual rhythm by alternating quotes and paraphrases to retain readers' interest and move the story forward. Chotzinoff's story "Life of the Party," provides a good example of how quotes can be used to establish this rhythm and mobility:

On the night of January 26, in fact, Shaun and Louie discussed their marriage while walking their dogs. The talk ended peacefully. Shaun went to bed but Louie stayed up—he planned to sharpen knives and then make bullets for the next day's shooting. He had his fatal heart attack within the hour.

"Ooooh, and his father died of a heart attack in the same room, in 1978—whaddaya think of that?" Shaun asks, scrabbling through her lists in search of cigarettes. At that point, she remembered what Louie wanted done with the remains: "He didn't want to be filled with fluids. He wanted to do the death thing right. He said, have a big party. Do what you have to do."7

Chotzinoff chooses to involve Shaun in the storytelling without surrendering the story to this character. The author uses direct quotation to bring her characters to life, to illuminate the path—and indeed the whole ecology—of the story. The quotes are very personal and say things in a way that perhaps only Shaun could say because of who she is and because of the peculiarity of her life and relationships.

## Dialogue

Dialogue, a form of direct quotation, admits the reader into the conversion. Writers frequently use dialogue to involve the reader more actively in the action and to situate characters in focus in a revealing relationship with other characters and narrative elements. Instead of one person speaking, the writer captures compelling parts of a conversation between two people. In Chapter 7, we explored the use of dialogue in considerable detail. We determined that a person can learn more about a person's character by listening to that person than by having someone else, with limited knowledge of the person, interpret that character interpreted. Watching people in a movie or on stage is more evocative than having the playwright describe them.

## Paraphrasing

The paraphrase transmits the words or the thoughts of people without using their exact words. Used thoughtfully with the narration, paraphrasing frees the writer from burdening the story with quotes and, thus, losing control. Furthermore, paraphrasing establishes a connection between sources or characters and readers.

The paraphrase is the interpretation of sometimes complex statements from sources into the simple and clear language that suits a mass audience. For example, a doctor's account of a clinical procedure may be weighed down by medical terminology. The reporter must write the story from the reader's point of view. In this regard, the paraphrase also serves as a tool of exposition.

# Exposition

As we saw in Chapter 8, exposition means explaining things to readers. This may involve paraphrasing, listing, illustrating, translating, or giving background. Exposition explains, circumstances, procedures, expectations, expert interpretations, and helpful details obtained through extensive research and interviewing, follow-up questions, and reference to expert human and material sources.

# Ending

Traditionally, a story is divided into three parts—the introduction (lead), the body, and the ending—leaving out the fourth part, the descent, which precedes and heralds the ending. The introduction the descent is crucial to the understanding and construction of a narrative story.

We will imagine the story to be an airplane. It taxies and takes off after the passengers have been prepared and briefed (on flight rules, details, and destination) for take off, and tries to fly smoothly (cruises). Then, the plane makes what the cabin crew would call "our final descent into the John F. Kennedy International Airport." Following the announcement of arrival and the crew's preparation of the cabin and passengers for landing, the captain can now land the plane safely and let passengers out.

To illustrate the importance of the descent in the context of the entire story, we will use the highlights of Chotzinoff's story to construct a story model or miniature story. The lead sets the scene and engages our imagination or curiosity. It tells us what to expect and where we are going: Louie is dead and his wife Shaun is partying. Shaun is the type Chotzinoff is obsessed with. In fact, the author suggests that "obsessed eccentrics" like Shaun and Louie "ought to be famous."[8]

> **LEAD:** "If I had it do over again, I would use dry ice," Shaun Gothwaite says, "Louie began to turn a little purple without it."
>
> Other than that, it was a perfect wake. No one who knew Louie Aran could imagine him filled with embalming fluid or laid out among waxy flowers in a funeral home. So they had an enormous party the day after he died of a heart attack, at home, at age fifty. Louise's wife, Shaun was, stayed home to direct the revel, which stretched on into a week. Louie himself was in attendance, dead on the sofa.

Next, the writer uses anecdotes and illustrations to show actions that give the story and its characters a unique character. The following sentences use anecdotes and illustrations to replay the actions that represent the circumstances of the story—the eccentricity of Shaun's life and death. We gather the details of the couple's eccentricity—their preparation for death, the dog's vigil, and the wife's execution of the outlandish propositions of the husband. This paragraph in the body of the story encapsulates the story. We will call it the story statement.

> On the night of January 26, in fact, Shaun and Louie discussed their marriage while walking their dogs. The talk ended peacefully. Shaun went to bed but Louie stayed up—he planned to sharpen knives and then make bullets for the next day's shooting. He had his fatal heart attack within the hour . . . . I filled out the piece of paper they gave me, and they told me Louie was dead, and I told them to leave the body with me, and they left," Shaun continues. At that point, she remembered what Louie wanted done with the remains: "He didn't want to be filled with fluids. He wanted to do the death thing right. He said, have a big party. Do what you have to do.

The writer arranges the information in such a way that it will lead to a memorable end. We see Shaun sending out the ashes of her husband—to the mountains, friends, and to their own garden. Even this act reinforces the thematic thread of illegality and eccentricity. The story has started its descent down, draped in its defining and enduring symbolism, for a landing. Now readers, like passengers, are expectant.

**DESCENT**: On Tuesday she filled several vials with Louie's ashes to give to friends. On Wednesday she began making arrangements to scatter another handful of Louie over the mountains north of Black Hawk. And I think I will sprinkle him on my garden this spring," she decides, "and a lot of our friends want him in their gardens too. It's illegal I hear."

The rest of Louie will stay in a small pine box in the living room, five feet from the new fire extinguisher and one wall away from the rapidly depleting woodpile.

Because the descent prepared the readers for landing, the ending will be natural and effortless. The ending will derive its vigor from the deliberately chosen details that heralded it. Shaun is fulfilling her husband's wishes to the very end. She has to ask herself whether Louie's ashes, all gone now, signal the end of Louie the eccentric. The answer is a breath-snatching "Yes." One word.

"I have to maintain the place," Shaun says, "I have to learn how Louie did it. And then there's the obituary, I mean, what about it? Could this just be it?" Yes.

# Ending Tips

We can see from the construction of Chotzinoff's story that the end of a story does not just happen. Storytellers build endings based on a strategic plan.

- **Outline**: It is important to create a story map or outline before you start writing and you determine the crossroads, the connection and correlation of action and people.
- **Alertness and Preparation**: You had used observation, anecdotes and deep research to gather lead and ending material at the reporting stage, for example at the scene of an event or while interviewing.
- **Mini-Story**: As part of the outlining, consider using the core elements of the story to build a mini-story model. As we can see from Chotzinoff's model this mini-story serves as a blueprint that can be expanded and supported with corroborating and explanatory details. The model can help writer's maintain the story's focus and internal logic. It also facilitates the construction of a powerful ending that flows from the story. You could build a small, representative, and coherent story based on the lead (and/or its development), main body, descent toward the ending, and the ending.

- **Choice of Ending Type**: The ending of one story rarely suits another story. You would have determined during outlining how the story will end.
- **Managing the Energy Level**: The end of the story is not the conclusion or its point of exhaustion. Consider the 4 x 100 m. (relay) race in a track meet. The last lap is run with at least the same vigor as the first. The ending should be as energetic and captivating as the lead. Pacing helps conserve energy for the final thrust.
- **Support**: The ending, like the lead, relies on supporting material for its survival. The supporting material that sets up the story for landing is known as the descent.
- **Transition**: The lead, body, and ending all thrive on transition— between ideas and paragraphs that constitute these parts, and a macro transitional framework from the lead to the body, and the body to the ending.
- **Ending size**: The ending should be short and crisp. If it is fairly long and comprises more than a paragraph, consider keeping the parting sentence brief. The ending is a farewell, a curtain call, the final bow. It cannot be protracted. One way of keeping the ending short and succinct is to construct an appropriate descending paragraph that announces, and bears the burden of, the ending.

# Anatomy of the Ending

Returning to our athletics analogy, the sprinter tries to end the race memorably, according to his or her individual style, and in a way that will leave a pleasant lasting impression in the minds of the fans. Likewise, the ending seeks to provide a clear, uniquely graceful, and compelling finish and to leave a lasting impression on the hearts and minds of readers. Successful endings respond principally to the unique perception and stylistic motivations of the writer, the richness and precision of the action-propelled details, and the type and mood of the story. Writers don't need to memorize the names of ending styles. The common labels for endings include:

- Circular endings
- A Direct quote
- A segment of a dialogue
- An anecdote
- A descriptive paragraph
- A narrative
- A kicker/teaser
- Poetic—offering final insight or a witty and sobering thought often relying on symbolism, quotation, or a summary observation
- Looking ahead —projecting future events, actions, circumstances

- That's that—ending a chronological account. "There is not more to say."
- See what I mean? This ending asks if the reader finally grasps what the writer was trying to say.

If we must pay any attention to lead categories, we would lump these ending types into two categories: the circular ending, which explains how the writer constructs an ending, and the rest, which merely label information contained in the lead is nicknamed without showing how the story components are interrelated.

The circular ending, far from being just a label, emphasizes the relationship between the components of the story, notably the lead and the ending. The circular ending restates the point of the lead. Here is how it works:

A child is born in a leaking thatched house, and his first bed is a wad of banana leaves. He grows up to win the Nobel Prize for Medicine. But he starts taking drugs and loses all his money, fame, and hope. He returns to his village, and to his mother's thatched house. The return to the village is circular because it transports the reader back to the start of the story (which is also the character's story).

# Ending Frame

Sustained, good reporting and writing result from reflection. Journalists must first think about how they will approach the story idea, reporting and writing. In addition, they must think ahead, planning, and resolving before the writing stage how the story will unfold and end. If the material for the ending is not preselected, weak material or the writer's opinion may stray into the ending.

Evidence of good writing is in the creation of a written or mental outline for the story. With an outline, no information will surprise the writer at any point of the story. The writer is in control. Control is manifested in the clarity of the story and its structure, as well as an inherent logic in its flow and outcome. At this level, skilled writers determine what feelings or sensations they should expose readers to, what readers will leave the scene and the story with, and what readers' frame of mind should be—perplexity, a smile, anguish, sense of salvation or redemption, justice, vindication, indifference, or complicity.

It is obvious that Chotzinoff knew how she was going to end her story and had determined an appropriate tone for the ending at the planning and outlining stage. Evidently, she had picked a narrative thread, the narrative equivalent of deciding on the route she was going to take before embarking on the journey. The narrative thread she picked would guide the story from the beginning. This thread would also guide her pursuit and selection of narrative details, including quotes and anecdotes. It would make it easier for her to discard information that does not support or develop the thread. She deliberately started her story with death—a husband attending his own funeral party, reclined on a sofa, dead. The story shows the intrigues and other angles of the marital relationship, defined by eccentricity and death. The story ends with the wife giving out the last particle of the husband and wondering whether that was really the end of him. Because his life and relationships were defined and driven by death and eccentricity, the answer—and the ending—would be a definitive "yes".

Now, join me on my beat and let me show you I planned the story I wrote for the *Daily News* at the newsgathering stage and how I thought the story through to the ending. I built the story titled "Senators Grill Fire Service Head Over Amendment," cited in Chapter 8, on the following information obtained while I was covering the senate of the US Virgin Islands: The Senate sat to deliberate on five bills, among them Bill Number 23-0106 on the management and funding of the Fire Department of St. Thomas. The Acting Fire Director Ricardo Santos, in his prim uniform, read the senators four pages of a proposed amendment to enhance the operations of the Fire Department. The fire chief wanted the senate to approve a $400,000 extra-budgetary allocation for Fiscal Year 2000, to be kept in an emergency fund. He also wanted funds for equipment. One senator expressed his concerns about the "direction and leadership of the Fire Department," saying he had received complaints from firemen. Another senator asked the fire chief what the procedure was for a fire emergency. His answer: "It depends on what it is." After the session, I asked Santos how many firemen he had under his command. First he said he was not sure. When I persisted, he said, "200, maybe more, maybe less."

Senators had made several complaints against the leadership of the Fire Department. The most striking complaint was that fire chiefs were out of touch with procedure and reality. For example, one senator pointed out, the bill that Santos had tabled had already been passed into law as the Revenue Enhancement Act of 1999.

"An existing law has been sent to this house to be passed as a law. Someone is sleeping at the switch," Senator Donald Cole said. Another senator said the people who made decisions at the fire department did "not have stellar qualities."

I determined that the fire story was the highlight of the Senate deliberations that afternoon. When I got back to the newsroom that evening, I laid out the information I had gathered and determined (after walking through the material) that the mood, or should I say temperament, of the story was that a fairly overwhelmed and confused official became fair game for the usually vicious senators. That was my narrative statement. I noted that Santos' seemingly calm demeanor and reflexes erupted into a form of aggression that made life even more uncomfortable for him in the senate chambers. I also allocated information for the body, the descent, and the ending before I started writing.

The lead portrayed the bravado of an unruffled fire chief "under fire".

The next paragraph developed the lead, showing the fire chief reading the four pages of demands that had been passed as law the year before as the Revenue Enhancement Act of 1999. I quoted an exasperated senator to support that information. The body of the story gave background and details of the aggression, the arguments, and the fireman's responses.

Then came the descent and ending for which I had reserved the witty exchanges:

Santos told the Daily News after the hearing that he was not sure how many firemen the Fire Service had. When pressed, he said, "200, maybe more, maybe less."

If the senators took Santos on a rough ride, they did not escape the fireman's treatment.

[Senator] Petrus: "What is the standard procedure when a fire is reported?"

Santos, with a smile: "It depends on what it is."

I had walked through all the details I collected and picked a narrative thread. Because I knew the ending in advance, I was able to prepare a place for the ending material. Planning also helped me to prepare the story for landing—the descent, which used the findings from additional interviewing to demonstrate how out-of-touch the Fire Chief appeared to be. That insight set the stage for the ending, amplified by the exchange between the fire chief and the senator in the Senate chambers.

My biggest challenge was resisting the temptation of making the ending my opinion. But I knew that a story that ends with a reporter's opinion is weak story. One major problem with opinion-driven story endings is the use of abstraction instead of action. An opinion is an idea, not an action. Good endings—just like good leads—thrive on and through action, details, evidence..

The *TIME* article, "Growing Their Own Future," (August 27, 2001), which we discussed in Chapter 8, ends grimly: "And her dreams are growing with it." That was the reporter's opinion, made up of an abstraction—no substance, evidence, and no action.

The writer cannot, however, approach a story from a neutral perspective. Once you walk through your material, you will have your thoughts or hunches on the story's direction, mood, and significance. This thought process—what you make of the material you have collected—should determine your approach. I determined (based on the facts, actions, and characters of the story) that the fire chief was going through a rough time, and was fighting back with his peculiar tragic-comic wit. Instead of describing him or his attitude (telling), I put the characters and the circumstances in action and used the action to illustrate (and show) attitudes. I put Mr. Santos through, as if on the phone, to readers.

# Structuring the End

Now we have established a story frame and an ending frame, structuring the information we have gathered becomes simple. Remember that a collection of details can produce different outcomes, depending on how they are sorted or arranged. The reflective process will enable you to try out one or two possible arrangements of details and therefore a number of possible endings. For example, if I had taken the emphasis off the acting fire chief, and placed it instead on the substantive fire chief who was away, Santos' "performance" would not have been such a key issue. The story would have run differently and ended differently. The ending of the story is the result of the logical arrangement and association of select details. These details, in turn, govern the interaction of the different elements and details to produce their own deductions or perspectives.

At this point, the writer crosschecks the taste the story will leave in the mouths of readers, so to speak. You do not want to come across as either callous or frivolous.

# Mechanics of the Ending

The key to understanding the working and the building techniques of a story ending is reflecting on the construction of a lead. While the lead takes a few seconds to persuade readers to start reading the story, the ending convinces readers to reflect on and cherish what they have read, and possibly to come back for more (from the same publication or author).

Imagine that at the end of a play at the theatre, the lead actor comes down to say hello to you, or after a long flight, the pilot steps out of the cockpit to chat with you. With these gestures, the pilot or lead actor would have left an imprint of your mind—just as the ending of a story should. Chances are, if you were promised those final sweet moments, you might want to fly that airline again and even recommend it to others. In other words, the same promise that is used to say goodbye to you, could be used to entice you.

So, quote, tease, narrate, describe, anything that will give the reader the star treatment. If you can write an engaging lead, you can probably also write a memorable ending. The same mechanics, and the same framework, apply in most cases.

You could say that an ending is a lead facing the other way.

# 11

## Greed and Grit: Guided Tour of a Storyteller's Mind

*It is an act of self contempt to write well. It is horrible.* —Mark Kramer.

In this chapter, award-winning reporter and writing coach Gary Tippet (*The Age*, Melbourne, Australia) dissects two of his major narrative feature stories, "A Deadly Game" and "Slaying the Monster" (*Sunday Age*, Melbourne). He pieces the stories together by offering blow by blow accounts of how he gathered and sorted the compelling details. He explains his choices, his tricks and his techniques. Tippet outlines the mental twists and turns and professional decisions that produced those powerful leads and engaging supporting paragraphs. He also explains how he used his greed to capture details that set the scene and mood of the story.

Except for the "Background" sections, which explain the circumstances and contexts of the stories, this chapter is Tippet's first-person account of the challenges he faced and the decisions he made. He also tells us how he selected and organized story details in his award-winning stories.

## A Deadly Game

### Background

A bunch of teenage boys are playing at Yarra Bend near Melbourne's Eastern Freeway. They start pushing rocks off an overpass as traffic passed beneath. Dr. Malcolm Goodall, a university professor, is driving toward Clifton Hill, a suburb of Melbourne, when the boys' last rock smashes though his windscreen and hits him in the chest. Dr. Goodall dies later.

After proceedings in the Children's Court, the boys, aged 13 and 14, are tried in the Supreme Court of the Australian state of Victoria on charges of manslaughter.

"A Deadly Game", a 2500-word narrative story, published on 10 September 1995 in the *Sunday Age*, ran along each side of detailed graphics of the freeway with pointers to where various parts of the action that shocked the whole region unfolded. Tippet obtained police records and an interview with the mother of one of the boys. He reconstructed the story from evidence given to the Children's Court and Supreme Court trials, including *voir dire* sessions (preliminary hearings by a judge in the absence of the jury). Australian law (Section 26 of the Victorian Children's and Young Person's Act) forbids the disclosure of the identity or publication of the names of the boys and witnesses. So Tippet called the boys T and R and identified other participants using initials and professions, where possible.

The major challenge was to tell a simple and engaging story that was not bogged down by the "overwhelming documentary material and legal strictures". Tippet says did not want to drape his story in blankets of jargon and "unavoidable artificiality" that would make it hard to read.

---

## Excerpts

## A Deadly Game *By Gary Tippet*

First thing Sunday morning—same as most weekend mornings—doors slammed, gates banged and the boys were gone: flown away to do all sorts of terrific boy things until the lowering dark drove them reluctantly home again.

They crashed together, as planned, outside the Welcome Mart, then rode, trailing shouts and insults and laughter, to the primary school where they crossed paths with the two younger kids. "Do you want to go for a bike ride down the track?" they asked. "Yeah," said the others, and that was the day all laid out.

All day on their mountain bikes and BMXs, backwards and forwards through the Yarra scrub from Fairfield Boathouse to the Yarra Bend Golf Course, Dights Falls and the Children's Farm. Burnouts and skids through a mud patch on the track, until their clothes were wonderfully splattered.

They watched golfers tee off at the first hole, ducks at the boathouse and mad blokes on mountain bikes tumbling down a wild slope near the golf course. They bought lollies for lunch at the Fairfield Hospital kiosk and took turns going over this great jump near there. Late in the afternoon they played tiggy down by the Yarra Bend Overpass.

Then one boy said to his mate "Do you want to throw some rocks at cars?" "Yeah,"said the other boy. "Yeah."

DOCTOR Malcolm Goodall had spent the afternoon that Sunday, 12 June, last year, at his wife Jacqui's grandmother's home in Ormond, helping the old lady with some handyman work around the house. That's the sort of person he was, everyone agreed: friendly, popular and committed to looking after others.

Dr Goodall, 36, a senior lecturer in microbiology at the Werribee campus of the Victoria University of Technology, had come to Australia from the north of England in about 1985.

He began teaching at the university's food technology department in 1989 after receiving a Bachelor of Science degree at Sterling University, Scotland, and completing his PhD at Monash. At Monash he met fellow microbiologist Jacqueline and they had married on February 26, just 15 weeks ago.

At the moment Jacqui Goodall was in Dubai, visiting her parents, so now he was driving home alone in his green Volvo to the weatherboard house in Claude Street,

Northcote, that they had bought just before Christmas. He drove north along Burke Road and at about 5.30 turned left onto the on-ramp of the Eastern Freeway. He stopped and gave way to the nurse turning right in her Alfa Romeo.

"DON'T do it," said the youngest boy and rode away. Later he remembered, "I thought it was dangerous." He was just 11.

His friend, the other primary school boy, followed and caught up with him just around the bend, but as he was leaving he saw one of the older boys walking near the southern end of the Yarra Bend overpass. The other was picking up a large, whitish rock.

# Reporting and writing *A Deadly Game*

The story had to be constructed from evidence the boys gave. To turn something like this into a story, I knew I had to take the reader to the scenes I was describing and give them the fullest possible experience. I needed to paint a picture full of impressions, give them a sense of immediacy, of being there. And the secret to that is greedy reporting—vacuuming up every forensic piece of detail.

I followed the final part of the trial and decided to tell the story as a detailed reconstruction. I wanted to follow the boys and their mates as they made their way to the overpass, to track Dr. Goodall as he drove along the freeway, and, in a sense, watch what happened when their paths intersected.

Luckily, I happen to like hitting the transcripts of long criminal trials because they are chock full of detail: the little, careful observations and impressions of witnesses, the different ways those individuals talk, the minutiae, the weighed-and-measured physical and expert evidence. These are the kind of details that, for space reasons, daily court reporters often leave out. This story had it all if you took the time to sift.

This story also had an abundance of movement. It had a trajectory, a momentum. Not just a beginning, a middle and an end but an arc, an almost relentless sequence of events that could keep the story moving—and hopefully carry the reader along with it.

I decided to tell the story cinematically, in a series of short scenes, or acts, swinging between the boys and Dr. Goodall and some of the other people in cars on the freeway as they inevitably headed toward each other.

Narrative doesn't have to proceed chronologically. It doesn't have to begin at the beginning. I searched for and found that storytelling moment. I could have started from the storytelling moment and used a flash back to connect the strands of the story. Starting the story from that dramatic moment when the stone hit Dr. Goodall would have said it all, and left readers little to look forward to. I felt this one worked best in a fairly straight chronological fashion to capture the momentum.

# Conceiving and constructing the lead

Where to begin seemed easy. How to begin was another thing.

But as I read over my notes and bits of the briefs of evidence, particularly from the boys and their mates, I was struck by how innocently and harmlessly the day had begun. These were just kids mucking around on their bikes on a winter Sunday. And then they did the dumb thing.

I'm a great fan of Ray Bradbury, the great science fiction and horror writer. I particularly love the nostalgic evocations of youth in his *Dandelion Wine* and *Something Wicked This Way Comes*: the simple everyday pleasures of summer vacations, exploration, running through long grass and just being alive enjoyed by the boys in those books. So I pretty much pinched my lead—or at least its tone, its energy and enthusiasm—from Bradbury.

I liked the quotes, "Do you want to throw some rocks at cars?" "Yeah," said the other boy. "Yeah." This was a terrific point to abruptly shift focus to Dr. Goodall turning onto the freeway. I like to stop at a dramatic moment and come at the story from a different point of view, add a new layer. You can do this by taking advantage of a natural pause in the story or you can suddenly stop and leave your reader in suspense. Readers want to know what's going to happen next but you say, "No. I'm not telling right now. We're moving to something else." You make them wait. You make them wonder.

Making readers wait can be a powerful technique. A while back, I read a piece by 1998 Pulitzer Prize winner Tom French. He said suspense leaves the reader with "that delicious sense of enforced waiting". It's drama.

# Telling the story—vacuuming up details

I was back with the boys after four paragraphs and picked up with another seemingly ordinary but telling quote that allowed me to pick up from where I'd left off:

"DON'T do it," said the youngest boy and rode away. Later he recalls, "I thought it was dangerous." He was just 11.

See what I mean about vacuuming up the detail? Same goes for what I guess you could call storytelling quotes. Those first three words seem pretty pedestrian sitting in a police record of interview, but in a way they sum up the dangerousness of what the other boys were planning. The fact that the kid was just 11 invigorated the action.

Another thing is illustrated here. To get a vividly detailed narrative, I always think about the shape my story will take even while I am reporting or researching it. I am always on the lookout for structural ideas like those quotes that are just right for ending a scene or introducing a new one, someone's perfect description of a piece of action, a throwaway line, something about what they were thinking at the time, what my characters are doing. If they're drinking a coffee, I want to know if it is it latte or espresso. If they're reading a book, I want to know the particular book they are reading, even the page.

In this yarn, the rock couldn't be just a rock. I wanted to find as much about it as possible. R found it beneath a tree. It was whitish, about 20cm long, oval, pointed at one end and, he estimated, about one-and-a-half kilograms. A pretty good guess as it turned out: the rock was exactly 1.76kg. Note that I had cross-checked the weight of the rock. I got it weighed. Precise details power story details and storytelling.

You like to think you'll remember these little flashes of inspiration, but you don't. I've scribbled notes to myself about how I might use them. I've even drawn sketches of things, such as surgical instruments, so I can better describe them later.

# Using the details

Sucking up detail doesn't mean I empty everything into the story. As much as it hurts, you have to be selective. I take it all in, but I leave a lot out. I heard someone say once 'you have to kill your babies'.

But you can also squeeze a lot of detail into a very small space. I described the fatal moment like this:

> The rock tumbled end over end for 12-and-a-half metres, punched a hole through the windscreen with a noise that sounded like a 'pssst!' to the boys on the bridge. It slammed into Dr. Malcolm Goodall's chest with the force of a five kilogram sledgehammer given a full swing and tore open his heart.

I think there were five separate pieces of information, or different sources, in those two sentences. There was evidence from a police accident investigation officer on the re-enactment of the rock falling and hitting the car. The police jacked up a test car at an angle to simulate the way the stone would hit the windscreen when the car was moving at about 90 to 100 kilometers per hour. A witness described how the rock tumbled end over end. One of the kids used the 'pssst!' sound to describe what he heard. A forensic pathologist used the sledgehammer analogy during the trial to describe the force with which the stone hit the wind screen (windshield) and the victim. And I knew the result had torn Dr. Goodall's heart open because the police informant took me aside one day to show me photos of the Volvo after the accident, and some other bits and pieces. Among them was a post-mortem photo of the organ with a deep split running from top to bottom.

You can tip a lot of information out of your notebook and into your story by compressing it—grabbing the really important aspects and putting them all together. Thinking about that, I'm reminded of something else I read a year or two ago from Tom French, which I think is relevant. French wrote that in narrative you need to know when to speed up the pace and when to slow down.

> The paradox is that when you're in the boring stuff that's when you need to speed up and when you're in the best stuff when things are moving really rapidly, you slow down . . . so that the reader can really feel and process and really enter that scene.

I completely agree. But in this case I did the opposite and got it over really quickly. I guess the moment when the boys push the rock off the overpass is the dramatic central point of the whole story, yet I knock it off in one paragraph of two sentences. Fifty six words.

It felt right. I guess it illustrates one of my other writing rules—that rules are made to be broken.

# *Slaying the Monster*

## Background

Reporter Andrew Rule sat next desk to Gary Tippet's in the newsroom of the *Sunday Age* newspaper in downtown Melbourne. A reporter working at a women's magazine alerted Rule to the story of a man called Tony Lock. Rule didn't have time to chase the story so he asked Tippet if he would like to give it a shot. "That was nice of him;" Tippet says because the story published on June 22 1997, won him Australian journalism's most prestigious award, the Walkley, for best newspaper feature.

Tony Lock had served time—19 months for manslaughter in Melbourne's Pentridge Prison some time before Gary Tippet spoke to him. Gordon Kerr's history of abuse and the awful job the local cops did in investigating complaints of the abuse two decades later was the reason Tony Lock got such a short sentence—time he'd already served awaiting trial. His offense: killing Gordon Kerr, the family 'friend' who had raped him, on average twice a week, from the time he was four until he turned 14.

Lock came for Kerr one early morning in April 1995. He smashed the door, charged into Kerr's house and attacked him with an axe. He walked away leaving the axe wedged in Kerr's buttocks.

The lead homicide investigator told Tippet the scene of the axe attack was one of the most confronting things he'd ever experienced.

Lock had avoided the media since his release but felt he was ready to talk. Gary Tippet pored over the trial transcripts, witness statements and parts of the police brief. He drove out to Trentham for a long interview with Tony Lock. He described the interview in his story, *Slaying the Monster*.

Fortunately for Tippet, Lock wanted his story told and "didn't want to stop talking, a gift to a feature writer".

---

*Excerpts*

### Slaying the Monster *By Gary Tippet*

THESE were the creatures of Tony Lock's stolen childhood: The Rainbow Bird of his daydreams and The Monster of his nightmares.

The Rainbow Bird was big and bright and beautiful. He'd climb on its back and be lifted high above the paddocks and cold, wet forest, far from the lonely timber huts and the hard, rough-handed men, away to somewhere he wanted to be: to the Safe Place. But it could never keep him there.

And at night The Monster would come.

From behind. Breathing hard and gaining on him as he ran towards home. And the door would open and his parents would be there and he'd scream for help and they'd just stand there in silence, looking on. And it would take him down, pushing his little face into the earth.

And then it would fill him up with pain.

He grew up and the Rainbow Bird went away, but the other lurked on, running him down again and again and again through 30 years of night terrors.

Then one star-bright morning, long after he'd become a man, the little boy came back, took an axe and slew The Monster.

TONY LOCK came crashing and crying to the door of a farmhouse outside Trentham, in the tall eucalypt ranges south-east of Daylesford, just after three o'clock on a bitter Sunday morning, 9 April 1995. He was sobbing so hard the poor woman who found him there could barely understand what he was trying to say.

All she could decipher was a single misery-ridden mantra: "Bad man hurt me. Me hurt bad man".

She called the police. The first officers to arrive, from Trentham's two-man station, found Lock curled up in a fetal position on the veranda, still weeping uncontrollably. As they approached, he rolled onto his back and said something like: "Help me please. I've just killed someone." Then he added: "Could you please hold me? Could someone just touch me?"

"The best way to describe him," a senior constable said later," is almost like a child that had, you know, hurt themselves badly and just wanted comforting".

Eventually Lock pointed the police to another farmhouse, in Bullengarook Road, East Trentham. Its front door had been battered down and inside, lying face down on a .22 rifle, they found the body of a retired farm laborer and timber worker, Gordon Lindsay Kerr, 67. His skull had been fractured on both sides—he had six head injuries in all, as well as four broken ribs and a ruptured spleen.

The axe that had killed him was still buried in his buttocks.

"I wanted to see him bleed from the arse and he did," Lock, then 38, told detectives later that morning." You know, I just wanted to do to him what he did to me."

# Reporting and writing *Slaying the Monster*

Tony Lock is the gentlest of axe killers: Solicitous, softly-spoken and tentative, with pale, haunted eyes beneath anarchy of hair and an edgy, frozen-in-the-headlights vulnerability. Rangy and gaunt, he brews you honeyed tea and wraps himself in a rough-knit, homespun jumper with a Wilderness Society badge at the neck. He's sorry but unapologetic.

Tony felt he had a good reason for that last blow: "You know, I just wanted to do to him what he did to me."

During the interview, Tony also showed me some of his poetry, written while he sat awaiting trial in a bluestone cell in Pentridge. They were mainly short fragments but tremendously affecting and I decided to weave a couple of them into the story. I felt that they, more than anything, revealed the damaged child who still lived within Tony. They were also a tool to show the enormity of what happened when Tony was raped. He wrote the poems with vividness and sensitivity, but stepping back from the physical details.

The man promised to take the boy to Melbourne overnight in his pulp truck. Instead he took him to a lonely timber hut in the bush. In his poems, Tony replays the night vividly: callused hands and rough whiskers, a little face pushed into a dirty black stinking pillow, searing white pain.

Elsewhere, I quoted one, written in prison but in the voice of a child where he recalled the first time it happened: "hurt so much monster crush me nothing now me see me like broken teddy me not no nothing now".

# Conceiving and constructing the lead

I was sitting with Tony, looking at his poetry and scraps of photographs from his childhood. He seemed terribly lonely. I asked him if he had any friends as a kid, and he said, "Not really". He said at lunchtimes he would wander into paddocks near the school, lie on his back and daydream about a mythical creature he called the Rainbow Bird. In his daydreams he would ride it away to safety.

Later we were talking about the damage done to his young mind and he said he used to have constant nightmares in which another creature lurked that he'd named The Monster.

I suffer an almost constant case of writer's block. I agonize over every paragraph, every phrase, and every word. Jill Baker, one of my editors at the *Sunday Age* at the time, used to say:

> I come in the morning and Gary is sitting there staring at a sentence on the screen. I go home that night and he's still sitting there staring at a sentence on the screen. Trouble is, it's the same bloody sentence.

I guess I'm not a natural at this game. Getting it hard is hard work. The hardest bit for me has always been the lead. I can't go anywhere until I get that intro. Some people can map out the story and come back to the start, but not me. If I don't have the lead I'm not going anywhere. Michael Gordon, our National Affairs Editor, and I were talking to our trainee journalists one day, and he said we were "bricklayers, nor architects". We can't begin until we lay that first brick down.

But this lead came to me fairly easily. In a sense it is fairly straight, the sort of intro I sometimes define as a scene setter, which takes the reader to a place. This one did that in a way, but what it was detailing was Tony's internal landscape. The idea was to take his daydreams and night terrors, as he had described them to me in the interview, and use them to illustrate the reality of his abuse and what it led him to do.

The Monster is Gordon Kerr and his parents standing there in silence and doing nothing all those 10 years. And the nightmare itself is about anal rape. But what it let me do was describe the act of rape with power but also sensitivity by coming at it in that roundabout and sort of circumspect manner—"And then it would fill him up with pain". I was pretty happy with it. I think it hooked the reader from the start.

# 12

## Persuasive Storytelling: Not a Matter of Opinion

*There is much to be said in favor of modern journalism. By giving us the opinions of the uneducated, it keeps us in touch with the ignorance of the community.* —Oscar Wilde

Journalism informs, educates, and entertains the public. It also generates and sustains debate and reinforces our democratic and socio-cultural values. News writers inform us about events near us or of interest or relevance to us. They make us aware of our environment and the larger world. News writers are expected to report "facts," and not impose their personal opinions on readers.

Narrative helps news, feature, opinion, art, review and other kinds of writers to tease out our humanity and our sense of community as they inform, sensitize, challenge and entertain their audience. Narrative puts the news in the context of our humanity and, in doing so, makes people laugh, cry, get angry or feel disturbed or reassured. Narrative writers too are not allowed to insert their own opinion in stories.

It is the responsibility of opinion writers to initiate, develop, sustain, and sometimes arbitrate the public's response to the news, features, and even people's attitudes. Opinion writers start a debate, make suggestions, challenge the system, or tease society into asking questions. They define the nature (and sometimes the magnitude or hopelessness) of a problem or situation. Editorial opinion sometimes makes us throw our collective hands in the air in helpless resignation. Opinion can entertain us.

The opinion writer is society's master of ceremonies and umpire. While news and feature stories point to what has happened, is happening, or could happen, opinion stories try to determine what society (the rulers, the ruled, the stake-holders, and the bystanders) should think about, and how the public should respond to issues that affect the immediate or larger society. Because the opinion article challenges people to reflect on issues and events that touch or shape society, opinion writing has become the soul of quality journalism. It has often been said that the concern of politics is to win the debate, while journalism's pre-occupation is to ensure that the debate does take place.

In the 20th and 21st centuries, the role of editorial opinion became as important as that of news and feature writers. The introduction of opinion writing into daily journalism is important to the business of journalism because it offers committed journalistic storytellers and knowledgeable reporters the opportunity to blow off steam. It offers reporters an avenue to vent pent-up subjectivity, ideally leaving news stories free of personal opinion. The public has always been suspicious of reporters, even the specialists among them, who inject their opinion into their news stories and analyses. Editors now advise reporters who have developed an expertise, interest or flair in certain areas, or who have built an opinion while working on a story, to express themselves in an opinion piece—an op-ed—or a review. Reporters need to understand how journalistic opinion is written. Because contributors write a high percentage of op-ed pieces in major publications, this chapter will be of interest to non-journalists as well.

Before now, the newspaper editor or a group of smart-mouthed reporters wrote the "leader" or opinion. Now, following the American model, newspapers around the world have created editorial boards composed of experienced journalists and industry or sectoral experts, and academics. In the latter part of the 20th Century, more non-journalists got their opinion published in op-ed pages of newspapers and magazines. In fact, many major newspapers rely on external contributors to fill their op-ed pages. The good thing about this is that experts in different areas of knowledge and human activity, and people with a wide variety of views enrich national and community debate. It is not surprising, then, that the quality and appeal of columns and op-ed pieces, to some extent, determines the seriousness and popularity of a quality newspaper. Opinion writers are among the most influential contributors to a newspaper or news magazine. Their columns are syndicated to hundreds of other newspapers. In the United States, William Safire, Roger Rosenblatt, George F. Will, and Art Buchwald are good examples of influential opinion writers.

# Persuasive Writing

The term *opinion* can be misleading. An opinion piece is not an opinion, as such. Opinion writers are not expected to download their personal opinion on readers. Instead opinion writers process facts and use these selected facts to deduce or construct a new reality, a new set of conceptual possibilities. The opinion writer's job is similar to the task of building with Lego tiles. Children do not manufacture the tiles. They take existing tiles and build them into unique shapes of their choice. Out of the same box of Lego tiles, one child may build, say, a boat, while another may prefer to build a rocket, a plane or a police officer. Each object is built from the same collection of tiles, and each boat, rocket, plane or cop had better have the attributes or personality of the object the tiles were combined to create. The same collection of tiles used to create a car can also be used to create a boat or house. If the Lego versions of these objects look different than the real things, the recreated reality had better be convincing.

The main purpose of the editorial opinion, therefore, is to persuade readers—to use a selection of information and "facts" to channel people's thinking toward awareness (or preferably a revelation), a conviction, a feeling, a mental frame or action.

Although the newspaper opinion pieces are aimed principally at the intellectual audience, they should also appeal to the type of people who read news and feature stories. Strong opinion pieces appeal to the senses (feelings, including our social morality) and the intellect (questioning, justification, debate). The opinion writer must, therefore, be conscious of people's sensibilities. No opinion, no matter how cleverly argued or upheld, is law. Every opinion is subject to public debate and negotiation. That is probably why opinion articles receive more reader reactions than most other types of journalistic writing.

There are four major forms of opinion pieces: the op-ed, the editorial, letters to the editor, and reviews. Letters to the editor will not be treated here because journalists rarely write them. Review writing, which is a shade of opinion, will be treated in Chapter 13.

# 1. Opinion or op-ed

Editors of major newspapers and magazines receive hundreds of opinion articles every week, but they end up publishing only one or two.

## Shortcuts to the Trash Bin

Some of the major reasons opinion page editors turn down submissions are:

- opinionated writing
- stale or irrelevant subjects
- lack of profile
- insensitivity
- shaky reasoning
- skimpy research.

### Opinionated Writing

One would have thought that an opinion article should contain the writer's opinion about the state of affairs of society. As we saw earlier, this is untrue. Readers and editors don't care what you think. They do not care about your moral, political, or philosophical views. They do care, however, about events, life, ideas, and your ability to collect and analyze facts in a refreshing and unique way that persuades the reader and leads to new ways of seeing things, or to further debate, even dissent. This is a careful and systematic process enlivened by the distinction of facts, the freshness of approach, the persuasiveness and logic of the argument and adept use of language.

## Stale or Irrelevant Subjects

Editorial page editors favor op-eds relating to events in the news, people's consciousness, or anniversary of major events. They also welcome op-ed pieces on timely or current affairs and matters of concern to the community or the larger society, especially if these issues can generate interest and debate or trigger reactions or redeeming action.

## Lack of Profile or Qualification

Unfortunately, the profile of the writer is often more important than the subject itself. An opinion piece about sexual assault written by a victim of rape (or a rapist, for that matter), a social worker, a civil rights campaigner, or a policy maker will be more authoritative than a similar article from a basketball star or a professor of physics. Likewise, an op-ed piece on the price of Christmas turkey from a professor of nuclear physics may attract the same suspicion reserved for an opinion piece on nuclear physics written by a sales clerk. Op-ed writers must be know a lot about a subject or have substantial direct personal or professional experience in the area they are writing about. The op-ed piece is nearly as important as the person writing it. Readers want to know the competence of the writer. Access to strategic information, depth of conviction, and the prospect of an ensuing debate are some of the things op-ed editors—and readers—value most in contributors. A brief career or biographical detail often accompanies many opinion articles. The bio brief tells readers that the writer knows what he or she is talking about.

## Insensitivity

Editorial page editors often reject articles that contain offensive language or promote shrill and unwholesome causes such as hatred, racism, and open immorality. Editors welcome articles that challenge existing institutions and values, such as democracy, government, communism, human rights, and law, as long as the arguments are sober, persuasive, sophisticated, and instructive. The difference between offensiveness and freedom of speech is very much like the difference between pornography and biology. One is an expression of weakness, and the other is a contribution to knowledge or debate, an expansion of the human experience and intellect. It is possible to write a well-reasoned and sober (even if unpopular) reflective piece on the merits of unemployment or poverty without using prejudicial, offensive, or hate-ridden language. Opinion pieces are not about right or wrong answers, but about the exercise of the intellect and democratic ideals of free expression and debate.

## Shaky Reasoning

Editors throw away articles that are emotional or partisan and, therefore, devoid of logical, persuasive reasoning. Some op-ed writers attempt to address too many issues, take sideswipes at people and institutions, and do not cause people to reflect. Such pieces are often excessively subjective; they are not built on blocks of knowledge and reason.

## Skimpy Research

Research is the soul of the opinion story. Research generates authority and facilitates reading. Specific details, anecdotes, hot quotes, unique background, and rare or implicative facts and figures are all hallmarks of good reporting. For example, in his op-ed piece titled "Neck and Neck in Gory" (*Newsweek*, March 7, 2001), Malcolm Jones argued that the racehorse Seabiscuit in 1938 "garnered more column inches in the newspapers than either Roosevelt or Hitler."

In her op-ed on American presidential candidate Senator John McCain, Margaret Carlson took us to the senator's political event at which "a 1,500-lb pig named Rootie" was in attendance. To have your opinion piece published in a major newspaper, you must show evidence of thorough research and a keen eye for factual and logical detail.

# Anatomy of the Op-ed

The structure and methodology of the opinion piece depend to a great extent on the type of op-ed one is writing. I will divide op-eds into three broad groups based on goal, structure, and content. These are: functional, intellectual, and entertainment or literary. However, some of the best op-ed stories incorporate elements of all three types. The type of op-ed determines its writing style.

## 1. Functional Op-ed

The functional op-ed deals with practical, relevant issues and seeks to bring about policy changes or changes in attitude. Its chief role is advocacy for change or preservation of life, values and standards. Among a legion of other things, the functional op-ed could argue for the initiation, maintenance, restoration, implementation, or cancellation of policy or action. It could call for improved health care, better education, human rights, or accountability. It could want to preserve the environment, rights, or safety. An op-ed arguing for the banning of cigarette smoking or advocating for action against child abuse or truancy, would be considered a functional op-ed. Intellectual and functional op-ed stories can lend themselves— reluctantly—to what we can call "hard opinion," the methodical hard-facts-only geometrical argument and structure:

Problem or situation ⌁ existing arguments for it ⌁ weaknesses of those arguments ⌁ the writer's points and arguments ⌁ mitigating or attenuating considerations ⌁ a conclusion that recaps the writer's arguments and drives home the point.

## 2. Intellectual Op-ed

The intellectual opinion or commentary seeks to elevate scholarship and develop or challenge the intellect, cultural, or moral codes and principles. It rarely brings about immediate social or political change. Instead, it prepares people's minds and offers options and possibilities of action and being. In the long term, the intellectual opinion may lead to action. For example, an op-ed writer about discussing the urgent need for democracy in North Korea may not see immediate change. Nor would the op-ed in India's *Hindu Times* exhorting the U.S. government to release Indian prisoners from U.S. jails immediately. While the U.S. government is unlikely to change its policy because an Indian newspaper asked it to, the article may stoke the fires of justice, peace, and fairness among Indians and, indeed, Americans. Intellectual opinion articles primarily target changes in perception rather than instant action, but the seeds may one day germinate and bring about the popular rejection of autocratic rule, as happened in Philippines and South Africa. Opinion pieces on utopia, capitalism, education, and the like, would qualify as intellectual op-ed pieces.

## 3. Entertainment or Literary Op-ed

This type of op-ed makes us laugh, cry, and feel excited or ashamed. It is a commentary on society (culture, life, trends, people, and special interests) and harbors hardly any elements of advocacy. It could contain personal anecdotes or an entreaty on life's ironies quirks.

The best op-ed writers typically use anecdotes, quotes, dialogue, imagery, and other storytelling tools, paying special attention to telling details, scene, and mood.

It is also possible to integrate elements of storytelling into the hard op-ed story. Because journalistic writing is heading steadily into storytelling, this chapter will concentrate on how to apply narrative techniques to opinion stories.

# The Lead

The lead sets the scene and presents the issue or an educated position. Op-ed writers present the issue in the lead principally by:

- Reporting (giving fresh information or building on a verified news report);
- Presenting a point of view;
- Raising an alarm.

In standard narrative stories, the writer uses one or more lead paragraphs to draw readers into the story. The nut graph or *so-what paragraph* states or emphasizes the importance and context of the story. In op-ed pieces the nut-graph is part of the lead, and often functions as the lead. The writer says up front why the issue is important, or states the impact or relevance of the issue on the community.

A good opinion lead is illuminating, surprising, provocative, or thought provoking. It is the beginning of the journey into the essence of opinion writing—getting readers to take a stand, or reconsider their stand on known issues, and challenging them to admit new knowledge and alternative options and perspectives.

An op-ed is a journalistic story, and requires the same reporting and writing skills expected of a narrative writer—complete with such elements as eloquent scenes, quotes, dialogue, scene and action. As a guide, let us say that an opinion piece that lacks the attributes of an excellent narrative news or feature story may not be particularly inviting.

There are innumerable ways of constructing a compelling opinion lead. The nature of the lead will be determined by the factual base, personality, exposure, imaginativeness, or creative energy of the writer. This section will point to a few common techniques opinion writers use to construct their leads.

It is sometimes easier to appreciate good writing after seeing an example of bad writing and understanding what makes it bad. One of the worst habits of opinion lead writing is tradition—the tradition of hard news and hard opinion. The hard opinion—that cold, martial opinion—starts by tabling a known and current thought and proceeds to argue it systematically.

One op-ed article in Singapore's *Straits Times,* (January 30, 2002), "What Lies Behind the *Tudung* Debate," started this way:

> From cute little kerchiefs to the tent-like burqa worn by women in Saudi Arabia, the question of how the female of the human species should protect their modesty, according to Islam, is one that has reared its head periodically over the centuries.
>
> So many issues are intertwined, and so many forces are at work that it becomes easy for reason to take a back seat.
>
> Islam being a highly contextual religion, there remains little consensus among Muslims worldwide over the rights and wrongs of wearing the headscarf, or indeed over the extent the body should be covered.

Despite the descsriptive beginning (cute little kerchief, tent-like burqa), the lead elements are common and as predictable as a traffic stop sign or a bag of McDonald's French fries. The lead only succeeded in telling us that the issue has been on the human agenda for centuries. Well, that is exactly why we do not want to hear any more of it.

The paragraphs that follow dwell on the difficulty and complexity of the issue—something readers already know. The sterile lead also lacked implicative connections. A perceptive reader would easily spot the wild assumption (little consensus among Muslims worldwide) in the lead.

Now let us look at how the author of another coiffure-guided opinion piece elicited and held the reader's unblinking attention. *TIME* Asia correspondent Tim Larimer's opinion piece, "A New Look" (May 1, 2001), on the Japanese prime minister's shaky government, started this way:

> That the most notable characteristic of Japan's new Prime Minister is his hair-style might not sound encouraging news. But in a country of cookie-cutter Breel-Creemed coiffures, the Koizimi perm is downright revolutionary. His ample gray locks cascade high above his head and swirl in waves down the back of his neck, brushing over his shirt collar. The rakish look of the tall, angular 59-year-old bachelor enhances his image as an iconoclast, a Don Quixote-style politician tilting the windmills of Japan's crusty political establishment. And many Japanese like what they see. "If we don't change the politics, we cannot go on," says Toshiaki Okazaki, a 59-year-old whale meat vendor in Kita-Kyushu. "Koizumi brings new blood."
>
> It's that fresh image that Junichiro Koizumi was selling, and the rest of Japan was devouring, when he was named . . . Prime Minister last week.

Larimer was telling a story, one he enjoyed telling—a human story with implicative political associations. Koizumi's new look and new-fangled approach gave him the job. A nut graph is hooked onto the lead. The writer creates a link between the prime minister's looks and his ascension to power and even to the politics of Japan. Koizumi's looks foreshadow his politics and the political scene, and the sensibilities, aspirations, and expectations of the Japanese people and the world.

It is this connection, this appeal, and this energy, that make this story more readable, more persuasive than the *Straits Times* piece. A good opinion story is designed to persuade the reader.

There are many ways of killing a mosquito. Some writers choose to open the article with a known position or scenario, which is no longer news on its own. By adding the new dimension or interpretation, or by pointing the known facts in a new direction, the op-ed writer can make readers understand how the situation relates to them and why they should bother to read yet another argument on the issue.

Some opinion writers flip familiar issues around to show fresh and illuminating perspectives that pose a nagging question or invite people to give the idea a thought (or a shrug, even a laugh) and retain it in the social and national agenda. Take the beginning of this op-ed article "Howard is Sacrificing our Interests," by Kenneth Davidson in the Australian newspaper, *The Age*, (June 13, 2002):

> Is John Howard mad, or is he just looking for an excuse during his visit to Washington to bask in the reflected glory of George Bush and his unilateral war on terror?
>
> What, precisely, does Howard expect to gain for Australia out of an Australia-US free-trade agreement (AUSFTA)? Is there anything in the words or actions of Bush, his administration or the US Congress that suggests Washington would make any trading concessions to Australia that might hurt some domestic US interest? 1

Instead of judging, the writer decides to (literally) question the prime minister's judgment—his decision to negotiate a free-trade treaty with the United States.

Lance Morrow, writing for *TIME* online (April 30, 2001), reached into his bag of the known to conjure the unexpected, the inevitable. This is how the piece mischievously titled, "Is George W. Heading for a Crash on the Newt Gingrich Highway?" started:

> Even where we find ourselves now—on the far side of the Bridge to the Twenty-First Century, in a post-millennial America so long at peace abroad that it has entered into a chronic state of warfare with itself at home, just to have nothing to do with the nastiness—even here, there are rules of decorum. And there are rules of political physics.
>
> There are things that we can and cannot do. George W. Bush and his friends don't seem to know this. I am afraid they are going to find it out the hard way, in November 2002.
>
> That's a guess.

It does not matter that the guess may be inaccurate. The piece is persuasive. The writer juggled the familiar into a new shape, a new and realistic perspective. The known could be an item of news, a commonly known occurrence or situation, or words written or spoken especially by newsworthy people.

In this op-ed piece, Sebastian Mallaby built his argument on a familiar situation and debate and the ringing words of a newsworthy public figure.

> Last month Harvey Pitt, chairman of the Securities and Exchange Commission, declared, "There is nothing rotten in the accounting profession." After the weekend's revelations about Enron, nobody believes this nonsense. Yet sane audit reform is not ensured, because the Enron scandal also exposes other shocks that divert attention from accountants. Wall Street analysts recommended Enron right up to the moment it went bust. Enron's board signed off on financial tricks that deceived the shareholders it was meant to represent. And shouldn't we step back and ask whether the root problem lies with stock options?
>
> No, actually, we shouldn't. The challenge, as a string of Enron protagonists parades before Congress this week, is to remember what this scandal is about: Companies are lying about their balance sheets, and only audit reform can restore faith in the numbers that make capitalism function.[2]

What makes the lead catchy is the writer's ability to interpret and convert a forgettable off-the-cuff remark or statement into a revealing, image-laden, and poignant argument.

In this op-ed published in the *Independent on Sunday*, British Foreign Secretary Jack Straw starts by stating known facts (that the British ambassador to the Congo and his family—like all foreigners—live in danger). Before he drops his real bomb (that Prime Minister Tony Blair should visit Kinshasa), he puts in a little reporting. He uses implicative scenic details to depict the danger lurking even within the ambassador's secure residence.

> There is a broken pane of glass in the British ambassador's home in Kinshasa. It has purposely been left unrepaired as a reminder of the day when a bullet whis-

tled through the window and embedded itself in the wall opposite. The hole in the wall remains unrepaired too.

But our ambassador, Jim Atkinson, and his wife, Annemiek, need little reminding of the violent nature of the Democratic Republic of Congo. The dangers of venturing outside their high-security compound were very obvious to me last week when I visited Kinshasa with the French foreign minister, Hubert Vedrine.

Straw's nut graph is interesting. Other top foreign western politicians are going to Kinshasa, a discreet announcement that the place may be dangerous. But if Kinshasa is safe and important enough for other western politicians, it should be safe enough for Prime Minister Blair. Blair needs to defy personal danger to bring peace to that African country.

Mr. Straw, who is not a journalist, belabored the issue of danger, thus losing readers who are not interested in the Secretary's travel diary and in the protracted pursuit of the stereotype that Kinshasa is dangerous. The nut graph could have presented a unique or dramatic Mr. Blair, or supplied information or an argument that could change our opinion on the subject.

You might have noticed that the lead of the *Washington Post* op-ed derived its appeal and crispness from the simplicity of the words, and from the simplicity of the sharp focus. Let's now look at the lead of Lance Morrow's op-ed in *TIME*, "Why Gore Should Embrace Clinton," (October 30, 2000).

What a dilemma for Al Gore. He should be well ahead of George W. Bush by now. He should be on cruise control, barreling down the interstate toward an electoral inevitability. He should have won all three debates by knockout or unanimous decision, exercising his famous command of fact and argument. He should be the unarguable favorite in the race—the Expected One. Instead . . . .

And so the dilemma on which Gore chews—over which, I suspect, he gnashes his teeth—is this: whether to go up to the Oval Office and say, "Mr. President, I need help. Unless you come out and start campaigning for me—now!—I am going to lose the election. And if I lose, there goes the vindication of the Clinton years. There goes the legacy.

The lead is playfully simple: it restates the known (that Al Gore is lagging behind), using foreshadowing and progression to heighten impact and interest. The lead's nut graph, introduced by a punchy elliptical word (Instead . . . ) to heighten the notion of Gore's blunder, offers a graphic, sound-backed scenario, and amplifies the consequence of Gore's insistence on a solo act. The lead is focused.

The basic rules of journalistic storytelling apply to opinion writing, among them a thread (a coherent argument and flow), and short and simple words, sentences, and paragraphs. The other requirement is progression: presentation of an idea, explanation or development of the idea, and smooth transition to another idea. The lead must be appealing and flow into a developed argument. Writing good opinion leads is particularly important because enlightened public discourse appeals to a limited section of the population. A lot of the issues opinion writers discuss things that transcend the immediate needs of the average reader: security, safety, food, shelter, and social amenities. Sloppy thinking, presentation, and writing can reduce the number of people interested in reading an op-ed.

Writing an op-ed on issues that the public knows or cares little about poses peculiar challenges. Teasing the reader into the story with captivating, sometimes entertaining, information and then hooking in a home angle as a nut graph has worked for many writers. The wider the gap between cultures, experiences, expectations, and realities, the tougher the job of creating perceptual connections becomes.

Drawing the fairly insular American newspaper audience to Nigerian issues can be tough. I tried to entice readers on America's West Coast into reading about Nigeria in an op-ed for a major U.S. newspaper, the *San Jose Mercury News,* (June 13, 1999). The story shrilly titled "Nigeria Elects High-Living Ex-general Disguised as Democrat" started this way:

> Nigeria has just inaugurated an army general as its first recent civilian president after a series of military rulers. A paradox to the West, maybe. But this is the beginning of Nigeria's political contribution to the world: democracy with an attitude.

Professor Reese Cleghorn, then dean of the School of Journalism at the University of Maryland, who taught opinion writing at the university, said what most captivated him about the piece was the lead, especially the expression "democracy with an attitude." I used a popular American expression as a cultural and political bridge to the Nigerian reality. It was like speaking to Americans in their own language about an unknown political reality.

Hat Lau more successfully charmed Americans into contemplating Chinese life, politics, and religiosity with his opinion piece "The Real Reason for Crack Down on Falun Gong," (*San Jose Mercury News*, August 8, 1999), which started this way:

> By and large, people growing up in the Western society believe that only one person can walk on water or change water to wine: God. By and large, Westerners don't try to become God.
>
> That is not how we Chinese think.
>
> Deep in the Chinese psyche is the belief that a person can become a supernatural being through some process or spiritual pathway. Understanding this is key to understanding the movement known as Falun Gong.

Both op-ed pieces, and Lau's in particular, used known or familiar symbols to communicate the unknown. While I used the American phrase "with an attitude" as a connecting symbol, Lau used familiar concepts of Western life and beliefs to explain the mysterious. His transitional sentence, "This is not how we Chinese think," establishes a contrast and uses that contrast to lure, challenge, and inform readers, and create a sense of relevance or connection. If the Chinese explain how they think, Americans might be interested in knowing how the Chinese think. A careful portrayal of unique perspectives of the known often generates interest in the contrasting, therefore connecting, unknown—or an unexpected aspect of the known.

I started another op-ed this way:

The outgoing military regime in Nigeria spent a whole week and some $4 million preparing for Saturday's handover of power to President-elect, Gen. Olusegun Obasanjo—a man who already been sentenced to death.

The edict did not come from the military high command that had earlier sentenced Obasanjo to life in prison on bogus charges of plotting a coup. It came from a religious man who can make Nigerian military dictators quake from fear: Tunde Bakare, a Pentecostal pastor and head of the influential Latter Rain church.

The United States and the rest of the Western world are blissfully oblivious of the pervasive influence of the supernatural on African political and social life. But as Nigeria embraces its first democratically elected president since 1984, outsiders would do well to understand the entire spectrum of the African political and belief system—both human and superhuman (*San Jose Mercury News*, May 30, 1999).

I wanted to lure readers into the story with the unexpected, gee-whiz detail. To succeed, the lead has to be focused, concentrating on one fresh strand of argument. Trying to juggle two points at the same time throws the op-ed piece into confusion, as the following piece in *The Guardian,* (Lagos, Nigeria), showed.

In the lead of the piece titled "Wondering in the Wilderness," (February 4, 2002), the writer offered:

By way of an acknowledgement, let me confess that brilliance and pungency of Rev. Fr. Hassan Kukah's televised review of the three publications recently launched by the Ministry of Information and National Orientation informed the conception of this write-up. I was wondering if the Awards for Excellence in Democracy Dividends were nationally widespread until it occurred to me that the Alliance for Democracy states rebuffed the National Media Tours. Be that as it may, if we are convinced that the appraisals were truly objective, it constitutes a very welcome approach towards encouraging healthy rivalry or competition among the states.

In the words of Rev. Fr. Kukah, military regimes anywhere have always had some positive sides to them. He cited examples of military dictatorships that exercised salutary influences on their peoples: Hitler's in Germany, Mussolini's in Italy, Pinochet's in Chile. In Nigeria, it helped to force the citizens into some degree of disciplined behavior, albeit very briefly and without long-lasting effect. In Nigeria, the tendency has always been to ascribe our lack of meaningful progress, firstly to deliberate plunder and lack of commitment by our colonial masters and secondly to "very monumental damage caused by many years of military rule." For how long do we continue to cry over spilt milk and hide under the cloak of diversionary, evasive and escapist tactics? Whether colonially or militarily caused, what have successive post-independence governments, military or civilian, done to right the developmental wrongs earlier perpetrated? Let us take a cursory look at some sorry aspects of our national life since political independence.

Even if we overlook the wordiness of the piece ("by way of an acknowledgement, let me confess"), it is clear that the reader may not be able to follow the argument. The first part of the lead ropes in Father Kukah, the brilliance of his review, the inherently satirical Awards for Excellence in Democracy Dividends, the spread of these awards, and public conviction on the appropriateness of the awards. The second paragraph should have sharpened the focus and explained why the story was important enough to be written. Instead, it started off with abstractions and unresolved and unfocused issues. This piece revealed the difficulty writers encounter in trying to capture and sustain the attention of readers. We will now explore some of the devices opinion writers use to grab and retain readers' attention.

# Lead Devices

## *Biography or Autobiography*

The writer may draw on their own or other people's experiences to establish an argument. This is an anecdotal device used frequently in opinion leads, like this op-ed, "Health Care to Drive Next Economic Boom," by Theodore Roszak (*San Jose Mercury News,* Augusts 8 1999).

> Her name was Mamie. When I finished lecturing, she was the first person to come up and shake my hand. She was 84, bright-eyed, smiling and looking not the least bit burdened by her years.
>
> "Thank God somebody finally recognized how much I'm worth," she exclaimed. "What you see is high maintenance body. There must be 50 people making a living off of me. Why, I'm a walking gold mine."
>
> The scene was a California retirement community. My subject for the day was the rising cost of health care.

The writer takes up the mantle of a storyteller: showing, explaining. The writer transports readers to the scene and lets them see and hear the key characters. The description is controlled and selective. The writer unleashes only details that heighten readers' appreciation of the theme. For example, Mamie's age and looks illustrate the success of the expensive medical attention she has received, which in turn supports the writer's thesis. Although Mamie is in the story, she is not the story. She is just the hook that pulls readers into the story. The op-ed writer must move quickly from the relevant biographical detail to the point of the story.

## *Hard-Nosed Details*

All journalistic writing is built on the foundation of accurate and fresh details. Opinion stories rely on precise details exactly the way news and feature stories do. Reporting is a critical part of opinion writing. Some of the information ignored by hard-news reporters could give an opinion lead a lift. In her op-ed on John McCain, Margaret Carlson introduced the presidential candidate this way:.

> Sitting behind the wheel of his Lincoln, wearing wraparound shades and a deep melanoma scar on his face, John McCain looks like a B-Movie hitman. As a matter of fact, he is trying to kill something: Washington's seamy money culture. The Arizona senator has just finished an event with a 1,500-lb pig named Rootie, his accomplice in an annual unveiling of the pork hidden in the federal

budget. Now he is tearing the wrong way up a one-way drive into the Capitol for a press conference with conservative Blue Dog Democrats supporting his effort to drive the pigs from the trough. After a decade of frustration, McCain's campaign-finance-reform bill will finally get its hearing on the Senate floor, without threat of filibuster this week ("A Death Match Between Friends", TIME).

Carlson used precise details along with foreshadowing imagery and elements of surprise to introduce to whisper to readers McCain's quaint political agenda.

The reader can see strong evidence of observation, keen interviewing, and research in the lead. Rare, personal details give the lead its punch and elegance. If you try to run the sentence without the unique facts, you would have something like this: "Sitting behind the wheel of his car, John McCain looks like a B-Movie hitman." But then you would be lying because sitting behind the wheel does not make anyone look like a hitman. You would lose your lead and nut graph.

Most op-ed writers start their pieces with known or accessible details. Information has to be newsworthy, except when the writer is commenting on the failure of society to see the information as newsworthy. An example would be the media and society paying no attention to the president's frequent nodding in meetings. An op-ed writer could flag that fact as newsworthy, discuss it as such, or use it to establish important points or insights.

Writers also use personal observation or the observation of others, but the key is the writer's ability to develop a context or perspective out of the news, anecdote, or observation.

## Fiction or Allegory

Some op-ed writers may choose to use fictional scenarios and allegory to explain a social phenomenon. An allegory is the expression of human truths and generalizations using symbolic figures, such as the pork and hitman imagery that threaded through Carlson's tantalizing story.

Part of the fictional scenario can be the deliberate overstepping of the bounds of news and conventional interpretation or perception. TIME columnist, Joel Stein's opinion playfully titled "Miss Get-Me-the-Hell-Out-of-Here," (March 6, 2001), started his hammering of the Miss USA pageant this way:

Straight guys don't watch beauty pageants. That's because pageants take a normal pastime—ranking women by how they look in bathing suits and turn it into something boring, with dance numbers. Plus, all the contestants are teenagers who look like 40-year-old anchorwomen and talk a lot about Jesus. You don't have to deal with that by the pool at the Delano.

Using fictional techniques, Stein manipulated our vision and perceptions to get our attention. His imagery is simple, witty, and streetwise. Half-nude teenage girls with the worn-out looks of ageing U.S. anchorwomen, putting on religious airs beside a swimming pool—is that what they call a beauty pageant?

# The Body

The body of the standard op-ed, written for a quality large-circulation English language publication, is constructed just like any narrative story. It has no preset shape. Its final shape is determined by interactions between the details and other story elements.

The body has a central theme supported by threads of narration, quotations, anecdotes, illustrations, scenes and images woven together into one coherent, cohesive thread of reasoning. The first few paragraphs that follow the lead develop and focus the contents of the lead.

While the lead identifies the conflicts or compelling issues or sets the scene for the presentation of the central question of the article, the body moves the story away from the writer's turf to the reader's. The lead is the writer's antics to attract the reader's interest and attention. In the body, the writer states the case before the people's court. In doing so, the writer may also present the previously unknown perspectives or untapped sources, details, and perspectives.

The body often poses questions or challenges people to pose them. It disagrees with generalized, traditional or opposing notions, or supports a given position. To do this successfully, the writer must offer expert knowledge and novel perspectives. The writer relies on associations, comparisons and contrasts to articulate these arguments.

So far, we have looked at some principles that guide our articulation of opinion articles. In isolation, these ideas cannot prepare one adequately for the writing task. Let us put this idea in a practical perspective by analyzing the nature and flow of arguments in an opinion article. Although there is no fixed way of writing the body, there are some guiding principles drawn from the structures of a variety of respected writers. Every writer has a unique style of writing and persuasion. But by studying the logical content and form of a good op-ed story, we should be able to grasp some of the principles and techniques.

Let us see how Thomas Friedman marshaled his arguments in this *New York Times* op-ed, "Jordan Gets It" (April 3, 2001). For the purpose of structural cohesion and a sustained perspective, we will start with the lead. The piece advocates the ratification of a trade treaty with a modest Arab desert kingdom.

> The U.S. Congress has a chance to do something really good for an ally and really interesting for global trade with one vote. And it has the chance to do something really reckless for both by shying away from this vote. Hold your breath and hope for the best.
>
> Friedman throws his hat into the ring, challenging Congress to choose between patriotism and recklessness. Using elements of suspense to cajole the reader into the story, he offers an interesting definition of recklessness—shying away from this vote, which would benefit the friendly Kingdom of Jordan. Hold your breath, reader, for what is to come. Ladies and gentlemen, please put your hands together and welcome the two lovable American Jordans (the beloved Michael Jordan and the equally beloved Kingdom of Jordan, whose "savvy young" king was born, incidentally, to an American woman).
>
> The story starts with Jordan, the desert kingdom whose exports to the U.S. probably don't equal Michael Jordan's annual salary from endorsements. But

Jordan's savvy young King Abdullah (who arrives in Washington today) figured out sooner than most of his Arab colleagues that trade, not aid, was the way to grow his country, drive domestic reform and differentiate Jordan from the oil states. After the peace treaty with Israel, Jordan arranged with the U.S. to set up several small trade-free zones inside the country, and they have already produced 13,0000 new jobs—a big deal for a country with no oil.

The writer sneaks behind counterarguments (Jordan's low trade with the United States), by appealing to American sentiments (basketball star Michael Jordan's appeal and the youth and savvy of the king of Jordan). He uses Jordan the flying American to get Americans interested in Jordan the pro-American kingdom. The Washington visit of the Jordanian king adds immediacy and appeal to the king and kingdom's relationship with America and Americans. Next, citing facts and figures, the writer sets the stage for the argument that the United States should enter a free-trade agreement with Jordan. After all, Jordan had signed a peace treaty with Israel.

The third paragraph recalls the "total free-trade treaty" the Clinton Administration worked out with Jordan, making it the only Arab country and the fourth country after U.S. neighbors Canada and Mexico and U.S. staunch ally Israel. It also states why Jordan is the country to do business with: it is a "staunch U.S. ally," it is democratizing, and it is a strategically placed buffer zone between Israel and belligerent Arab states. In short, "This is a treaty worth supporting."

In the fourth paragraph, the writer offers other reasons the treaty with Jordan should be ratified, and questions the logic and the sense of duty and responsibility of Congress: "Given all this, you would assume the Jordan free-trade treaty would be easily ratified by Congress. I wish."

In the fifth and sixth paragraphs, Friedman analyzes and pokes holes in the arguments of groups (labor and environmental lobbies) opposed to the treaty. Next, he explores the other dimension of the problem: partisan politics. After appealing to GOP's Republican ideals, he challenges the government's political maturity and sense of fairness: "Does the Bush team push the Jordan free-trade deal that is important for US national security but includes pro-labor, Clinton-installed provisions? Or does it let the accord languish?"

The next three paragraphs identify the mechanisms within the Bush administration that can facilitate the ratification of the treaty, and sum up the importance and social and political benefits of the treaty.

# The Ending

Like the lead, the structure and content of the ending depend on the type of op-ed (functional, philosophical or entertainment).

In a functional op-ed, the ending of an opinion piece can be the author's biggest reason for writing the piece. It is the philosophical or ideological statement of the piece. Friedman's functional piece ended emphatically: "This is a good idea. This is an important trade accord, and could be a good precedent for the future. Congress should act now." That was the point of the piece. It sums up the argument (not the individual points) of the piece. Jordan should get it. As you can see, the ending circles back to the lead and even the headline of the story.

To understand the role of the functional ending, it is important to acknowledge the intellectual op-ed's logical or syllogistic framework: Insects have six legs. The ant has six legs. Therefore, the ant is an insect. Or more befuddlingly: a table has four legs, a cat has four legs; therefore a cat is a table. Or should be a table!

Larimer's piece (*The Australian*) on Japanese Prime Minister Junichiro Koizumi analyzed Japanese politics and the prime minister's chances of survival. The writer uses the political symbolism of Koizumi's looks to situate him in the Japanese political context. Conclusion: In this land of fleeting prime ministership, does Koizumi have what it really takes to survive?

> Dating back to 1989 and the apex of Japan's economy, the prime ministerial names run together like menu offerings at a sushi restaurant: Takeshita, Uno, Kaifu, Maiyazawa, Hosokawa. A dozen years. Eleven prime ministers. Zero successes. The last time Japan was talking about change of this magnitude was 1973, when the fossilized LDP was booted from power for the first time in four decades and Morihiro Hosokawa took the helm. He too was celebrated as a great reformer, delighting Japanese with his sartorial style and samurai roots. Eight months later, he was history. Where is Hosakawa today? Late last month, he was peddling his pottery at an exhibition in the Ginza. Kiozumi will have to work fast if he wants to avoid such a fate.

Lance Morrow, assessing President George W. Bush's political vulnerability, ends his piece on a shorter, sharper note: "He's in greater danger than he thinks."

Davidson ends his op-ed for *The Age*, which started with a barrage of questions, with a declaration disguised as a rhetorical question, so tellingly similar to one the opposition would lob at the prime minister during Question Time.

> It is reported that John Howard is going soft on signing up to the International Criminal Court, on the grounds that it would undermine our sovereignty. This is nonsense.
>
> But why is he apparently eager to sign up to an agreement, which, if it follows the NAFTA rules, will cripple Australia's sovereignty in favor of foreign investors?

Opinion writing is not about right and wrong. It is about public debate, engagement, sensitization and entertainment. Joel Stein's opinion story, like most entertainment op-ed stories, does not end with any suggestion or challenge.

> Friday night, I watched Miss Texas win, the woman who answered my "Would you sleep with Donald Trump?" question with the misinformed, "I think he's a little old for me." After it was over, the only thing I felt was that I'd wasted two valuable TV viewing hours, and that I was the only one who knew which state really won.

Stein sums up his opinion of beauty pageants: a time-squandering, tawdry show that the public does not give a hoot about. Using a personal anecdote, he highlights the resulting issues or sensation and gets the reader to say something like: Imagine that!

In another *TIME* essay, "Having Sex Museum Style," (October 21, 2000), Stein mocks the opening of the Museum of Sex in New York City and the attempt to intellectualize sex this way:

> Academics ruin sex. They analyze it, explain it, deconstruct it, and by the time they're done, you wish they had stuck to talking about Kant's Prolegomena to Any Future Metaphysics. So when the Museum of Sex opened in New York City. I shouldn't have been surprised that it was heavy on the museum and light on the sex . . . . But when I heard about the Museum of Sex, my mind shot right past the museum and straight to the sex part. I think my past experiences at the end of the Hershey and Guinness factory tours built unreasonable expectations.
>
> In fact, the most shocking thing about the museum, besides the $17 admission fee, is that it exists at all: a Fifth Avenue building completely devoted to sex.

The way the ending echoes and amplifies the lead and the body of the story makes Joel's piece stand out. He begins the descent toward the end by quoting a retired porn star who said that curators who managed the sex museum had lewd interests but tried to hide them behind a stiff upper lip, "otherwise they'll stutter." The piece ends this way:

> And that's the problem: no matter what they do, academics always ruin sex by refusing to stutter. They intellectualize it until you realize why they spend so much time alone "writing dissertations." Museums are designed to illuminate the inanimate mummies, Renaissance paintings, Richard Nixon. Flash freezing the ephemeral is too difficult. If you think too long about kissing, it starts to seem like a ridiculous impossibility. (It also means you are very, very lonely). And honestly, that's the problem: the Museum of Sex undermines the real purpose of museums—which is to pick up women. Coming up with a line while you are staring at a Picasso is a lot easier than when you are looking at a statue of a murdered 19th Century prostitute.

Note that, although his arguments serve no mountain-moving social function, they are built on sound reporting—observation, interviews and research. They are persuasive, even brain teasing. The ending of this piece leaves us tipsy with delight. You walk away from the piece with a naughty conspiratorial smile.

# 2. The Personal Column

The personal column is the designer op-ed.. Columnists are considered the most powerful journalists. They seem to have more access to people in power more than any other media writers. I wrote my first column for a not so widely read evening paper. But everyone from the unemployed to the political elite and the military high command read the column. I became the first journalist to be granted a one-on-one by a Nigerian president after I challenged the president to a one-on-one meeting. Military President Ibrahim Babangida instantly took up the offer. "I read your column regularly," President Babangida said we first met in his office.

One possible explanation for the attention columnists get is that because columnists are influential (political columnists in particular), people in power realize the need to pay them respect. In addition, politicians realize that it would be to their own detriment if they failed to give the columnist their perspective on things. Columnists are usually more experienced writers, more likely to understand intricate political nuances, and less likely to misquote sources. They often have contacts in high places. For people in power, or those seeking greater influence or public appeal, being quoted or featured by a widely read columnist is like appearing on the national news in prime time. It makes the columnist a high-profile reporter. The columnist is the people's chief campaigner, entertainer, and hero—or villain. Often the columnist's picture appears in his or her column, lending a celebrity status to the columnist. Although more and more publications illustrate op-ed pieces with the photo of the author, it is more traditional to include the author's photo in a personal column. As a child, I believed that to be called a journalist one had to be a columnist. Columnists were the only journalists whose names I knew, whose pictures I saw.

Columnists, like op-ed writers seek to persuade readers to accompany them on a jolly ride. They both want to sensitize the public on issues that touch society, and to initiate and moderate public debate. Many op-ed writers are columnists.

Although columnists use the skills and techniques of op-ed writers, there are significant differences between columnists and writers. Op-ed writers get published when they write publishable articles. A columnist is allocated a regular slot, with a deadline, which can be daily, weekly, or periodical. In other words, the op-ed writer with a regular slot and a deadline is a columnist.

There are, however, differences between a generic column and a personal column. The generic column appears on a designated opinion page, whether it is written by a (regular) columnist or an op-ed contributor. A personal column is placed on a page the editors believe will give it the best advantage. It could be on the front page, back page, or anywhere else in the paper, depending partially on the clout or appeal of the columnist or the relevance or impact of the area the columnist specializes in.

# Writing the Personal Column

The personal column adopts the structure of the op-ed, but the nut-graph is optional. The columnist teases, cajoles, and sometimes angers readers into a reaction and an addictive loyalty to the column. A column elicits strong public interest and reactions. Another difference between the op-ed and the personal column, therefore, is that the op-ed writer seeks a passionate one-day stand, so to speak. The columnist wants to sign on the dotted line. The columnist seeks to build followership and a relationship with readers. To achieve these, the columnist must:

- Establish a very personal style: This means the columnist will write to individuals not to a crowd. This involves using a few personal details to illustrate or introduce points and a communication scheme, such as the use of personalized turns of phrase, and imagery. It also means a fresh and personal perception of life derived from voracious reading, attention to detail, and considerable exposure, and openness.
- Research and observe authoritatively: The columnist must establish a reputation as a reporter capable of picking details lesser reporters and writers would overlook. For example, Carlson, captured U.S. presidential candidate John McCain "sitting behind the wheel of his Lincoln, wearing wraparound shades and a deep melanoma scar on his face". That strong introduction was the work of keen observation and deep research. That mean look, we soon see, made McCain look "like a B-Movie hitman. As a matter of fact, he is trying to kill something: Washington's seamy money culture."
- Master the art of association and irony: Writing a column is a very personal endeavor. Columnists tap into the deepest recesses of their personality—their quirks, streaks of their peculiar brand of humor, and their humanity to explain issues. It is this personal humor, enlivened by a unique sense of the absurd, that helped Carlson to associate a senator with a hitman. This reemphasizes cultural and intellectual versatility. A columnist is not one to turn off the television because a trashy black-and-white 1954 movie has come on. There is a message, an irony, and a possible interpretable association, lurking in every experience. This association is manifested in the allegories, the comparisons, the wit, and the uniqueness of the information writers use. It is this knack for unique associations that defines a columnist's identity and success.
- Relate to the audience: For a column to be successful, the columnist needs to know and appreciate the audience, and vice versa. Columnists must trim their writing to the level of their audience. Whatever the intellectual level or stature of the readers, columnists must write simply, using cues that the audience can relate and respond to.

# The Columnist's Message

The op-ed article discusses issues of the day. The personal column discusses any issue the columnist chooses. It could be cats, interns, words, food, and it could be nothing. The columnist must whip up a subject and supporting material that will appeal to readers. The columnist's message can be deeply subjective.

The cardinal attribute of a successful column is the writer's ability to show his or her distinct love for people. In their exposition of societal pains, triumphs, and questions, columnists should exude a mastery of—and the ability to understand and explain—their nature and human nature. They must also be able to judge character.

It is impossible to explain all the intricacies of column writing in one section of a book. It would require a whole book and a different audience to do justice to this subject. Therefore, rather than teaching how to write a column, this section will look at elements of column writing that can help anyone interested in future column writing—its principles and challenges.

# The Tools of the Columnist

Columnists use a combination of techniques to get their message across. These tools include:

- Humor (forcing people and society to laugh at themselves)
- Satire (using cheeky humor to portray reality and to criticize action or inaction)
- Argumentation (advancing sturdy arguments for or against actions)
- Plain entertainment (taking people for a pleasant ride)
- Technical exposé (simplifying and contextualizing complex issues)
- Shock/calming treatment (Columnists may decide to shock and/or calm or reassure the readers.)
- Originality of insight (offering unusual insights or perspectives, which can then be subjectively but intelligently illustrated or substantiated. E.g. Shakespeare: fat men are reliable; Joel Stein, *TIME*—Straight guys don't watch beauty pageants

Escape is one of the biggest reasons people read. Life has too much gloom, and humor offers an escape from the harshness of modern life. Humorists and satirists are among the most popular columnists in the major media because they make people laugh and forget their troubles. Humor comes alive in journalistic writing and more so in columns, through the author's use of observation (detail), overview, association and chronicle

# Quick Tips on Column Writing

1. Columnists are writers who can appeal to readers' emotional and critical faculties.
2. Columnists cannot operate without a trust-driven relationship with readers.
3. Columnists must stand for something, even if that means an unpopular position.
4. The column must display variety and freshness. Columnists must read widely, socialize, specialize, observe and, if possible, take breaks to refresh their minds.
5. Columnists show interest in and compassion for people of all classes.
6. Columnist should carve out a well articulated area of specialization or expertise.

# Task

Read an opinion piece from one local, one regional and one international newspaper, and attempt to answer the following questions:

1. What type of op-ed is it?
2. What is the central message of the op-ed?
3. What are the writer's main arguments and how persuasive are they?
4. What devices did the author use in constructing the lead, body and ending?
5. How successfully do the lead and the ending play their roles in this article?
6. How does the writer use a current and familiar event to create and develop his or her arguments?
7. In what way is this op-ed different (structure, persuasive techniques, voice) from a recent one you have read in a quality newspaper?

# 13

## Between Typing and Writing: The Narrative Art of Reviewing Art

*The audience expects storytelling to take art and life to the limit—the depth and breadth of human experience.* —Robert McKee

Reviews combine the functions of a news feature, and an op-ed. All the techniques of op-ed and column writing, as well as the conceptual and professional framework of narrative writing, operate in review writing.

In a review I read long ago, a critic had something memorably cruel to say about a book. The reviewer said something like this: "This is not writing; this is typing." That assessment not only captured the motivation and reputation of the old reviewer (a devourer, a cannibal), but it also created an apt distinction between two major kinds of reviews we read today.

The first type of review is typing. The reviewer types out the promotional blurb from publishers or producers, throws in a dash of personal opinion and snippets of the story. The typing reviewer then comments on the cast. This type of review is common in provincial newspapers, where review pages serve as community bulletin boards. If these "reviews" fulfill the community service roles of journalism, we cannot complain, but then these insertions should be listed under announcements or a "cultural calendar" of emerging books, movies, music, and exhibitions that are scheduled or planned.

The key feature of the typing review is the reviewer's personal opinion. The opinion is often not supported by any evidence. It tells the reader the preferences of the writer instead of giving the reader information needed to understand the work and decide whether to see, read or listen to it.

The *New Zealand Herald* offers an example of the old-time review.

> This suspense thriller—occasionally engaging though never entirely convincing—earned the opprobrium of the American press for the unfortunate combination of its timing and content.
>
> Released barely a fortnight after September 11, it has shots of the Twin Towers and its climactic scene, which involves a character being buried in an avalanche of falling beams and earth, recalled images still seared on the public retina.

At this distance, those associations are not so raw. But if the film doesn't distress, neither does it impress, largely thanks to some implausible plotting.

The reviewer does not end there.

In the end, there's a faintly antiseptic, production-line feel to it all. Though Bean is demonstrably ruthless, he is slack and sloppy at crucial moments so the sense of menace just evaporates, and the climax—despite the echoes of Ground Zero—verges on the laughable. Even fans of slick, violent thrillers will be disappointed.

# What Is a Review?

We shall start with what a review is *not.* A review is not a journalist's opinion of an artistic work. In a book, for example, it is not the statement of the theme, plot, characters, and the recommendations of the reviewer, as we can see from the review above.

What then is a review? It is a story that explains a work, and breathes life into a work. The reviewer selectively activates select elements to tell the story of the work. A review is the story behind the work.

Works of art are like cars. We need someone to start the engine and swing her onto the road to release the beauty and the beast under the hood. One has to be able to separate the performance of the car from its packaging (color and superficial comforts and gadgets, which can distract from a car's performance on the road). The review is the test drive, the release of the car's inner power.

So, should we discard all that we learned in college about literary criticism? Well, um, yes. The reason we must unlearn old habits is that there is no standard or customary method of reviewing. Reviews and audience expectations are evolving.

Our review of Graham Greene's book, *The Quiet American,* would therefore not be merely the assessment of Greene's characters (Phuong, Pyle, Granger, and the rest) and an abridged reenactment of the story. The story is also about the interaction of the characters in their peculiar Vietnamese setting, revealing in the lives of these characters a universal statement, a universal humanity. It is the revelation and reenactment of Vietnam, with its political, social, and human dramas—Greene's Vietnam, Phuong's Vietnam, and now our collective Vietnam. The story is the blending (think of a kitchen blender or cocktail shaker) of the dynamic moral, intellectual and cultural forces to produce the Greene who, in turn, created or powered his characters.

To illustrate this point, let us see how a reviewer captured the social and political drama of the movie, *Slogans.* David D'Arcy, reviewing this Albanian film for *The Guardian* ("Rocks and hard places," February 1, 2002), recreated and refreshed the life of the movie this way:

The setting is Enver Hoxha's Albania of the 1970s. Joseph Stalin's picture is on almost every wall. In a poor mountain village, communist officials conscript locals to gather rocks, the only natural resource, to spell out party slogans on the steep barren hillsides. After a long day memorizing the sayings of Comrade Hoxha, the paranoid strongman who ruled Albania from 1945 to 1985, schoolchildren are deployed to pick out, stone by stone, phrases like: "Enver Party", "Albania: Rock of Granite", and "The Worst Enemy Is a Forgotten One". If the stones roll down the hill, the children haul them up the slopes again. It is Sisyphus, Albanian-style.

Gjergj Xhuvani's *Slogans* is set in deep Stalinism and even deeper poverty. Peasants are punished for any perceived ideological deviation, even if they can't read the slogans that they're commanded to construct in stone. As officials pursue petty goals with deadpan doggedness, you find yourself sharing the gallows humor of a people who, as the slogan goes, have nothing to lose but their chains.

D'Arcy went beyond the content of the movie and his personal thoughts. His review confirms that reading a book or watching a movie does not give us sufficient material to review it. Imagine a movie actor reading a script and acting the role at the same time. Imagine Will Smith, watching a Muhammed Ali boxing match at the same time as he is trying to portray Ali in the movie, *Ali*. Instead, Smith and the producer of the biographical movie read a lot about Ali. They interviewed Ali and the people who knew him. They spoke to former cotenants and landlords. Based on the information and insights he obtained from his research, and on his personal and spiritual contact with the boxing legend, Smith was able to present a living, surprising and stunningly human Ali to the audience. That is how a good reviewer presents a literary work or production. The reviewer strives to present the story of the story and the life of the life that the author, producer, or artist had created, using the work as one of the ingredients or backdrops of this recreation. Recreation brings a faraway and unfamiliar person or object close and familiar enough for the audience to respond to.

The book (with its plot, characters, settings, story line) is just a container, a container of incense. The importance of the shape, size, and texture of the bottle or what it is made of is marginal. It would be foolish to concentrate on the bottle and neglect the aroma that fills the room and charms its occupants when the incense is heated. The aroma leaves the bowl, fills the room, and sifts out onto the balcony, to the garden, onto the street and the apartment across the street, creating new life, meaning, implications, and associations, and eliciting diverse responses. Maybe it offends and maybe it titillates people next door. Maybe it sticks to the clothes of a visiting husband who later gets kicked out on suspicions of infidelity. Maybe a religious person associates it with an angelic visitation and makes a wish. The interaction of the incense with the world becomes the story. The review should be the incense, not the container or just the manufacturers of the incense.

Let us look at a sports analogy. To play basketball, you need to work out, do push-ups, and sprints, and maybe some muscle toning. The game itself uses some elements of the training and a lot of other skills. Imagine a player who, at the whistle, starts doing push-ups and other muscle-toning or body-building exercises. This is what reviewers who write about plot, characters, settings, and climaxes, often end up doing. They miss the game. They miss the big picture.

It is not the reviewer's business to tell the readers whether they should read a book, buy a new music CD, or see a movie. Oprah Winfrey is a promoter, not a reviewer. The public has the habit of going to see movies that critics have violated with turgid, opinionated reviews. In any case, reviewers and audiences probably have different tastes. It is the business of promoters to publicize a production. The responsibility of reviewers is to interpret that work and situate it in an audience-friendly social context.

So, should critics totally ignore the plot, setting, techniques (suspense, imagery and other tools of persuasion), and the captivating characters? Not necessarily, but neither should they dwell on those peripheral elements. Instead critics should draw on relevant elements that help them tell a captivating story, a story that articulates collective human experience (the aroma of the incense), emanating from the work (the bottle of incense).

Literary criticism concentrates on one tiny aspect of the reviewing process—dissecting works of art, rather than explaining them. Let's take the review of a book. The book review has four stages:

1. Preparation
2. Reading the book
3. Extensive research
4. Writing.

# 1. Preparation

Preparation means working hard to become a world citizen intellectually and culturally. It involves reading many books, newspapers and magazines, watching loads of movies, listening to people, networking, and listening to all sorts of music. Preparation is all about being connected and being culturally exposed or assimilated. You can call it an initiation into global art culture or an induction into the global literary fraternity. It is a lifelong engagement. Reading comes before writing. Reviewers need to read good reviews in major publications. If you do not love reading, you cannot be a good writer of any kind. Preparation means getting to know art, places and people and opening ourselves to new perceptions and possibilities. It also means understanding our society and our world.

# 2. Reading the Book

There are many ways of reading a book: casually, intently, and purposefully. The reviewer should be able to read each book in all these ways, but spend time reading the book with a purpose, to assess its different components and the author's execution of the book. To be able to read the book with some focus, reviewers pay attention to the following:

## The Plot

The plot is the development of events and character—how the story flows along the writer's outline, and how characters through their actions, order and propel themselves from the beginning, past the crossroads, to the resolution. In Chapter 8, we also described the plot as the alignment of progressively developed actions, scenes, and events with the theme or focus of a story. Central characters usually propel the plot.

## Setting

The setting is the world in which the characters live, work, grow, play and die.

## Characters

The reviewer takes into account internal and external forces that propel the characters in the story, and the character's relationship with other characters and with their environment to achieve the goal of the book. The movie reviewer will explore the characters actions and reactions, what happens to them and how what happens to them changes them and others.

## Techniques

The reviewers explain how the author or producer of the work creates or captures the scene, how he or she makes the characters and setting interact, the rhythm of the story (suspense, digressions, etc.), and the effect the techniques have on the outcome.

## Language

The reviewer examines how the writer uses this vehicle, combined with other elements of writing, to create an emotional experience and to recreate a persuasive and pleasurable universalized reality.

## Reader Response

The reviewer steps out of the role of critic to embrace life like an inquisitive human being to be able to make a sound and inclusive judgment of the emotional or intellectual stimuli the work transmits to the audience. The fact that you enjoyed a work does not necessarily mean that most readers would enjoy it—another reason the reviewer's personal opinion is not really welcome. The reviewer should learn enough about the writer or artist's world to be able to offer a convincing translation of that unfamiliar world to the audience. It is not about the reviewer's personal response to the work.

# 3. Research

In his book, *A Short Guide to Writing about Film,* Timothy Corrigan observes that "research improves any piece of writing" and makes writing about a subject more satisfying. Research broadens the understanding of the writer and the audience. In explaining the importance of research, Corrigan amplified the role of the reviewer as an interpreter of life, culture and art this way:

> Two equally intelligent friends may watch Paul Schader's *Mishima* (1985), and although each may have perfectly sensitive and sensible responses to it, the one who has knowledge of Japanese culture or the facts of Mishima's life will have a richer and more detailed reading of the movie and will be able to support her or his evaluation better. Although both may understand the themes and recognize that the elaborate structure and style are central ingredients in their reaction to those themes, the viewer who can connect them to other Schrader films, such as *American Gigolo* (1980) or *Affliction* (1998), will be able to detect variations and complexities in motifs concerning obsessiveness and alienation that escape the less knowledgeable viewer.[2]

Few newspaper readers can do such in-depth research on a movie or book. That is where reviewers come in. Now, the reviewer, having gotten one tiny piece of the picture from a casual encounter with the work, goes out to search of the missing pieces. The reviewer looks up the setting of the story in geography, history, literature, and politics, for example. If it is not possible to visit the setting, the reviewer can look it up on the web, get postcards, find people from those parts, read a book, or see a movie set in that place. The reviewer is seeking to discover the basis, message, meaning, direction and implications of the work.

The reviewer gets acquainted with similar or dissimilar works or events that happened in the setting. If the work was set in the past, the reviewer should grasp not just that past but also the present (and vice versa).

The reviewer does a rigorous background check on the author, including personal details. Even things like dressing come in handy. Based on such familiarity, one reviewer wrote that an author was dressed like one of his sentences.

A lot of literary works are disguised autobiographies. Graham Greene acknowledged the relationship between novelists and the characters they create. In his literary memoir, *Ways of Escape,* a kind of footnote to his own writing, he wrote that a novel's major characters "must necessarily have some kinship to the author; they come out of his body as a child comes from the womb".

Reviewers discover the relationship between authors and their characters by interviewing authors and their friends and associates, and visiting the authors' worlds and the settings of their work. Reviewers can explore the person behind the book by reading other works by the author, and the works of the author's contemporaries or critics.

This search offers reviewers a superior grasp of the mechanics of the work, to enable them to interpret it. Art reviewers must collect information that will make it possible for them to create awareness by showing what the work contributes to life and how it situates itself in our communal culture.

# 4. Writing the Review

We saw earlier that the reviewer's responsibility is to interpret or decode a production or creation and to situate it in a social, people-friendly context. Reviewers prepare readers for a heightened appreciation of the work. The art of abstract representation requires discipline. This leaves the writer or producer little room for broad sweeps of explanation and context. Without context and interpretation, most of the audience would be lost. This is why God made the reviewer.

A good example of persuasive writing that oozes with the writer's versatility is this review of Allan Ahlberg and Raymond Brigg's children's book, *The Adventures of Bert*. Belinda Luscombe, (*TIME*, February 6, 2002), uses her knowledge of tennis to interpret the work:

> Ahlberg and Briggs are the Andre Agassi and Pete Sampras of British kid lit. But—like most British tennis players, actually—they have not made much of an impression in the U.S. Reading a book by both is like seeing Agassi and Sampras play doubles: it's nimble, apparently effortless, playful work. The adventures of said Bert, who has a wife and easily waked baby, aren't too perilous. In one chapter (a concept the book cleverly introduces to younger readers), he puts on a shirt, falls into a truck and is taken to Scotland.

Whether the work is a gem or trash, the critic should break the news to the public with style. The review is, after all, a work about a work, a story about a story. It is a story that nudges, tickles, and excites the reader.

Like op-ed writers, reviewers have to convince readers to accept, if not approve, their perception or interpretation of life. That is called persuasion, and is distinct from opinion.

Like columnists and novelists, reviewers nudge readers into seeing things the reviewers' way. Reviewers do not just make logical deductions from known premises. They jump on the backs of readers, and playfully point the way, an alternative exciting way of seeing life. The review, like the lead of a good story, generates interest in the work and in the world that conferred on the work its unique universal credentials.

The reader must find the review pleasurable. Most people who read reviews will not actually buy the book. The review puts the book on the reader's résumé of works read or seen. The review is like a vitamin pill. With the pressure of work and family, not too many people finish all emerging good books. A good review can sometimes be more enjoyable than the work itself.

Because writing is a form of construction, some great writers, especially famous ones, may bore their readers, clogging their works with arcane literary devices. A *TIME* reviewer once wrote that a certain book was so impenetrably boring; only a prominent and respected writer could have achieved such a level of drabness.

Reviews are becoming increasingly fluid in form. The reviewer adopts a conversational style. Many factors determine the audience reception of a review. These factors include: the reputation of the publication, the reputation or profile of the reviewer, the reviewer's style, and the type or profile of work reviewed. Although there is no rigid formula for writing or judging reviews, few would challenge the notion that a good review is, quite simply, one that attracts and engages readers, while at the same time, doing justice to the work reviewed.

# Attracting and Engaging Readers

As writers, reviewers can attract and retain the interest and goodwill of their readers by, among other things:

- Showing evidence that they are having fun;
- Writing an enjoyable story;
- Exuding a personal style;
- Balancing authority with humility.

## Having Fun

You can tell whether the reviewer is skipping, cart wheeling, and singing. You can also tell whether the reviewer has a gun to his or her head, or is writing under great pain or a spell of boredom. It is possible to tell from the tone of a telephone conversation whether the person on the other side is smiling or sulking. Deciphering whether a writer is having fun is much easier.

Take the introduction to this review titled "Tsui Hark's New Spark," for the film *Time and Tide,* (*TIME*, October 30, 2000, page 63). Richard Corliss starts the piece by saying:

God said, Let there be light. In Tsui Hark's universe, that means fancy cigarette lighters lighting big cigars and bigger scams in Hongkong's neon night.

You can picture the reviewer's mind skipping and somersaulting with glee. The reviewer conjures knowledge of the word, the world, and of life, to give the reader an evocative and insightful interpretation of the film.

Compare Corliss' liberating start with this preachy book review extract from the *New Zealand Herald*:

"So I say truly," wrote Sir John Mandeville in the late 1350s, "that a man could go all round the world, above and below, and return to his own country, provided he had his health, good company, and a ship. And all the way he would find men, lands, islands, cities and towns."

Prophetic words, and the question of how Mandeville formed his opinions has been debated since.

The latter starts with a wordy quotation and unfocussed commentary. The lead forces the reader to ask the question: so what? The start of a book review in one of Canada's biggest newspapers, *The Globe and Mail,* (February 2, 2002), offers a competing example of grumpiness:

> About three years ago, I discovered *The Yellow Pear*, a vibrant book of reminiscences and drawings. The maker of the book was Gu Xiong, and the publisher was Vancouver's Arsenal Pulp. A year later, this newspaper asked me to review a wordbook from Arsenal Pulp.
>
> It was not very good. My crest fell. Now comes another word book from Arsenal Pulp, under the editorial imprimatur of Michael Turner, who is one of our better and riskier writers (*Hard Core Logo, The Pornographer's Poem*).

Here, the writer imposed what seemed like the contents of a personal diary on readers. The review is not an avenue for writers to pour their opinion or personal experiences and preferences on readers. It is better to write in the third person than in a moody first person, especially when the first-person account fails to provide readers illuminating insights. Compare the first-person subjectivity of this review with the following compressed extract of Jonathan Farley's perceptive first-person review. Farley used his own nerdy world of mathematics to hook readers into the message and significance of a major movie that featured Russell Crowe:

> A few months ago, I was at a party when somebody said, "Listen to this joke: Let epsilon be a large negative number . . . ." Those of us who were mathematicians cracked up laughing; everybody else stood around looking puzzled.
>
> I would have never laughed at that same joke fourteen years ago. That was the year before I entered college, and I visited the Math Department at Harvard University along with a few other students who, like me, intended to major in math. When a physicist talks, at least, about atoms and stars, his audience will nod meaningfully. An artist can show us her canvas; an economist, money and markets. We mathematicians have nothing to show. That's why the new movies about math hold such promise. They're opportunities for others to tell our stories better than we could hope to.
>
> *A Beautiful Mind*, starring Russell Crowe, is the latest film to make this daring attempt. It's the true story of John Nash, the man who set the mathematical world ablaze at twenty-one, but went mad at age thirty; a genius who believed he could speak with extraterrestrials and who still won the Nobel Prize (in economics—there is no prize for mathematics). [3]

The reviewer who is having fun writes with telling precision, explores a variety of approaches, tells a story, relates to the reader, avoids the beaten path, and heads for a world of sensuous freedom of expression and perception. This freedom is evident in the reviewer's creative selection and association.

In the earlier example, Corliss creatively selected a catchy and awe-inspiringly (not idly) familiar line from the film *Time and Tide*. "And God said, 'Let there be light.'" He lets his mind loose in this sensuous freedom. Instead of the familiar "And there was light" which we all know, the author conspiratorially flipped the unexpected at us: "in Tsui Hark's universe, that means fancy cigarette lighters lighting big cigars and bigger scams in Hong Kong's neon night."

# An Enjoyable Story

No matter how technically accurate, how deeply philosophical, and how factually rich a review might be, it would fail if readers do not enjoy reading it. The review has to be an engaging narrative story.

James Ponewozic's review of the book, *The Autograph Man*, was a narrative story. Titled, "A Frenzy of Renown", the review published in *TIME* started this way:

> Of the many subjects in Zadie Smith's second novel—Budhism, Jewish mysticism, the Hollywood studio system—one that she presumably did not have to research was the bug-light allure of celebrity. In 2000, at the age of 24, she became deservedly famous for *White Teeth*, a sprawling erudite comedy about culture clash and bioengineering in postcolonial Britain. Brilliant, young and beautiful, she became a favorite of the British media, which followed her love life, her hair style changes with a fervor Americans reserve for cast members of *Friends*.
>
> The hunger to get a piece of the famous and the psychology behind the desire are the substance of her [second novel].

The reviewer used narrative journalistic storytelling techniques. Good reviews have an enticing beginning and a rapturous end. They have a thread—a set of events, a setting, and strong characters—that weaves its way from the lead to the end of the story. The story is cohesive, threaded all the way through, and stitched together imperceptibly by an internal transition. The language is evocative, and the action and associations fresh, and possibly offbeat. Even if the review takes the readers on a journey to hell, that journey is fun; the reader sees beyond the devil's obvious pitchfork, tail, and horns.

# Personal Style

The main characteristics of good writing were discussed in Chapters 6 and 7. Astute writers learn those protocols and then use their own personalities to interpret them. It is the ability to massage our experiences, unique attributes and the sum total of our social and intellectual orientation, into a story that gives a piece of writing a distinct personality. Readers can tell a chef's original cordon bleu creation from a Big Mac.

This personal style is sometimes known as originality. Originality breeds irreverence. Irreverence breeds wit. And wit breeds readers' reverence for the writer. It is such freshness of perception that drove Samuel Butler to upturn traditional thinking when he said that the hen is an egg's clever method of producing another egg.

## Balance of Authoritativeness and Humility

Reviewers need to be familiar with the world they are recreating and explaining. This is where humility comes in. The reviewer's humility does not manifest itself in self-effacing pretensions. Humility means avoiding sweeping opinions. This implies the selective use of what the writer knows and supporting and validating that knowledge with illustrations, anecdotes and quotes. You should interview experts to obtain supporting insights, quotes, and nuances. This shows your acknowledgement of alternative or new perspectives and approaches—an acknowledgement that you do not know it all. Such humility, celebrated by a ceaseless lust for knowledge came brightly across in Sacha Guiltry's unforgettable admission: "The little I know I owe it to my ignorance."

# Doing Justice to the Work

A good review is a tour of a work of art, and not the stocktaking of its characteristics. While reviewers are at liberty to discuss any part of the work they consider illuminating, most would pay special attention to the following aspects:

- Spirit
- Purpose
- Effect and significance

## Spirit

The spirit of the work is the story's essence. It is a kind of conceptual nut graph. It defines the driving force of the work. It is more than the theme. The theme is the central subject, but the spirit is the location of that theme in a personal and social context. In Graham Greene's novel, Dr Fischer of Geneva or the Bomb Party, the theme is greed that transcends social structures and levels of wealth. The relationships between the major and insignificant characters, the physical, emotional, and political setting, combined with the author's near-sinful compassion for the wicked, present a fresh human option. That resultant revelation of humanity—a now universalized and sympathetic humanity we and the people and life in Greene's artistic world share—is the spirit of the story.

D'Arcy's review of *Slogans*, cited earlier in this chapter, revealed the spirit of the movie by capturing the Albania that produced the movie. Placing the movie in a contemporary context, the reviewer took readers on a tour of the filmmaker's world and mind:

> While Xhuvani had not carried stones up hillsides and written slogans, he did remember calling out and applauding on the roadside with other students when Prince Norodom Sihanouk of Cambodia made an official visit to Albania.

Everyone in Albania remembers doing that kind of thing, Xhuvani says. In *Slogans*, party officials hope for the day when Hoxha will read their work as his black Mercedes thunders through their village.

Weak reviews fail to identify the spirit of the work and dwell on the surface of the work, what the work is about. Good reviews say what the work is, what it represents (its connotations and implications), and what purpose it serves.

## Purpose

Every work of art has a purpose. The creator must have a reason, other than reward or recognition. The creator might, for example, want to sensitize or warn people. He or she could want to record reality for future instruction or for entertainment. The creator also has a personal purpose or motivation, which we shall call a personal statement, which is often coded.

By researching the society and the creator of the work, the reviewer is able to identify, decipher and explain the purpose of the work.

## Effect and Significance:

A work worth reviewing must be relevant to people. The significance of the work could be the effect the events portrayed have on the global village. It could make us think, laugh, scream, cry, or just shrug. If the work elicits no reaction, then it should not have been produced. The work should be placed alongside our values, our consciousness, our humanity, or the other works that exist or should exist.

A book, for example, can have an effect on the world of literature, on the government, on young or old people, and on people's perceptions. Corrigan stresses the importance of making connections between the work reviewed and "other artistic traditions, such as literature and painting". Through research and interviews, reviewers can become acquainted with the artistic terrain, the dynamics of society, and the author's personality and works. Once a work is produced, whether we revile or worship it, it enters the ecological cycle of our human experience, and will have an effect on life and art. Every work, no matter how mediocre, adds something to its field and to life. Every work worth reviewing, no matter how pedestrian it is, deserves a brilliant review.

# Things to Remember

1. There is a difference between literary appreciation and media reviews.
2. Reviewers use the techniques of literary appreciation to read or appreciate a work—its anatomy and literary techniques. The reviewer should drop the jargon and attitude of literary appreciation and tell the story of the book.
3. A review is a journalistic story, not an essay or an opinion.
4. The reviewer's main job is not to promote or crucify a work of art. Nor is it to retell the story and recast the characters.
5. Reviewing is a four-step process involving: preparation, reading (or viewing or listening to), research, and writing.
6. The reviewer's main job is to explain the work by putting it in a human context, by placing the story within a human social, cultural, political, or cosmic context.
7. Good reviews attract and engage readers. Some ways of engaging readers include: showing evidence the reviewer is having fun, writing an enjoyable story, exuding a personal style, and balancing authoritativeness with humility.
8. The reviewer must do justice to the work and capture the spirit, meaning, effect, purpose, and significance of the work.

# 14

## A Story about Getting Hired

*As every author—and every reader—knows, writing well is the best trip of them all.*
—Gore Vidal

What do hiring editors want? This purpose of this chapter is to apply journalistic storytelling techniques to job-hunting.

## Searching for the Job

Although the media job market seems to be shrinking, there are probably as many job openings as there are well-prepared and competent or promising journalists to fill them. Almost every major newspaper in the world—including those reducing their staff—is looking for excellent reporters and writers. A news organization's image, ratings, and fortune depend on its ability to attract enthusiastic and competent reporters. Knowledge of narrative gives you a distinct advantage.

Preparation, reading, and catching up with writing and working trends and challenges, are as important as, and probably more difficult than, getting jobs.

## Preparation

As with writing, the reporter or staff writer's job search starts with preparation. If you tell yourself you want to write for *TIME* and not the *Boozer's Digest,* then you will read *TIME,* study the writing and the people, and start thinking like a *TIME* writer. As the aphorism goes, if you want to be a millionaire, you need to think and walk like a millionaire.

The next level of preparation is, of course, instruction. Read widely, and experiment with new writing approaches and story type, especially narrative.

# Networking

Seek out people who are in the business and related to the business at public engagements, such as conferences and workshops. Of all the writing workshops, I opted for the National Writers Workshop in Hartford, Connecticut, because syndicated satirical columnist Art Buchwald was giving the keynote address. I pulled him aside to discuss his satire, my work, and my aspirations. I returned with his business card and an open invitation to contact him if I ever needed anything.

A note from an esteemed colleague, friend, or associate of an editor is worth its weight in gold. You will get recommended if you can prove your determination, skills, and career plans. I got invited to work with a major U.S. newspaper based on a recommendation from one of my professors at the University of Maryland, who happened to be the editor's former professor. I can't emphasize enough the need to make connections with your college's alumni. At the University of Maryland, a bulletin board at the College of Journalism features alumni's names, positions, work samples, and contact information. Students are encouraged to contact these alumni. Even big stars are sentimental about their former college and want to know how things are going at their old school.

Do not hesitate to show your work, share your plans, and seek the advice of successful or highly placed journalists. Feel free to e-mail or e-mail a writer you admire and, after complementing his or her work, ask if he or she could look at a few articles you have written. Consider telling an established writer that you aspire to write like him or her, and asking for advice. People generally have a soft spot for those who come to them for advice.

Networking is important because the better writing jobs are not always advertised. They are given to people who come well recommended. Many newspapers create new positions to fit the skills of a well-recommended writer. Brad Schultz recommends a visit to media organizations. "By making an effort, you introduce yourself to the decision makers and get your 'foot in the door'," he observes. "It also communicates that you're serious about your work and are thinking about the future."[1]

Job searches become more productive if they are combined with serious networking. Sell yourself to the organization. Show how hiring you would benefit the paper.

# General Search

The Internet is a great place to search for jobs locally and around the world. For instance, on search engines like www.google.com, you may search by keyword and location—region, country, state, or town, such as the Caribbean, Nigeria, California, Singapore, New Zealand, Costa Rica, or Prague  by typing in a phrase like "journalism jobs AND Singapore." A list of specific journalism job sites can be found at the bottom of this chapter.

# Specific Search

You may choose to search for jobs with specific newspapers or magazines. If you do not know the web site of a specific newspaper, you may search for it using a search engine, such as Yahoo or Google. If you know the newspaper's name or reputation, but not the web site, type the newspaper's name, say, *The Indian Times*, into a search engine and click on the appropriate result. Journalism jobs would normally be found in classified sections of newspapers, but many organizations, including the media, create a slot for jobs within the organization. If you cannot find a link to Job Opportunities or Employment on the Internet home page, go to "About us" or "About the company," or to the human resources page. Most web sites have a Site Map, a kind of table of contents, listing all sections and links featured on the web site. Sometimes a link for vacancies not featured on the Index page can be found on the site map.

Another way of conducting a specific search is to choose a country and search for a list of newspapers in that country (national, regional, or local) and then use the method described above to find writing jobs available for a specific newspaper. You may also e-mail newspaper editors to introduce yourself and ask for employment. Universities with journalism programs, such as University of California (Berkeley), have links to journalism jobs.

# E-mail Notification

Many listservs and web sites can e-mail journalism jobs in your areas of interest directly to you. The web sites for the University of California, Berkeley Graduate School of Journalism (http://www.journalism.berkeley.edu/jobs) and Louisiana Tech University (http://eb.journ.latech.edu/jobs.html) host journalism jobs and internships listings. You may sign up for regular notification of emerging jobs and internships.

# Researching the Newspaper or Magazine

One of the most important steps in journalism job searching is studying the specific media outlet's interests, style, and audience. Read the letters and editorial pages. Identify the paper's strengths and weaknesses and think of how you can add to its strengths or help redress some of its weaknesses. If you want to work for *The Independent* (UK), read the paper regularly. Find out as much as you can about the editors or other hiring officers.

If the organization is not far from you, you may try the Gene Roberts method. Roberts, a former managing editor of *The New York Times*, and a journalism professor at the University of Maryland (College Park), said he got his first job by keeping vigil outside the newsroom. One day, the editor of the newspaper stopped and asked the young Roberts to come to his office. The editor told the young man he has seen him sitting there everyday. Roberts went in prepared. For his persistence and resourcefulness, he got hired as reporter.

For most reporters, however, finding the right job is not that straightforward. They have to prepare an application package, including a cover letter, a portfolio, and a résumé

# The Cover Letter

The cover letter is an employer's first encounter with you, and you know what they say about first impressions. You only get one chance, so you need to put your best foot forward. The cover letter tells an employer what he or she really wants to know, which is, what you can do for the company, why you are unique, and if you are enthusiastic about the organization and the position. It is, therefore, important to articulate simply, naturally, and assertively what you can do.

Research is a major part of good writing. Researching the newspaper and the people who work for it indicates that you are knowledgeable, sharp, committed, curious, and prepared. A good cover letter reveals the writer's insight into the present and impending needs of the organization. Is the company trying to move ahead of the competition? If so, how would your skills and background be critical to its success? Is the newspaper particularly strong on personality profiles? Then how can you add to the reputation? If the company leads the competition, it needs to consolidate and improve its lead. What skills and qualities do you have that could contribute to this progress?

The ability to read the signs of the times singles out an application. From your research, you discovered that the newspaper was not covering certain types of stories. A good cover letter will point this out and state skills the candidate has that will make this happen.

Because you are applying for a writing position, your letter should be in the narrative and have a strong lead, a body and a crisp ending. Now you see why it is important to have a storytelling frame of mind and to grasp the storytelling skills and practices.

# The Cover Lead

The lead of your cover letter states why you are writing (responding to an ad, testing the waters, introducing yourself to the news organization). The hidden purpose of the opening paragraph is to create an impression, to tell the employer you are a storyteller—vibrant, original, and fresh. You should avoid yawn-inducing platitudes like "With reference to your recent advertisement in…" or "Enclosed, please find." These expressions do not exude the warmth, friendliness, originality, and the vibrancy hiring editors look for.

Joe Grimm, recruiting editor at the *Detroit Free Press,* says a good cover letter should "tease the editor" into reading your clips.[2] "Open your cover letter in an interesting way. We want to see that you can write. Show us...Take a risk. With the odds so high, it makes sense and can pay off," he advises applicants.

A well written opening will also tease the editor into reading the rest of your cover letter, and your résumé. Grimm lists one innovative autobiographical teaser that thrilled hiring editors: "I have been yelled at, lied to, had the door slammed in my face and been shot at—all in the pursuit of journalism. What a great business."

Grimm offers another interesting opener for a reporter who has already done significant stories: "They said it couldn't be done, but I did it." You would then describe a story you did under extreme pressure and deadline. If you are able to hook your cover on an interesting story you have done or a challenge you have faced, you are likely to get the hiring editor's attention. If you haven't done major stories, you can present your writing ability, curiosity, or other demonstrable attributes.

Another option is to drop the name of a respected journalist you know. Remember courting respected journalists, and getting their suggestions is an excellent step toward getting a journalism job. Say, you had asked a highly regarded current or former reporter what editors look for. You may quote what this person said—Mike Gore, *The Guardian's* White House bureau chief, said . . . —and relate your skills or dream to it.

For example, Gene Roberts also often shared personal stories about his blind editor who told reporters to make him "see" a story. As editor, I would take a second look at an applicant who says he or she was one of Roberts' students. Judicious name-dropping pays.

The cover letter is not an appeal for help. Offering people a livelihood is not the hiring editor's priority. Even if you are desperate for a job, with huge bills to worry about, and probably seeking your first media job, you must flee from such refugee cover leads as:

"I am currently searching for a chance to enhance my skills as a reporter with another newspaper, and I am hoping the *Detroit Free Press* can provide me with that opportunity." (Tell not what the newspaper can do for you; tell what you can do for the newspaper, says Grimm.) "I am a recent graduate." Great, but so are thousands of others. Being a recent graduate does not make you stand out. College degrees do not guarantee jobs. State what makes you stand out and where you are going, not where you have been. Let your lead illustrate what you are made of—you are and possess the stuff of which resounding leads are made. As with all good news stories, you must also connect the lead to the body with a hook.

# The Body: Ask Not What the Company Can Do for You

The lead enticed the hiring officer. Now the body must keep the hiring editor or manager hooked. Engage the hiring editor or manager by addressing the company's needs and saying what the company stands to gain by hiring you. The body may demonstrate your awareness of the status or needs of the company and make a statement about how you can be an asset to the company. If the job was advertised, the body of the cover letter very briefly addresses the key points of the search criteria with a not-too-specific anecdotal illustration. You might include the impact of your work, evidence of your commitment, dedication, and excellence. Perhaps your story on teenage drug use earned you a community commendation. Your accolades do not have to be earth shaking, but the body of your letter must respect the rules of good writing—show; don't tell. Do not enumerate or list things you have done. Illustrate them with anecdotes.

# The Ending

The final paragraph is the clincher. Use it to restate your suitability and ask for an interview. The smooth way of doing this is by saying you look forward to the opportunity of meeting the hirers to personally explain how your key skills (state them) will help the employer's organization in a specific way (state it).

# Addressing the Letter

The cover letter should be addressed to a specific person, not to "To Whom it May Concern" or "The Editor." Hiring editors believe that if you are interested enough in the newspaper, you will find out the name of the person who does the hiring. Look up the names of officials on the newspaper's web site or call or e-mail the newspaper to confirm names and spellings, as well as the exact designations of hiring officers. You should address the person as "Dear Ms. Cartwheels" rather than "Dear Sir or Madam." Note that the preferred punctuation for this address is a colon: "Dear Ms Cartwheels:".

Close the letter with "Sincerely" (no punctuation), and leave a gap of two double spaces (four lines) between this and your full name. This space is for your signature. Sign your letter with blue or black ink. Below the signature, write "Enclosure" (without the quotation marks, of course). That shows that your letter is accompanied by some documentation, including a résumé.

Justify subject headings and signatures to the left-hand side of the page. If in doubt about format, follow the prompts of the letter-writing assistant provided by Windows 98 (and later versions).

# Review

One of the most important stages of preparing the cover letter is the review. Check your grammar and spelling and be sure they are error-free. Relying on the "Spelling and Grammar" on the Window's Word program can be disastrous. The program has limited vocabulary and grammar. It often asks users to replace their correct construction with an atrocious alternative. Always do a manual check after the computerized spell check. Finally, check for flow of ideas, repetition, trivialities, and clichés. Get someone else to review the letter.

# In a Nutshell

Here is an example of what your cover letter should look like:


Date

Mr. Paul Hogan
Hiring Editor
Daily Mountain Newspapers Ltd
7015 Street Address
Townsville, Postcode 20709


Dear Mr. Hogan:

CATCHY TITLE

Now, imagine you met Mr. Hogan at the park. Breathe in and tell him briefly, in a personal and conversational tone that you came across his announcement and that he should cheer up for the man or woman he is looking for is here—you.

Say why your background makes you the ideal candidate for the position. As you articulate your ideas, put yourself in Mr. Hogan's place. Show how your qualities and motivation should both excite and benefit Mr. Hogan's newspaper, now and in the future. Remember that Mr. Hogan had been approached by hundreds of other candidates— which is why he came to the park for a whiff of fresh air. Refresh him with your originality, brevity and determination, not desperation.

Throw in a word about your research on and strong interest in his or her newspaper: its strengths, weaknesses and challenges. Now indicate in about two lines how your employment would help the company in these areas.

In closing, tell Mr. Hogan you would welcome the opportunity to explain in greater detail and in a more appropriate setting (at an interview) how your background (sum it up here: stories, skills, education, track record, the sum of your personal attributes) could add to the success of the *Daily Mountain*. End the letter this way:

Sincerely

Diana Stories (Your full name, no title)

Encl: résumé and samples of my work

Your cover letter will be a waste of the hiring editor's time and yours if it did not:

- Grab attention and identify and present you as unique and enterprising (based on who you are, what and who you know).
- Identify a reason your application package should be plucked out of the pile for further consideration.
- Create some chemistry between the hirer and your background
- Highlight compelling information in your résumé
- Show an impressive grasp of grammar, spelling, and storytelling skills.
- Use the name the company at least once in the body of the letter to show that this is not a generic letter.

# Preparing a Killer Résumé

Your cover letter showed the hiring editor that you can think and write. This editor now wants to see what you have done. That is where the résumé comes in. The résumé tells the employer that, from what you have done so far, it is worth reading a sample of your work, and eventually meeting you. Adapt your résumé specifically for each job, addressing the needs of that employer. Avoid all-purpose résumés.

Hiring editors are busy people. Make your résumé short, about 1.5 pages and taut. The hiring officer is interested in your skills and proof of the deployment of these skills in real or convincing circumstances. This includes jobs at the college newspaper, the local rag sheet, or any significant publication. Include education. The editor wants to know you are not illiterate.

Arrange the headings in an inverted pyramid, most important elements first. List courses or workshops that could be useful to a journalism job. If you graduated from a highly rated journalism school, you may place your education heading up front. Always list your strongest points up front and other particulars in descending order of benefit to your application. For example, if you had an internship at the *Wall Street Journal*, that should feature both in your cover letter and at the top of the first page of your résumé.

Experience, not education, however, should lead the page unless you graduated with a first class honors degree or went to an Ivy League university. If the only experience you got was in the form of an internship, list it.

Journalism recruiters are not impressed with subheads such as:

*Experience*: Education reporter, *The Nightly Vision*, Bradford, N.Y. 1987 to 1991.

State what your job involved, what skills you used, the major stories you covered, any groundbreaking accomplishments, or how you interpreted your journalistic role.

"Mention the more complicated, difficult or humorous accomplishments you had in those jobs," says Grimm. Stress what makes you stand out. Editors want to see your uniqueness, achievements, your attitudes, and your approach to your job.

If your journalism experience is thin, you may include jobs outside journalism. Even if those jobs do not highlight your reporting and writing skills, they will draw attention to relevant attributes, such as responsibility, drive, punctuality, ability to work under pressure, curiosity, interviewing skills, circumspection and the ability to handle complex and multiple tasks.

Under "Education," list all relevant journalism and non-journalism courses (politics, environmental studies, etc) that show the level of your training and all-round preparation to work as a general or specialized reporter or communicator.

Next, and only if applicable, you may create a heading for "Awards" or "Achievements" to list your achievements, awards, scholarships, fellowships and activities that demonstrate success, leadership and personal achievements. If you have a high grade point average, state it here. One of my students interviewed John Howard (Australian Prime Minister) in his first year at college and another student interviewed President Bill Clinton. Such achievements should be featured both in the cover letter (in context, to illustrate your drive and winning newsgathering techniques) and in you résumé.

Consider listing additional skills, such as familiarity with newsroom software and traditions, language skills, and any evidence of cross-cultural communication.

You may list other outstanding qualities you possess and interests, attributes and engagements that portray you as versatile, well-rounded, creative, enterprising, and unique.

# The Tyro's Résumé

One of the greatest headaches of the job-searching student or recent graduate is the lack of experience. Employers demand experience, even from first-time job seekers. This may seem unfair. If you don't work, you don't have work experience, and if you don't have work experience, you may not get hired. However, it is not that bad. Everyone had to start looking for work without formal "job experience." College employment, including summer jobs, work for the college media, and internships count as work experience.[3] An assignment highly praised by a lecturer or professor, or some notable members of the community, can attract a hiring editor. The big challenge is identifying the skills you possess and applying them to the requirements of the job you are searching for. Almost all jobs require evidence of the following qualities:

- Communication (interpersonal and cross-cultural, oral and written)
- Management (resources, time, including deadlines, people)
- Judgment (decisions, priorities, social responsibility, work ethics, etc)
- Adaptability (reflected in such attributes as flexibility, ability to work required hours, mobility, work ethics, and human relations).

Journalism has industry-specific generic skills, which include communication, ability to write, appreciation of good writing, grasp of grammar and style, curiosity, openness, social awareness, extensive reading, current affairs, public and human interest, handling pressure and deadlines, and passion for journalistic storytelling. These skills manifest themselves in many areas of life: the classroom, clubs, school newspapers, other writing avenues, internships, and workshops, even classes and excursions.

The beginner's résumé should take into account portable skills that address the generic and specific skills of journalism. A priest could cite his interviewing and communication skills. A hooker could claim strong communication and negotiation skills, extensive interpersonal and cross-cultural communication, financial management, self-motivation, ability to work without supervision, and most importantly, a "high rate of customer satisfaction."[4] Now, try identifying the marketable skills for the following professional or managerial positions: bank robber, serial killer, or drugs dealer.

# Assessing Your Résumé

The following generic résumé assessment criteria may be useful in reviewing your journalism résumé:

1. Is the look of the résumé easy on the eyes?
2. Are your strongest assets easily and quickly discernable and do they immediately catch the reader's eye?

3. Have you proofread the résumé several times, ensuring all words and figures, including names and dates, are accurate?
4. Do you express yourself clearly, using where necessary, buzzwords of the particular industry?
5. Under your experience heading, did you begin statements with action verbs and communicate accomplishments and results?
6. Does your résumé emphasize accomplishments and skills over responsibilities and duties?
7. Are your informal skills, such as cross-cultural communication, featured in this résumé?
8. Did you account for all periods of time, including informal pursuits?
9. Have you eradicated all irrelevant information like age, nationality, marital status, and membership in obscure clubs?
10. Does the format you have chosen (functional, chronological, or combined) reflect your experience and skills?
11. If your résumé is more than one page, is your name on the top of each page?[5]

# Courting References

As with most jobs, references play an important part in the decision to hire a reporter. Sometimes, when hiring managers have to choose between two equally appealing candidates, the one with the stronger reference often gets the job. You must make a conscious effort to line up referees—people who can attest *positively* to your personal qualities and academic and professional potentials.

Preferably, your referees should be mentors and people whose opinion you occasionally seek. Recruiting a referee is an art. The first part of the process involves preparation. You must maintain a network of referees. Initiate the contact, stay in touch, share your work or career plans, and ask for the person's opinion. After a while, ask if the person would be happy to write you a reference. Share with the potential referee your strengths and career plans. The best and most handy referees would usually be your professors, especially those with a public or professional profile. While college professors and supervisors are often the primary references, it is important to confirm that your professor or supervisor has something very positive to say about you, before listing him or her as a referee. As a member of a hiring committee, I watched with exasperation as our preferred candidate lost the job because his referee said he was a fine, but unreliable, journalist. The candidate would have saved himself the stress and embarrassment by simply asking the person if he would be able to write him a positive reference.

Professionals you come in contact with, from any field, can make good referees. Three major factors define a referee's suitability and effectiveness. The referee should:

- know enough about the nature of the job you are applying for;

- believe in you and be able to write about you persuasively, forcefully, and informally;
- confirm that he or she will write very positively about you.

It might help if the person likes you.

It is not a good idea to have permanent referees on you résumé. References written by people who had written you several references previously may lack the freshness and vigor of a first-time, enthusiastic, new referee.

If you did an internship, your supervisor will probably be a good referee. You must cultivate a relationship of mutual respect with your supervisor and other senior journalists and editors at the newspaper.[6]

# The Job Interview

If you are invited in for an interview, the employer is willing, on the basis of your cover letter, résumé, and clips, to give you the job, but needs to confirm that you are who you claimed to be and that you are a likeable and enthusiastic person.

At the interview, there are no gratuitous actions and questions. The questions interviewers ask are a projection of their desires and concerns. Well-prepared candidates will identify and address these concerns in the questions, and their answers will attempt to address the motives behind questions the interviewer asks. The newspaper's hiring managers want to ascertain your skills and abilities, as well as your personal qualities.

## Skills and Abilities

- The employer wants to ascertain that that you have the requisite skills, principal among them being the ability to identify and gather news, talk to people, and write good copy.
- Do your experience and outlook on life show the use of the essential skills and aptitudes necessary for the job, even if your specific background is different?
- Does your employment history (if cited), your education, and other developmental areas show constant application of your skills and energies?

## Personal Qualities

The employer wants to determine whether:

- you have demonstrable motivation, enthusiasm, and self-confidence required to do the job.
- your previous experience and your personal character show that you will be a loyal, committed, conscientious, fair, and determined journalist.
- you are sufficiently interested in the position and the organization to remain and make significant contributions, with a substantial long-term commitment.
- you know what you want. Is there a consistent interest in a specific area or career path?
- you are a sociable person and a team player who will have a good influence on colleagues and who would be a good ambassador of the organization.

- you are well confident and adjusted to fit in socially and professionally into the fold?

Some of the questions you may be asked are as follows:

## *Why do you want to work for this newspaper?*

The interviewer wants to confirm that you have done substantial research on the newspaper (what it publishes, how it rates against the competition, the quality of its stories, awards or prizes it has won or not won, its policies, its treatment of its employees, career options, and level of stability). It would be a good idea to mention both what the company has done well (altruistic and complimentary) as well as how you would fit into the social structure of the company (your interests). If the newspaper is a prestigious publication, highly acclaimed employer, or offers career growth, say so. Organizations feel comfortable with workers who believe in them enough to want to make a career there. The recruiter watches for things like the candidate's social and communication skills and sense of humor. Remember the saying that a laughing jury is not a hanging jury. The general notion is that if you cannot relate well to someone as wonderful as your recruiter (who is probably your prospective boss), you cannot possibly get along well with lesser mortals in the newsroom.

## *Why should I hire you?*

The interviewer wants to see how well you can think and communicate, and whether you are calm, mature, and skillful enough to balance self worth with modesty and truthfulness.

You should restate your professional and personal qualities and skills. This profile should naturally match or surpass the requirements for the job. In addition, address the needs and strengths of the organization and say why hiring you could add to the strength of the newspaper. Let the interviewer know you did some research.

## *What books, newspapers, and magazines do you read?*

Here, the interviewer is testing your passion for knowledge as well as your critical faculties. Start now to read the major publications and be prepared to cite, comment on, or discuss a specific article or writer. You should be able to cite specific works and authors and the reasons you like them. Reading widely is the ultimate preparation for a job application. Read books about newspapers, reporters, reporting, writing, editing, interviewing or other journalistic skills and practices. You should have read two or three classics and at least one best seller and perhaps some biographies. Reading shows your intellectual and professional preparedness. It also shows character, a critical mind, and teachability, among other key qualities.

*Where do you see yourself in ten years time?*

The interviewer is not interested in your travel plans to Egypt or Hawaii. Nor is he or she interested in your ambition to become governor, or Miss World or Mr. Universe. The interviewer is checking for your stability, career goals, and level of determination.

Many interviewees get themselves into trouble by stating specific positions in the company they would like to occupy, including salary levels they wish to attain. The danger of this type of answer is that you may either be venturing into risky political grounds.

A good response to this question is a turn-around question of your own to ascertain what qualities are required for the senior positions in the organization. You could ask:

"According to your existing structures, how far up the ladder could a hard working reporter get in ten years?"

You may also ask how hard work, dedication, initiative, and other attributes you believe you possess are rewarded. If you do not ask this question at this point, you should ask it when they pop the inevitable question: Do you have any questions for us? You may refer to your attributes of being a quick and eager learner and to your existing skills that fit the framework of the organization.[7]

*What do you think of this newspaper?*

This question tests your researching skills and your projected contributions and not your skills as a judge. Start with the positive aspects (good stories, good reputation). Be specific. State a story you liked particularly, who wrote it, and what techniques you learned from it. If you contactor a star writer, tell the interviewer something about the exchange. You will be respected for your initiative, boldness, determination, enthusiasm, and ambition. Discuss the newspaper's weaknesses in the context of what you read heard from experts.

# Journalism jobs on the web

News jobs www.newsjobs.com
Editor and Publisher www.mediainfo.com,
Detroit Free Press www.freep.com
UC Berkeley - Journalism Jobs http://www.journalism.berkeley.edu/jobs
Louisiana Tech University Journalism Department: Jobs in Journalism
http://eb.journ.latech.edu/jobs.html
Freelance Journalism http://freepages.writing.rootsweb.com/~petersplace/
JournalismJobs.com www.journalismjobs.com
Media Bistro www.mediabistro.com
California Journalism Job Bank http://www.csne.org/jobs/postings.html
UK journalism jobs www.honk.co.uk/fleetstreet

American Press Institute
http://www.journaliststoolbox.com/newswriting/jobs.html
Journalism Toolbox (www.journalismtoolbox.com)
provides links to many job sites, notes on cover letters and
resumes, and leads to internships.

# 15

---

## Freelancing: Narrative for Hire

*A gifted editor once told me that what she most looked for in a new writer was 'the glint of obsession'.* —Sarah Harrison

Freelance articles sustain most newspapers and magazines. Many publications, especially magazines, rely primarily on freelance contributors to fill their pages. There is a serious shortage of reporters and writers with narrative skills. Some freelance contributors write more regularly than full-time media employees. News organizations are always on the look out for excellent freelance reporters and writers.

A lot of good articles emerge from everyday occurrences in life or leisure. I once read a fascinating freelance story in an international magazine on the march of a tribe of soldier ants under a bed in an African village. Most vacations—domestic or international—could produce freelance stories.

Many freelance writers are stringers. Editors value stringers because, depending on the contract, they can rely on them for exclusive breaking stories. Editors may suggest story ideas, or ask stringers to check on a story, interview a personality, or write sidebars, color stories or back-up stories to accompany a wire story following a major newsbreak. Despite the availability of newswire reports, which are supplied to all subscribing newspapers, editors want exclusive stories.

Few people get published by tossing an article in the mailbox. Getting published and paid is a process. Here are some of the steps.

# 1. Skill Acquisition

The first step is to read widely and to acquire appropriate writing skills for the type of writing you wish to do. Read articles by the experts. Pick up a good book on media writing. Talk to people.

# 2. Familiarization

Study the particular publication you wish to write for. Note the writing style, the type and range of topics, the people who commission articles, and conditions of acceptance of articles. Find out what the newspaper lacks. Some freelancers erroneously believe that editors will welcome only the type of stories their publications normally run. On the contrary, in the very competitive market, editors want novel ideas, topics and approaches. Editors always welcome proposals and stories that "stop them in their tracks or at least intrigue them sufficiently to contact you," observes Jill Nick.[1]

Read rival publications and look out for similar publications. This will give you a better understanding of the market. It will give you story ideas and options. It will also make you aware of what stories or angles have already appeared in that paper or magazine.

Build a network. Networking is very important. See the section on networking in Chapter 14.

Find out the name and position of the editor who commissions articles for the section you wish to write for. While some newspapers have one central commissioning editor, most allow the line or section editors to commission or discuss stories. Major newspapers, such as the *New York Times, San Jose Mercury News, The Washington Post, The Australian,* and *The Independent,* have commissioning editors for different sections of the paper.

Many big newspapers have guidelines for freelancers as well as a stylebook. Familiarization goes both ways. You have to make the editor familiar with your skills or profile by describing your skills and experience. You may send clips of your work along with a query letter, especially if you have not written for major publications and are not very sure of your story idea.

# 3. Story Ideas

Without a story idea, your work becomes an unsolicited submission. Sending a story proposal or pitch is a way of testing the waters, and introducing yourself— proving that your idea or approach would suit the needs of the publication at that time. It is also possible that the editor may have already received or commissioned a story on that subject. Your language use and articulation tell the editor whether you can write and whether you possess the experience, competence, enthusiasm, knowledge and credentials to be trusted with a story.

It is important to distinguish between a story idea and a pitch. To understand the difference, take a man who wants to build a high-rise mall in Los Angeles. The thought that it would be a good, useful, and profitable idea to build the mall is an idea—a bright and potentially lucrative one at that. For that idea to become a proposal, the promoter must first conduct a feasibility study—state the financial implications, funding sources, administrative and legal procedures, profitability, and interested partners, for example. Bankers and investors work with proposals, not mere ideas or flashes of inspiration from unknown people. Editors work the same way.

# The Query

The query letter is the freelancer's cover letter. It is short (200–300 words) single-spaced, and usually on no more than one page. The best query, like the good narrative lead, should captivate the reader. The query should let on a vibrant personality. It is the best way to show how well you can write. The query has the attributes of a good story—it is based on thorough research and planning. It is structured as a narrative story. The lead is short and seeks to capture and retain the editor's attention.

The body is a bit longer. The second paragraph may develop the opening paragraph. It may alternatively act as the pitch, which would explain what you are offering, probably with a working title. For example, perhaps you are offering a 2,000-word travelogue about the modern Aztecs in South America. You might also be writing the follow-up of a story previously published by the newspaper or magazine, or even a rival publication.

Next, you will state what the story involves, including the following information:

- Why it is significant or interesting;
- What research you have done;
- What key information and documentation you already have;
- What is left to find out;
- Your proposed approach to the story;
- Who you will be talking to;
- What access you might have to sources;
- Any binding rules (anonymity, embargo, etc.);
- When the story might be ready
- Why you should be the one to write the story.

The ending may address your suitability for the task. State your relevant qualifications, including publications you have written for and proof of your familiarity with or expertise in the subject. You might also mention your ability to secure exclusive interviews, documents, or photographs, especially if you are dealing with a big, enthralling, or sensitive issue.

# Query Format

Not all query letters take the traditional format. Some freelancers demonstrate their storytelling skills in the query letter. Freelander & Lee offer this memorable example:

> Dear Mr. Hudddlestone:
>
> If you find out your spouse is being unfaithful, you can bite off his nose. If your luck has turned from poor to worse, you can visit your local evil-eye lady who will move the evil spirits and restore your happiness. If your daughter's fiancé runs out at the last minute, your sons and husband can kill him.
> That is, if you happen to be a Cretan.
> To the average tourist, Crete is the largest and one of the most fascinating of the Greek isles . . . . But there is another side of the Cretan way of life.[2]

That query letter, written by a young woman just breaking into the freelancing world, would tease many an editor into wanting to know more. It is the kind of writing and the kind of story editors want to take a look at. The letter contrasted the Crete everyone knew with the one the writer had discovered. She said the article would be 2,000 words long and would reveal the mystery of the "evil eye" and the intrigues and betrayals of arranged marriages and other "offbeat cultural facts." The writer established her suitability and resourcefulness by telling the editor she had spent five summers living with a Cretan family and had collected many anecdotes.

Take another example from one of the students in Clarence Schoenfeld's class. It shows elements of research and highlights the significance of the story. Surely, people want to know about rats that may save America from cancer.

> Probably every Madison resident realizes that this city is capital of "America's Dairyland" and the "City of Four Lakes," but Madison also has the distinction of being the white rat capital of the nation. The tiny creature who may some day save us from cancer, heart disease, or arthritis will very possibly be a Madisonian.
> Each month about 100,000 white rats are shipped throughout the country for scientific research.[3]

The writer proved she had done substantial research and some interviewing. She suggested that the story would interest people living in or near Madison (significance and relevance). She ended the query by asking the editor: "Would you like to see it?"

There are probably as many query writing styles as there are writers. What is most important is making the letter inviting, engaging, and lucid.

These examples show that the freelancer cannot base the query letter entirely on a whim. The freelancer must research the story, do some ground work, obtain documents and illustrations, find anecdotes, conduct preliminary interviews, and, if possible, line up sources for full interviews or explore the prospect of interviews with key individuals. Such affirmative steps help determine the feasibility and marketability of the story.

# Facing Realities

Freelancing is fun and rewarding, but it can be a risky pursuit. While anticipating the gains, you must be equipped to handle the frustrations of freelancing. The main negatives involved in freelancing are:

- Rejection;
- Delayed publication;
- Changes in the story;
- Copyright ownership;
- Payment.

## *Rejection*

Authors will tell you about the inevitability of rejection. Many of William Shakespeare's major works got turned down, even ridiculed by publishers. Graham Greene never found publishers for his first two books. Writers are not the only ones to face rejection. Top physicists mocked the idea of a plane ever flying, not to mention carrying people across the sea.

Freelance writers must be prepared for bad news or no news about their queries. Perhaps it was the wrong publication. Well, then you should be happy that it was a query letter—not a full story—that was sneezed at. Try other publications or review your query. You may seek a second opinion, including the opinion of an established freelance writer who gets published regularly. This is not a tall order. Some freelancers respond to e-mail, if you massage their ego a bit and show your willingness to learn from them.

## *Delays*

The publication of feature stories is governed by space availability but narrative news stories can be short and sharp. Major publications have story calendars. Your story may be accepted in January, but not get published until July the next year. Even scheduled stories can be upstaged by commemorative stories or topical.

## *Hostile Editing*

Many freelance writers are distressed or angered by changes in their stories, including changes to facts, syntax, structure, angle, or even deletion and addition of facts. The newspaper has to protect its reputation—and the idiosyncrasies of its copy editors. Researchers and copy editors have the right to alter your story for clarity, balance, style, and space, and for ethical and legal reasons. Annoying editorial changes are the fate of every writer, even those employed fulltime by the newspaper.

## Copyright

Some top publications demand the copyright of stories you write for them. *The New York Times* will not publish your article unless you sign a paper relinquishing your right to the copyright. Many other newspapers, however, will grant you your rights.

## Payment

Many freelancers write for money. In fact, some people—well, not beginners—live on their freelance earnings. It would be foolish, however, to make a financial commitment on the basis of an expected check for a freelance contribution.

Many big newspapers take six to eight weeks after publication to process freelance payment. Different newspapers have their own payment schedules. While eight weeks is the average processing time, it is good to find out from the commissioning editor what the specific payment structure is.

## The Market

It is always wise to start freelancing for newspapers close to your town or city. For one, editors may be more accessible, and calling them might be cheaper. The Internet has now made it easier to write for newspapers around the world.

Additional web resources for freelancers can be found by searching with key words at www.google.com. The following books are invaluable tools. *Writer's Market* (Writer's Digest Books), and the *Writers' & Artists' Yearbook* (A & C Black). The 2003 edition ordered directly from the publishers, A & C Black, London (www.acblack.com) or from Amazon UK (www.amazon.co.uk) costs about $20. Amazon US (www.amazon.com) sells the book for between $40 and $50. You might find some of these books in local or college libraries. The book offers tips on how to prepare articles and what editors want. It lists the major North American, European, African, Asian and Australian newspapers and magazines, syndicates and news agencies, stating in most cases the editorial staff to contact, procedures and fees for freelance articles, as well as the type and lengths of articles the publications accept. For a fuller listing of international newspapers and freelance markets, please see *Willings Press Guide: World* (Gale Group).

# Notes

## Chapter One

1. David Conley, *The Daily Miracle* (Sydney: Oxford University Press, 1999), 220–221.

2. Steven Cohan & Linda Shires, *Telling Stories: A theoretical analysis of narrative fiction*, New York: Routledge, 1998, 1.

3. Kathleen Hansen & Nora Paul, *Behind the Message: Information Strategies for Communications*, Boston: Pearson, 2004, 25–26.

4. Allan Bell, *The language of news media*, (Oxford: Blackwell, 1991), 147.

5. Louise Woodstock, *Public Journalism's Talking Cure: An Analysis of The Movement's 'Problem' and 'Solution' Narratives*, Journalism 3, no. 1 (2002): 37–55

6. Dele Olojode, *Telling Africa's Stories*, Narrative Journalism South Africa. (2005), 51.

7. Olojode, *Telling Africa's Stories*, 2005, 51.

8. Woodstock, *Public Journalism's Talking Cure*, 40.

9. Chip Scanlan, *What is Narrative, Anyway? A Craft Dialogue, Part 2: Feature Writers and Editors Weigh In*, 2003, <http://www.poynter.org/content/content_view.asp?id=499044> (5 September 2004).

10. Bell, *The language of news media*, 154.

11. Ndaeyo Uko, *Hard News is No News: The Changing Shape of News in The 21st Century* ANZCA Online Journal, 2002, <http://www.bond.edu.au/hss/communication/ANZCA/papers/NUkoPaper.pd> (29 May 2003).

12. Todd Hanson quoted in Nisar Keshvani and Sharon Tickle, *Online News: The Changing Digital Mediascape*, Journal of Australian Studies (December 2001), 99–105.

13 James Stovall, *Writing for the Mass Media*. Boston: Pearson, 2002, 157).

14. Wilber and Miller, *Modern Media Writing*, 130.

15. Readership Institute, *The Value of Feature-style Writing*, 2003, <http://readership.org/content/editorial/feature-style/main.htm> (15 April 2005).

16. Hemant Shah, *Journalism in an Age of Mass Media*, Globalization International Development Studies Network, 2000, <http://www.idsnet.org/Papers/Communications/HEMANT_SHAH.HTM> (30 August 2005).

17. Walter Fox, *Writing the News: A Guide for print Journalists*, 2nd edition, (Ames, IA: Iowa State University Press, 1998), 118.

18. Rick Bragg, *Weaving Storytelling into Breaking News*, (Nieman Report 54, no. 3 (Fall 2000), 29.

19. Rick Bragg, *Weaving Storytelling*, 29–30.

20. Rick Bragg, *Weaving Storytelling*, 29–30.

21. GlobeScan, *BBC/Reuters/Media Center Poll: Trust in the Media*, 2005, <*http://www.globescan.com/news_archives/bbcreut.html*> (10 June 2005).

22. Readership Institute, *The Value of Feature-style Writing*.

23. Walter Fox, *Writing the News: A Guide for Print Journalists*. (Ames: Iowa State University Press, 1998), 121.

## Chapter 2

1. Douglas Foster "It's all about reporting," *Narrative Journalism South Africa* (2005), 26–30.

2. Douglas McGill, "War-at-Home Narratives, Their Promise and Failures," Nieman Narrative Digest 2006, <http://www.nieman.harvard.edu/narrative/digest/essays/warstories-mcgill-nnd.html> (16 August 2006).

3. Christopher Callahan, *A Journalist's Guide to the Internet: The Net as a Reporting Tool* (Needham Heights, MA.: Allyn and Bacon, 1999), 30–31.

4. Roland De Wolk, *Introduction to Online Journalism: Publishing News and Information* (Needham Heights, MA.: Allyn and Bacon, 2001), 71.

5. Stephen Quinn, *Newsgathering on the Net* (Sydney: Macmillan, 2001), 44.

6. Bob Baker, *Newsthinking: The Secret of Making your Facts Fall into Place* (Boston: Allyn and Bacon, 2002), 100.

## Chapter 3

1.Ndaeyo Uko, *Daily News*, St Thomas, Virgin Islands, 16 August 1999, 2.

2. Lowe Davis, the Pulitzer-winning newspaper's Executive Editor, said the story was the most engaging accident story she had ever read.

## Chapter 4

1. Ken Metzler, *Creative Interviewing: The Writer's Guide to Gathering Information by Asking Questions* (Needham Heights, MA.: Allyn and Bacon, 1997), 60.

2. Alice Klement and Carolyn Matalene, *Telling Stories Taking Risks: Journalism Writing at the Century's Edge* (Belmont, WA: Wadsworth, 1998), 160.

3. Sally Adams, *Interviewing for Journalists* (London: Routledge 2001), 118.

4. Metzler, *Creative Interviewing*, 123.

5. Metzler, *Creative Interviewing*, 124.

## Chapter 5

1. Lisa Grunwald, "Betrayed: A Story of two Wives and Many Lives," *Esquire*, June 1990, in Alice Klement and Rosalyn Matalene, *Telling Stories, taking Risks: Journalism Writing at the century's Edge* (Belmont, WA: Wadsworth), 154.

2. Ken Metzler, *Creative Interviewing: The Writer's Guide to Gathering Information by Asking Questions* (Needham Heights, MA.: Allyn and Bacon, 1997), 202 – 203.

3. Sally Adams, *Interviewing for Journalists* (London: Routledge, 2001), 57.

4. Baden Eunson, *Negotiating Skills,* (Milton, U.K.: John Wiley & Sons, 1994), 42.

5. Louise Ritchie, "Getting the measure of soul on deadline: Interviewing tips from a psychologist," 2000, <www.freep.com/jobspage/academy/psych.html> (16 May 2002).

6. *The Australian*, 2 January 2002, 6.
7. *The Weekend Australian*, 8-9 December 2001, 23.
8. Metzler, *Creative Interviewing*, 104.

## Chapter 6

1. Meredith Hall, "Killing Chickens", *Creative Nonfiction*, Number 18, 2001, 32.
2. Jon Franklin, *Writing for Story* (New York: Penguin, 1994), p. 162.
3. *Weekend Australian*, 20–22 April 2002, 14.
4. *TIME*, (Australia/Pacific Edition), 13 May 2000, 23.
5. Katie McCabe, "Like Something the Lord Made", in Edward Jay Friedlander & John Lee Feature *Writing for Newspapers and Magazines: The Pursuits of Excellence* (Sydney: Longman, 2000), 93.

## Chapter 7

1. Peter Richardson, *Style: A Pragmatic Approach* (2nd ed.) (New York: Longman, 2002), 4.
2. James Stovall, *Writing for the Mass media* (5th ed.) (Needham Heights, MA.: Allyn and Bacon, 2002), 61.
3. Ndaeyo Uko, *The Rock 'N' Rule Years: A Satirist's View of Nigeria's Military Presidency* (Ibadan: Bookcraft, 1992), 84.
4. Walter Fox, *Writing the News: A Guide for Print Journalists* (2nd Ed), (Ames: IA.: Iowa State University Press, 1998), 50.
5. *Weekend Australian* (January 12-13, 2002), 11.
6. Maurice Dunlevy, *Feature Writing* (Victoria, Australia: Deakin University Press, 1998), 59.
7. Evelyn Waugh, "Critics on Graham Greene," 2000, <http://members.tripod.com/~greeneland/critics.htm> (14 August 2004).
8. Bob Baker, Newsthinking: *The Secrets of Making Your Facts Fall into Place* (Boston, MA.: Allyn and Bacon, 2002), 102.
9. Quoted in Carol Rich, *Writing and Reporting News: A Coaching Method* (3rd Ed), (Belmont, CA.: Wadsworth, 2000), 229.
10. Jon Franklin, *Writing for Story: Craft Secrets of Dramatic Nonfiction by a Two-time Pulitzer Prize Winner* (New York: Plume/Penguin1994), 181.
11. Jan Herman, "Cuba Where Time Has Stopped," *Newsweek*, 2002, <www.msnbc.com/news/733488.asp?0dm=H1ANL#BODY> (31 November 2002).
12. Quoted in *The Weekend Australian*, 8 – 9 June 2002, 14.

## Chapter 8

1. Tzvetan Todorov, quoted in Steven Cohan, and Linda Shires, *Telling Stories: A Theoretical Analysis of Narrative Fiction* (New York: Routledge, 1988), 54.
2. Ronald J. Nelson, *The Language of Love in Richard Selzer's "The Consultation"*, in River Teeth: *A Journal of Nonfiction Narrative*, Vol. 1, No. 1/ Fall 1999, 85.
3. Garry Disher, *Writing Fiction: An Introduction to the Craft* (Victoria, A: Penguin Books, 1983), 13.
4. Ron McIntosh, *The Quest for Revival* (Tulsa, OK, Harrison House, 1997), 201.
5. Maurice Dunlevy, *Feature Writing*, (Victoria: Deakin University Press, 1998), 61.

## Chapter 9

1. Joe Grimm, "The Art and Craft of Feature Writing,"1999, <www.freep.com/jobspage/academy/blundell.htm> (30 June 2002).
2. Clarence Schoenfeld, *Effective Feature Writing: How to Write Articles that Sell* (New York: Harper & Row, 1966), 30.
3. Patrick May, "Society Pays Awful Price for Violence," *Miami Herald*, July 25, 1993, cited in Klement and Matalene, 79–81.
4. George Vecsey, "England Beats Argentina," *International Herald Tribune*, 2002, www.iht.com/cgi-in/generic.cgi?template=articleprint.tmplh&ArticleId=60638, (31 December 2002).

## Chapter 10

1. Jon Franklin, *Writing for Story: Craft Secrets of Dramatic Nonfiction by a Two-Time Pulitzer Prize Winner* (New York: Penguin, 1994), 162.
2. Edward Jay Friedlander & John Lee, *Feature Writing for Newspapers and Magazines: The Pursuits of Excellence* (New York: Longman, 2000), 203.
3. Alice Klement & Carolyn Matalene, *Telling Stories Taking Risks: Journalism Writing at the Century's Edge* (Belmont, CA.: Wadsworth,, 1998), 64.
4. Quoted in Walter Fox, *Writing the News: A Guide for Print Journalists* (Ames, IA.: Iowa State University Press, 1998), 116.
5. Walter Fox, *Writing the News: A Guide for print Journalists*, second edition, (Ames, IA: Iowa State University Press, 1998), 25.
6. Clarence Schoenfeld, *Effective Feature Writing: How to Write Articles that Sell,* (New York: Harper & Row, 1966), 189.
7. Klement and Matalene, *Telling Stories Taking Risks*, 65.
8. Klement and Matalene, *Telling Stories Taking Risks,* 63.

## Chapter 12

1."Howard is sacrificing our interests," *The Age*, www.theage.com.au/articles/2002/06/12/1023864297100.html, June 6, 2002.
2. Sebastian Mallaby, *Washington Post* ("Accountable Accountants," p. A17, February 4, 2002).

## Chapter 13

1. Peter Calder, "Don't Say a Word" *New Zealand Herald*, 2002, <www.nzherald.co.nz> (2 February 2002).
2. Timothy Corrigan, *A Short Guide to Writing about Film* (New York: Longman), p. 144.
3. Jonathan Farley, "A Beautiful Mind: American Pi", *TIME*, 2002, <www.time.com/time/sampler/article/0,8599,190839,00.html> (5 January 2002).

## Chapter 14

1. Brad Schultz, *Sports Media: Reporting, Producing and Planning.* (Boston: Elsevier, 2005), p.251.

2. Joe Grimm, www.freep.com/jobspage/toolkit/cover.html

3. Schultz, *Sports Media*, 251.

4. Ndaeyo Uko, *Job Hunting: A Practical International Guide* (Ibadan, Nigeria/Jersey, U.K.: Spectrum Books, 2002), p. 25.

5. Uko, *Job Hunting,* 63.

6. For more on obtaining, managing and making the best out of internships, visit Newspaper Internships: Jobs Page, http://www.freep.com/jobspage/interns/index.htm

7. Uko, *Job Hunting,* 122.

## Chapter 15

1. Jill Nick, "Writing for Newspapers" in *Writers and Artistes Yearbook 2003* (London: A & C Black, 2003), 125.

2. Edward Jay Friedlander & John Lee, *Feature Writing for Newspapers and Magazines: The Pursuit of Excellence* (New York: Longman, 2000), 268.

3. Clarence Schoenfeld, *Effective Feature Writing: How to Write Articles that Sell* (New York: Harper & Row, 1966), 142.

# Index

abstract, 26, 78, 80, 91, 93, 125, 130, 131, 138, 139, 148, 200
abstraction, 63, 141, 158
accuracy, 41, 44, 80, 83, 85, 119, 149
Achebe, 51, 60, 61
alarm, 40, 174
Ali, 25, 196
analogy, 78, 96, 123, 155, 162, 197
analysis, 66
Anderson, 30
anecdote, 31, 55, 70, 71, 72, 129, 130, 146, 148, 155, 183, 187
angle, 7, 32, 54, 82, 162, 179, 230
appearance, 39, 107
Arafat, 24
arbitrate, 167
architecture, 83
arguments, 48, 99, 124, 129, 157, 171, 173, 184, 185, 187, 191, 193
art, 8, 48, 62, 101, 119, 135, 167, 184, 190, 194, 195, 197, 198, 199, 200, 205, 206, 207, 219
attack, 6, 26, 94, 118, 131, 136, 142, 149, 151, 152, 153, 163
attitude, 114, 136, 158, 173, 179, 207
Australia, 8, 21, 24, 26, 65, 71, 72, 101, 112, 117, 138, 157, 158, 176, 186
authoritativeness, 207
authority, 11, 40, 61, 70, 71, 80, 112, 172, 202

axe, 163, 164

Bennet, 10
Biafra, 31
Blair, 177, 178
body, 3, 41, 50, 55, 61, 85, 103, 106, 129, 141, 142, 145, 148, 152, 153, 154, 157, 164, 175, 181, 183, 184, 187, 193, 197, 200, 212, 214, 216, 227
Bragg, 5, 6, 47, 93
brevity, 30, 83, 85, 216
bridging, 62, 122
Bush, 66, 94, 111, 118, 176, 177, 178, 185, 186

Callahan, 10
carnival, 113, 143
characterization, 106, 110
chat, 11, 29, 31, 32, 41, 59, 118, 119, 159
Chomsky, 93
chronological account, 155
Chucky, 17, 18
circumstantial, 8
clarity, 36, 83, 85, 96, 97, 149, 156, 230
cliché, 98, 101
Clinton, 31, 46, 55, 178, 185, 218
color, 1, 10, 18, 24, 28, 39, 50, 51, 56, 71, 73, 78, 81, 142, 195, 225
column, 172, 188, 189, 190, 191, 193, 194
complication, 104, 105, 106

concrete, 8, 12, 26, 76, 79, 83, 86,
    91, 93, 97, 117, 119, 122, 123,
    125, 130, 131, 141, 148
condition, 25, 49, 69, 104, 108, 119
conflict, 15, 70, 101, 103, 104, 105,
    107, 118, 143, 145
constructing, 160, 165, 175, 193
construction, 25, 26, 86, 87, 98,
    119, 122, 123, 135, 152, 153,
    154, 159, 201, 215
contrast, 96, 102, 112, 121, 133,
    143, 180
conversation, 9, 11, 29, 30, 37, 42,
    43, 44, 45, 47, 55, 57, 58, 59,
    60, 63, 64, 127, 133, 136, 142,
    151, 202
Corinthians, 47, 93
corroborating, 4, 50, 154
corroborative, 8, 12, 24, 32, 75
cover letter, 212, 213, 214, 215,
    216, 217, 218, 221, 224, 227
crisis, 105, 107
crossroads, 48, 70, 105, 154, 198
cue, 100, 103
curiosity, 9, 35, 38, 41, 47, 49, 64,
    71, 81, 99, 104, 110, 135, 139,
    152, 213, 217, 218

Daily News, 22, 27, 37, 114, 120,
    145, 156, 157
deadline, 5, 10, 16, 59, 62, 188, 213
denouement, 106
descent, 152, 153, 154, 157, 158,
    187
description, 9, 26, 73, 74, 76, 77,
    78, 80, 82, 90, 102, 110, 111,
    112, 114, 115, 118, 121, 136,
    146, 149, 161, 181
detail, 8, 11, 12, 19, 21, 22, 23, 24,
    25, 28, 36, 39, 44, 50, 57, 59,
    71, 72, 73, 74, 75, 76, 77, 78,
    81, 88, 92, 93, 98, 110, 114,
    115, 116, 117, 120, 119, 127,
    129, 137, 139, 140, 148, 149,
    151, 159, 161, 171, 172, 180,
    182, 190, 192, 216

DeVito, 56, 57
dialogue, 10, 46, 57, 102, 109, 113,
    114, 130, 146, 151, 155, 174
dimensions, 7, 18, 24, 25, 33, 34,
    73, 79, 81, 91, 98
drama, 5, 12, 23, 27, 38, 48, 49, 73,
    75, 76, 79, 90, 107, 111, 118,
    119, 120, 121, 146, 160, 196
dramatization, 106, 110, 120

editor, 2, 42, 43, 60, 63, 84, 120,
    168, 169, 210, 212, 213, 214,
    216, 217, 218, 225, 226, 227,
    228, 230
editorial, 58, 168, 169, 203, 211,
    230
elegance, 8, 95, 182
e-mail, 10, 11, 36, 210, 211, 214,
    229
empathy, 42, 48, 57, 69, 136
ending, 46, 103, 106, 107, 135,
    145, 146, 150, 152, 153, 154,
    155, 156, 157, 158, 159, 161,
    185, 186, 187, 188, 193, 212,
    227
entertainment, 6, 71, 172, 185, 186,
    191, 206
evasiveness, 62
exposition, 107, 110, 112, 113,
    137, 138, 142, 146, 147, 148,
    151, 152, 191

fact, 4, 30, 39, 67, 69, 85, 89, 105,
    106, 121, 149, 151, 152, 153,
    161, 168, 178, 182, 187, 190,
    199, 230
fallible, 28, 46, 56
false, 39, 40, 67, 69
famous, 35, 38, 51, 52, 62, 141,
    152, 178, 201, 204
fantasies, 51, 109
fantasize, 52
feature writing, 5, 18, 46, 112
featurized, 7
fiction, 47, 94, 99-111, 114, 159,
    178, 183

film, 94, 102, 195, 196, 202, 203
flow, 57, 71, 77, 81, 87, 88, 99,
    103, 120, 121, 132, 133, 136,
    156, 178, 184, 215
forensic, 159, 162
foreshadowing, 82, 110, 127, 178,
    182
Foster, 9
Franklin, 73, 98, 101, 102, 104,
    106, 112, 132, 137

Garba, 45
Google, 10, 11, 211
Gore, 88, 178, 209, 213
grammar, 109, 215, 216, 218
Greene, 92, 100, 101, 102, 104,
    115, 195, 200, 205, 229
grenade, 53, 54, 55
Grunwald, 34, 55, 56

Hanson, 1, 4, 39, 67, 84
hard news, 2, 3, 4, 5, 6, 7, 9, 13, 15,
    19, 79, 103, 106, 111, 122, 123,
    134, 135, 136, 137, 145, 146,
    149, 150, 175
Hemmingway, 19, 73, 83, 95, 102
homicide, 59, 163
hostility, 60
humility, 202, 205, 207
humor, 7, 71, 84, 114, 143, 190,
    191, 192, 196, 222

ice breaker, 64
imagery, 23, 97, 98, 99, 100, 116,
    135, 150, 174, 182, 183, 190,
    197
images, 12, 76, 80, 97, 98, 99, 101,
    136, 143, 183, 195
implicative, 8, 12, 21, 24, 69, 76,
    78, 80, 88, 92, 93, 103, 109,
    110, 111, 112, 113, 115, 138,
    139, 150, 172, 175, 176, 177
interpret, 4, 151, 177, 197, 200, 204
interview, 11, 29, 30, 31, 32, 33,
    34, 35, 36, 37, 38, 42, 43, 44,
    45, 46, 47, 49, 53, 55, 56, 57,

58, 60, 61, 62, 63, 64, 65, 66,
    69, 73, 127, 158, 161, 163, 164,
    165, 205, 214, 216, 221, 225
inverted pyramid, 2, 3, 4, 6, 7, 8,
    145, 217
irony, 7, 22, 26, 27, 75, 77, 114,
    136, 143, 144, 190

jail, 65
jargon, 27, 29, 63, 86, 116, 119,
    158, 207
Jordan, 87, 184, 185, 186
journalism jobs, 211, 224
jumble, 112, 122, 124
justifier, 146, 148

Killenberg, 30
Kramer, 157

Lacey, 31
Lau, 179
lead
    conceiving, 140
    constructing, 140
        conceiving, 140
listserv, 10
lucidity, 83, 95

manic, 9, 37, 135
Mexican War, 3
Meyer, 12, 97
military coup, 45, 105
modifier, 88, 95, 96
mood, 7, 22, 26, 72, 79, 113, 114,
    115, 116, 117, 118, 125, 137,
    142, 155, 157, 158, 157, 174
Morrow, 176, 178, 186
motion, 9, 75, 77, 78, 93, 105, 108,
    110, 120, 124, 135, 149
motive, 39, 62, 101
movements, 26, 50
Myerhoff, 1

Nalder, 49, 58
Napley, 38

narrative, 1, 2, 4, 5, 6, 7, 8, 9, 12,
15, 16, 38, 46, 57, 70, 77, 79,
82, 83, 94, 98, 100, 101, 102,
103, 115, 117, 118, 120, 123,
129, 131, 133, 134, 135, 140,
144, 146, 148, 149, 150, 151,
152, 155, 156, 157, 158, 157,
158, 161, 162, 174, 183, 194,
204, 209, 212, 225, 227, 229
narrativity, 2, 101
negotiation, 66, 69, 169, 219
networking, 197, 210, 226
newsgathering, 11, 13, 38, 120,
123, 156, 218
Nigeria, 26, 31, 45, 84, 85, 179,
180, 210
Nixon, 65, 187
non-fiction, 118

Obasanjo, 180
observation, 9, 12, 13, 17, 18, 19,
28, 38, 46, 47, 50, 54, 73, 74,
80, 95, 98, 106, 115, 119, 123,
130, 137, 154, 155, 182, 183,
187, 190, 192
Olojode, 2
op-ed, 172, 173, 174, 188
opinion, 167, 168, 169, 171, 173,
182, 186
outline, 102, 120, 122, 154, 156,
198

paradox, 102, 143, 144, 162, 179
paraphrase, 149, 151
Paul, 1, 21, 109, 111, 136, 199, 215
perspective, 6, 14, 15, 59, 66, 76,
141, 158, 177, 183, 184, 188
persuasion, 120, 150, 184, 197, 201
planning, 31, 32, 34, 35, 45, 156,
161, 227
pleasure, 6, 12, 77, 79, 116, 136,
137, 139, 141
plot, 98, 103, 106, 107, 108, 120,
121, 195, 196, 197, 198
Plot, 198

point of view, 29, 96, 106, 115,
116, 118, 119, 151, 160, 174
police, 13, 22, 32, 37, 42, 46, 49,
54, 57, 66, 69, 90, 91, 95, 117,
132, 144, 158, 161, 163, 164,
169
Ponewozic, 204
preparation, 32, 38, 63, 152, 207,
209, 217, 219, 222
probe, 68
profile, 19, 36, 45, 46, 47, 48, 51,
109, 112, 169, 171, 188, 201,
220, 222, 226
Profile, 170
psychological planning, 35
public relations, 33, 41
publicity, 33, 59, 61
punctuation, 26, 83, 214, 215

query, 226, 227, 228, 229
question, 10, 23, 30, 34, 40, 50, 51,
53, 54, 55, 57, 58, 59, 61, 62,
64, 66, 67, 68, 69, 70, 73, 74,
90, 92, 100, 103, 105, 113, 127,
134, 140, 175, 176, 183, 186,
187, 202, 223
quotation, 4, 134, 140, 149, 150,
151, 155, 202, 215

rambling, 59, 60, 62, 68
reactive, 13, 14, 15
Readership Institute, 4, 7
redundancies, 87, 89, 90, 95
redundancy, 90, 95
reflective, 22, 158, 171
rejection, 173, 229
reporting, 2, 4, 5, 7, 8, 9, 10, 12,
13, 14, 15, 19, 22, 32, 33, 41,
60, 73, 84, 88, 93, 95, 112, 119,
120, 131, 137, 154, 156, 159,
161, 172, 174, 177, 187, 217,
222
research, 9, 10, 25, 28, 32, 36, 38,
39, 41, 44, 46, 47, 50, 62, 64,
66, 67, 81, 98, 120, 123, 137,
152, 154, 170, 172, 182, 187,

190, 196, 197, 199, 204, 206,
207, 212, 216, 222, 227, 228,
229
resolution, 105, 106, 107, 198
résumé, 201, 212, 213, 215, 216,
217, 218, 219, 220, 221
review, 1, 93, 126, 167, 168, 180,
181, 194, 195, 196, 197, 200,
201, 202, 203, 204, 205, 206,
207, 215, 229
Roberts, 212, 213

sensitivity, 135, 136, 164, 165
setting, 37, 48, 64, 75, 82, 105,
106, 114, 116, 117, 118, 120,
195, 196, 197, 198, 200, 204,
205, 216
shape, 7, 18, 23, 24, 28, 81, 100,
109, 121, 119, 120, 123, 146,
161, 167, 177, 183, 196
shoehorn, 20, 23, 73
shotgun, 137
Showing, 202
silence, 15, 53, 54, 69, 70, 87, 108,
133, 163, 165
simplicity, 61, 84, 85, 88, 99, 178
specification, 22, 25, 93, 94
spirit, 26, 39, 76, 101, 120, 148,
205, 206, 207
Spirit, 205
story lead, 140
story question, 127
storytelling, 1, 2, 3, 8, 28, 29, 101,
102, 106, 115, 119, 123, 132,
135, 136, 140, 146, 149, 151,
160, 161, 174, 178, 194, 204,
209, 212, 216, 218, 228
Stovall, 4, 83
Straits Times, 175, 176
Straw, 177, 178
structuring, 158
style, 2, 3, 4, 5, 7, 15, 27, 65, 73,
83, 84, 95, 97, 106, 135, 146,
155, 172, 175, 184, 186, 190,

196, 199, 201, 202, 204, 207,
211, 218, 226, 230
sympathy, 48

techniques, 1, 7, 11, 15, 43, 46, 61,
100, 102, 114, 119, 140, 149,
150, 159, 157, 174, 175, 183,
184, 188, 191, 193, 194, 197,
199, 204, 207, 209, 218, 223
telegraph, 3
television, 2, 3, 6, 30, 76, 79, 84,
102, 133, 190
terrorism, 6, 50, 118
texture, 24, 28, 120, 142, 146, 196
Thatcher, 38, 50, 72
theme, 8, 46, 50, 75, 76, 103, 107,
115, 117, 120, 121, 122, 130,
135, 136, 181, 183, 195, 198,
205
thread, 8, 46, 55, 71, 101, 103, 107,
115, 120, 121, 124, 153, 156,
158, 178, 183, 204
Tippet, 21, 27, 71, 100, 157, 158,
162, 163
transition, 77, 82, 103, 121, 122,
123, 124, 125, 126, 127, 129,
130, 131, 132, 133, 134, 135,
136, 137, 154, 178, 204
typing, 194, 211

vacuuming, 159, 160, 161
village, 17, 23, 79, 104, 156, 196,
206, 225
Virgin Islands, 22, 37, 52, 112,
113, 114, 134, 140, 143, 144,
157
vitality, 148
voice, 48, 91, 98, 130, 136, 165,
193

word play, 143

xenophobic, 84

# About the Author

**Ndaeyo Uko** has worked in the newsrooms of major newspapers in the United States, the United Kingdom and Nigeria. In the United States, he had a stint at the *San Jose Mercury News*, where he wrote op-ed pieces and news stories, and served as a visiting member of the editorial board. At the *Daily News* (St Thomas, USVI), he covered the Senate and the Governor's office in addition to his general beat, writing practically all his news stories in the narrative. In Nigeria, he reported and wrote columns for major national dailies including *The Guardian*, *Daily Times* and *Punch*. He became Editor (Sunday) of the *Post Express* and Deputy/Acting Editor of the Daily Times, both national newspapers in Lagos, Nigeria. He is a roving Asia-Pacific correspondent of *The Guardian*. He covered Nigeria for *The Independent* in London as a stringer and worked as a columnist, reporter, and editorial specialist for *West Africa* magazine, London.

He ran the journalism program at the University of the Virgin Islands and currently teaches journalism at Monash University, Melbourne, Australia.

Dr. Uko speaks regularly at narrative and other journalism conferences in the United States, Europe, Asia, Australia and Africa. His talks on narrative techniques are based principally on the contents of this book. He also coaches journalists on reporting and writing techniques in newsrooms across West and Central Africa.

His books include *The Rock 'N' Rule Years: A Satirist's View of Nigeria's Military Presidency* (1992) and *Romancing the Gun: The Press as a Promoter of Military Rule* (2004). He spent his Hubert Humphrey (Fulbright) fellowship year at the University of Maryland. In 2003, he was named the Rotary International Ambassadorial Scholar (Goodwill Ambassador—tertiary journalism teaching) to Ghana.